空知英秋

Hideaki Sorachi

I fought for it, but no luck. The world has become a hard place to live for smokers.

Hideaki Sorachi was born on May 25, 1979, and grew up in Hokkaido, Japan. His ongoing series, *GIN TAMA*, became a huge hit when it began running in the pages of Japan's *Weekly Shonen Jump* in 2004. A *GIN TAMA* animated series followed soon after, premiering on Japanese TV in April 2006. Sorachi made his manga debut with the one-shot story *DANDELION*.

GIN TAMA VOL. 16
SHONEN JUMP ADVANCED Manga Edition

STORY & ART BY HIDEAKI SORACHI

Translation/Kyoko Shapiro, Honyaku Center Inc.
English Adaptation/Lance Caselman
Touch-up Art & Lettering/Avril Averill
Design/Ronnie Casson
Editor/Alexis Kirsch & Jann Jones

VP, Production/Alvin Lu
VP, Publishing Licensing/Rika Inouye
VP, Sales & Product Marketing/Gonzalo Ferreyra
VP, Creative/Linda Espinosa
Publisher/Hyoe Narita

Printed in the U.S.A.

Published by VIZ Media, LLC
P.O. Box 77010
San Francisco, CA 94107

10 9 8 7 6 5 4 3 2 1
First printing, January 2010

THE WORLD'S MOST
CUTTING-EDGE MANGA

www.viz.com

www.shonenjump.com

GIN TAMA

Vol. 16 Germa
Suplex Any WomanWh
Asks, “Which Is Mor
Important, Me o
Your Work?

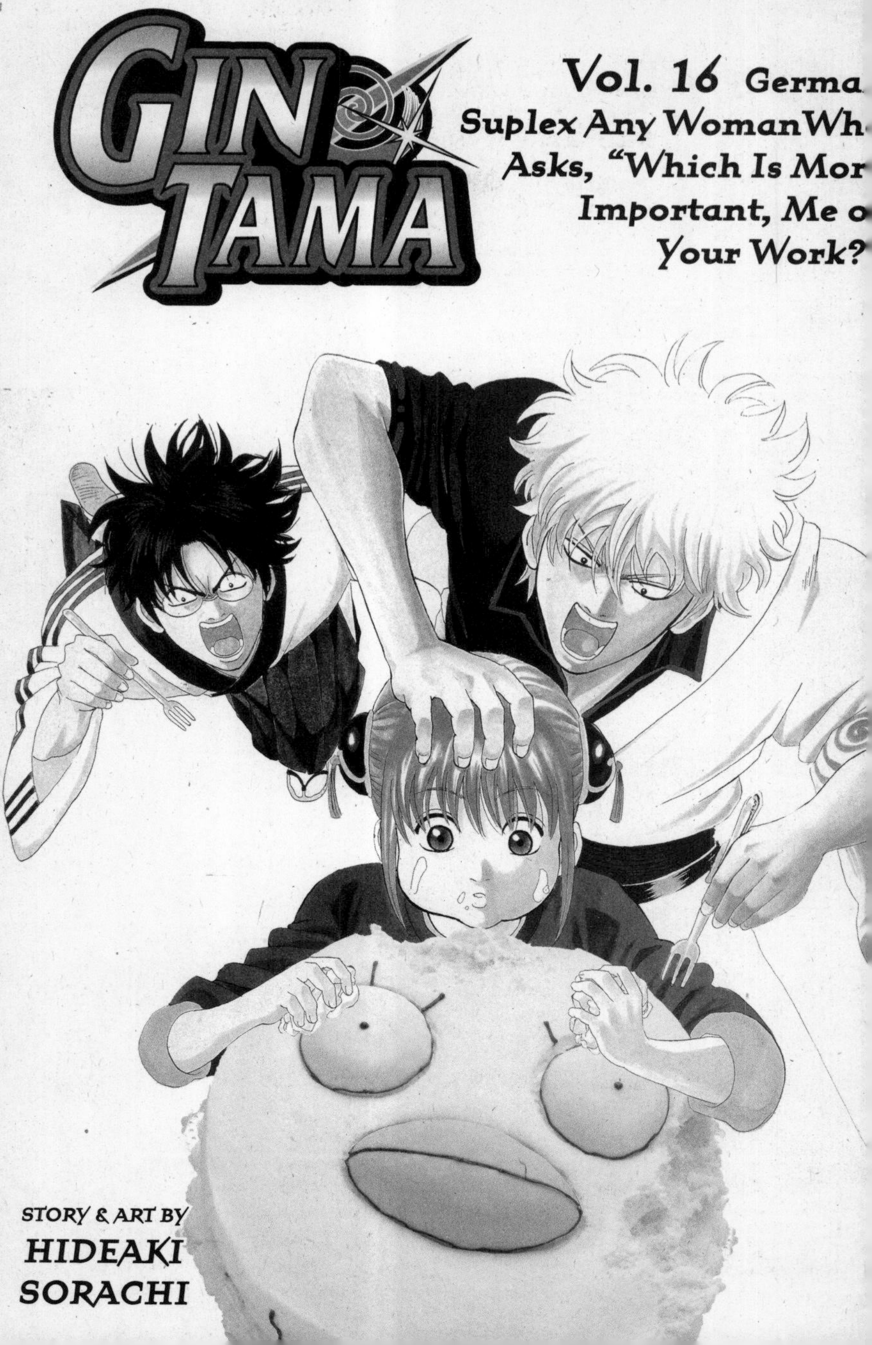

STORY & ART BY

HIDEAKI SORACHI

Cast of Characters

Yorozuya Members

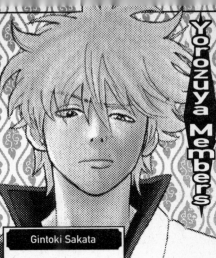

Gintoki Sakata

The hero of our story. If he doesn't eat something sweet periodically he gets cranky—really cranky. He boasts a powerful sword arm, but he's one step away from diabetes. A former member of the exclusionist faction that seeks to expel the space aliens and protect the nation.

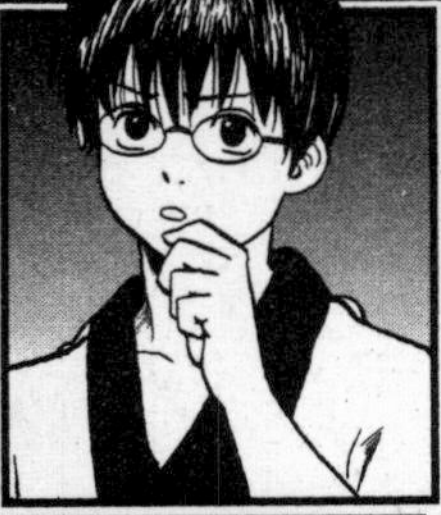

Shinpachi Shimura

Works under Gintoki in an attempt to learn about the samurai spirit, but has often come to regret his decision recently. President of the Tsu Terakado Fan Club.

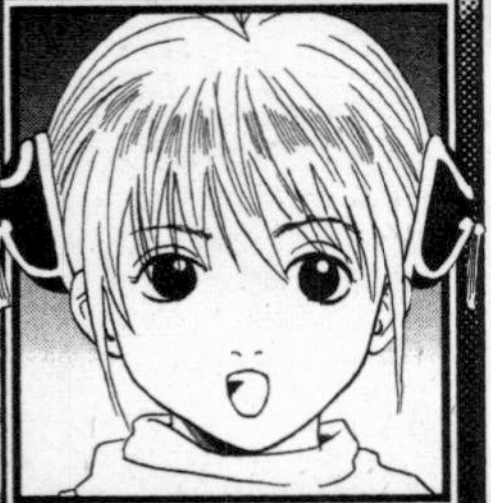

Kagura

A member of the "Yato Clan," the most powerful warrior race in the universe. Her voracious appetite and alien worldview lead frequently to laughter…and sometimes contusions.

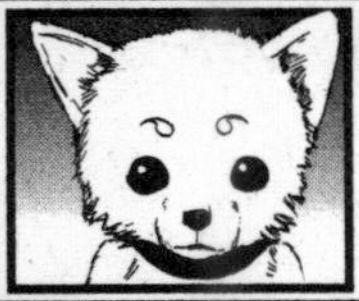

Sadaharu

A giant space creature turned office pet. Likes to bite people (especially Gin).

Shinsengumi Members

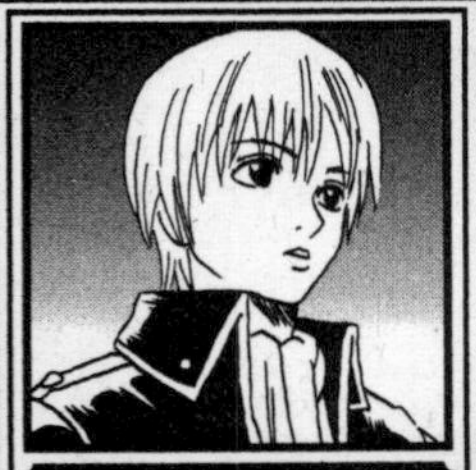

Okita

The Shinsengumi's most formidable swordsman. Behind a façade of amiability, he tirelessly schemes to eliminate Hijikata and usurp his position.

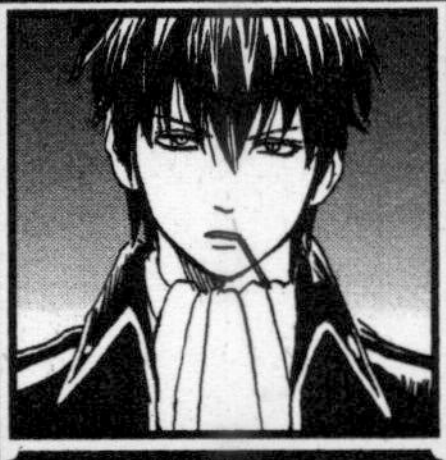

Hijikata

Vice-Chief of the Shinsengumi, Edo's elite counter-terrorist police unit. His air of detached cool transforms into hot rage the instant he draws his sword…or when someone disparages mayonnaise.

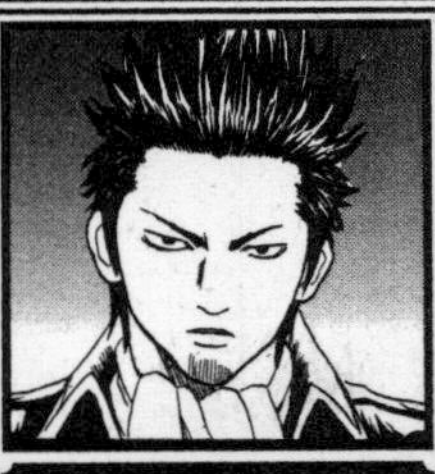

Kondo

The trusted chief of the Shinsengumi (and the remorseless stalker of Shinpachi's older sister Otae).

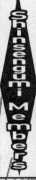

Other Characters

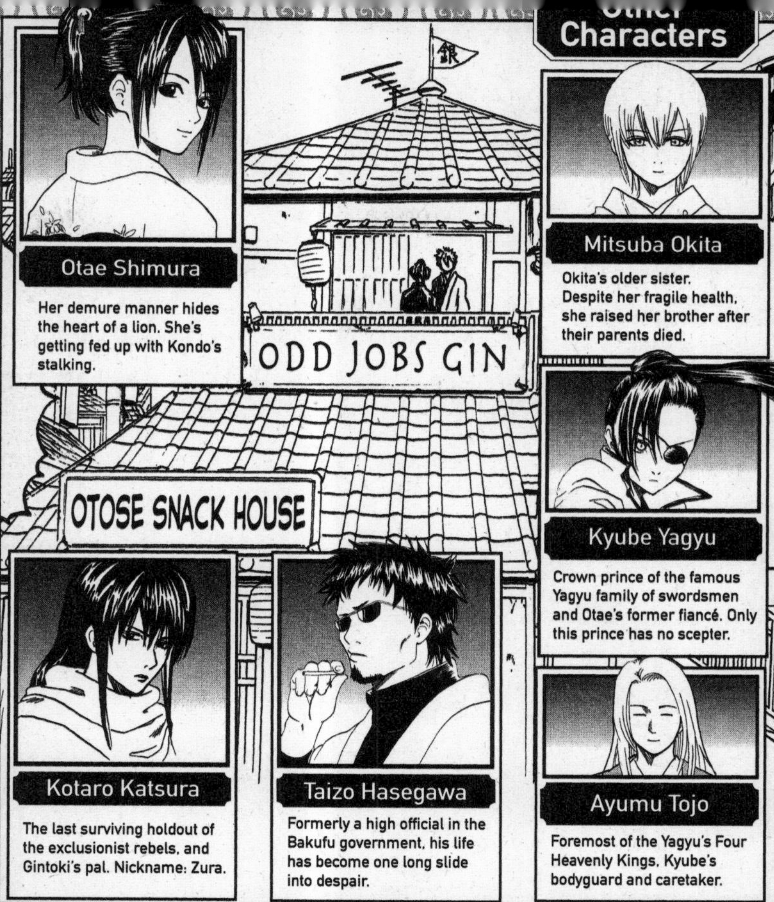
ODD JOBS GIN
OTOSE SNACK HOUSE

Otae Shimura

Her demure manner hides the heart of a lion. She's getting fed up with Kondo's stalking.

Mitsuba Okita

Okita's older sister. Despite her fragile health, she raised her brother after their parents died.

Kyube Yagyu

Crown prince of the famous Yagyu family of swordsmen and Otae's former fiancé. Only this prince has no scepter.

Kotaro Katsura

The last surviving holdout of the exclusionist rebels, and Gintoki's pal. Nickname: Zura.

Taizo Hasegawa

Formerly a high official in the Bakufu government, his life has become one long slide into despair.

Ayumu Tojo

Foremost of the Yagyu's Four Heavenly Kings, Kyube's bodyguard and caretaker.

The story thus far

In an alternate-universe Edo (Tokyo), extraterrestrials land in Japan and the new government issues an order outlawing swords. The samurai, who have reached the pinnacle of power and prosperity, fall into rapid decline.

Twenty years hence, only one samurai has managed to hold onto his fighting spirit: a somewhat eccentric fellow named Gintoki "Odd Jobs Gin" Sakata. A lover of sweets and near diabetic, our hero sets up shop as a *yorozuya*—an expert at managing trouble and handling the oddest of jobs.

Joining "Gin" in his business is Shinpachi Shimura, whose sister Gin saved from the clutches of nefarious debt collectors. After a series of unexpected circumstances, the trio meet a powerful alien named Kagura, who becomes—after some arm-twisting—a part-time team member.

Shinpachi and Kondo rescue Otae from the stronghold of the formidable Yagyu family; Kondo almost marries a gorilla; Katsura takes a driving lesson; Sadaharu finds love; and the shogun enjoys a trip to a nightclub. Now, as Okita's sister languishes in the hospital, Hijikata tries to bust her fiancé for selling weapons to the exclusionist ronin.

WHAT THIS MANGA'S FULL OF
vol. 16

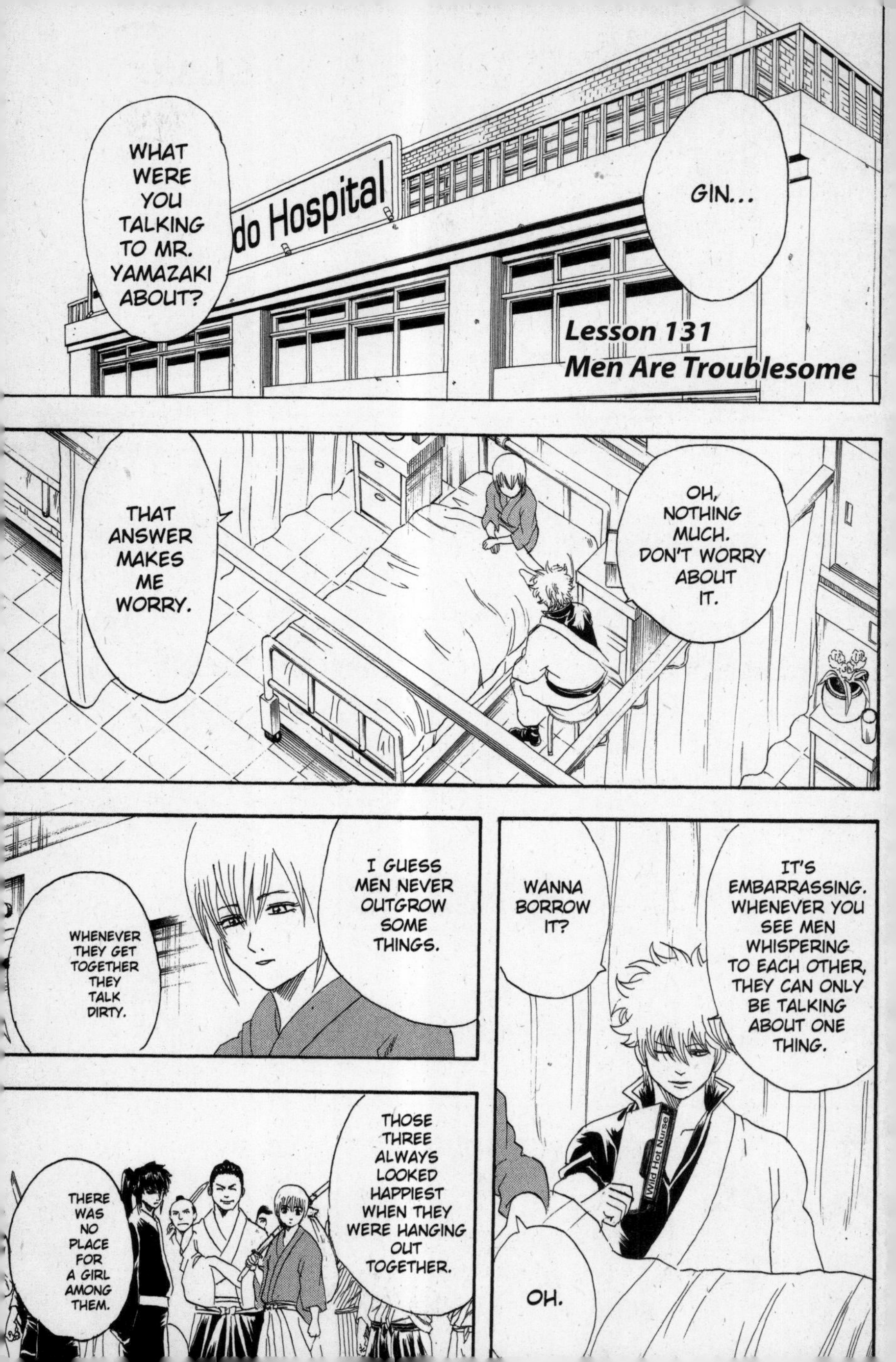
GIN...
WHAT WERE YOU TALKING TO MR. YAMAZAKI ABOUT?
do Hospital
Lesson 131
Men Are Troublesome
OH, NOTHING MUCH. DON'T WORRY ABOUT IT.
THAT ANSWER MAKES ME WORRY.
IT'S EMBARRASSING. WHENEVER YOU SEE MEN WHISPERING TO EACH OTHER, THEY CAN ONLY BE TALKING ABOUT ONE THING.
WANNA BORROW IT?
Wild Hot Nurse
OH.
I GUESS MEN NEVER OUTGROW SOME THINGS.
WHENEVER THEY GET TOGETHER THEY TALK DIRTY.
THOSE THREE ALWAYS LOOKED HAPPIEST WHEN THEY WERE HANGING OUT TOGETHER.
THERE WAS NO PLACE FOR A GIRL AMONG THEM.

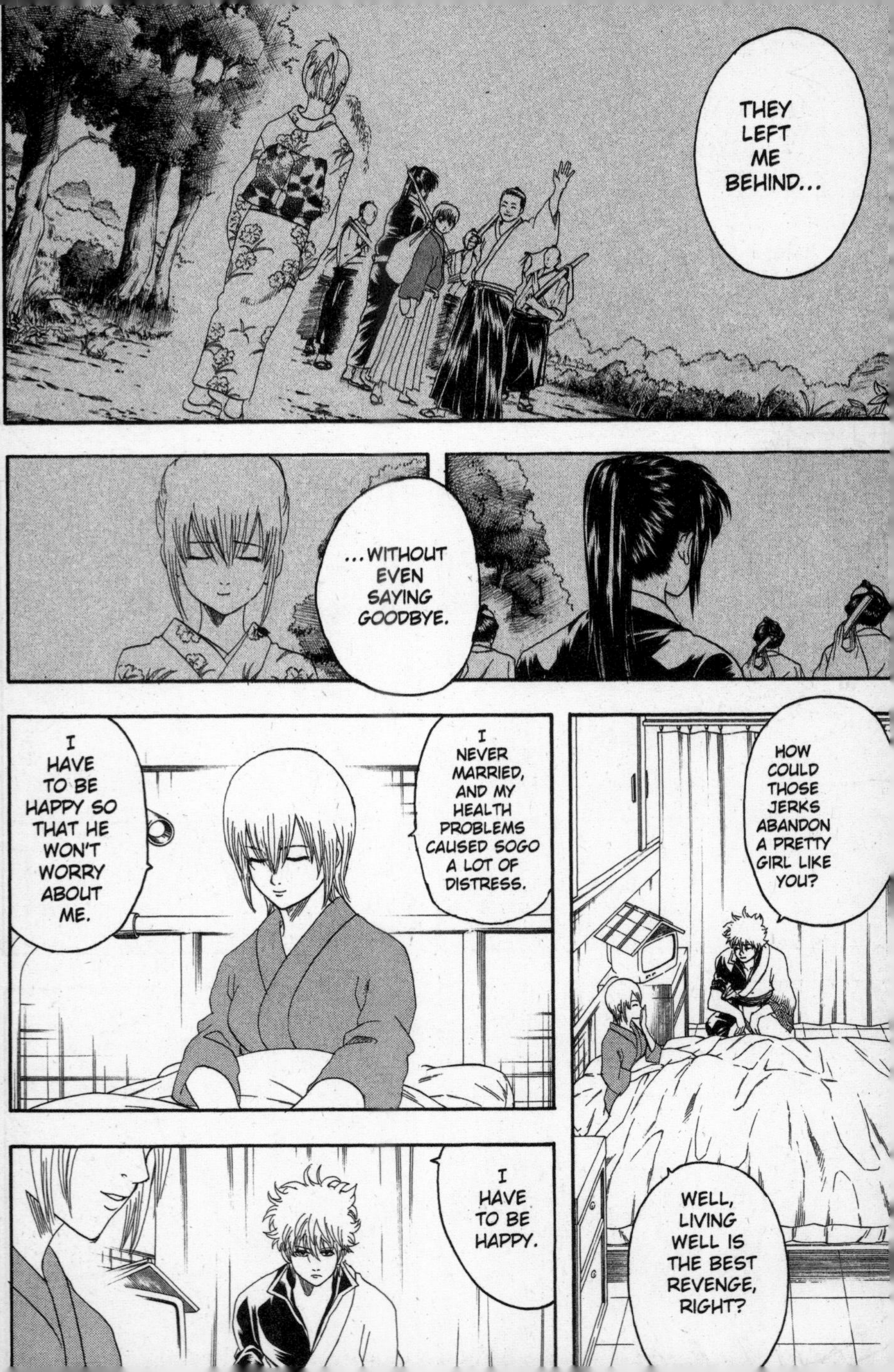
THEY LEFT ME BEHIND...
...WITHOUT EVEN SAYING GOODBYE.
HOW COULD THOSE JERKS ABANDON A PRETTY GIRL LIKE YOU?
WELL, LIVING WELL IS THE BEST REVENGE, RIGHT?
I NEVER MARRIED, AND MY HEALTH PROBLEMS CAUSED SOGO A LOT OF DISTRESS.
I HAVE TO BE HAPPY SO THAT HE WON'T WORRY ABOUT ME.
I HAVE TO BE HAPPY.

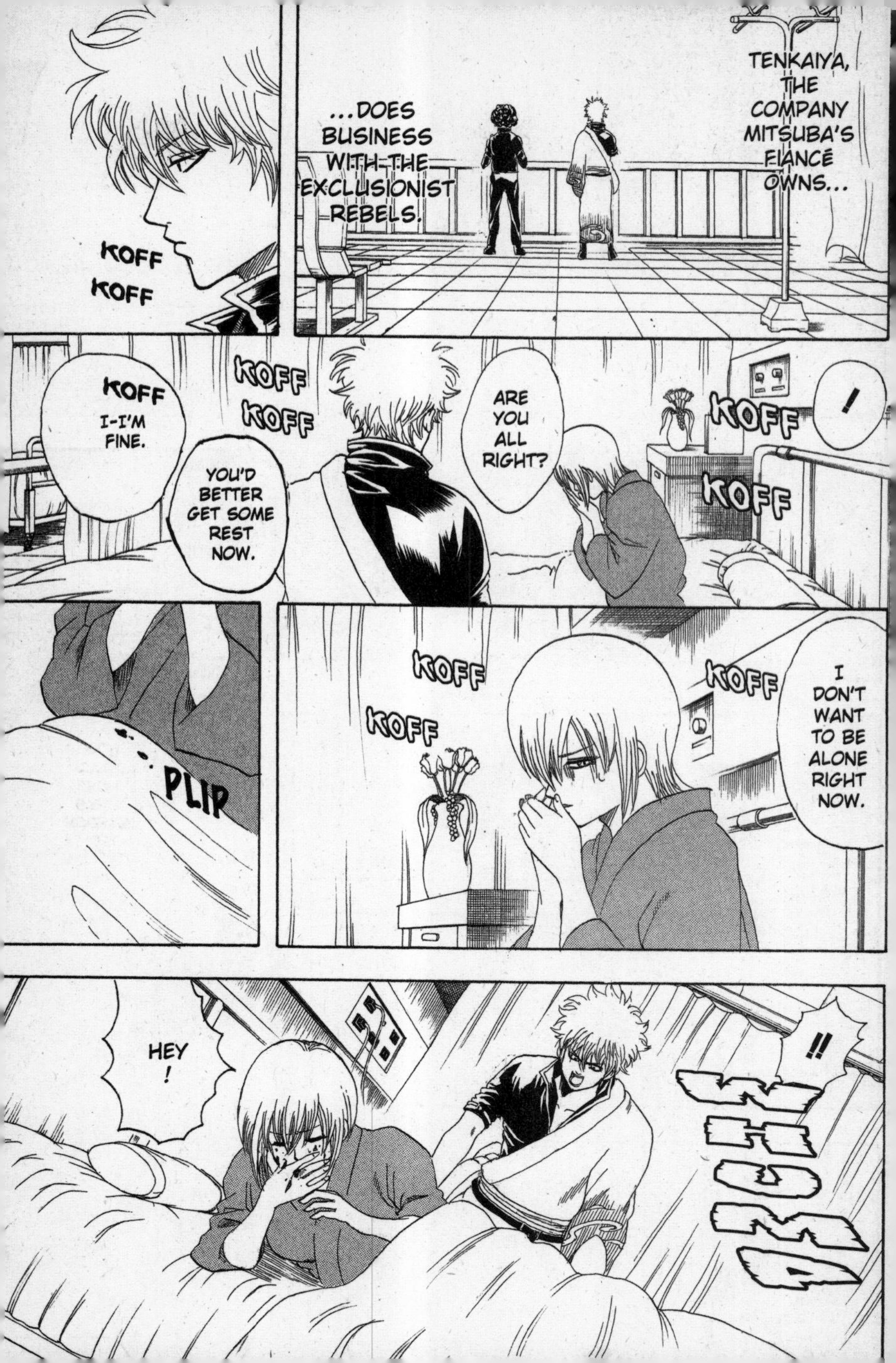
TENKAIYA, THE COMPANY MITSUBA'S FIANCÉ OWNS...
...DOES BUSINESS WITH THE EXCLUSIONIST REBELS.
KOFF
KOFF
!
KOFF
KOFF
ARE YOU ALL RIGHT?
KOFF
KOFF
YOU'D BETTER GET SOME REST NOW.
KOFF I-I'M FINE.
I DON'T WANT TO BE ALONE RIGHT NOW.
KOFF
KOFF
KOFF
PLIP
!!
WHUMP
HEY!

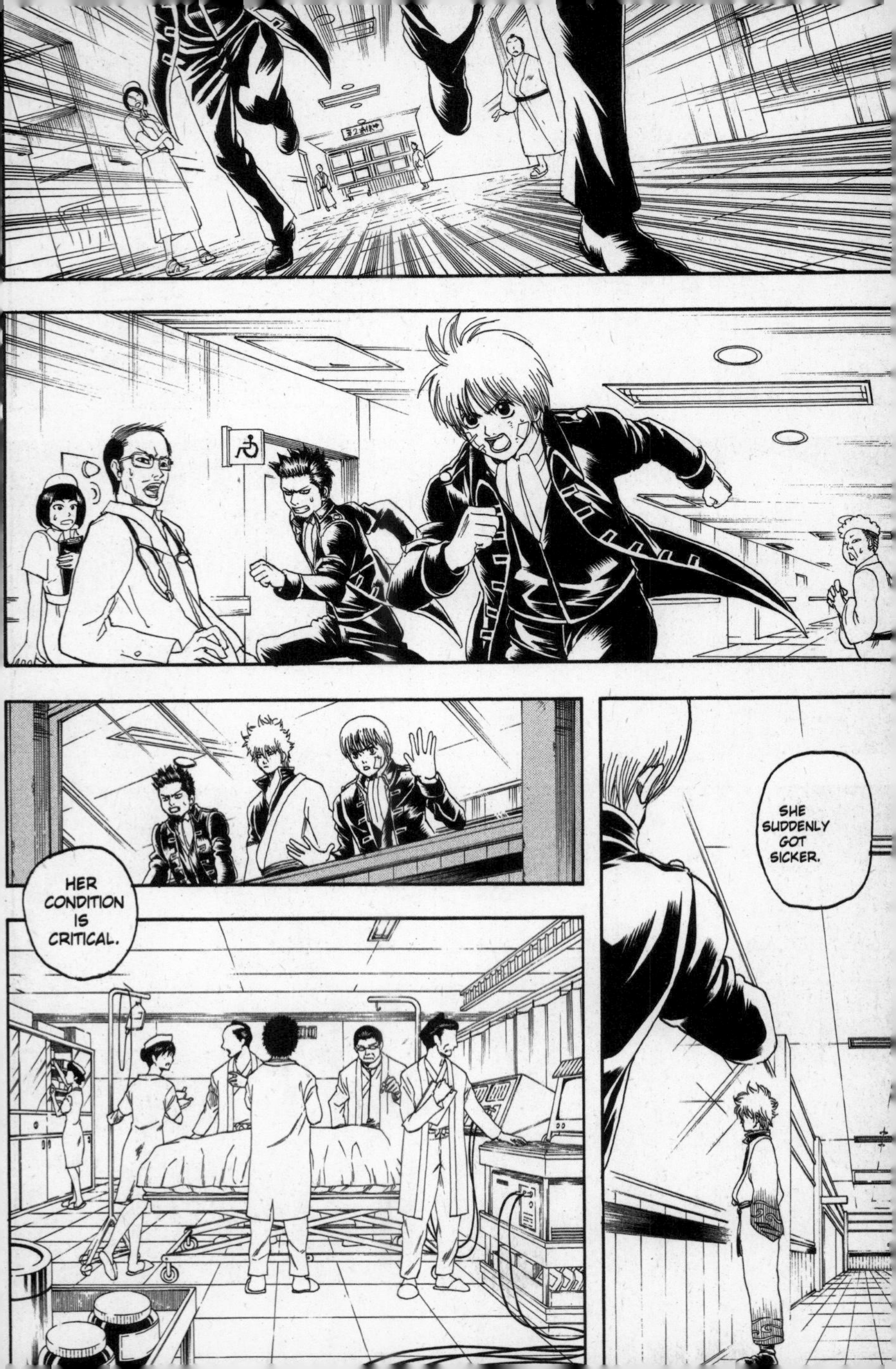
SHE SUDDENLY GOT SICKER.
HER CONDITION IS CRITICAL.

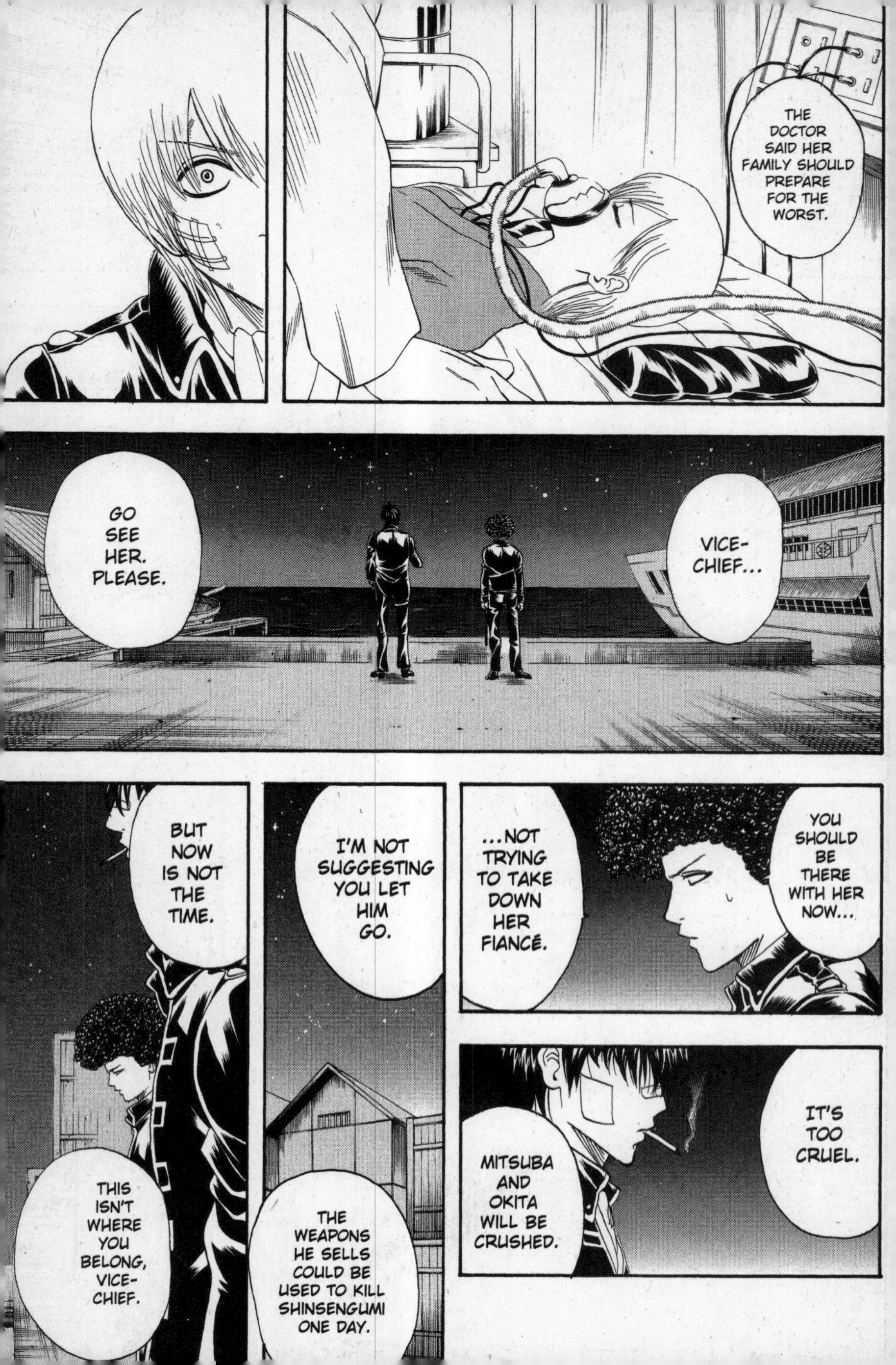
THE DOCTOR SAID HER FAMILY SHOULD PREPARE FOR THE WORST.
VICE-CHIEF...
GO SEE HER. PLEASE.
YOU SHOULD BE THERE WITH HER NOW...
...NOT TRYING TO TAKE DOWN HER FIANCÉ.
IT'S TOO CRUEL.
MITSUBA AND OKITA WILL BE CRUSHED.
I'M NOT SUGGESTING YOU LET HIM GO.
THE WEAPONS HE SELLS COULD BE USED TO KILL SHINSENGUMI ONE DAY.
BUT NOW IS NOT THE TIME.
THIS ISN'T WHERE YOU BELONG, VICE-CHIEF.

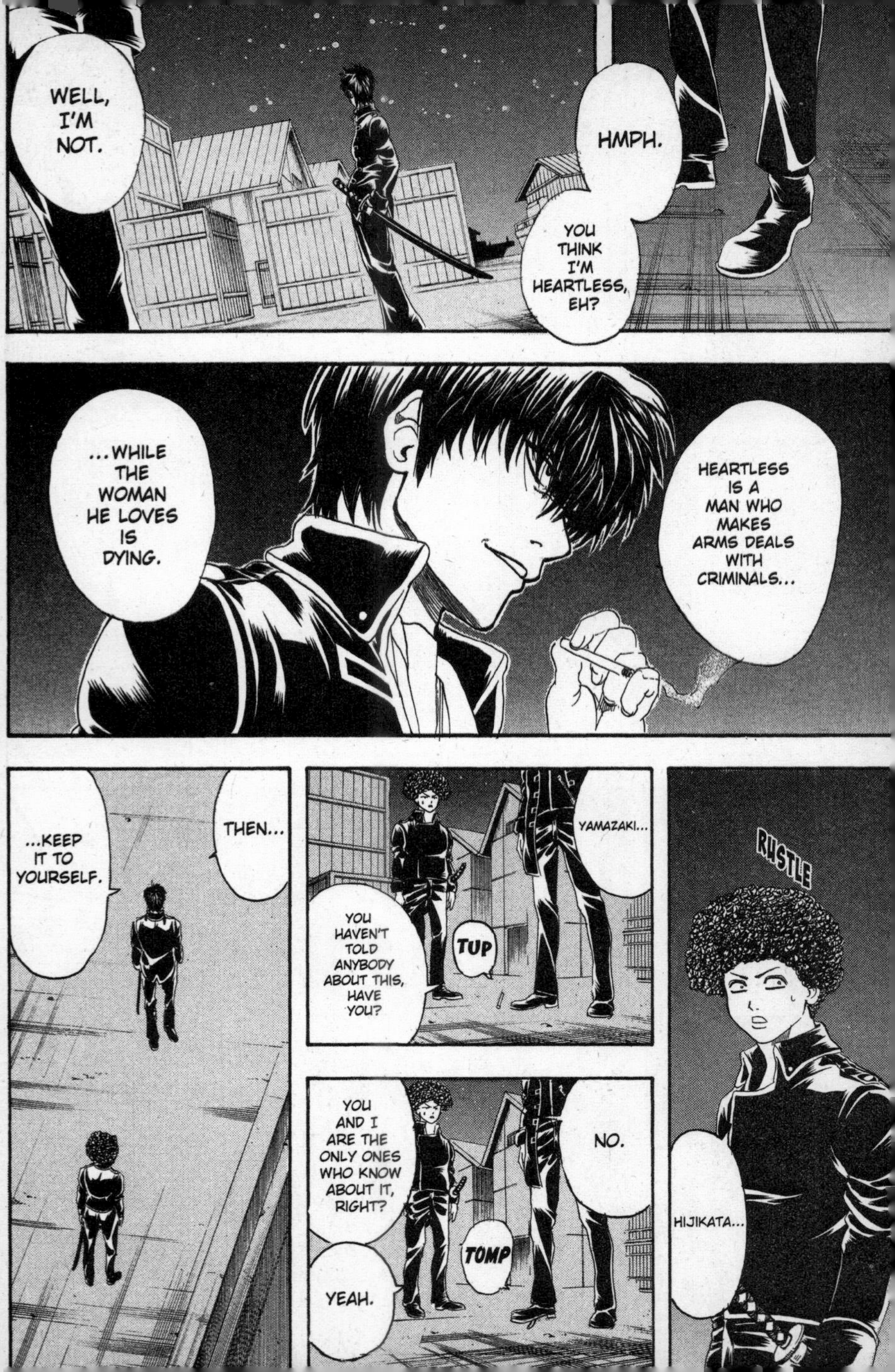
HMPH.
YOU THINK I'M HEARTLESS, EH?
WELL, I'M NOT.
HEARTLESS IS A MAN WHO MAKES ARMS DEALS WITH CRIMINALS...
...WHILE THE WOMAN HE LOVES IS DYING.
RUSTLE
HIJIKATA...
YAMAZAKI...
YOU HAVEN'T TOLD ANYBODY ABOUT THIS, HAVE YOU?
TUP
NO.
YOU AND I ARE THE ONLY ONES WHO KNOW ABOUT IT, RIGHT?
TOMP
YEAH.
THEN...
...KEEP IT TO YOURSELF.

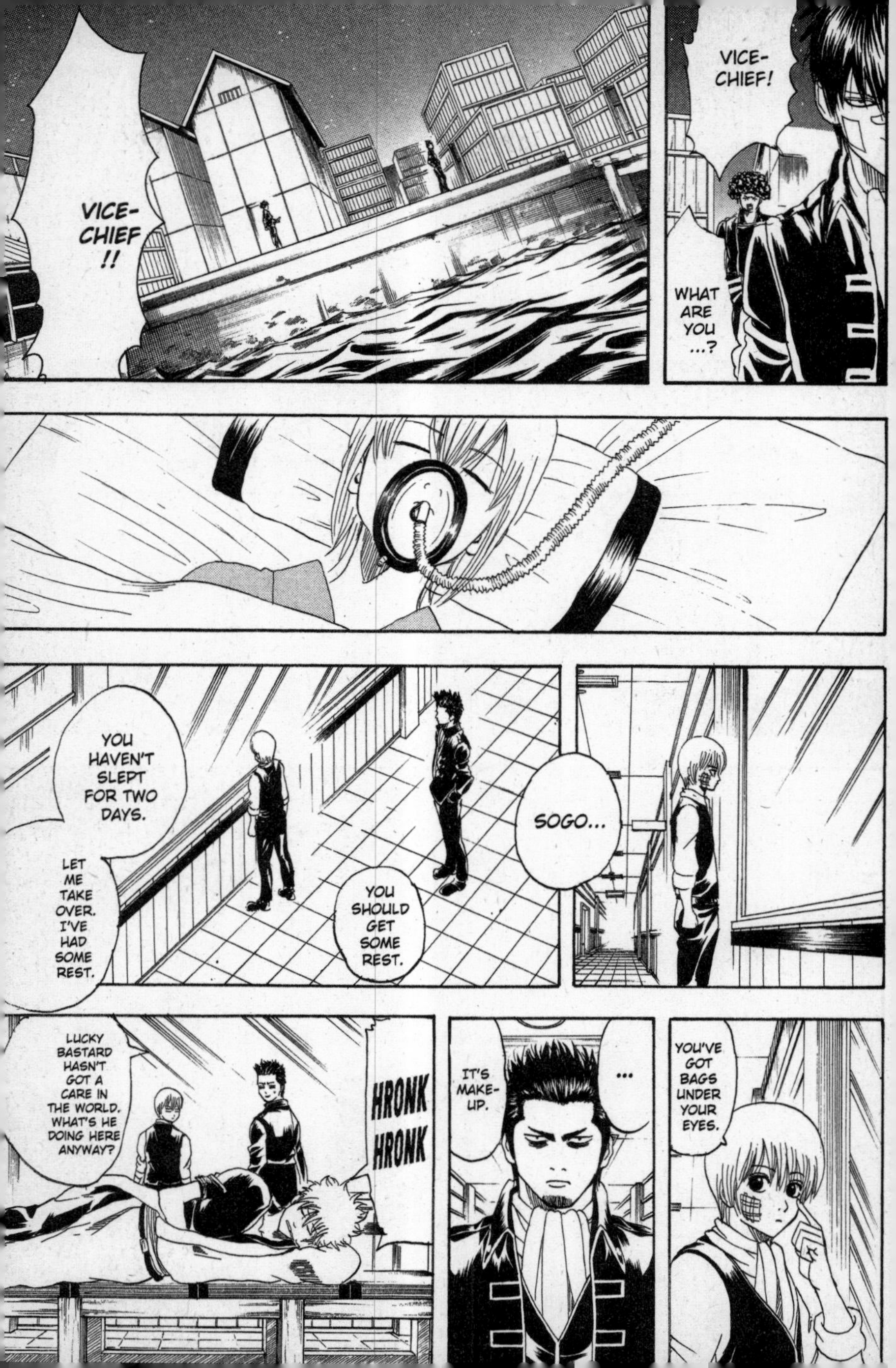
VICE-CHIEF!
WHAT ARE YOU ...?
VICE-CHIEF!!
SOGO...
YOU HAVEN'T SLEPT FOR TWO DAYS.
YOU SHOULD GET SOME REST.
LET ME TAKE OVER. I'VE HAD SOME REST.
YOU'VE GOT BAGS UNDER YOUR EYES.
...
IT'S MAKE-UP.
HRONK HRONK
LUCKY BASTARD HASN'T GOT A CARE IN THE WORLD. WHAT'S HE DOING HERE ANYWAY?

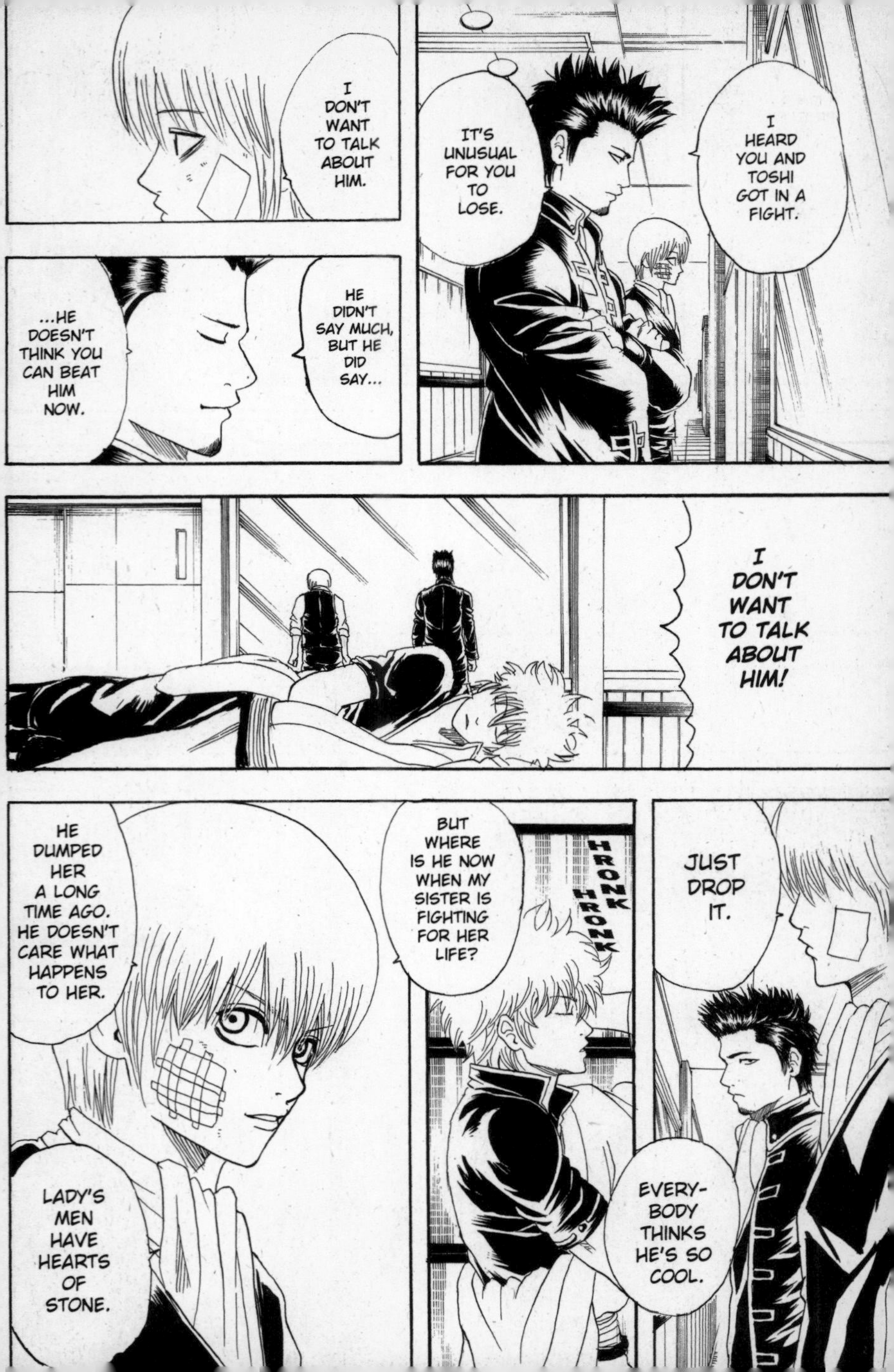
I HEARD YOU AND TOSHI GOT IN A FIGHT.
IT'S UNUSUAL FOR YOU TO LOSE.
I DON'T WANT TO TALK ABOUT HIM.
HE DIDN'T SAY MUCH, BUT HE DID SAY...
...HE DOESN'T THINK YOU CAN BEAT HIM NOW.
I DON'T WANT TO TALK ABOUT HIM!
JUST DROP IT.
EVERY-BODY THINKS HE'S SO COOL.
BUT WHERE IS HE NOW WHEN MY SISTER IS FIGHTING FOR HER LIFE?
HRONK
HRONK
HE DUMPED HER A LONG TIME AGO. HE DOESN'T CARE WHAT HAPPENS TO HER.
LADY'S MEN HAVE HEARTS OF STONE.

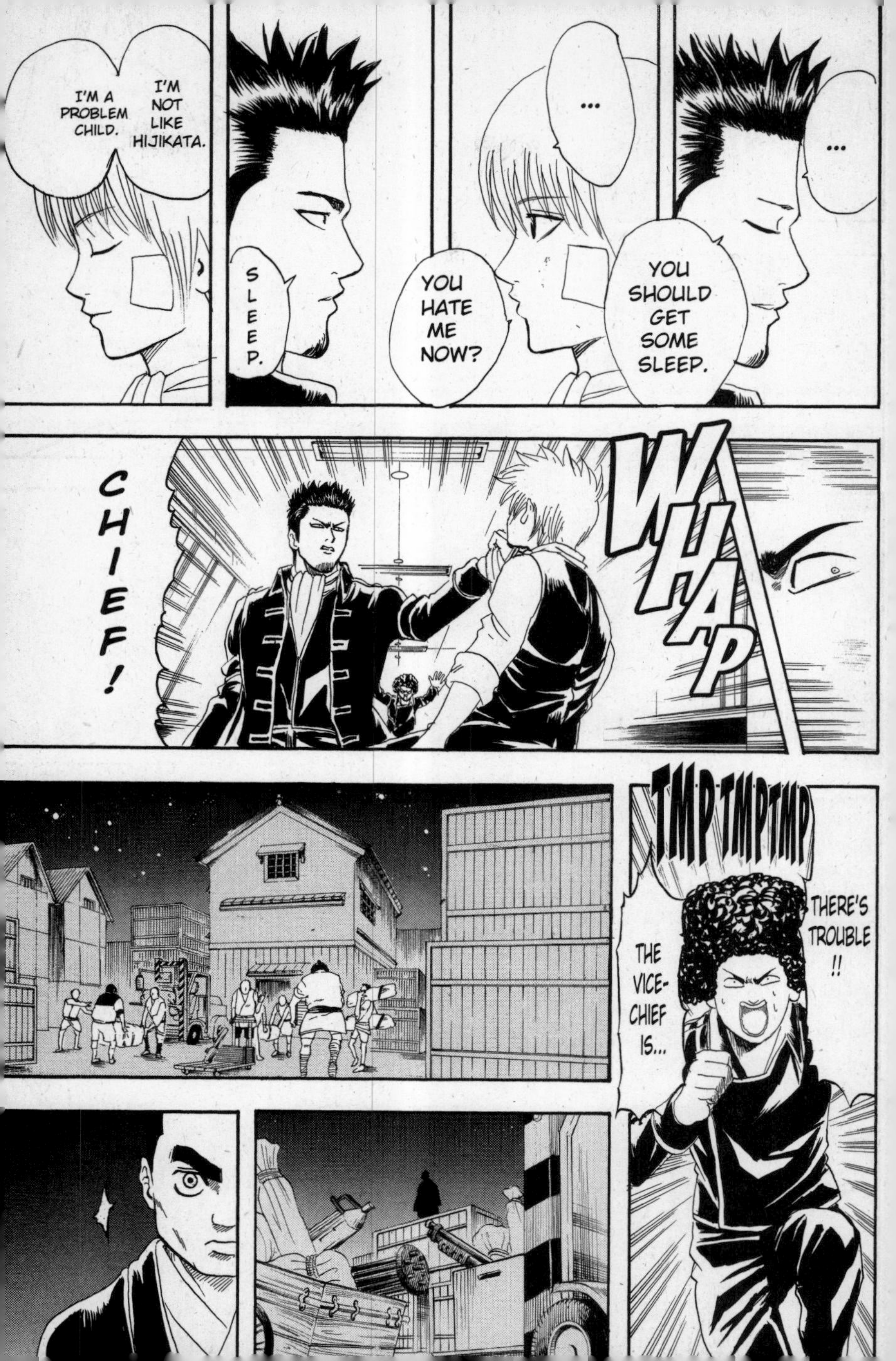
...
...
YOU SHOULD GET SOME SLEEP.
YOU HATE ME NOW?
SLEEP.
I'M NOT LIKE HIJIKATA.
I'M A PROBLEM CHILD.
WHAP
CHIEF!
TMP TMPTMP
THERE'S TROUBLE!!
THE VICE-CHIEF IS...

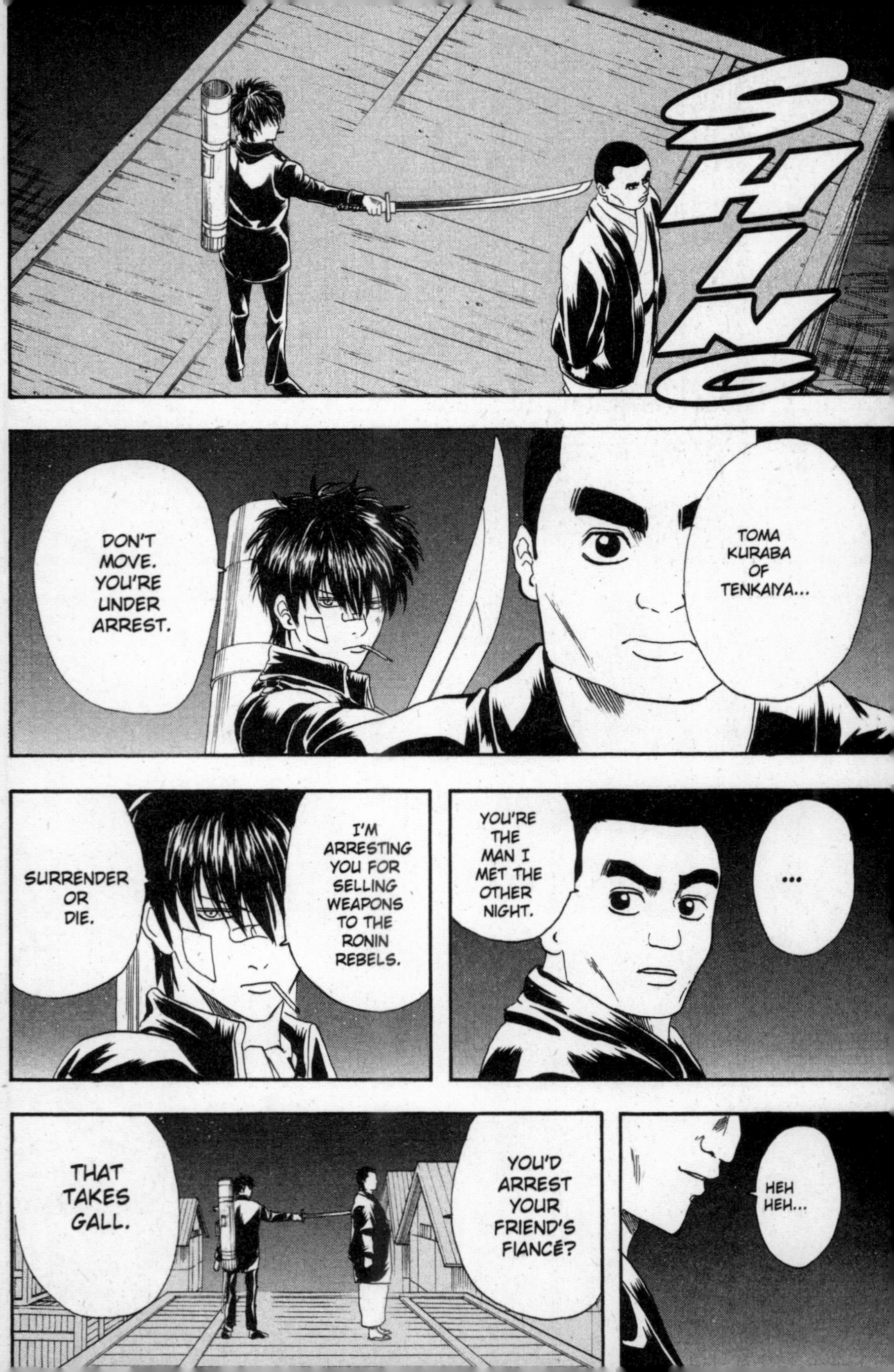
SHING
TOMA KURABA OF TENKAIYA...
DON'T MOVE. YOU'RE UNDER ARREST.
...
YOU'RE THE MAN I MET THE OTHER NIGHT.
I'M ARRESTING YOU FOR SELLING WEAPONS TO THE RONIN REBELS.
SURRENDER OR DIE.
HEH HEH...
YOU'D ARREST YOUR FRIEND'S FIANCE?
THAT TAKES GALL.

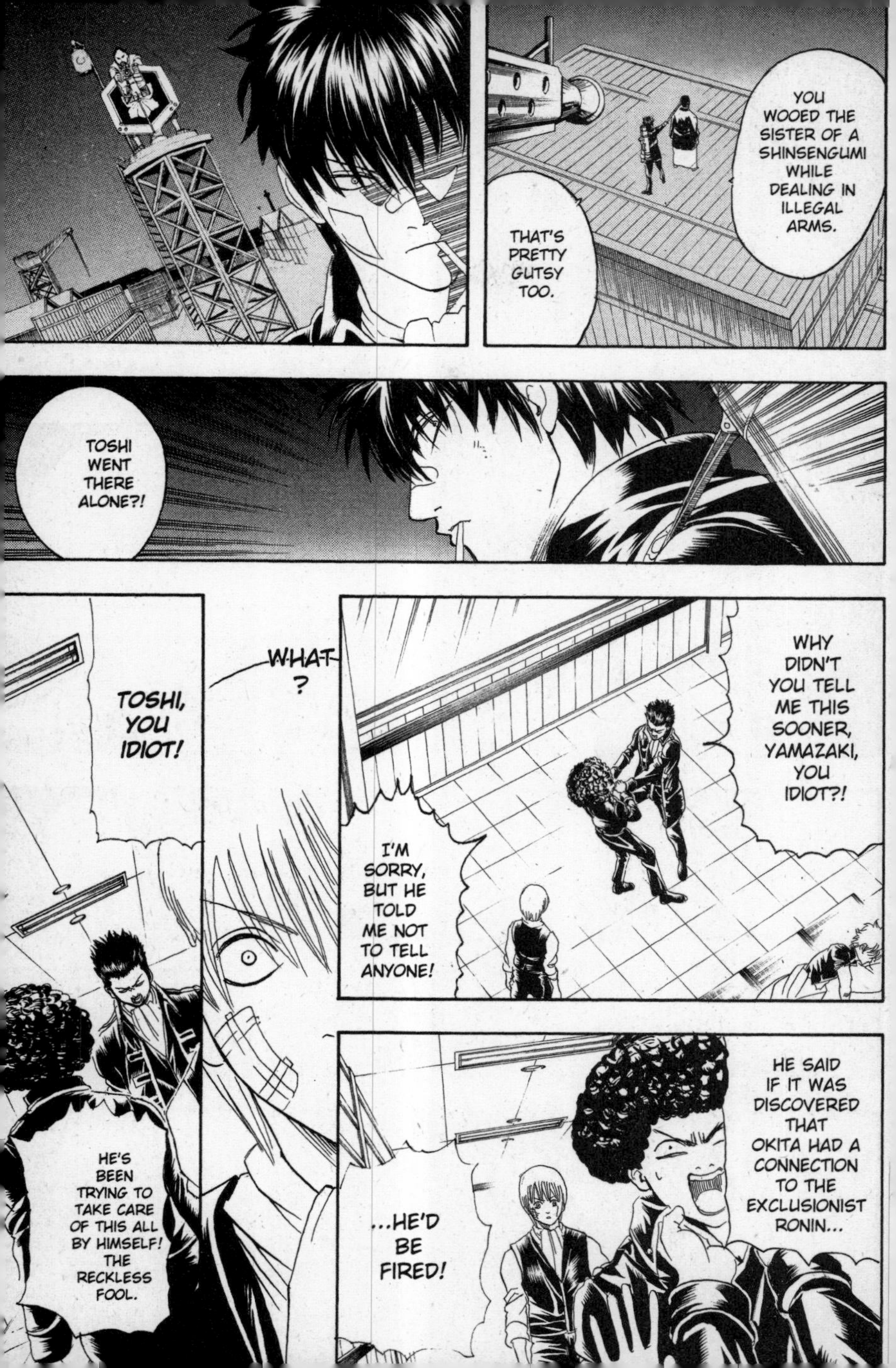
YOU WOOED THE SISTER OF A SHINSENGUMI WHILE DEALING IN ILLEGAL ARMS.
THAT'S PRETTY GUTSY TOO.
TOSHI WENT THERE ALONE?!
WHY DIDN'T YOU TELL ME THIS SOONER, YAMAZAKI, YOU IDIOT?!
I'M SORRY, BUT HE TOLD ME NOT TO TELL ANYONE!
HE SAID IF IT WAS DISCOVERED THAT OKITA HAD A CONNECTION TO THE EXCLUSIONIST RONIN...
...HE'D BE FIRED!
WHAT?
TOSHI, YOU IDIOT!
HE'S BEEN TRYING TO TAKE CARE OF THIS ALL BY HIMSELF! THE RECKLESS FOOL.

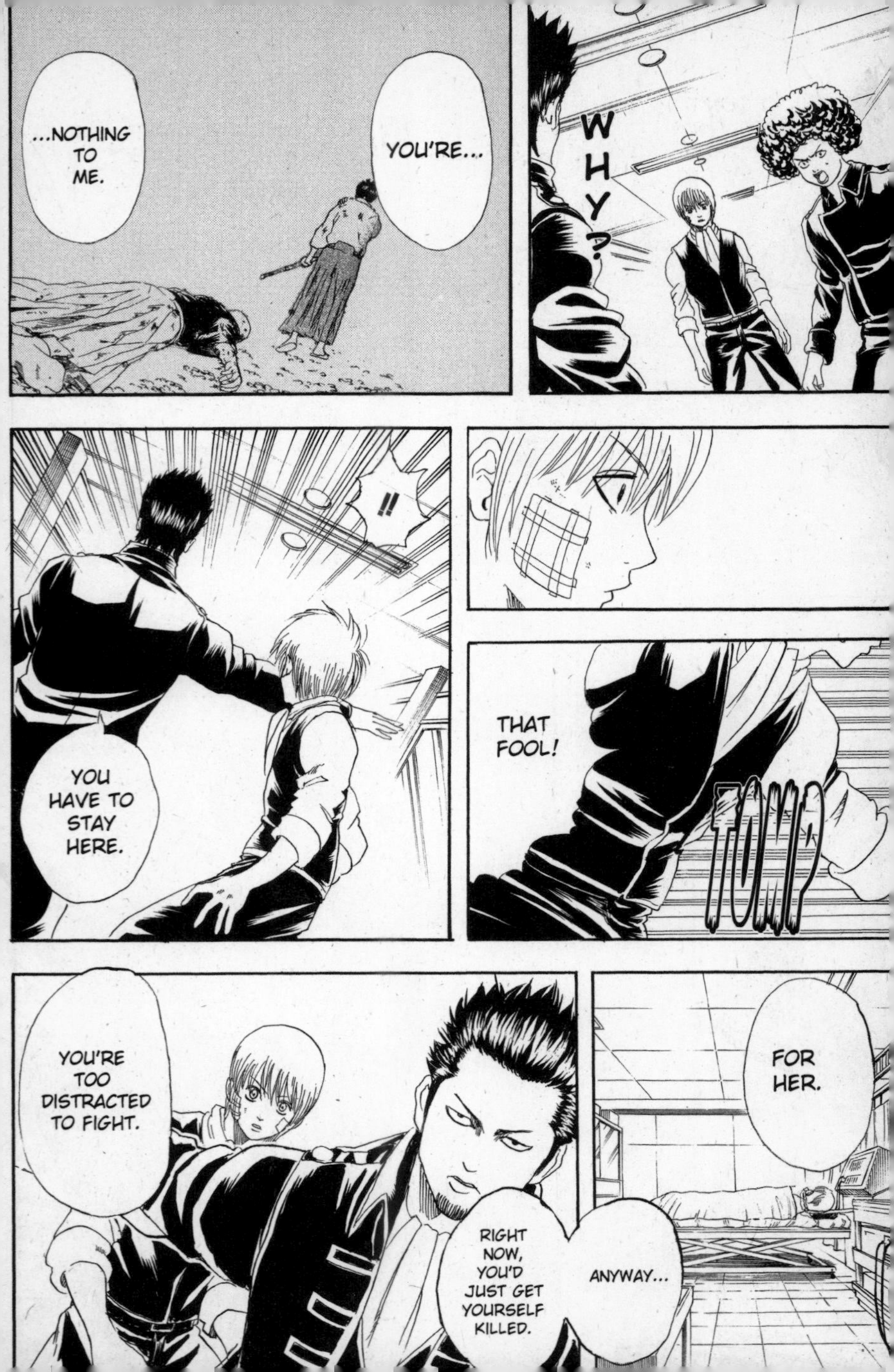
WHY?
YOU'RE...
...NOTHING TO ME.
THAT FOOL!
TOMP
!!
YOU HAVE TO STAY HERE.
FOR HER.
ANYWAY...
YOU'RE TOO DISTRACTED TO FIGHT.
RIGHT NOW, YOU'D JUST GET YOURSELF KILLED.

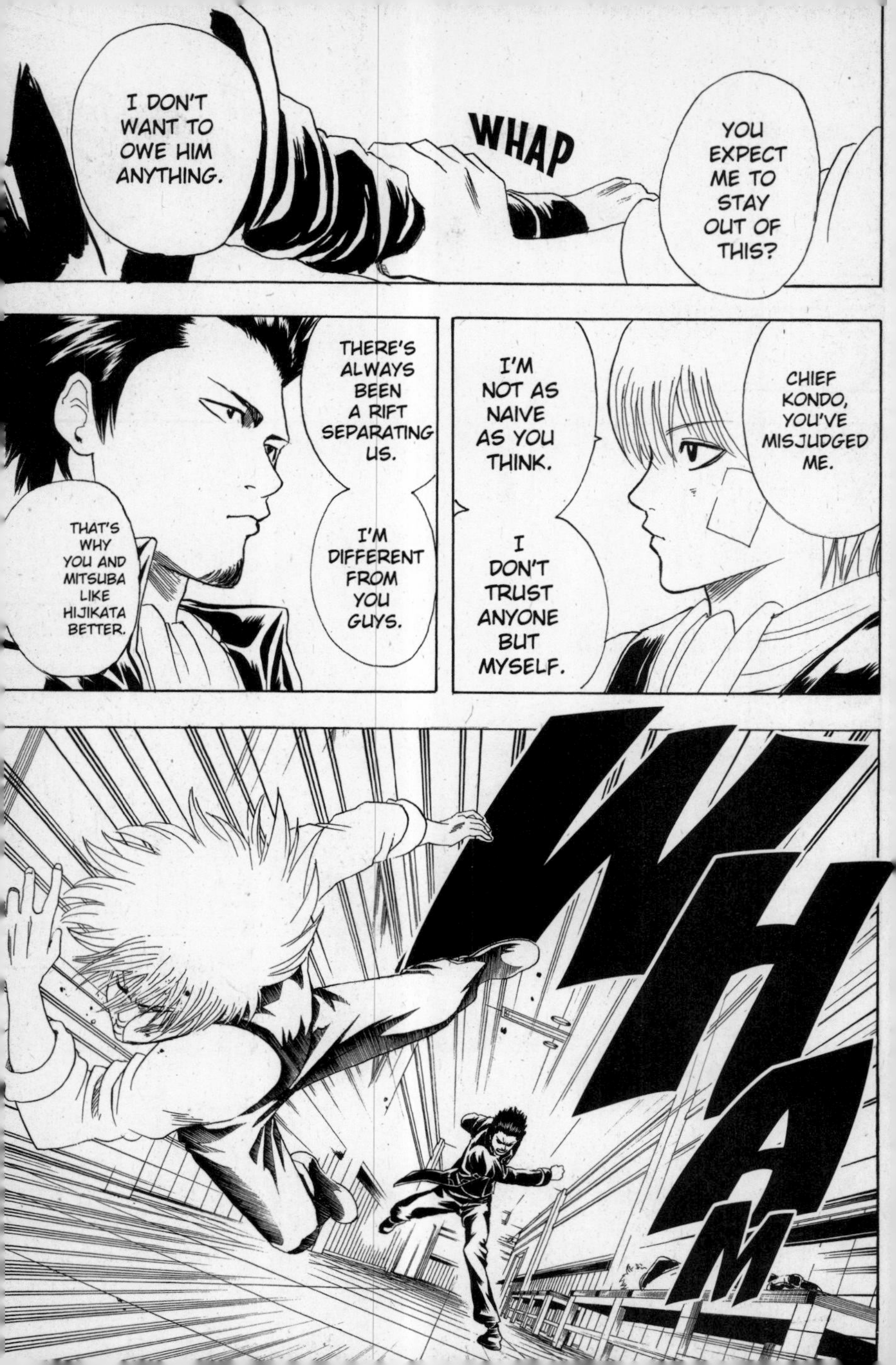
YOU EXPECT ME TO STAY OUT OF THIS?
WHAP
I DON'T WANT TO OWE HIM ANYTHING.
CHIEF KONDO, YOU'VE MISJUDGED ME.
I'M NOT AS NAIVE AS YOU THINK.
I DON'T TRUST ANYONE BUT MYSELF.
THERE'S ALWAYS BEEN A RIFT SEPARATING US.
I'M DIFFERENT FROM YOU GUYS.
THAT'S WHY YOU AND MITSUBA LIKE HIJIKATA BETTER.
WHAM

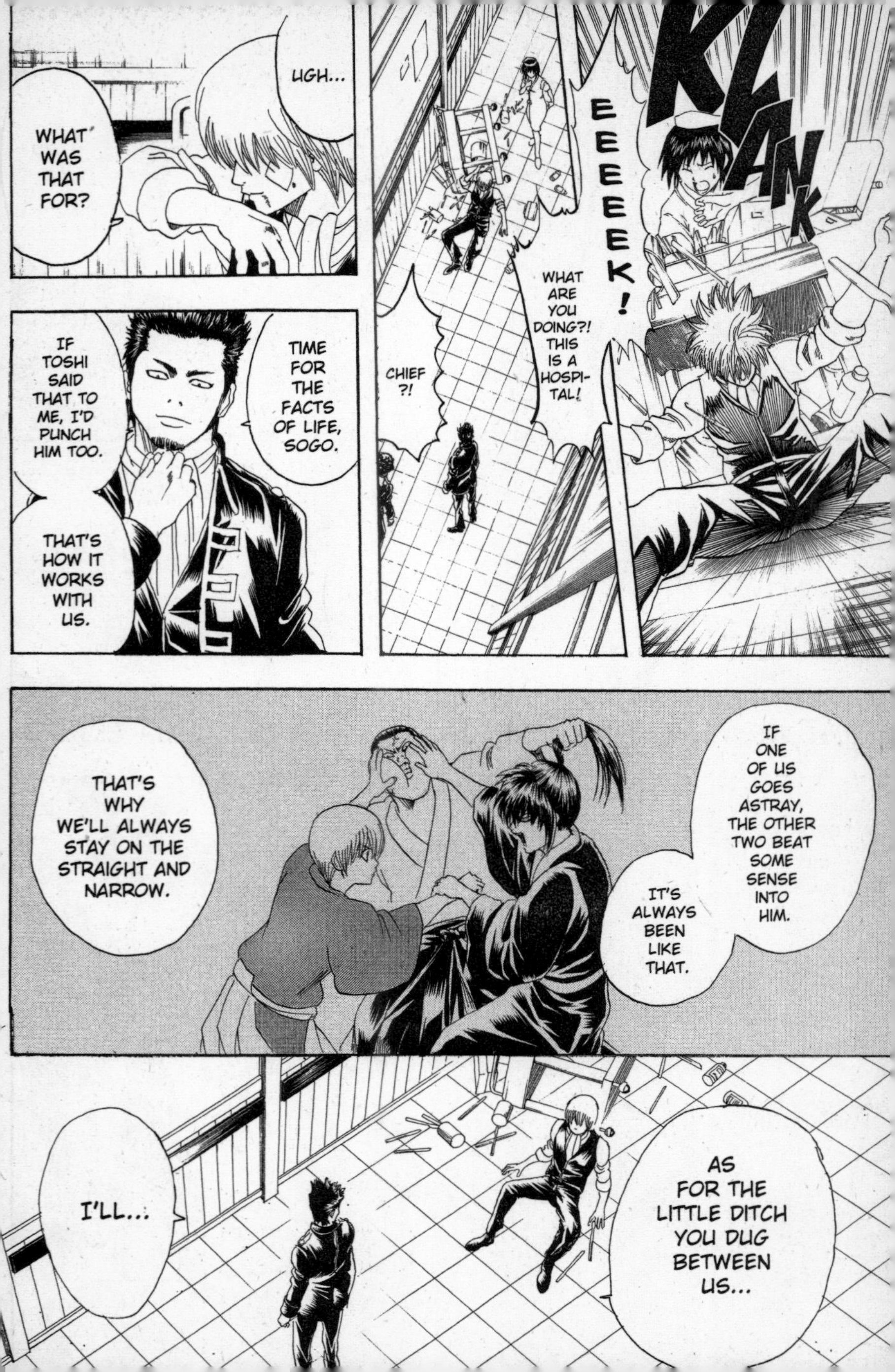
KLANK
EEEEEK!
WHAT ARE YOU DOING?! THIS IS A HOSPITAL!
CHIEF?!
UGH...
WHAT WAS THAT FOR?
TIME FOR THE FACTS OF LIFE, SOGO.
IF TOSHI SAID THAT TO ME, I'D PUNCH HIM TOO.
THAT'S HOW IT WORKS WITH US.
IF ONE OF US GOES ASTRAY, THE OTHER TWO BEAT SOME SENSE INTO HIM.
IT'S ALWAYS BEEN LIKE THAT.
THAT'S WHY WE'LL ALWAYS STAY ON THE STRAIGHT AND NARROW.
AS FOR THE LITTLE DITCH YOU DUG BETWEEN US...
I'LL...

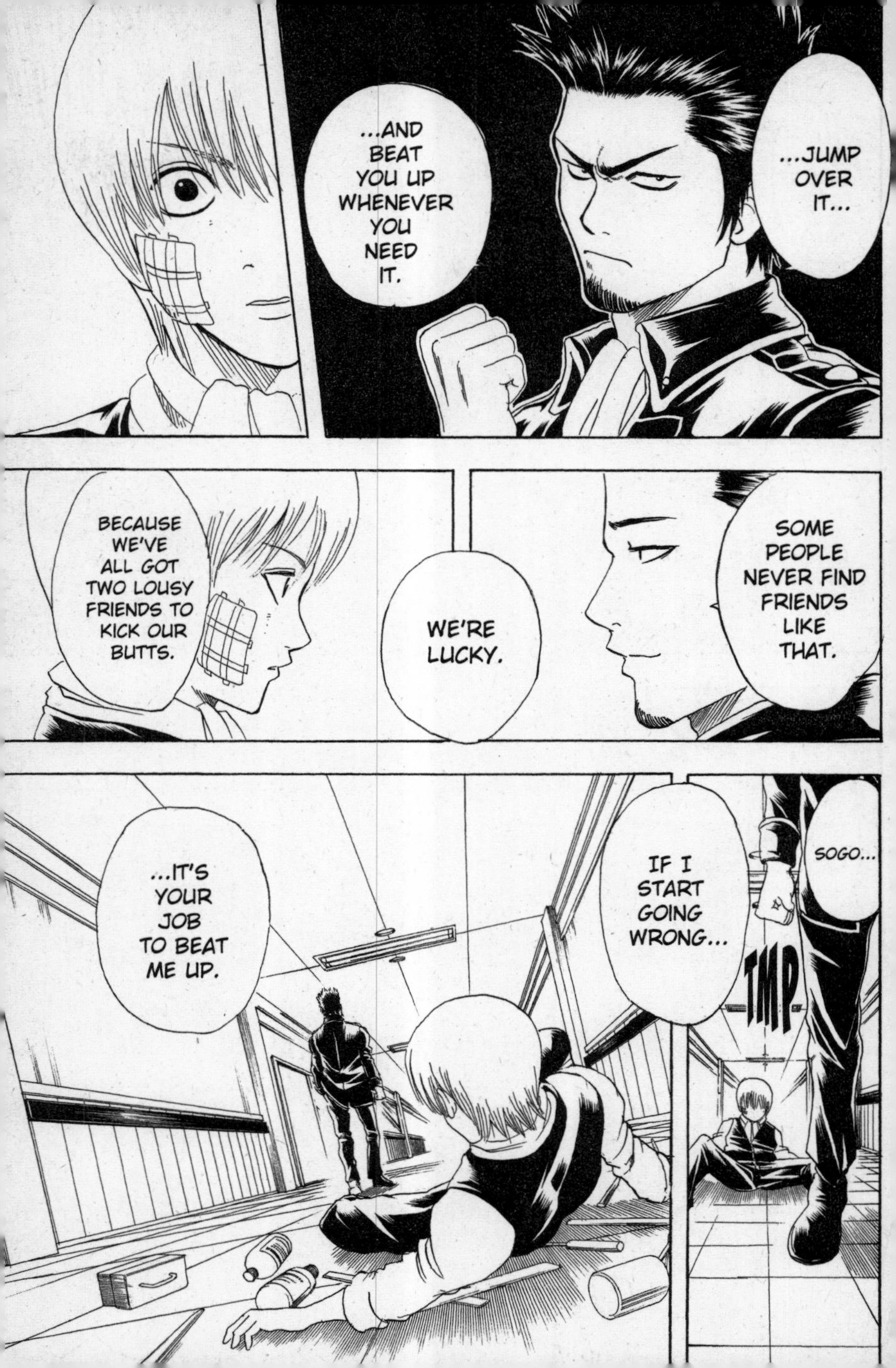
...JUMP OVER IT...
...AND BEAT YOU UP WHENEVER YOU NEED IT.
SOME PEOPLE NEVER FIND FRIENDS LIKE THAT.
WE'RE LUCKY.
BECAUSE WE'VE ALL GOT TWO LOUSY FRIENDS TO KICK OUR BUTTS.
SOGO...
IF I START GOING WRONG...
TMP
...IT'S YOUR JOB TO BEAT ME UP.

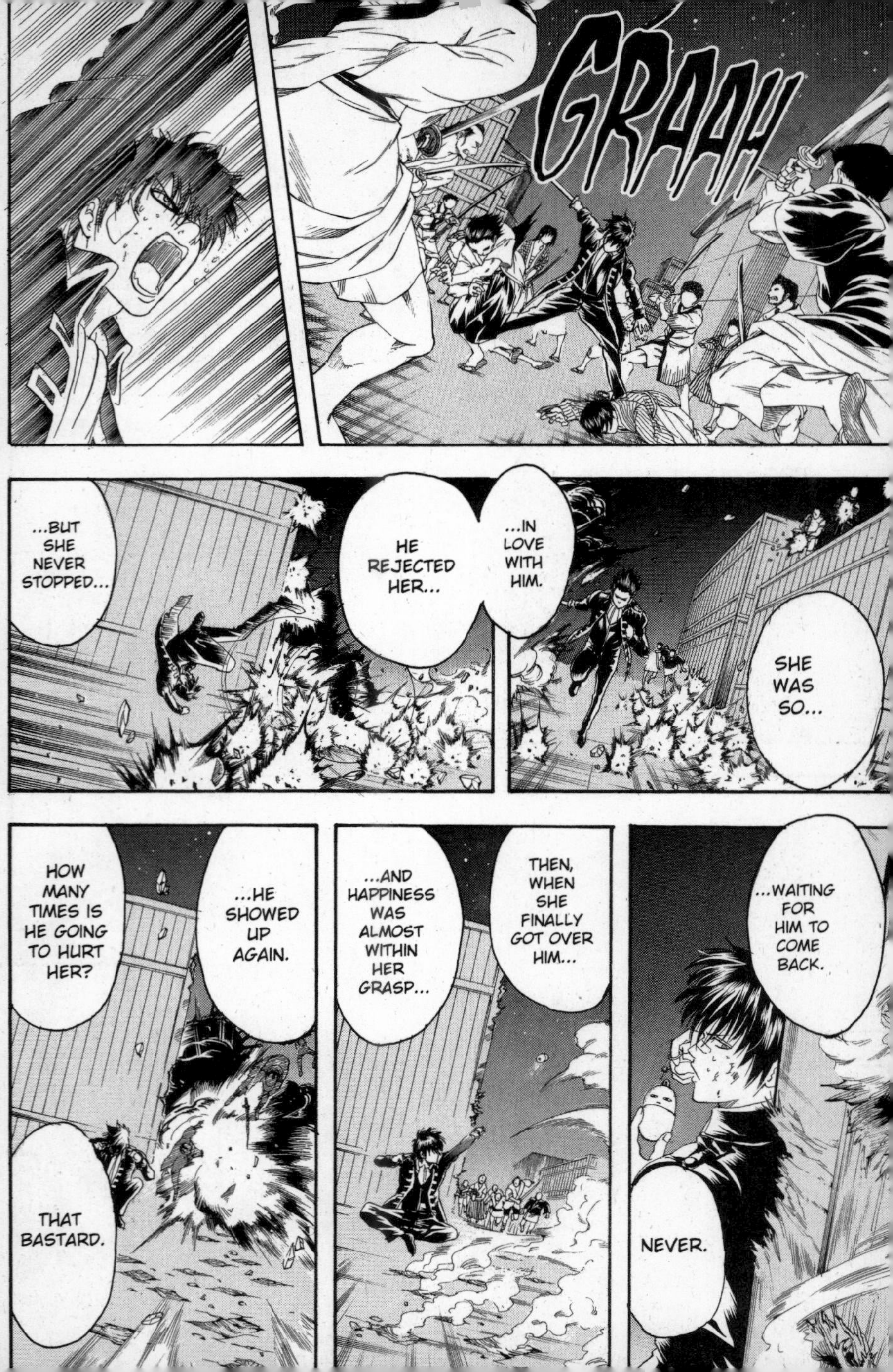
GRAAH
SHE WAS SO...
...IN LOVE WITH HIM.
HE REJECTED HER...
...BUT SHE NEVER STOPPED...
...WAITING FOR HIM TO COME BACK.
NEVER.
THEN, WHEN SHE FINALLY GOT OVER HIM...
...AND HAPPINESS WAS ALMOST WITHIN HER GRASP...
...HE SHOWED UP AGAIN.
HOW MANY TIMES IS HE GOING TO HURT HER?
THAT BASTARD.

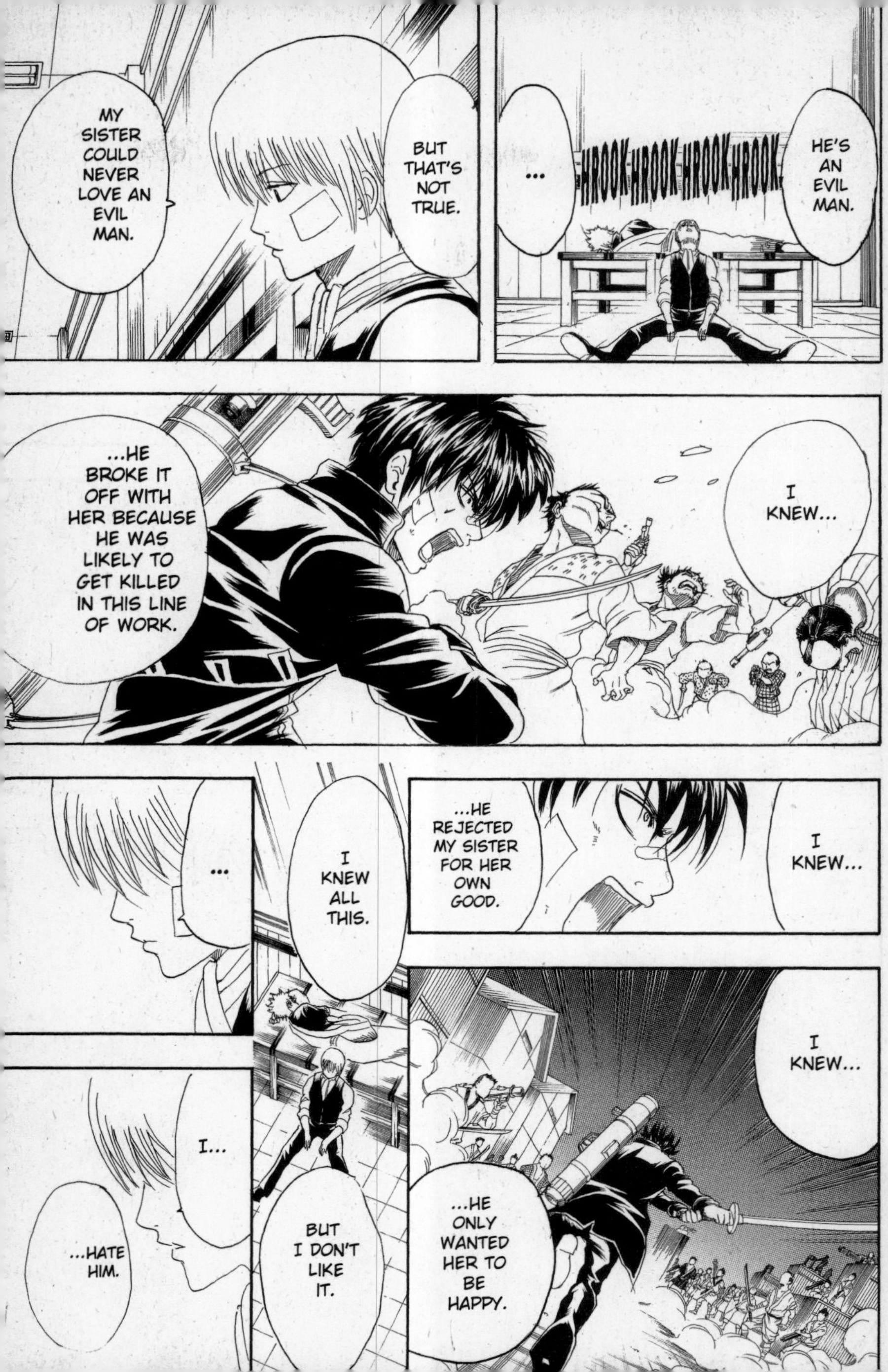
HE'S AN EVIL MAN.
HROOK HROOK HROOK HROOK
...
BUT THAT'S NOT TRUE.
MY SISTER COULD NEVER LOVE AN EVIL MAN.
I KNEW...
...HE BROKE IT OFF WITH HER BECAUSE HE WAS LIKELY TO GET KILLED IN THIS LINE OF WORK.
I KNEW...
...HE REJECTED MY SISTER FOR HER OWN GOOD.
I KNEW...
...HE ONLY WANTED HER TO BE HAPPY.
I KNEW ALL THIS.
...
BUT I DON'T LIKE IT.
I...
...HATE HIM.

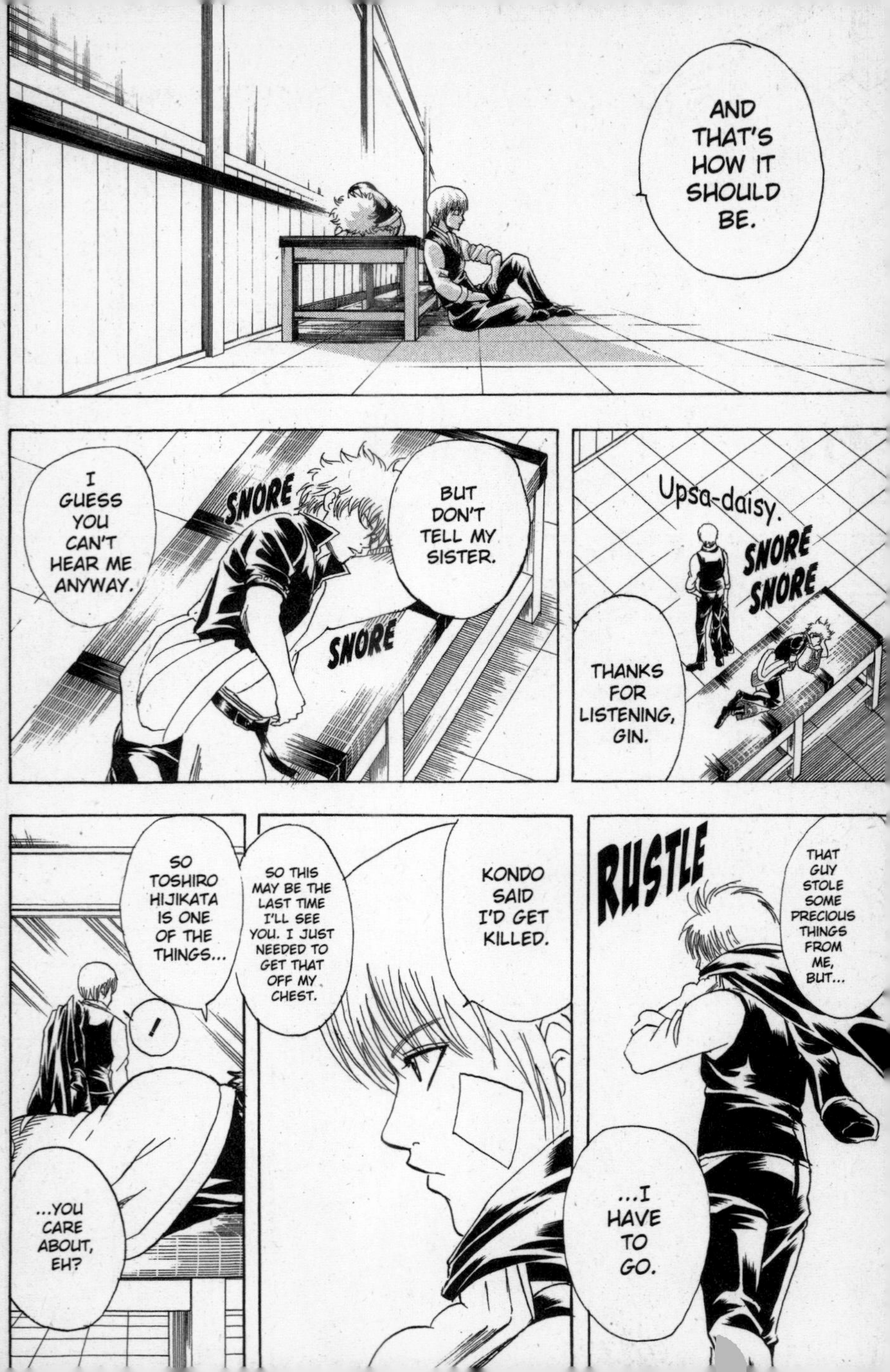
AND THAT'S HOW IT SHOULD BE.
Upsa-daisy.
SNORE SNORE
THANKS FOR LISTENING, GIN.
BUT DON'T TELL MY SISTER.
SNORE
I GUESS YOU CAN'T HEAR ME ANYWAY.
SNORE
RUSTLE
THAT GUY STOLE SOME PRECIOUS THINGS FROM ME, BUT...
...I HAVE TO GO.
KONDO SAID I'D GET KILLED.
SO THIS MAY BE THE LAST TIME I'LL SEE YOU. I JUST NEEDED TO GET THAT OFF MY CHEST.
SO TOSHIRO HIJIKATA IS ONE OF THE THINGS...
!
...YOU CARE ABOUT, EH?

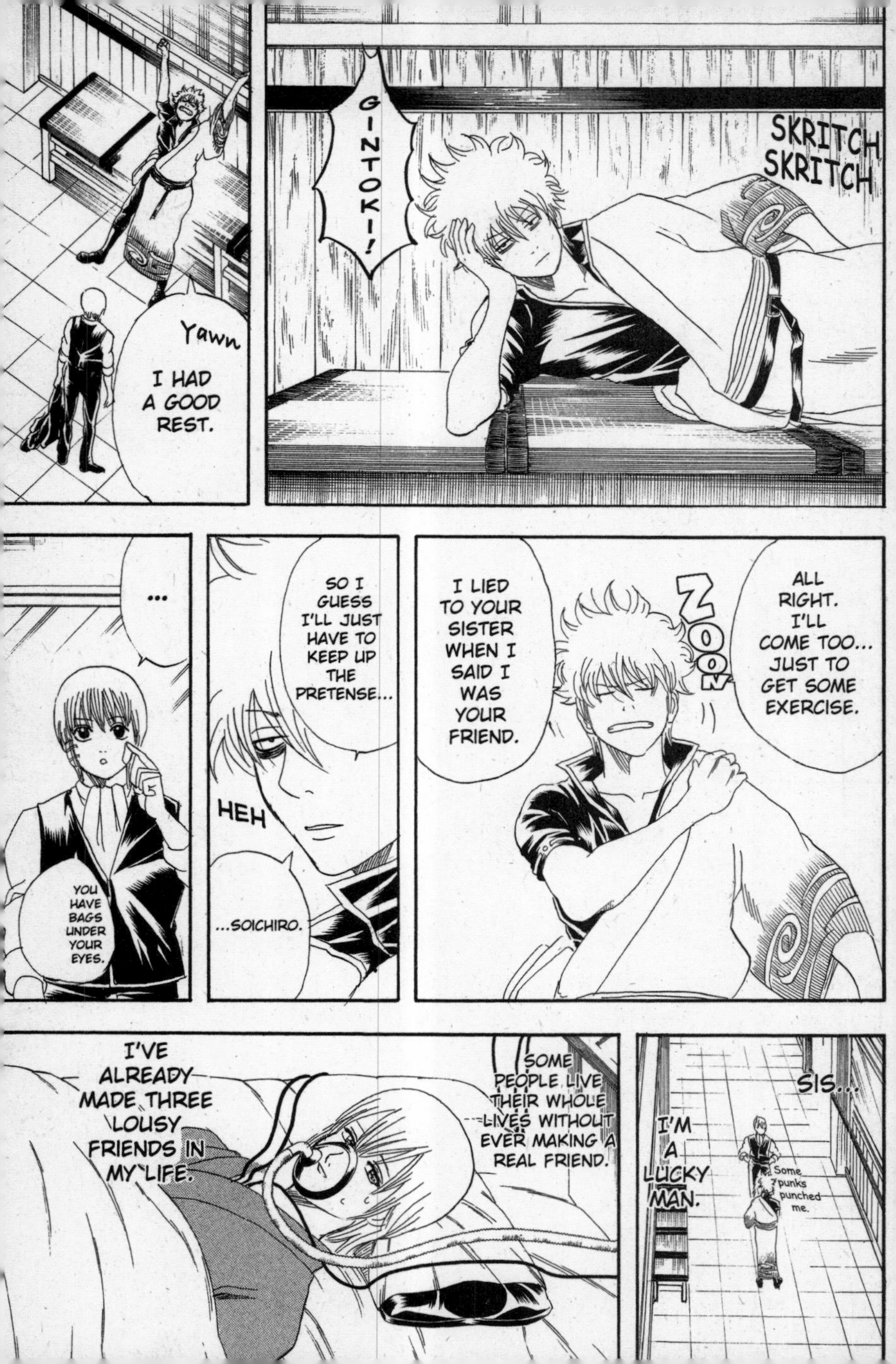
GINTOKI!
SKRITCH SKRITCH
Yawn
I HAD A GOOD REST.
ALL RIGHT. I'LL COME TOO... JUST TO GET SOME EXERCISE.
ZOOON
I LIED TO YOUR SISTER WHEN I SAID I WAS YOUR FRIEND.
SO I GUESS I'LL JUST HAVE TO KEEP UP THE PRETENSE...
HEH
...SOICHIRO.
...
YOU HAVE BAGS UNDER YOUR EYES.
SIS...
I'M A LUCKY MAN.
Some punks punched me.
SOME PEOPLE LIVE THEIR WHOLE LIVES WITHOUT EVER MAKING A REAL FRIEND.
I'VE ALREADY MADE THREE LOUSY FRIENDS IN MY LIFE.

Thank you for purchasing **Gin Tama** volume 16. The other day, I had a chance to party with the **Gin Tama** anime crew. I got to talk with the staff and the cast. Once again I came away feeling like I'd been abusing these people. It's like I'm sexually harassing them all, particularly the female voice actors. They really looked like they'd been having a hard time, and I felt sorry for them, but I was too shy to say so. A shy guy like me tends to say things in roundabout ways, like, "What's it like being a voice actor? You guys probably do naughty things like play with each other's nipples, huh?"

"No, we don't."

"Come on. I know you do. You do naughty things, right?"

In the cab on the way home, my editor gave me a lecture. "How could you say those things to people you just met for the first time? Behave yourself."

And as I was bemoaning the fact that nobody understands me and watching the night scenes slide by, I suddenly felt like I was about to die right there in the cab. When I finally got home I put my head in the toilet to throw up, but an entirely different substance came out the other end. Just another night in the life of a 27-year-old man.

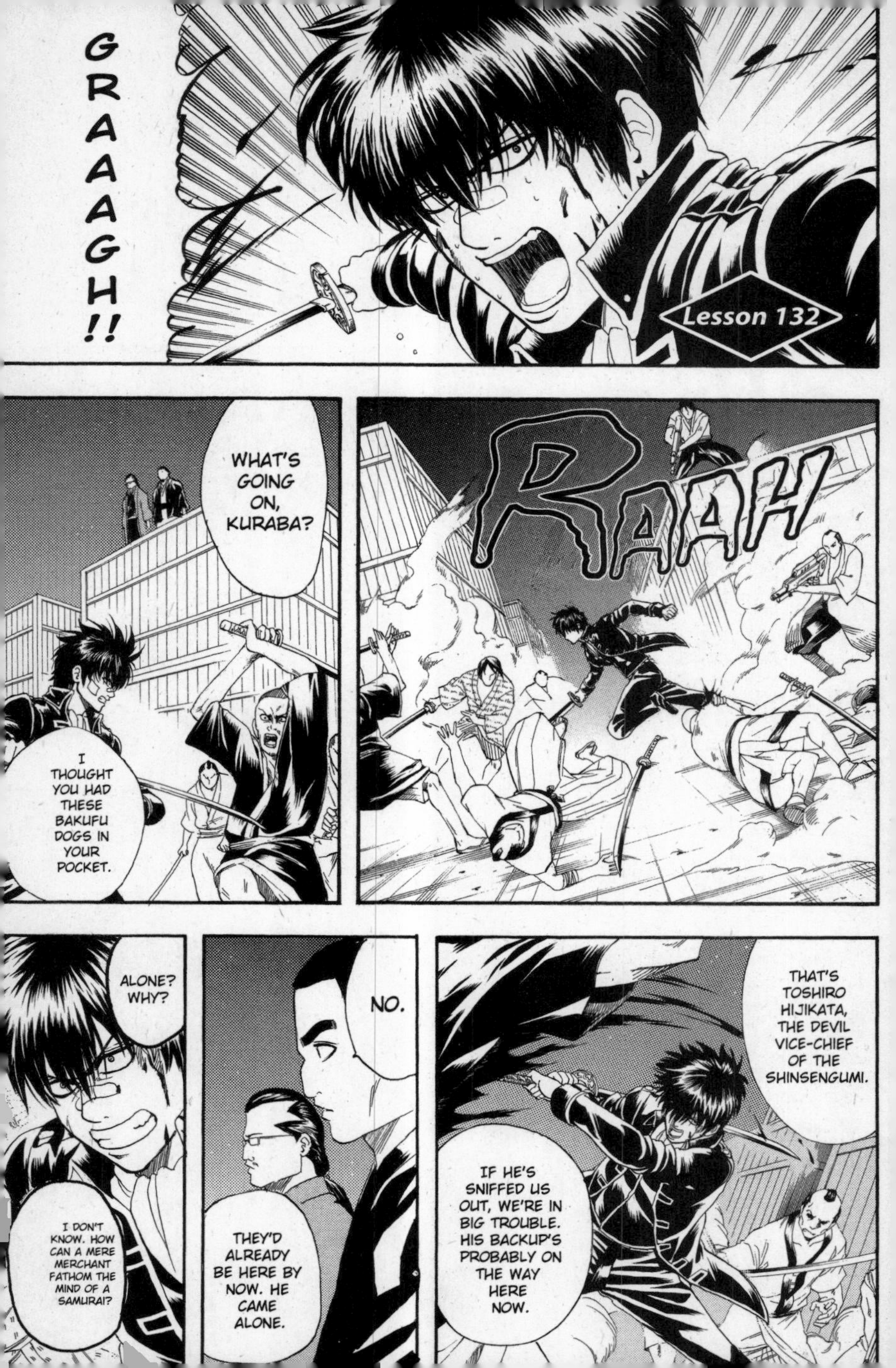
GRAAAGH!!
Lesson 132
RAAAH
WHAT'S GOING ON, KURABA?
I THOUGHT YOU HAD THESE BAKUFU DOGS IN YOUR POCKET.
THAT'S TOSHIRO HIJIKATA, THE DEVIL VICE-CHIEF OF THE SHINSENGUMI.
IF HE'S SNIFFED US OUT, WE'RE IN BIG TROUBLE. HIS BACKUP'S PROBABLY ON THE WAY HERE NOW.
NO.
THEY'D ALREADY BE HERE BY NOW. HE CAME ALONE.
ALONE? WHY?
I DON'T KNOW. HOW CAN A MERE MERCHANT FATHOM THE MIND OF A SAMURAI?

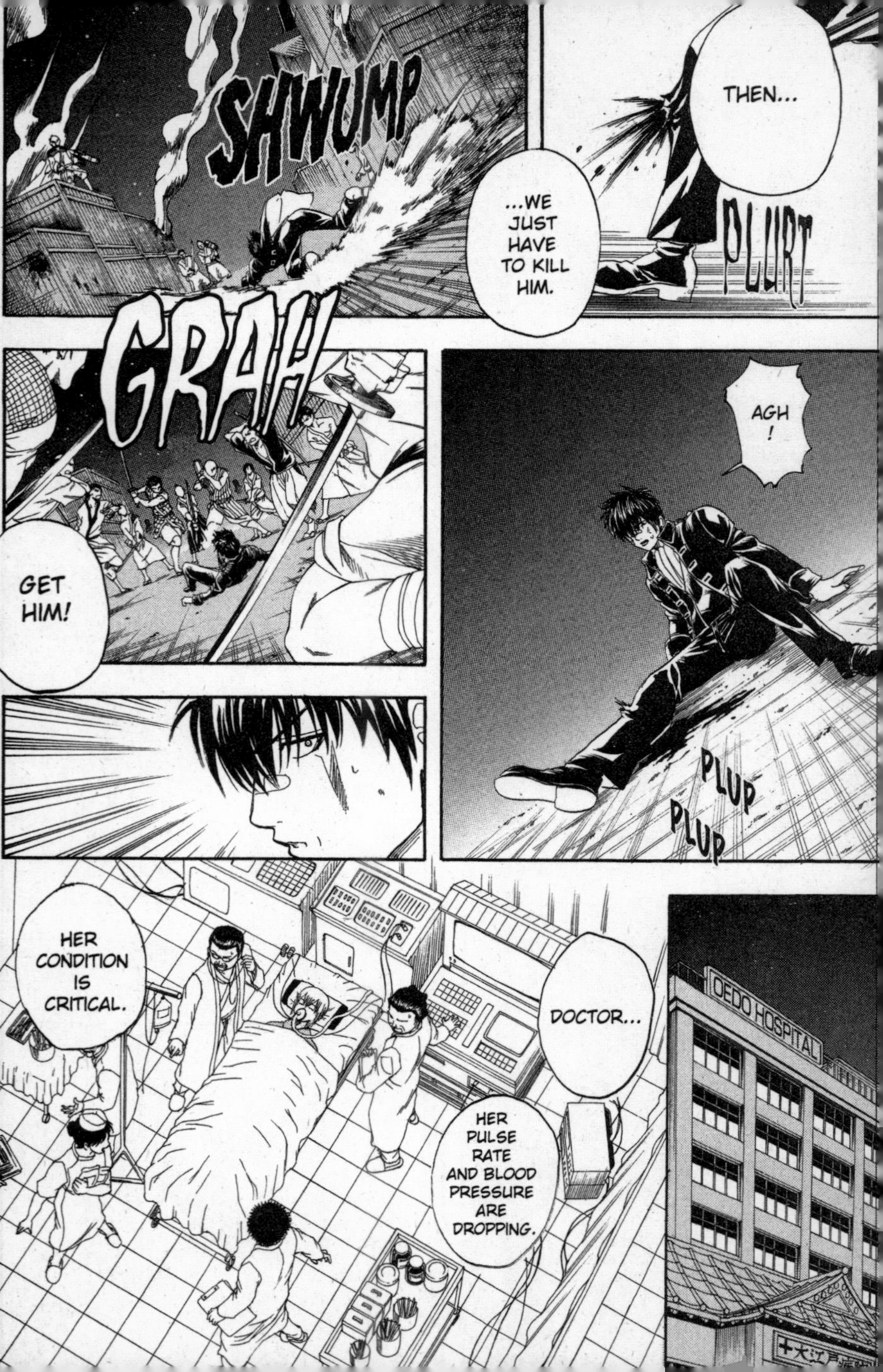
THEN...
...WE JUST HAVE TO KILL HIM.
PLURT
SHWUMP
AGH!
PLUP PLUP
GRAH
GET HIM!
OEDO HOSPITAL
DOCTOR...
HER PULSE RATE AND BLOOD PRESSURE ARE DROPPING.
HER CONDITION IS CRITICAL.

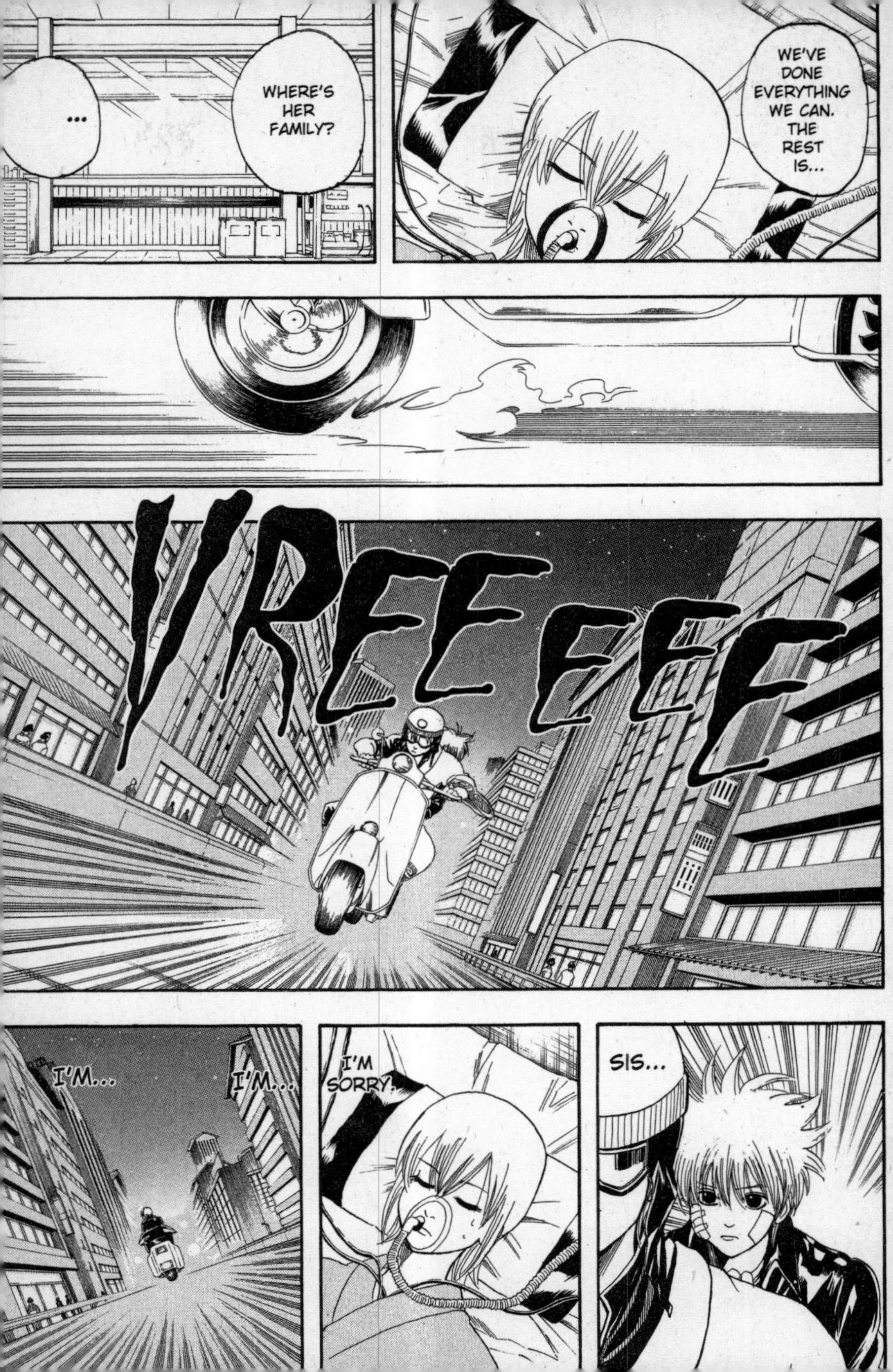
WE'VE DONE EVERYTHING WE CAN. THE REST IS...
WHERE'S HER FAMILY?
...
VREEEEE
SIS...
I'M SORRY.
I'M...
I'M...

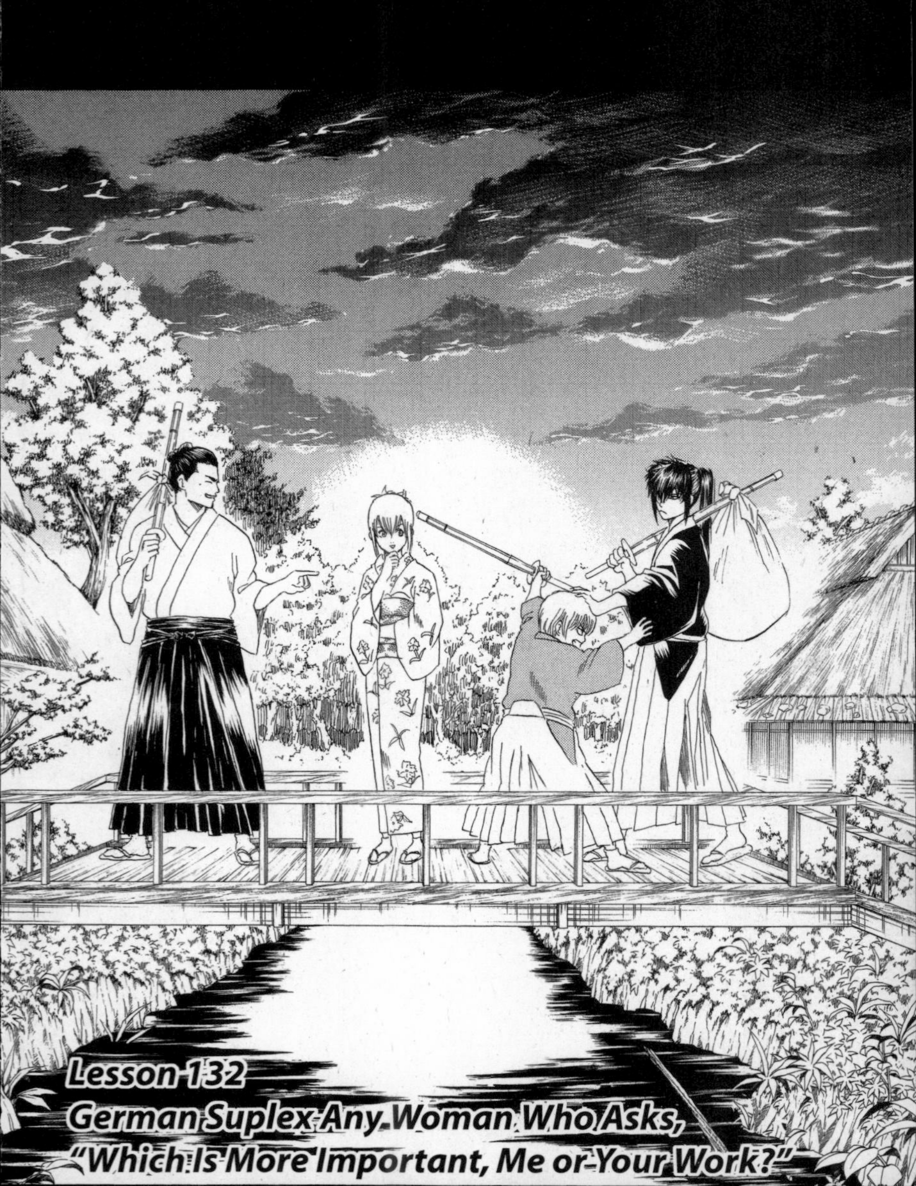
Lesson 132
German Suplex Any Woman Who Asks, "Which Is More Important, Me or Your Work?"

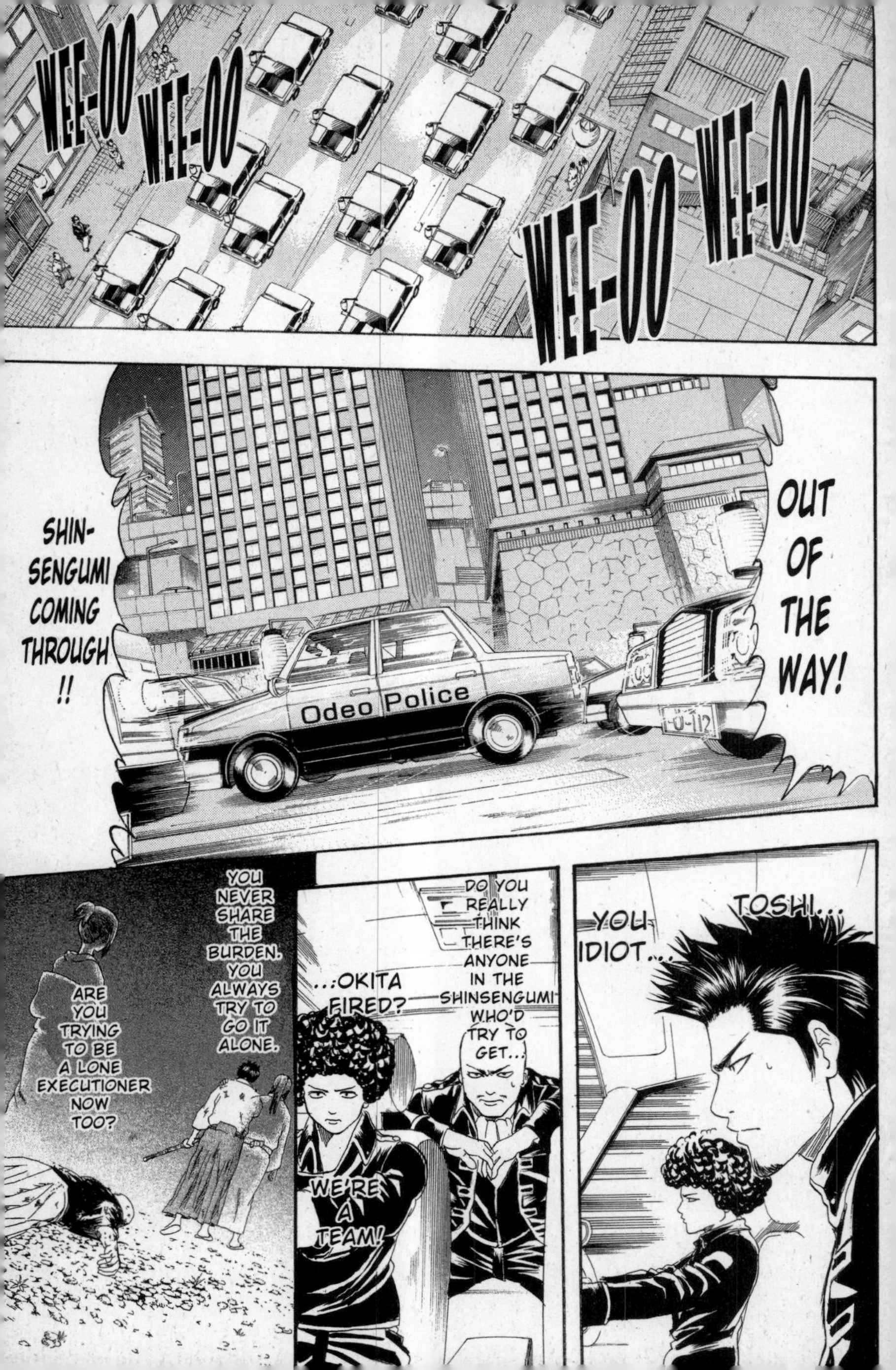
WEE-OO
WEE-OO
WEE-OO
WEE-OO
OUT OF THE WAY!
Odeo Police
SHIN-SENGUMI COMING THROUGH!!
TOSHI...
YOU IDIOT...
DO YOU REALLY THINK THERE'S ANYONE IN THE SHINSENGUMI WHO'D TRY TO GET...
...OKITA FIRED?
WE'RE A TEAM!
YOU NEVER SHARE THE BURDEN. YOU ALWAYS TRY TO GO IT ALONE.
ARE YOU TRYING TO BE A LONE EXECUTIONER NOW TOO?

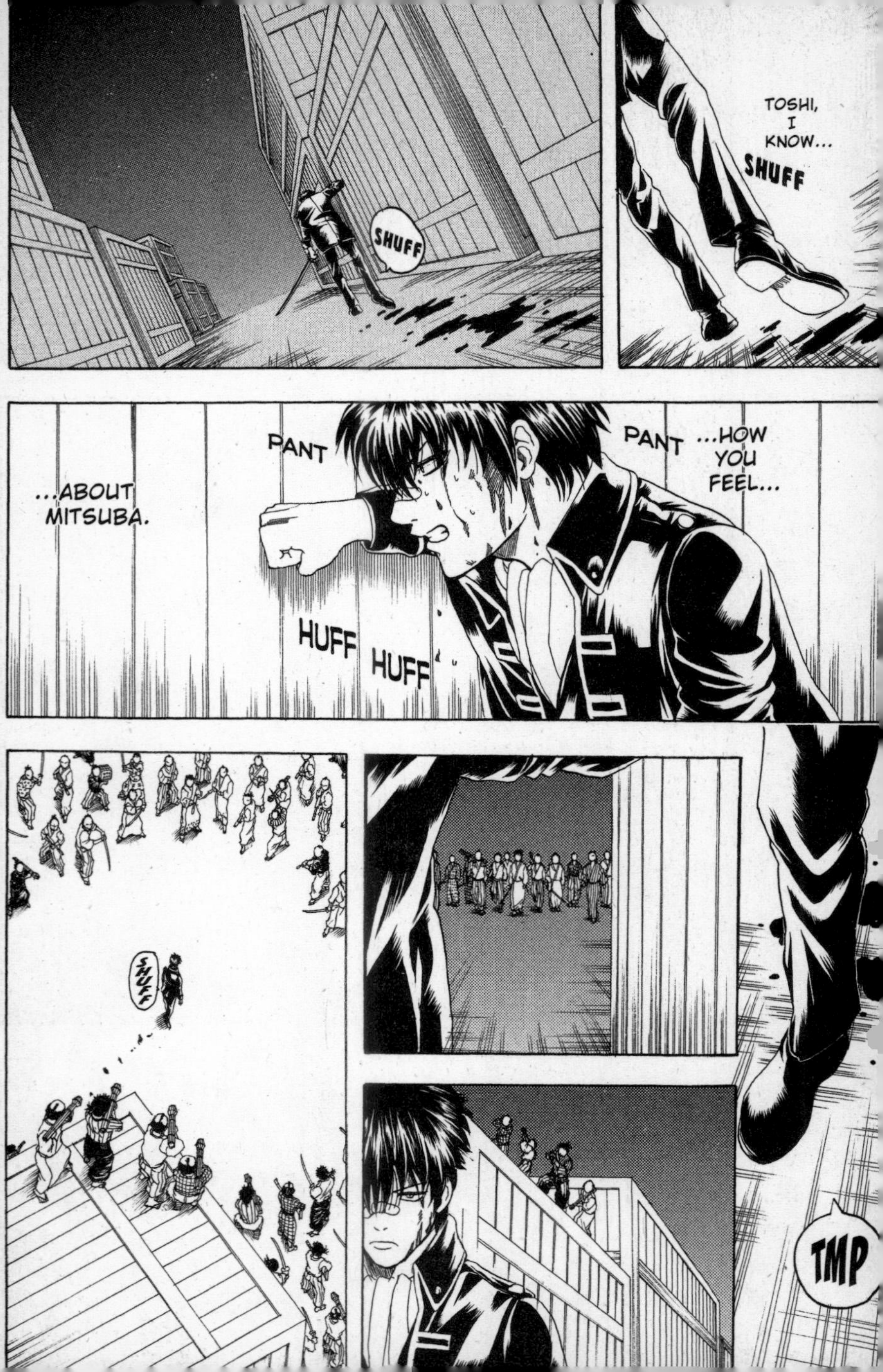
TOSHI, I KNOW...
SHUFF
SHUFF
PANT
...HOW YOU FEEL...
PANT
...ABOUT MITSUBA.
HUFF HUFF
TMP
SHUFF

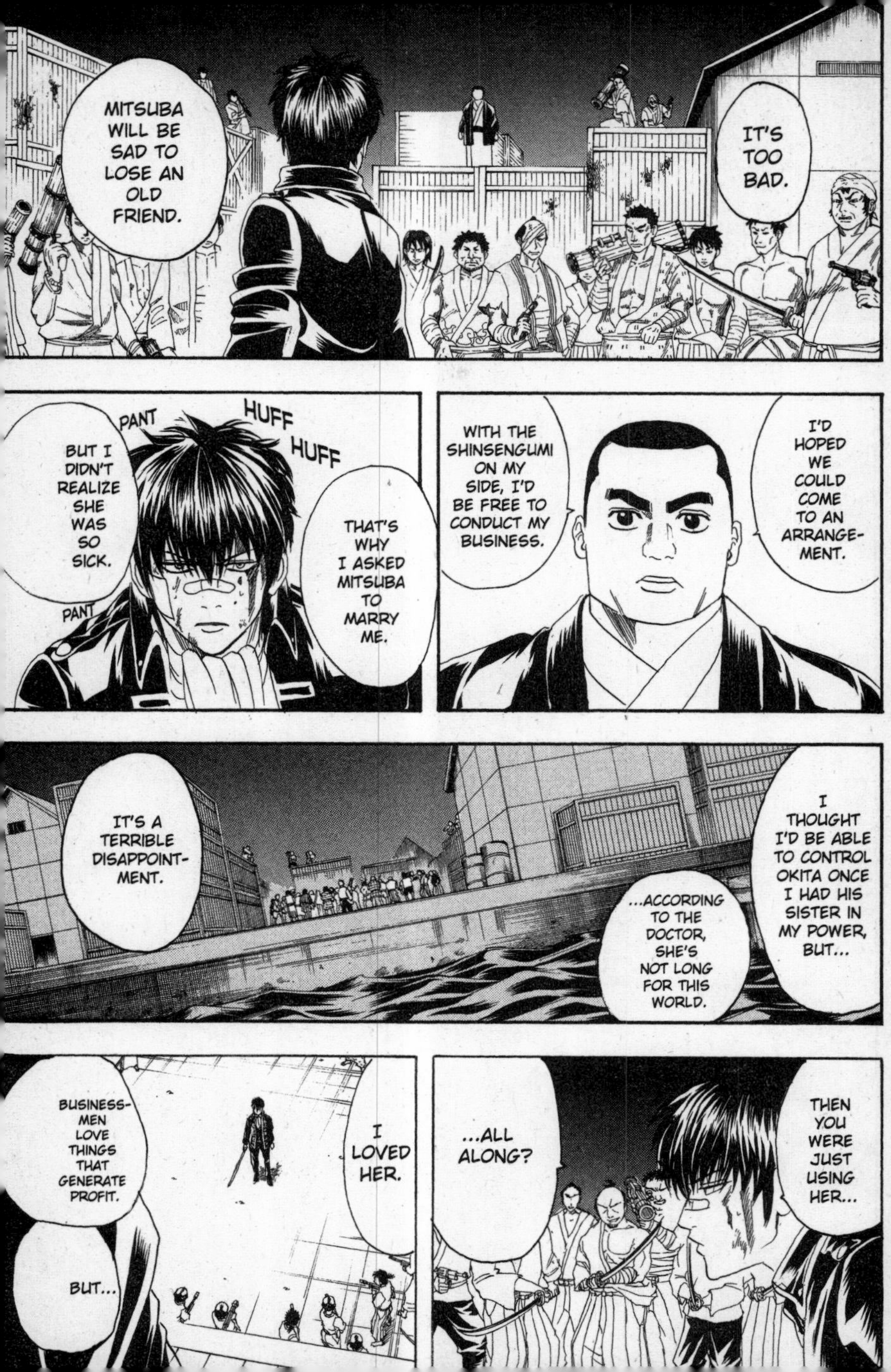
IT'S TOO BAD.
MITSUBA WILL BE SAD TO LOSE AN OLD FRIEND.
I'D HOPED WE COULD COME TO AN ARRANGE-MENT.
WITH THE SHINSENGUMI ON MY SIDE, I'D BE FREE TO CONDUCT MY BUSINESS.
THAT'S WHY I ASKED MITSUBA TO MARRY ME.
HUFF HUFF
PANT
BUT I DIDN'T REALIZE SHE WAS SO SICK.
PANT
I THOUGHT I'D BE ABLE TO CONTROL OKITA ONCE I HAD HIS SISTER IN MY POWER, BUT...
...ACCORDING TO THE DOCTOR, SHE'S NOT LONG FOR THIS WORLD.
IT'S A TERRIBLE DISAPPOINT-MENT.
THEN YOU WERE JUST USING HER...
...ALL ALONG?
I LOVED HER.
BUSINESS-MEN LOVE THINGS THAT GENERATE PROFIT.
BUT...

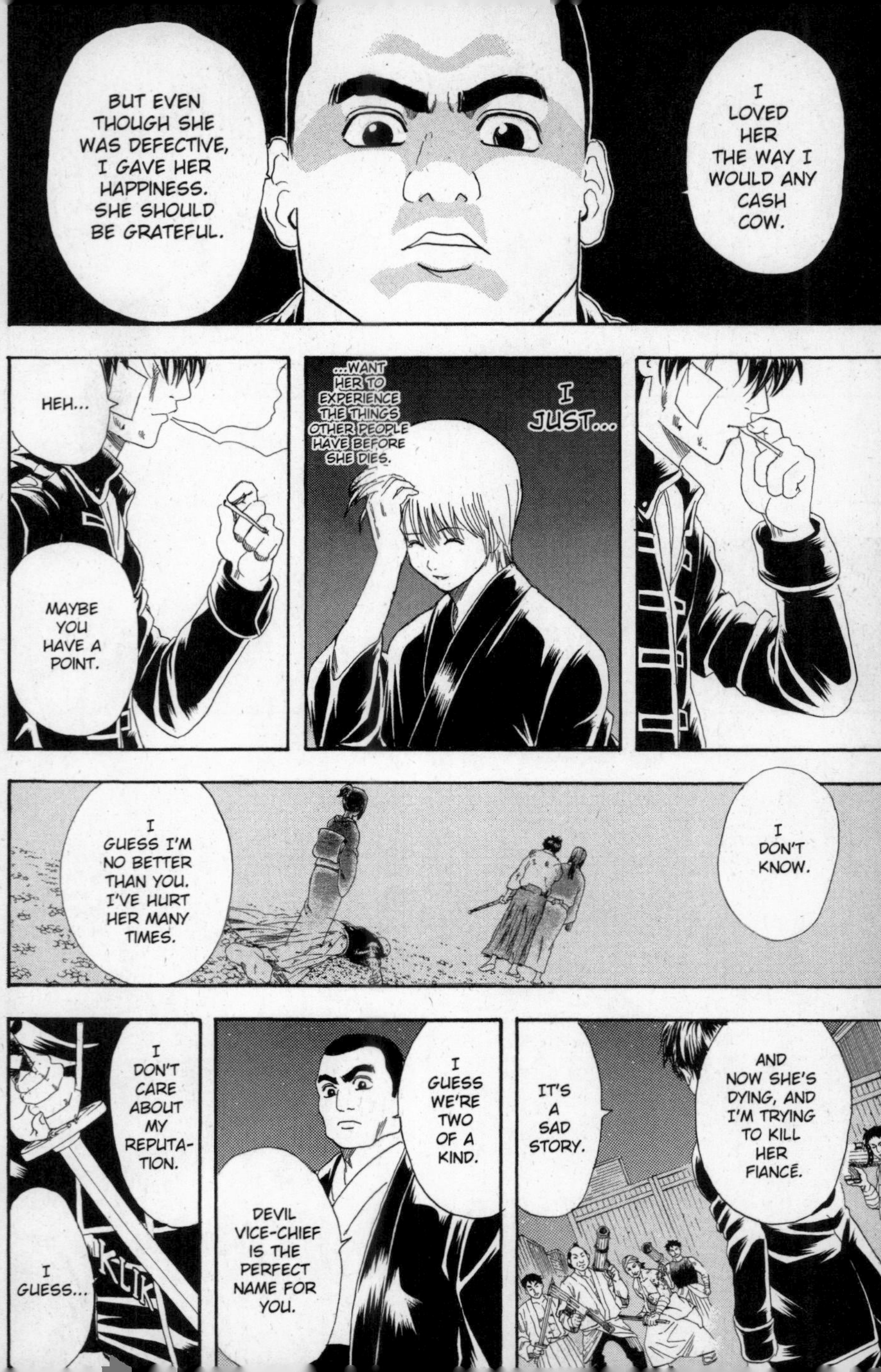
I LOVED HER THE WAY I WOULD ANY CASH COW.
BUT EVEN THOUGH SHE WAS DEFECTIVE, I GAVE HER HAPPINESS. SHE SHOULD BE GRATEFUL.
I JUST...
...WANT HER TO EXPERIENCE THE THINGS OTHER PEOPLE HAVE BEFORE SHE DIES.
HEH...
MAYBE YOU HAVE A POINT.
I DON'T KNOW.
I GUESS I'M NO BETTER THAN YOU. I'VE HURT HER MANY TIMES.
AND NOW SHE'S DYING, AND I'M TRYING TO KILL HER FIANCÉ.
IT'S A SAD STORY.
I GUESS WE'RE TWO OF A KIND.
DEVIL VICE-CHIEF IS THE PERFECT NAME FOR YOU.
I DON'T CARE ABOUT MY REPUTATION.
K-LIK
I GUESS...

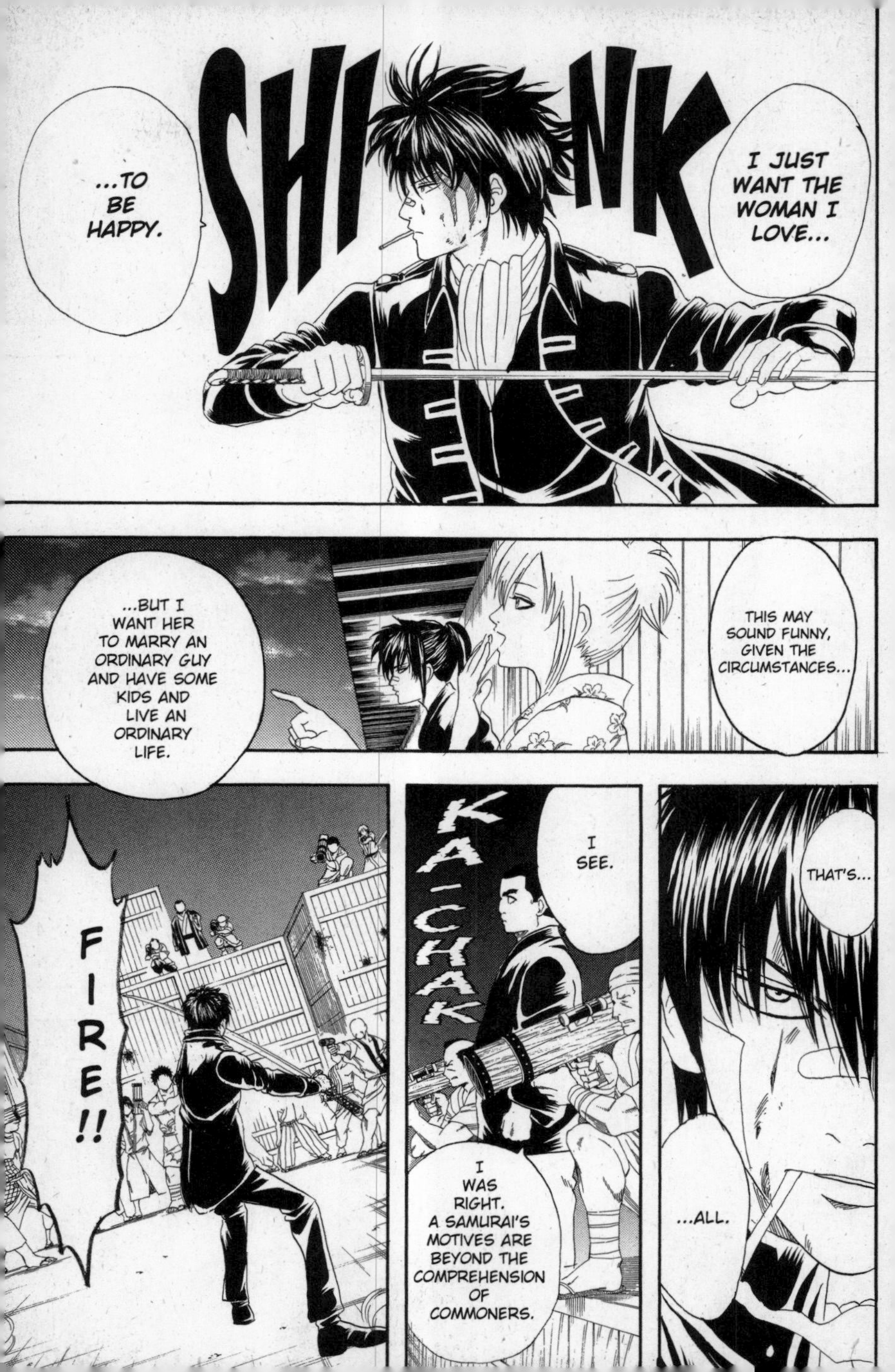
I JUST WANT THE WOMAN I LOVE...
SHI NK
...TO BE HAPPY.
THIS MAY SOUND FUNNY, GIVEN THE CIRCUMSTANCES...
...BUT I WANT HER TO MARRY AN ORDINARY GUY AND HAVE SOME KIDS AND LIVE AN ORDINARY LIFE.
THAT'S...
...ALL.
I SEE.
KA-CHAK
I WAS RIGHT. A SAMURAI'S MOTIVES ARE BEYOND THE COMPREHENSION OF COMMONERS.
FIRE!!

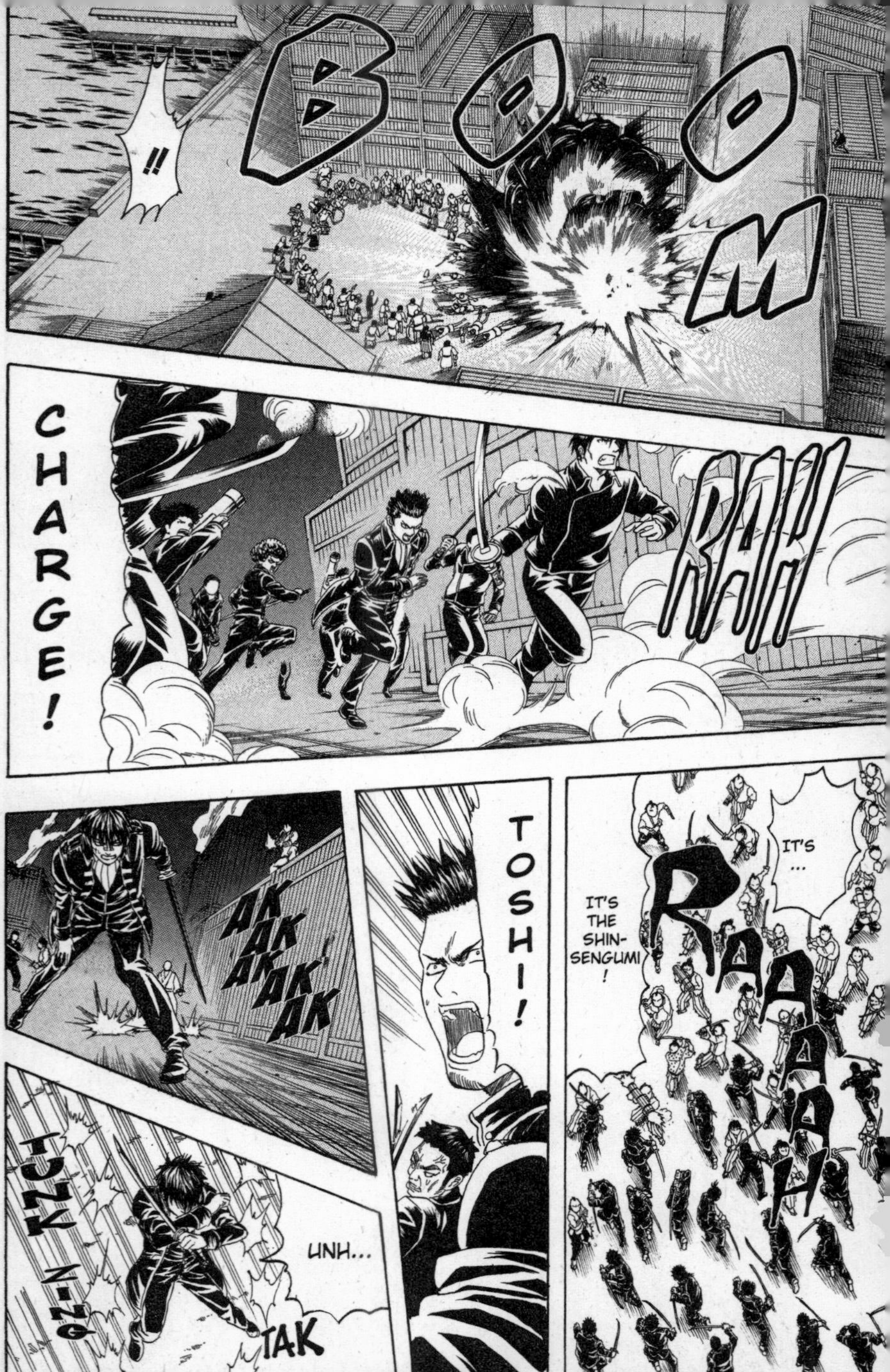
!!
BOOM
RAH
CHARGE!
IT'S ...
RAAAAH
IT'S THE SHIN-SENGUMI!
TOSHI!
UNH...
AKAK
AKAKAK
TUNK
ZING
TAK

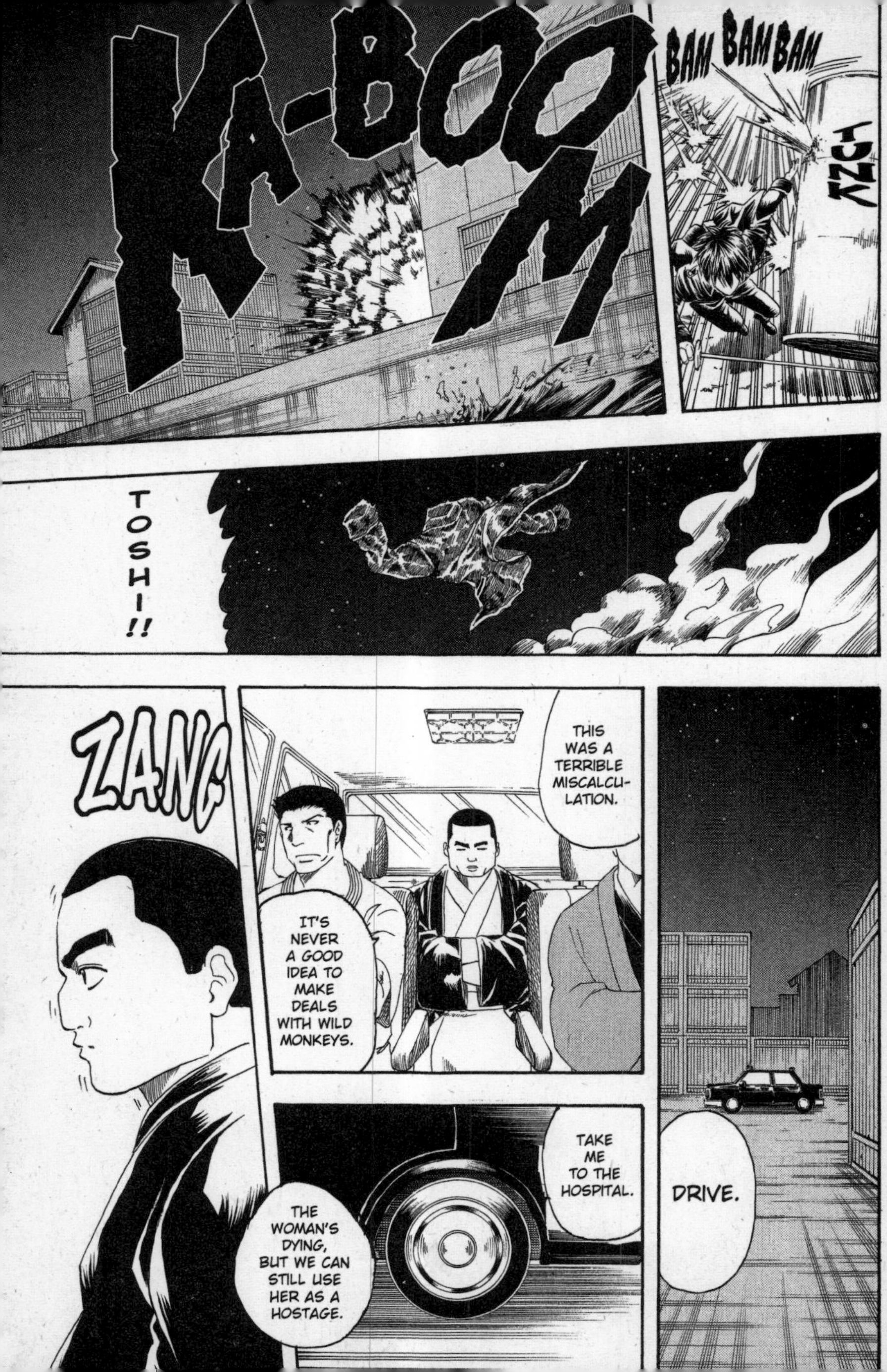

BAM BAMBAM
TUNK
KA-BOOM
TOSHI!!
DRIVE.
THIS WAS A TERRIBLE MISCALCULATION.
IT'S NEVER A GOOD IDEA TO MAKE DEALS WITH WILD MONKEYS.
TAKE ME TO THE HOSPITAL.
THE WOMAN'S DYING, BUT WE CAN STILL USE HER AS A HOSTAGE.
ZANG

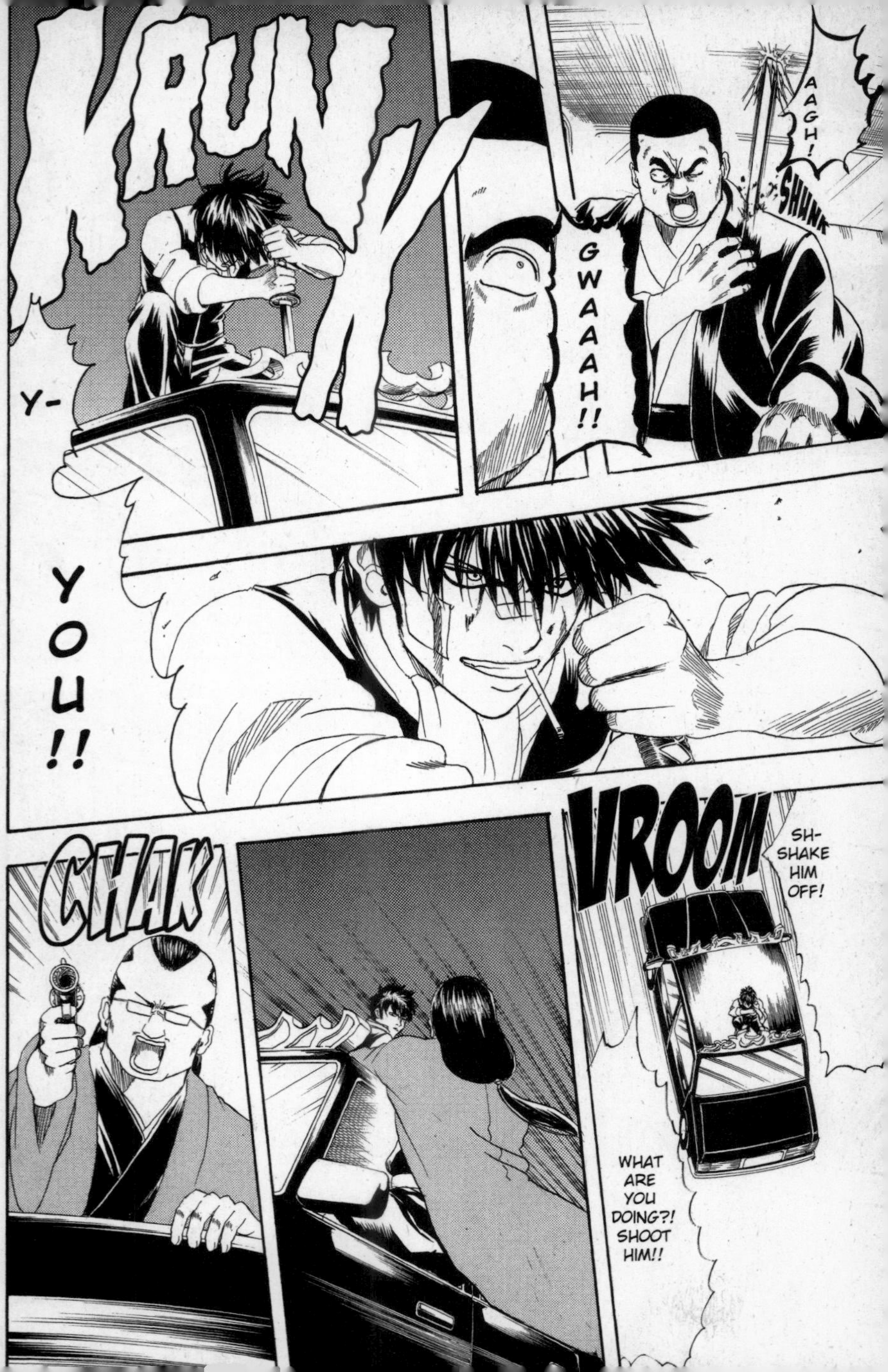
AAGH!
SHUNK
GWAAAAH!!
KRUNK
Y-
YOU!!
VROOM
SH-SHAKE HIM OFF!
WHAT ARE YOU DOING?! SHOOT HIM!!
CHAK

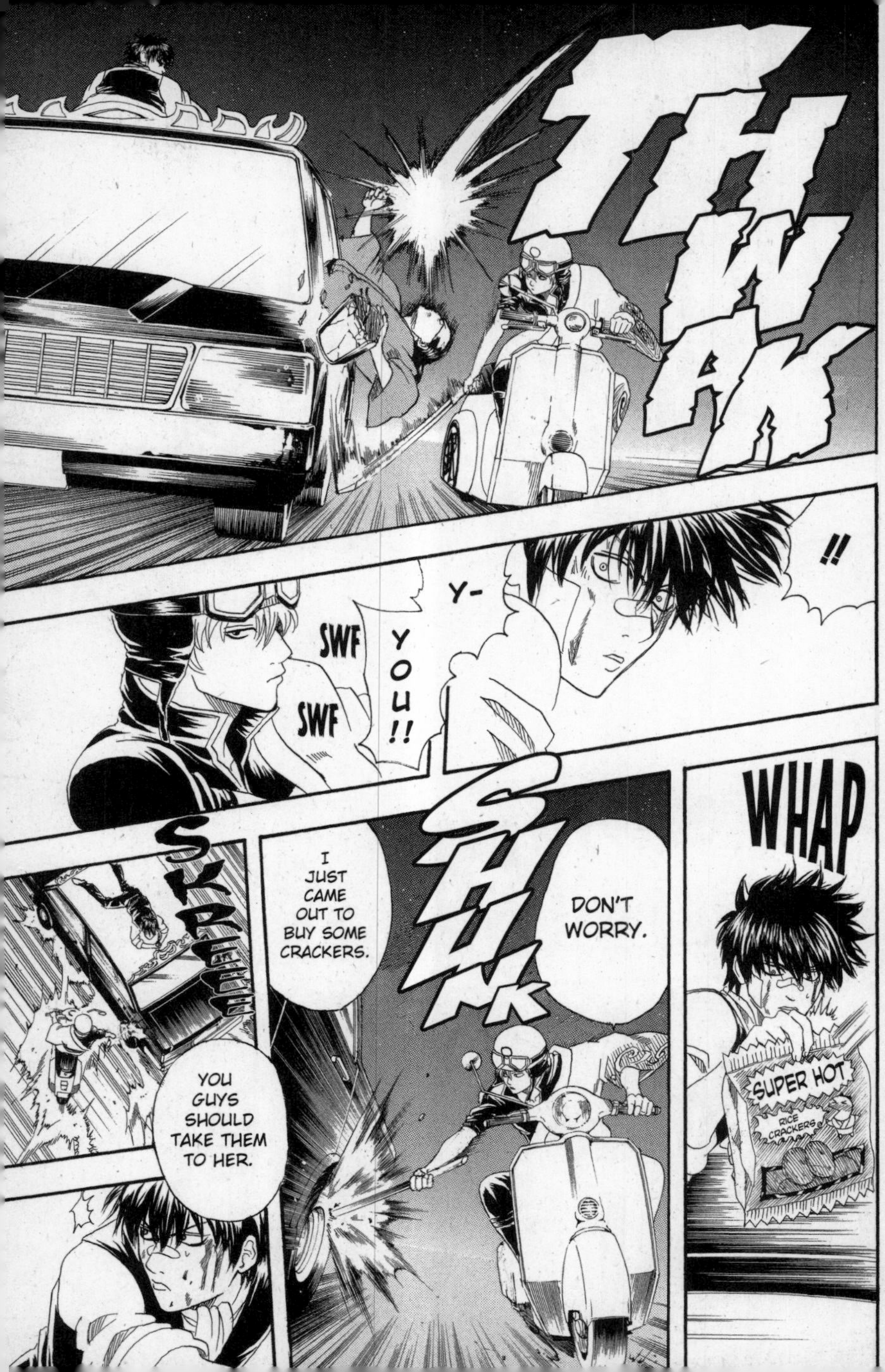
THWAK
!!
Y-
YOU!!
SWF
SWF
WHAP
SUPER HOT
RICE CRACKERS
SHUNK
DON'T WORRY.
I JUST CAME OUT TO BUY SOME CRACKERS.
SKREEE
YOU GUYS SHOULD TAKE THEM TO HER.

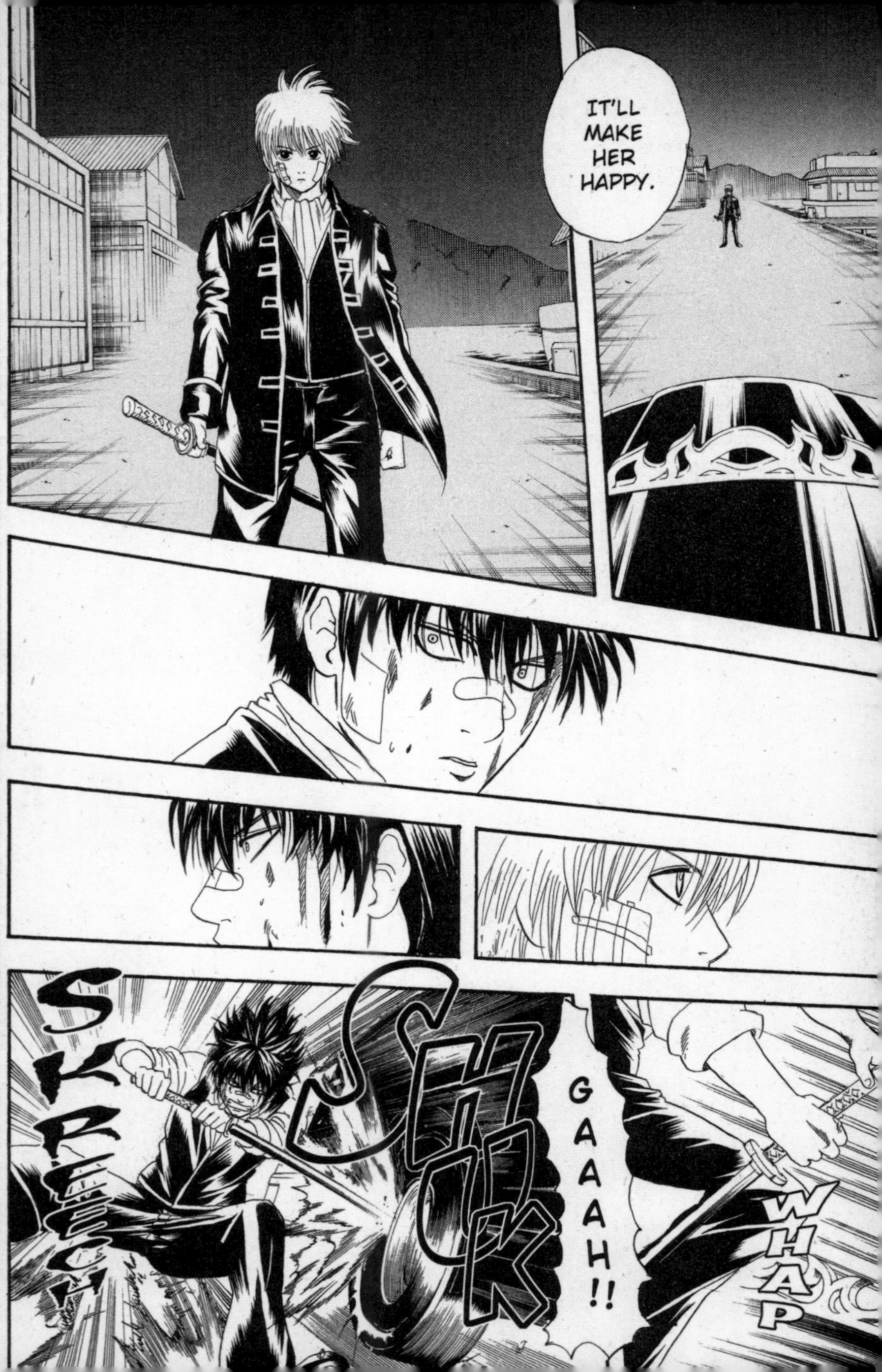
IT'LL MAKE HER HAPPY.
WHAP
GAAAH!!

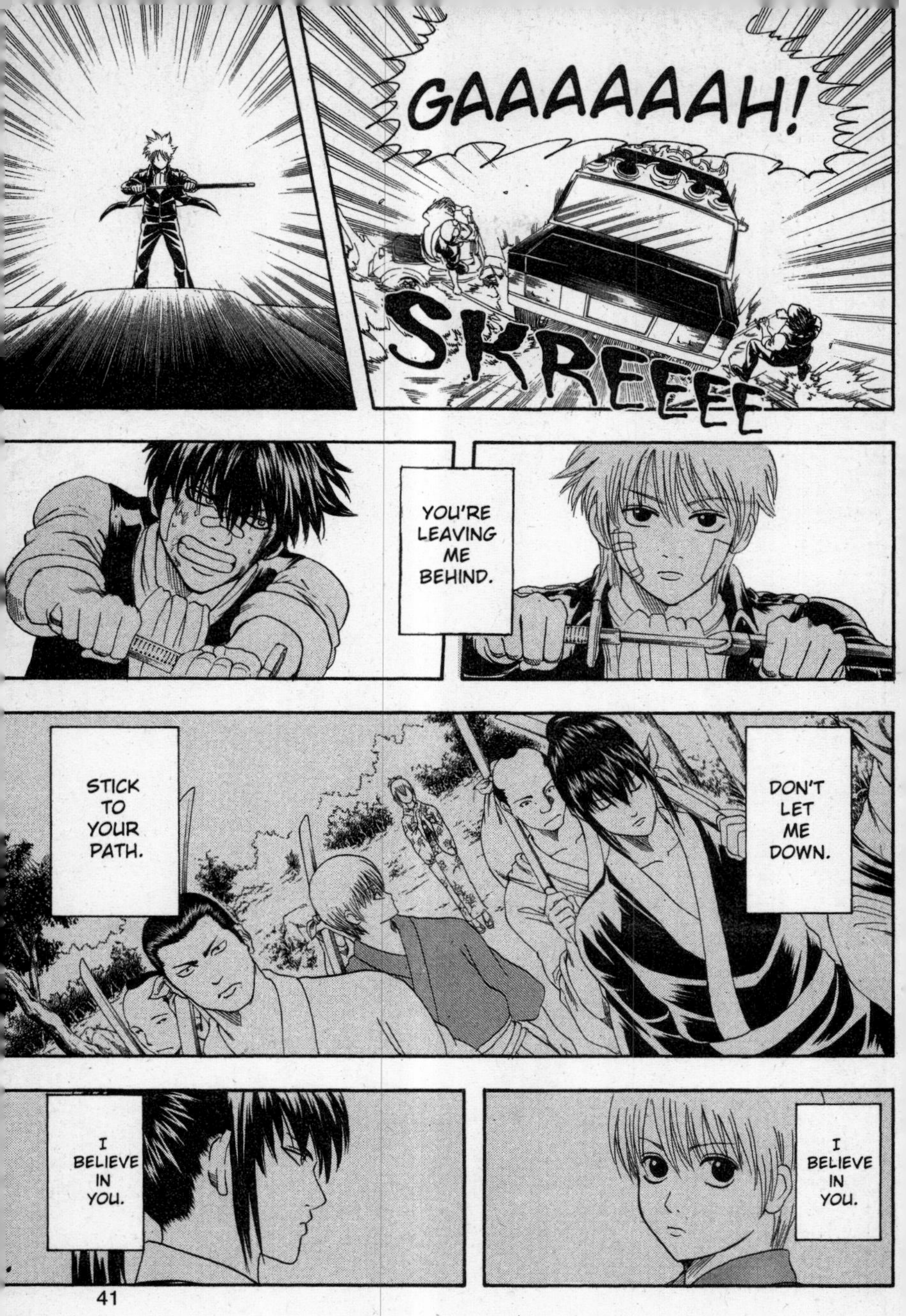
GAAAAAAH!
SKREEEE
YOU'RE LEAVING ME BEHIND.
DON'T LET ME DOWN.
STICK TO YOUR PATH.
I BELIEVE IN YOU.
I BELIEVE IN YOU.

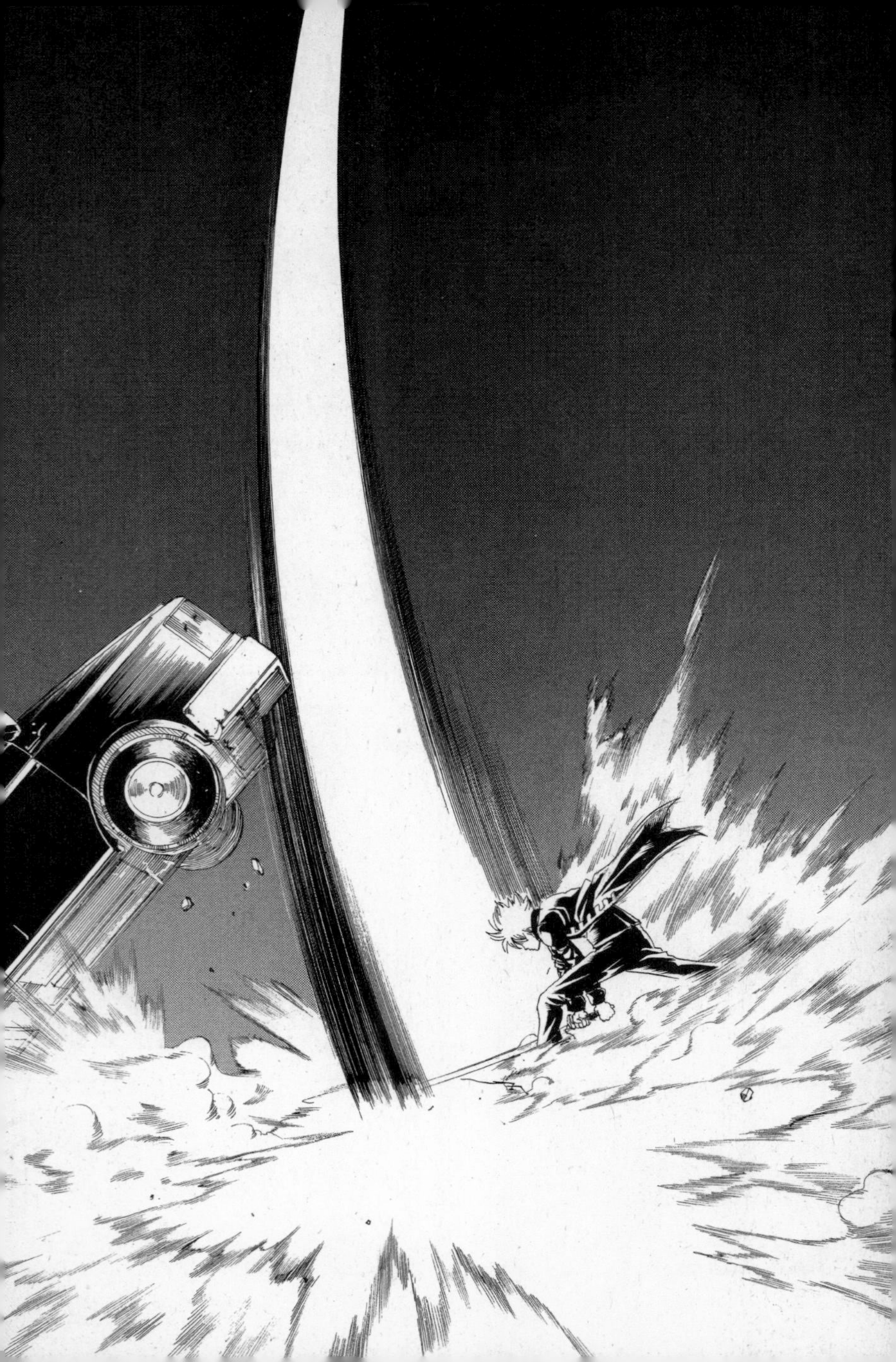

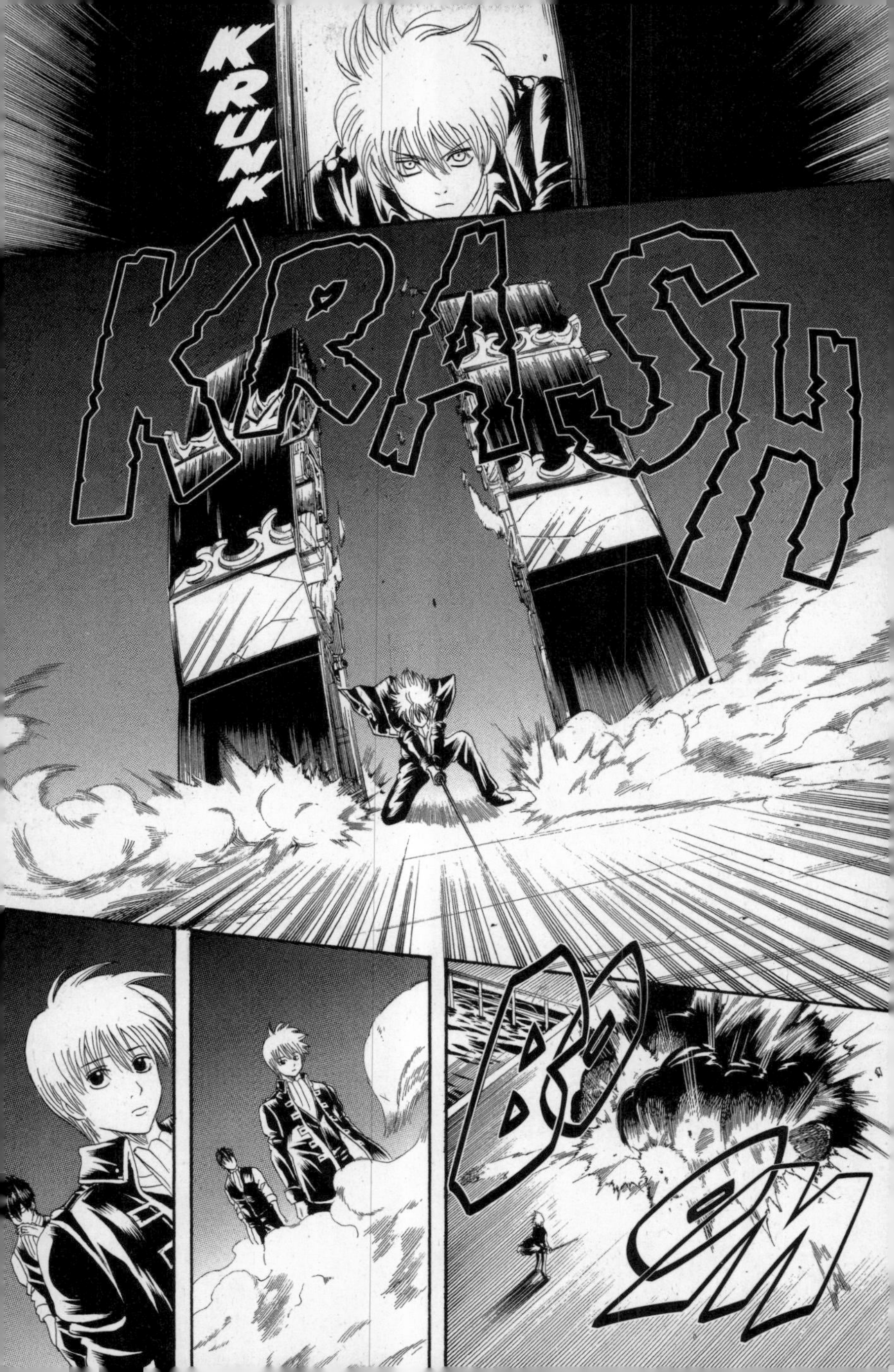
KRUNK
KRASH
BOOM

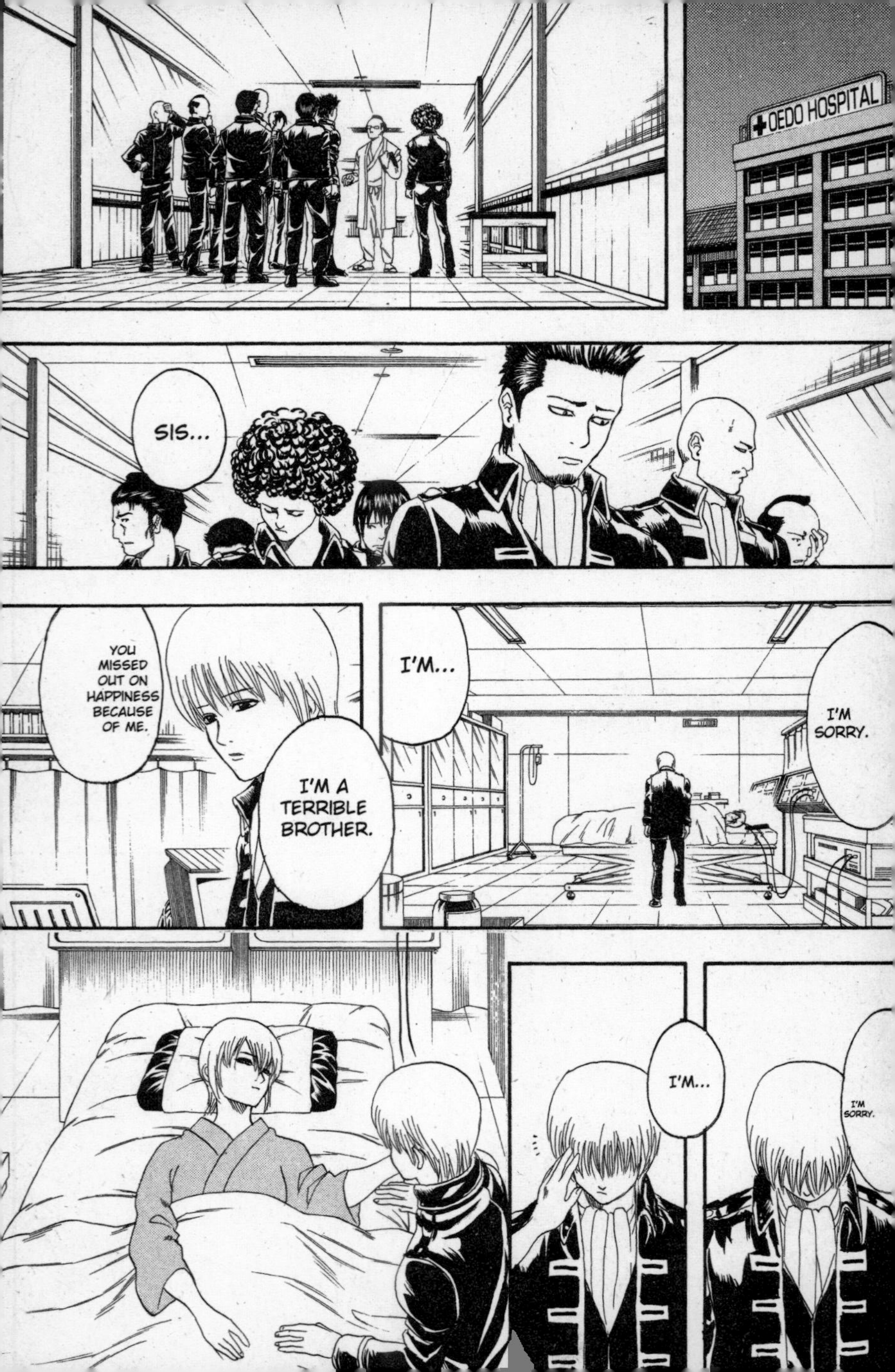
OEDO HOSPITAL
SIS...
I'M SORRY.
I'M...
I'M A TERRIBLE BROTHER.
YOU MISSED OUT ON HAPPINESS BECAUSE OF ME.
I'M SORRY.
I'M...

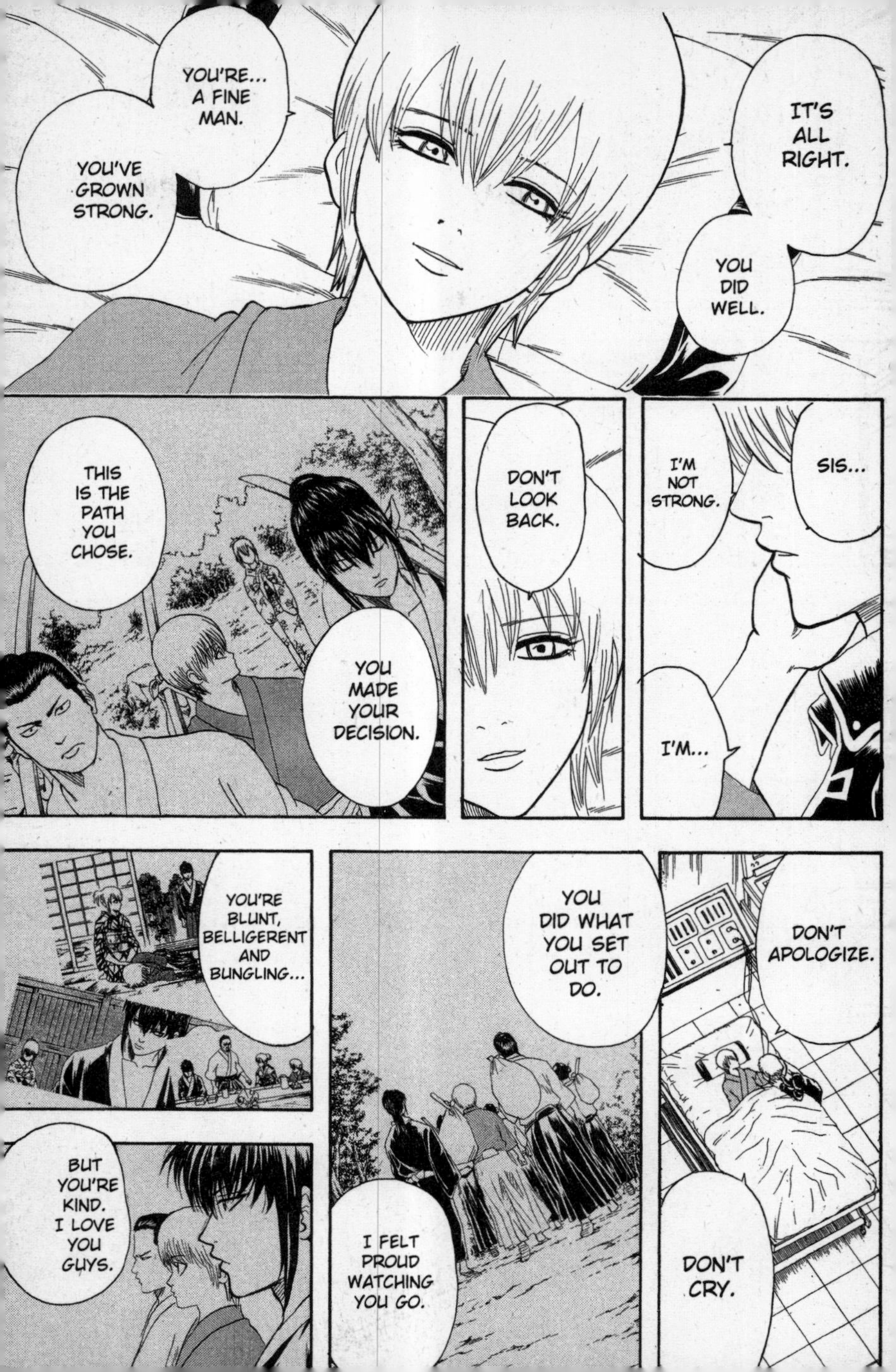

IT'S ALL RIGHT.
YOU DID WELL.
YOU'RE... A FINE MAN.
YOU'VE GROWN STRONG.
SIS...
I'M NOT STRONG.
I'M...
DON'T LOOK BACK.
THIS IS THE PATH YOU CHOSE.
YOU MADE YOUR DECISION.
DON'T APOLOGIZE.
DON'T CRY.
YOU DID WHAT YOU SET OUT TO DO.
I FELT PROUD WATCHING YOU GO.
YOU'RE BLUNT, BELLIGERENT AND BUNGLING...
BUT YOU'RE KIND. I LOVE YOU GUYS.

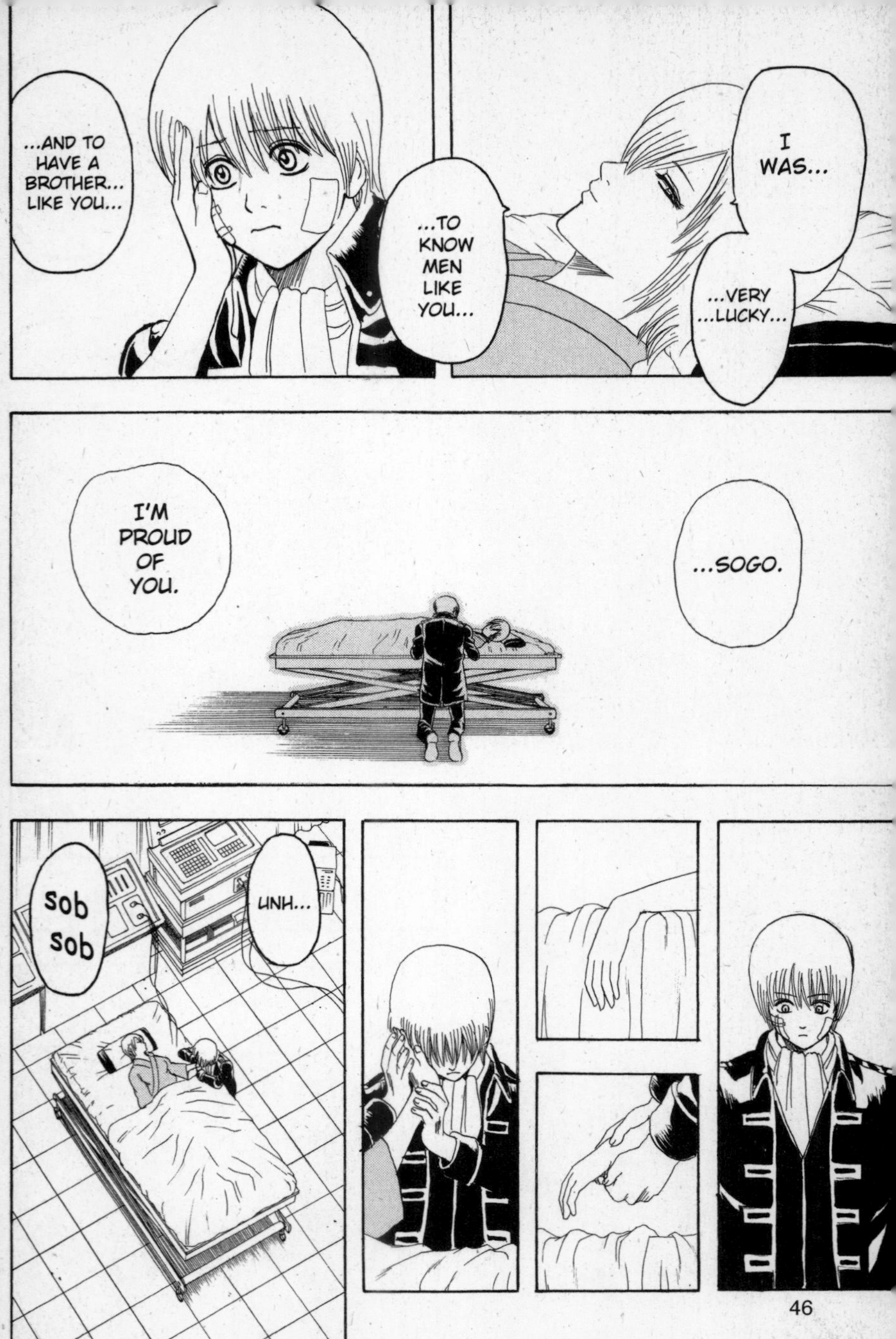
I WAS...
...VERY ...LUCKY...
...TO KNOW MEN LIKE YOU...
...AND TO HAVE A BROTHER... LIKE YOU...
...SOGO.
I'M PROUD OF YOU.
UNH...
sob sob

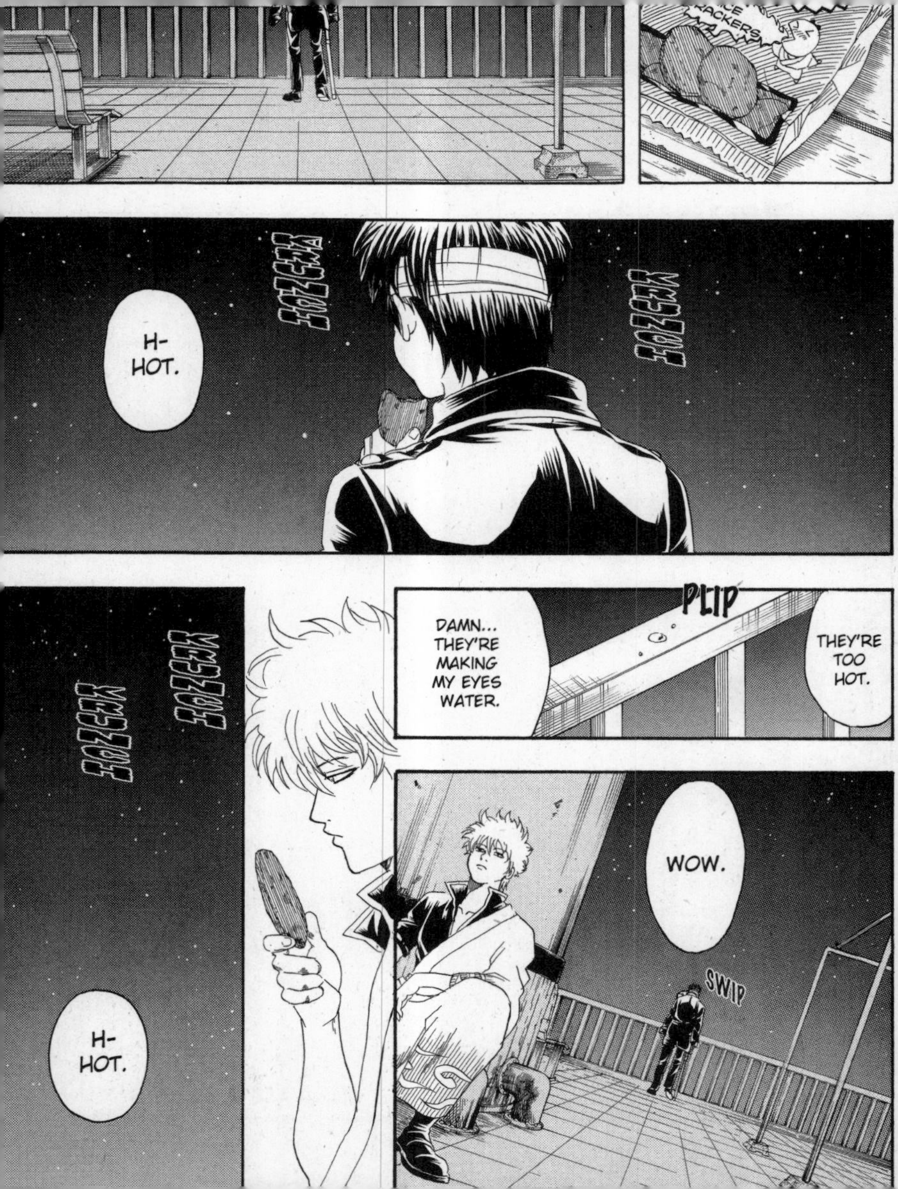
H-
HOT.
THEY'RE TOO HOT.
PLIP
DAMN... THEY'RE MAKING MY EYES WATER.
WOW.
SWIP
H-
HOT.

<Question from Marine Silver Samurai from Osaka>

Hello, Mr. Sorachi! Gin always reads *Jump*, but which manga does he like best?

<Answer>

Ginnikuman. (a pun on Kinnikuman)

(Q&A #48 is on page 68)

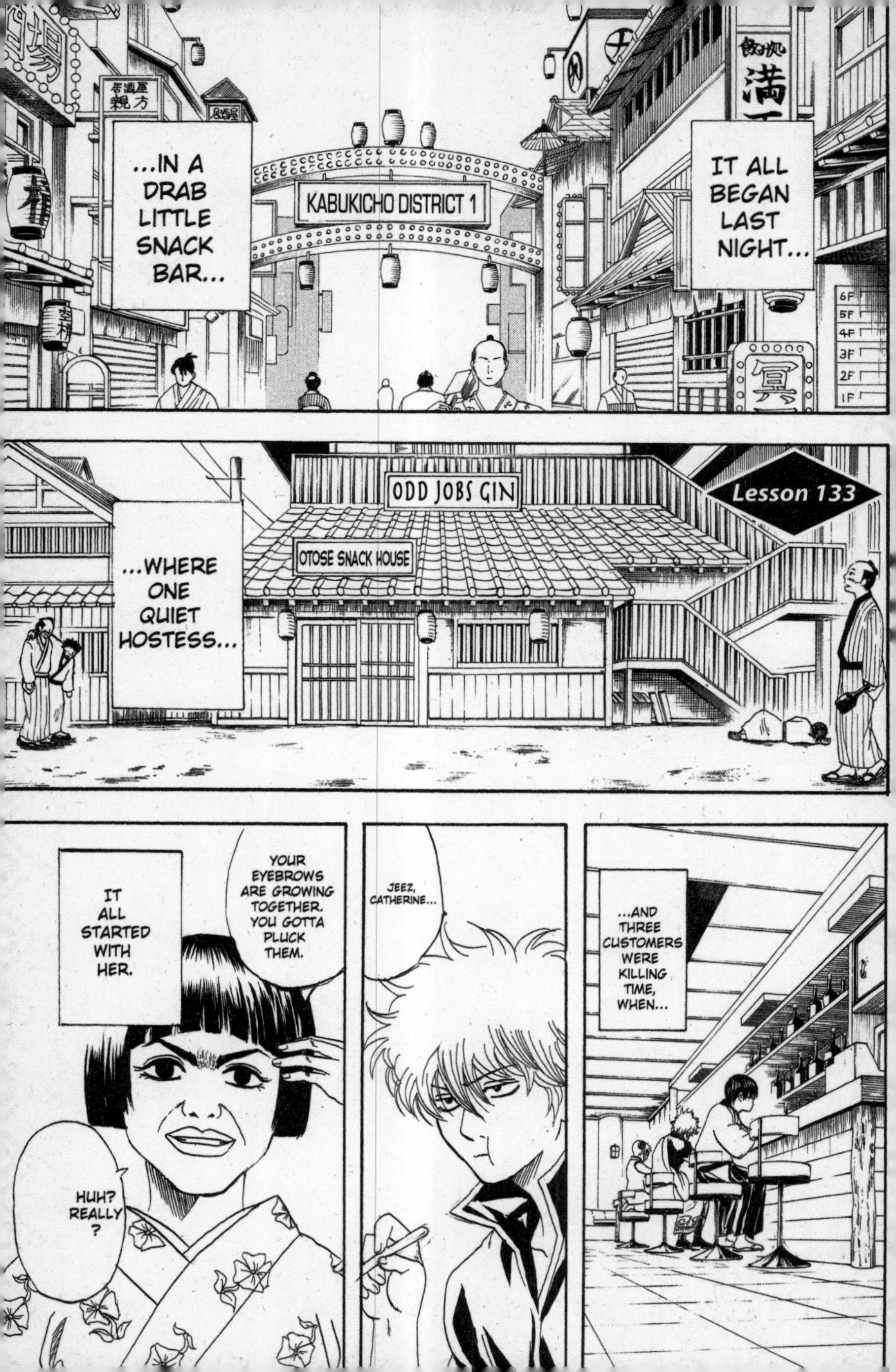

IT ALL BEGAN LAST NIGHT...
KABUKICHO DISTRICT 1
...IN A DRAB LITTLE SNACK BAR...
Lesson 133
ODD JOBS GIN
OTOSE SNACK HOUSE
...WHERE ONE QUIET HOSTESS...
...AND THREE CUSTOMERS WERE KILLING TIME, WHEN...
JEEZ, CATHERINE...
YOUR EYEBROWS ARE GROWING TOGETHER. YOU GOTTA PLUCK THEM.
IT ALL STARTED WITH HER.
HUH? REALLY?

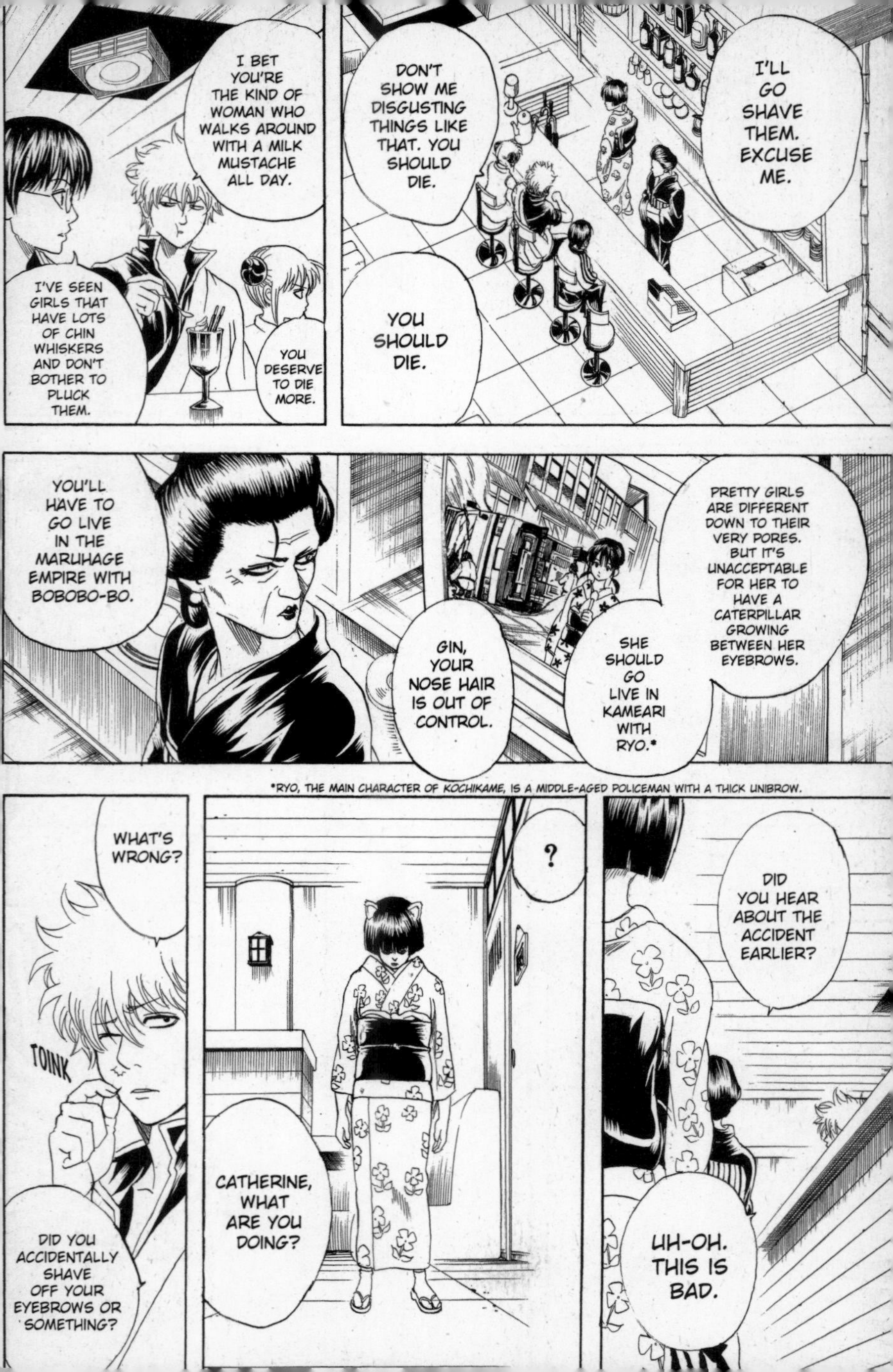
I'LL GO SHAVE THEM. EXCUSE ME.
DON'T SHOW ME DISGUSTING THINGS LIKE THAT. YOU SHOULD DIE.
YOU SHOULD DIE.
I BET YOU'RE THE KIND OF WOMAN WHO WALKS AROUND WITH A MILK MUSTACHE ALL DAY.
YOU DESERVE TO DIE MORE.
I'VE SEEN GIRLS THAT HAVE LOTS OF CHIN WHISKERS AND DON'T BOTHER TO PLUCK THEM.
PRETTY GIRLS ARE DIFFERENT DOWN TO THEIR VERY PORES. BUT IT'S UNACCEPTABLE FOR HER TO HAVE A CATERPILLAR GROWING BETWEEN HER EYEBROWS.
SHE SHOULD GO LIVE IN KAMEARI WITH RYO.*
GIN, YOUR NOSE HAIR IS OUT OF CONTROL.
YOU'LL HAVE TO GO LIVE IN THE MARUHAGE EMPIRE WITH BOBOBO-BO.
*RYO, THE MAIN CHARACTER OF KOCHIKAME, IS A MIDDLE-AGED POLICEMAN WITH A THICK UNIBROW.
DID YOU HEAR ABOUT THE ACCIDENT EARLIER?
UH-OH. THIS IS BAD.
?
CATHERINE, WHAT ARE YOU DOING?
WHAT'S WRONG?
TOINK
DID YOU ACCIDENTALLY SHAVE OFF YOUR EYEBROWS OR SOMETHING?

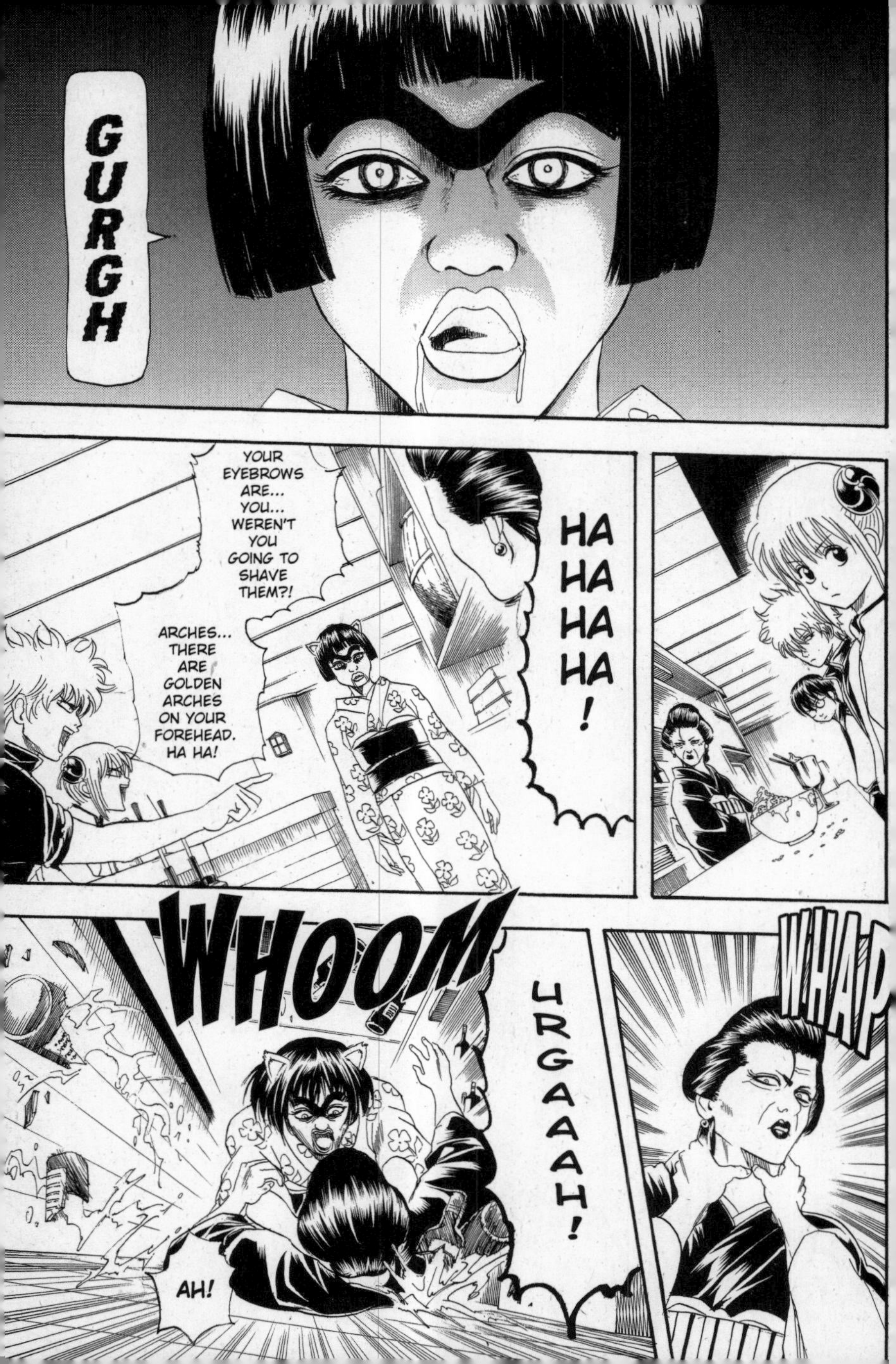
GURGH
HA HA HA HA HA!
YOUR EYEBROWS ARE... YOU... WEREN'T YOU GOING TO SHAVE THEM?!
ARCHES... THERE ARE GOLDEN ARCHES ON YOUR FOREHEAD. HA HA!
WHAP
WHOOM
URGAAAH!
AH!

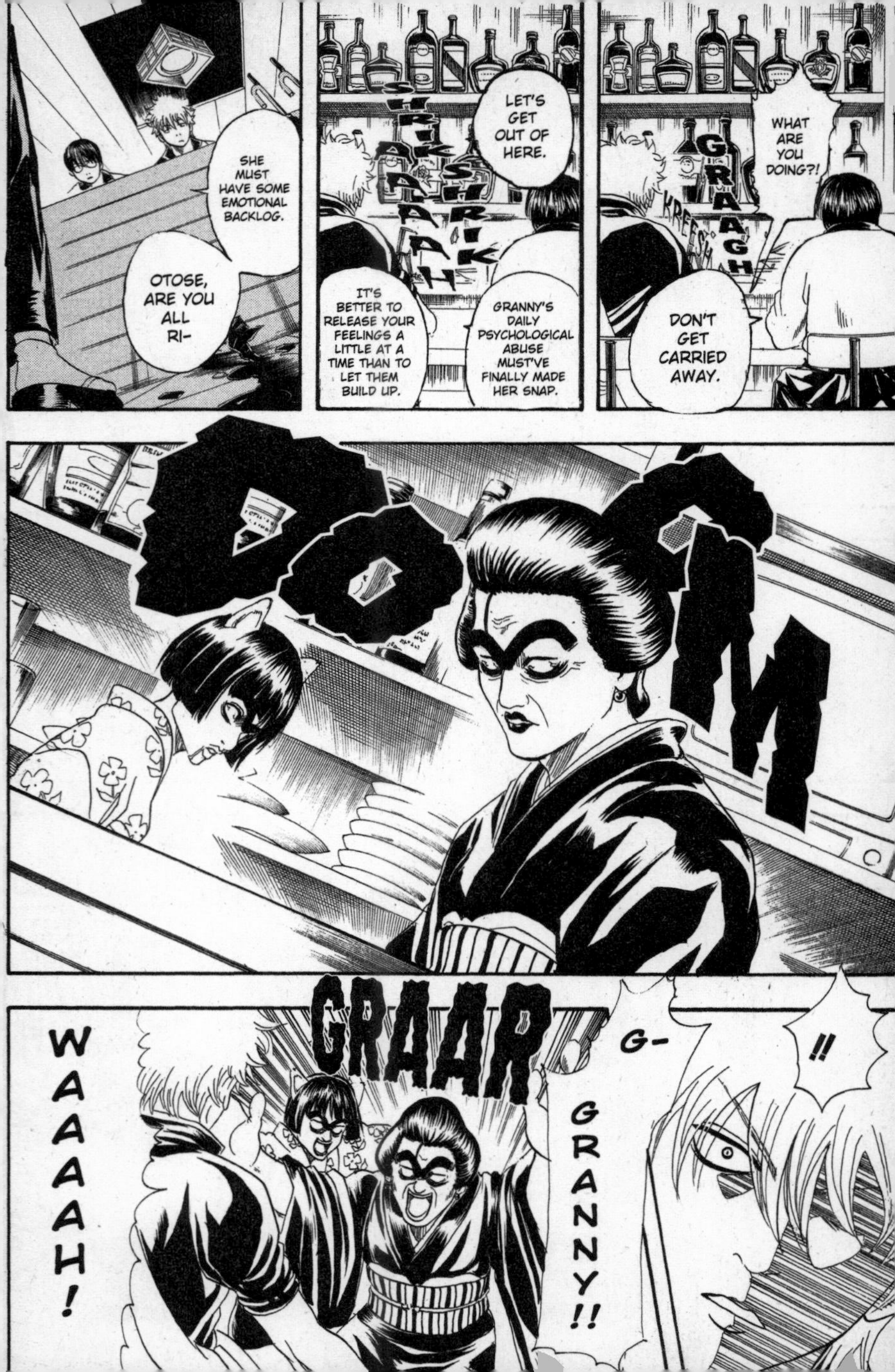

WHAT ARE YOU DOING?!
GRAGH
KREESH
DON'T GET CARRIED AWAY.
LET'S GET OUT OF HERE.
SHRIK
SHRIAKAAAH
GRANNY'S DAILY PSYCHOLOGICAL ABUSE MUST'VE FINALLY MADE HER SNAP.
IT'S BETTER TO RELEASE YOUR FEELINGS A LITTLE AT A TIME THAN TO LET THEM BUILD UP.
SHE MUST HAVE SOME EMOTIONAL BACKLOG.
OTOSE, ARE YOU ALL RI-
BOOM
!!
G-
GRAAR
GRANNY!!
WAAAAH!

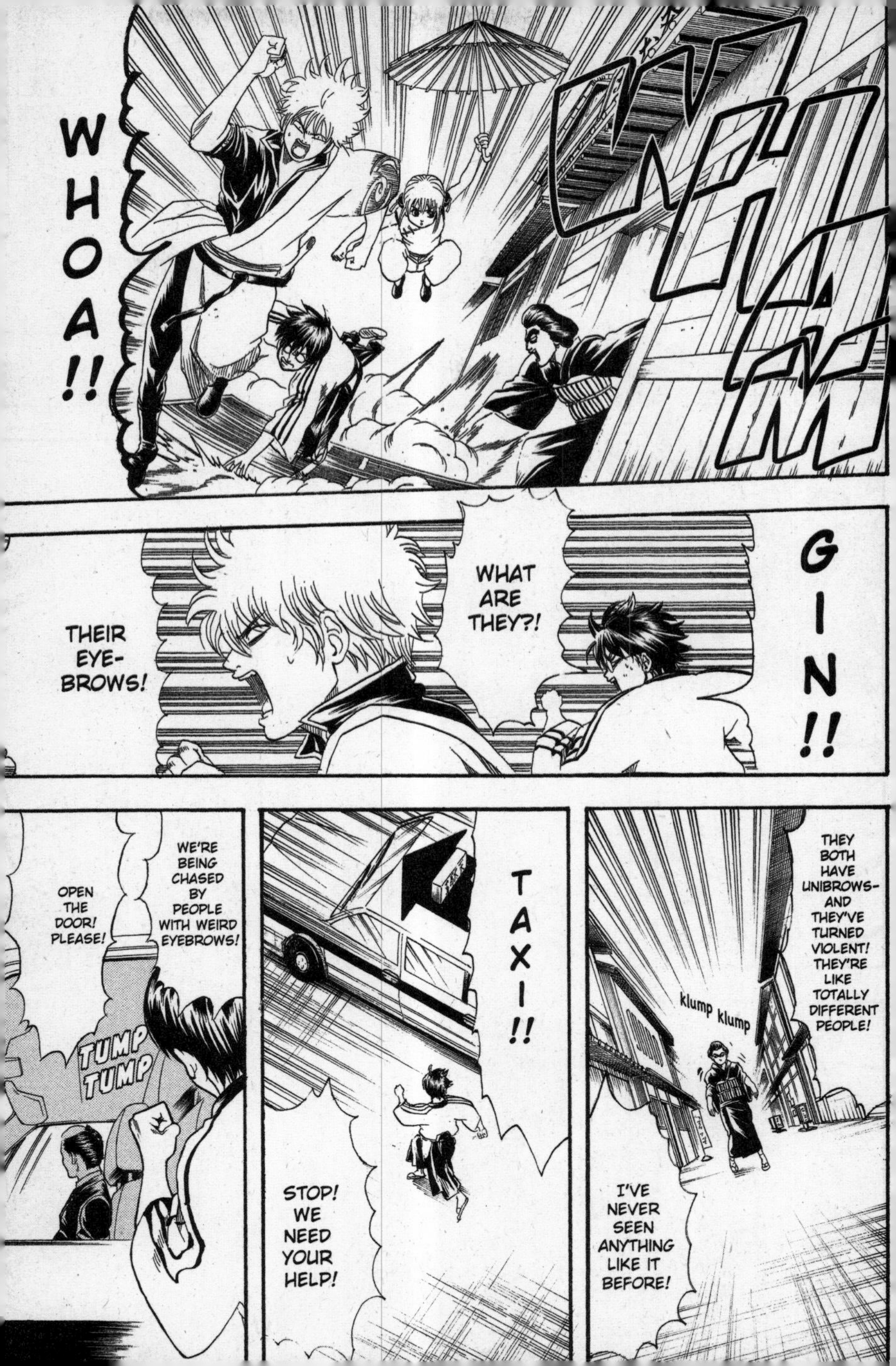
WHAM
WHOA!!
GIN!!
WHAT ARE THEY?!
THEIR EYE-BROWS!
THEY BOTH HAVE UNIBROWS-AND THEY'VE TURNED VIOLENT! THEY'RE LIKE TOTALLY DIFFERENT PEOPLE!
klump klump
I'VE NEVER SEEN ANYTHING LIKE IT BEFORE!
TAXI!!
STOP! WE NEED YOUR HELP!
WE'RE BEING CHASED BY PEOPLE WITH WEIRD EYEBROWS!
OPEN THE DOOR! PLEASE!
TUMP TUMP

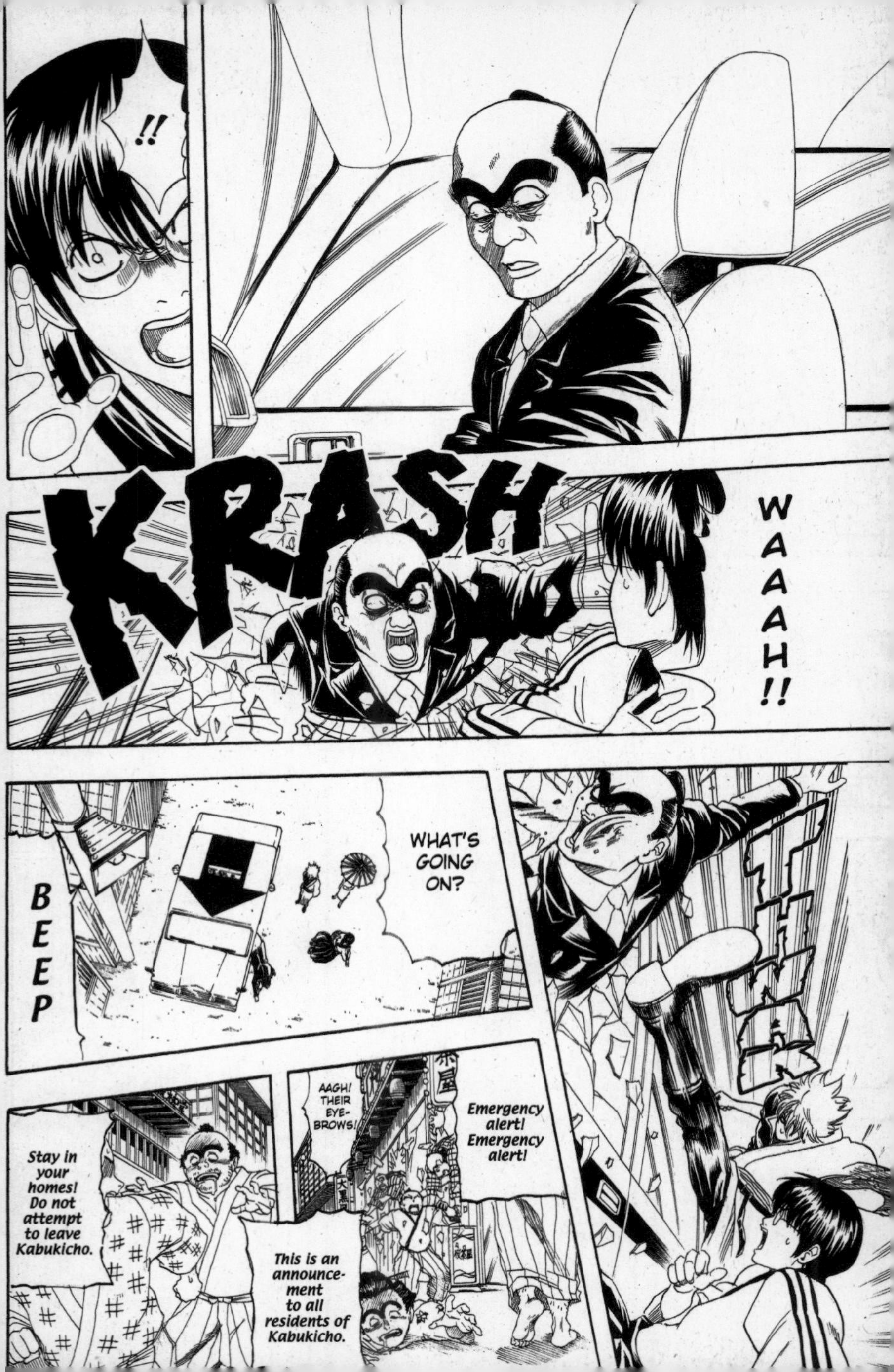
!!
WAAAAH!!
KRASH
THWAK
WHAT'S GOING ON?
BEEP
Emergency alert! Emergency alert!
AAGH! THEIR EYEBROWS!
This is an announcement to all residents of Kabukicho.
Stay in your homes! Do not attempt to leave Kabukicho.

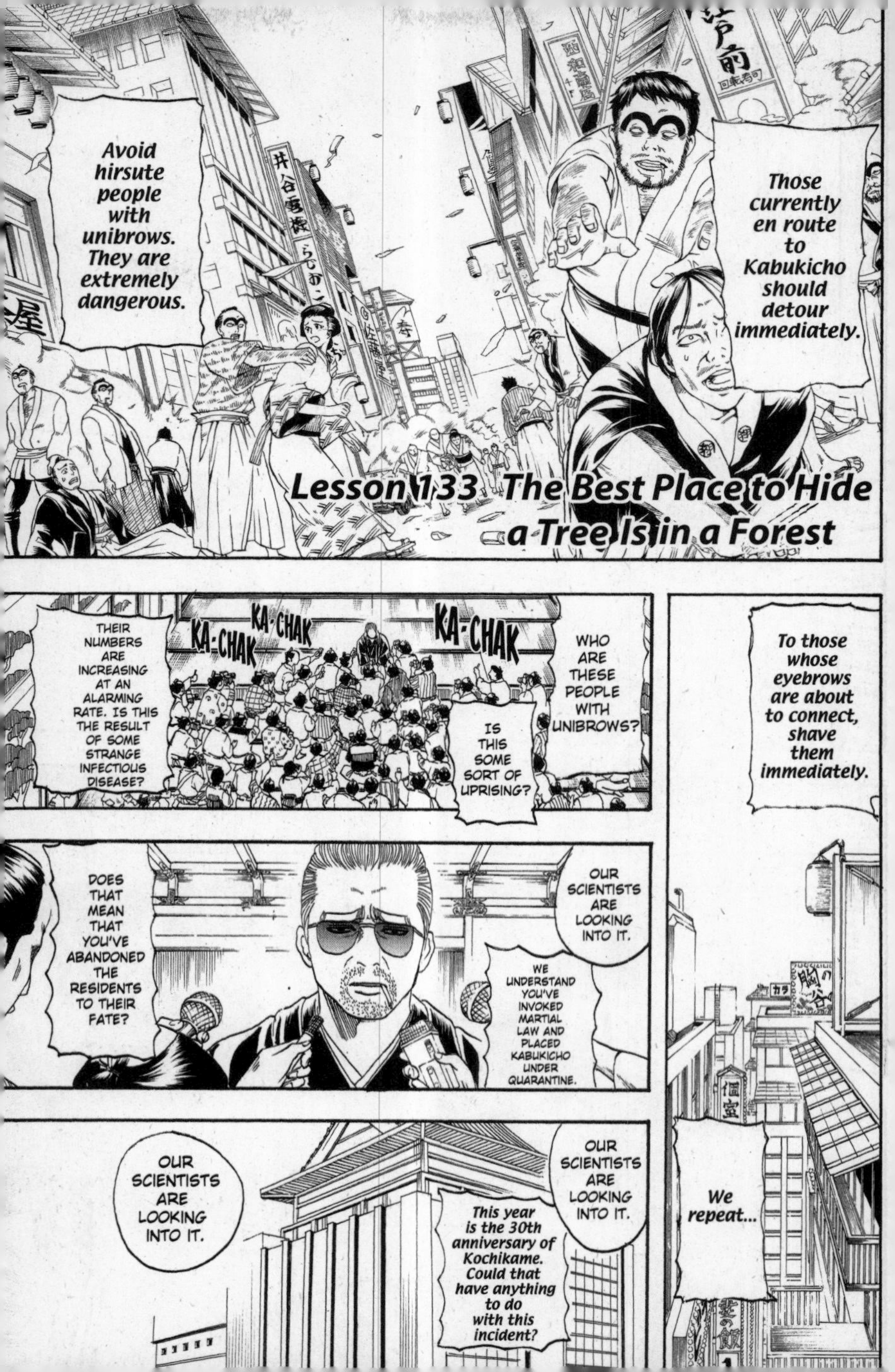
Those currently en route to Kabukicho should detour immediately.
Avoid hirsute people with unibrows. They are extremely dangerous.
Lesson 133 The Best Place to Hide a Tree Is in a Forest
To those whose eyebrows are about to connect, shave them immediately.
We repeat...
KA-CHAK
KA-CHAK
KA-CHAK
WHO ARE THESE PEOPLE WITH UNIBROWS?
IS THIS SOME SORT OF UPRISING?
THEIR NUMBERS ARE INCREASING AT AN ALARMING RATE. IS THIS THE RESULT OF SOME STRANGE INFECTIOUS DISEASE?
OUR SCIENTISTS ARE LOOKING INTO IT.
WE UNDERSTAND YOU'VE INVOKED MARTIAL LAW AND PLACED KABUKICHO UNDER QUARANTINE.
DOES THAT MEAN THAT YOU'VE ABANDONED THE RESIDENTS TO THEIR FATE?
OUR SCIENTISTS ARE LOOKING INTO IT.
This year is the 30th anniversary of Kochikame. Could that have anything to do with this incident?
OUR SCIENTISTS ARE LOOKING INTO IT.

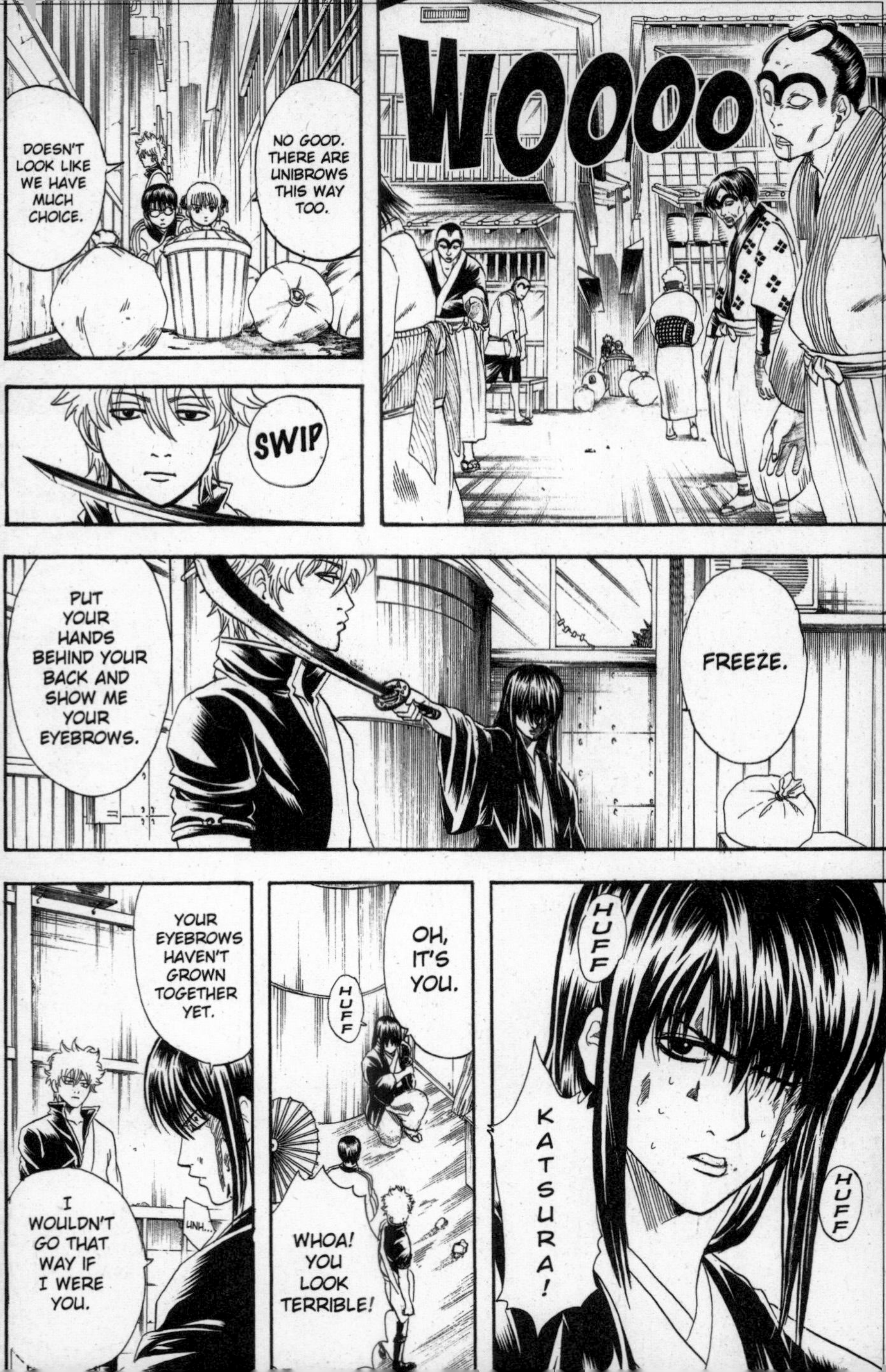
WOOOO
NO GOOD. THERE ARE UNIBROWS THIS WAY TOO.
DOESN'T LOOK LIKE WE HAVE MUCH CHOICE.
SWIP
FREEZE.
PUT YOUR HANDS BEHIND YOUR BACK AND SHOW ME YOUR EYEBROWS.
HUFF
KATSURA!
HUFF
OH, IT'S YOU.
HUFF
WHOA! YOU LOOK TERRIBLE!
YOUR EYEBROWS HAVEN'T GROWN TOGETHER YET.
UNH...
I WOULDN'T GO THAT WAY IF I WERE YOU.

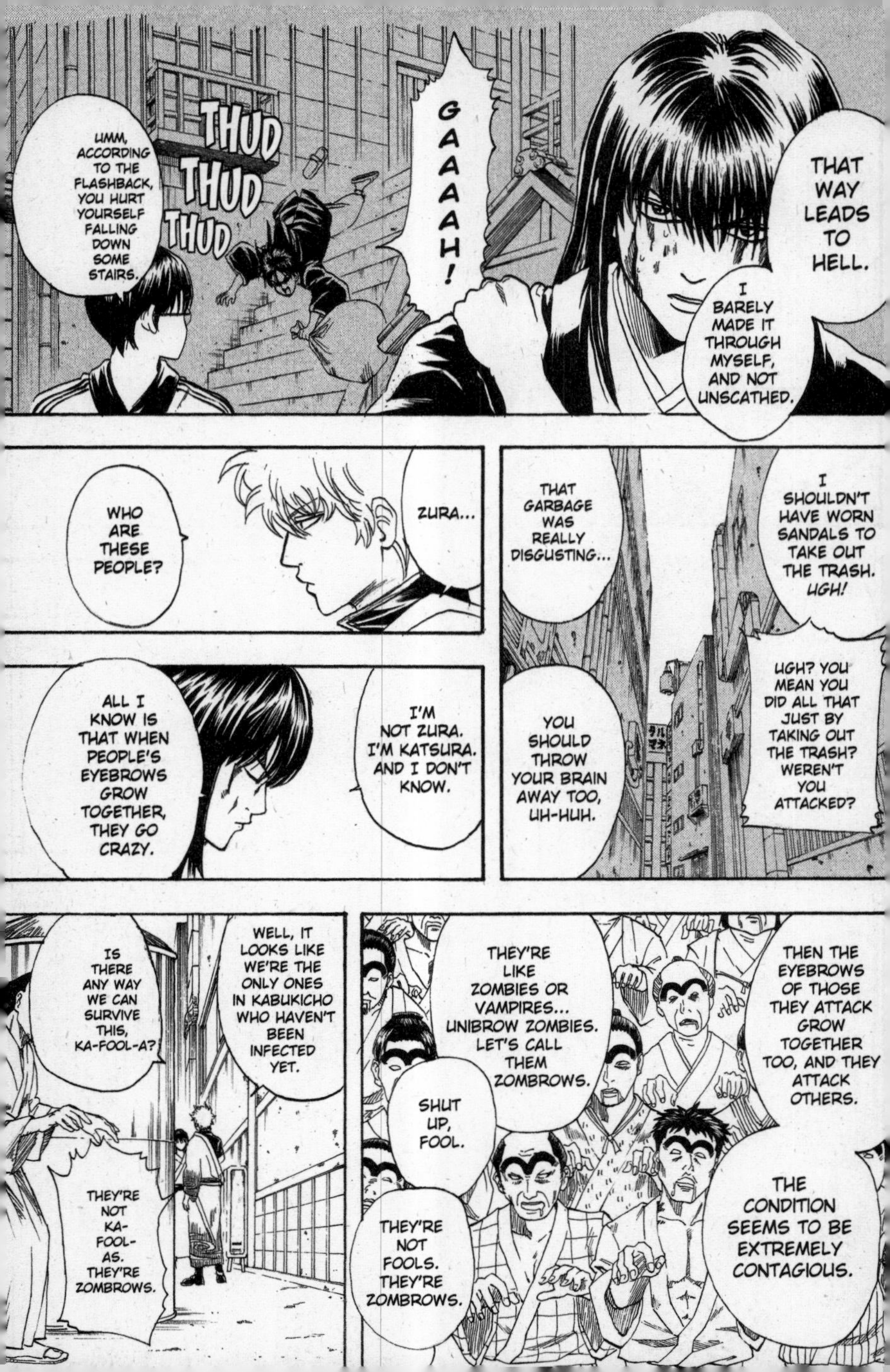
THAT WAY LEADS TO HELL.
I BARELY MADE IT THROUGH MYSELF, AND NOT UNSCATHED.
GAAAAAH!
THUD THUD THUD
UMM, ACCORDING TO THE FLASHBACK, YOU HURT YOURSELF FALLING DOWN SOME STAIRS.
I SHOULDN'T HAVE WORN SANDALS TO TAKE OUT THE TRASH. UGH!
THAT GARBAGE WAS REALLY DISGUSTING...
UGH? YOU MEAN YOU DID ALL THAT JUST BY TAKING OUT THE TRASH? WEREN'T YOU ATTACKED?
YOU SHOULD THROW YOUR BRAIN AWAY TOO, UH-HUH.
ZURA...
WHO ARE THESE PEOPLE?
I'M NOT ZURA. I'M KATSURA. AND I DON'T KNOW.
ALL I KNOW IS THAT WHEN PEOPLE'S EYEBROWS GROW TOGETHER, THEY GO CRAZY.
THEN THE EYEBROWS OF THOSE THEY ATTACK GROW TOGETHER TOO, AND THEY ATTACK OTHERS.
THEY'RE LIKE ZOMBIES OR VAMPIRES... UNIBROW ZOMBIES. LET'S CALL THEM ZOMBROWS.
THE CONDITION SEEMS TO BE EXTREMELY CONTAGIOUS.
SHUT UP, FOOL.
THEY'RE NOT FOOLS. THEY'RE ZOMBROWS.
WELL, IT LOOKS LIKE WE'RE THE ONLY ONES IN KABUKICHO WHO HAVEN'T BEEN INFECTED YET.
IS THERE ANY WAY WE CAN SURVIVE THIS, KA-FOOL-A?
THEY'RE NOT KA-FOOL-AS. THEY'RE ZOMBROWS.

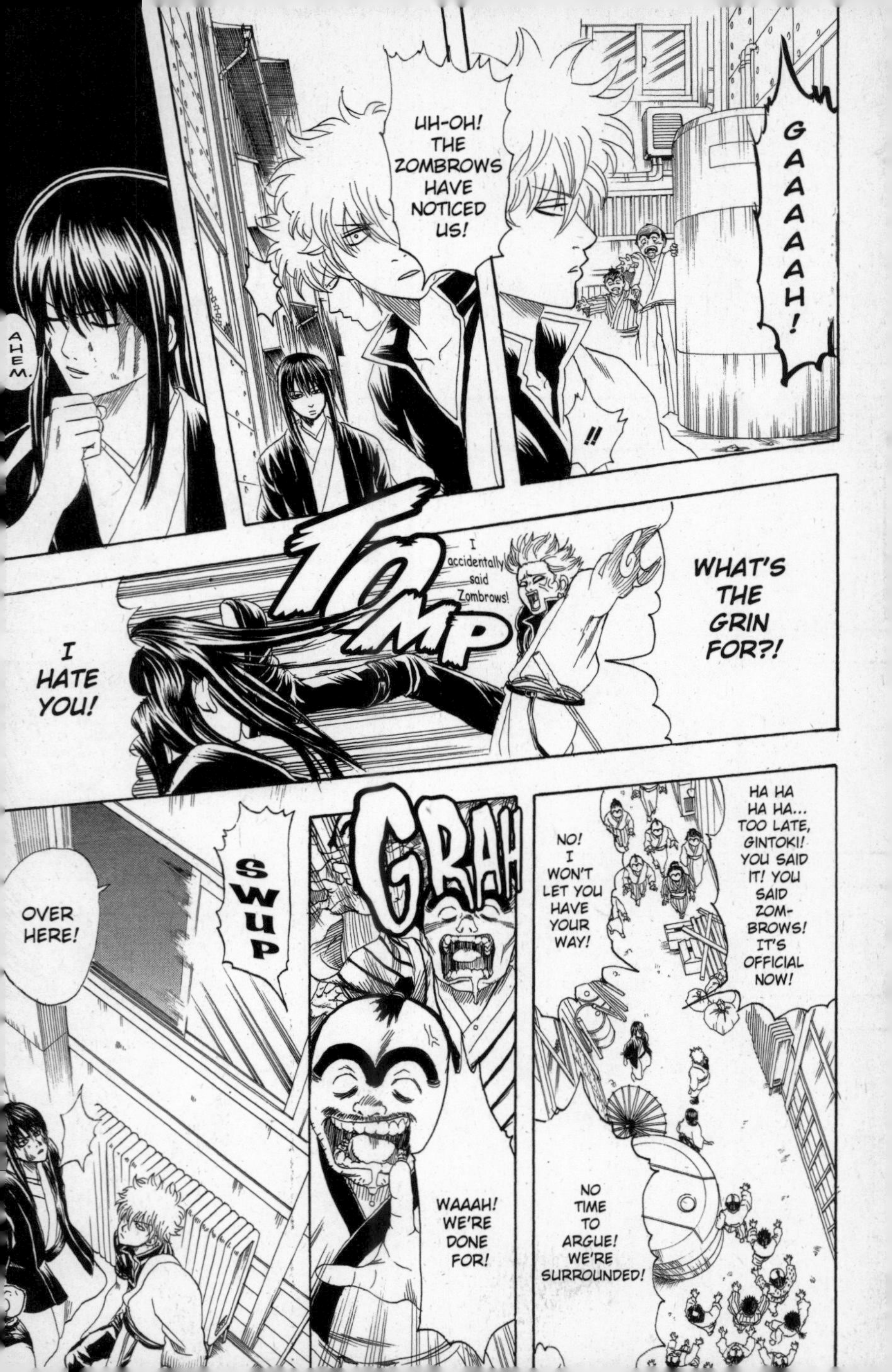
GAAAAAAH!
UH-OH! THE ZOMBROWS HAVE NOTICED US!
!!
AHEM.
WHAT'S THE GRIN FOR?!
I accidentally said Zombrows!
TOMP
I HATE YOU!
HA HA HA HA... TOO LATE, GINTOKI! YOU SAID IT! YOU SAID ZOM-BROWS! IT'S OFFICIAL NOW!
NO! I WON'T LET YOU HAVE YOUR WAY!
NO TIME TO ARGUE! WE'RE SURROUNDED!
GRAH
WAAAH! WE'RE DONE FOR!
SWUP
OVER HERE!

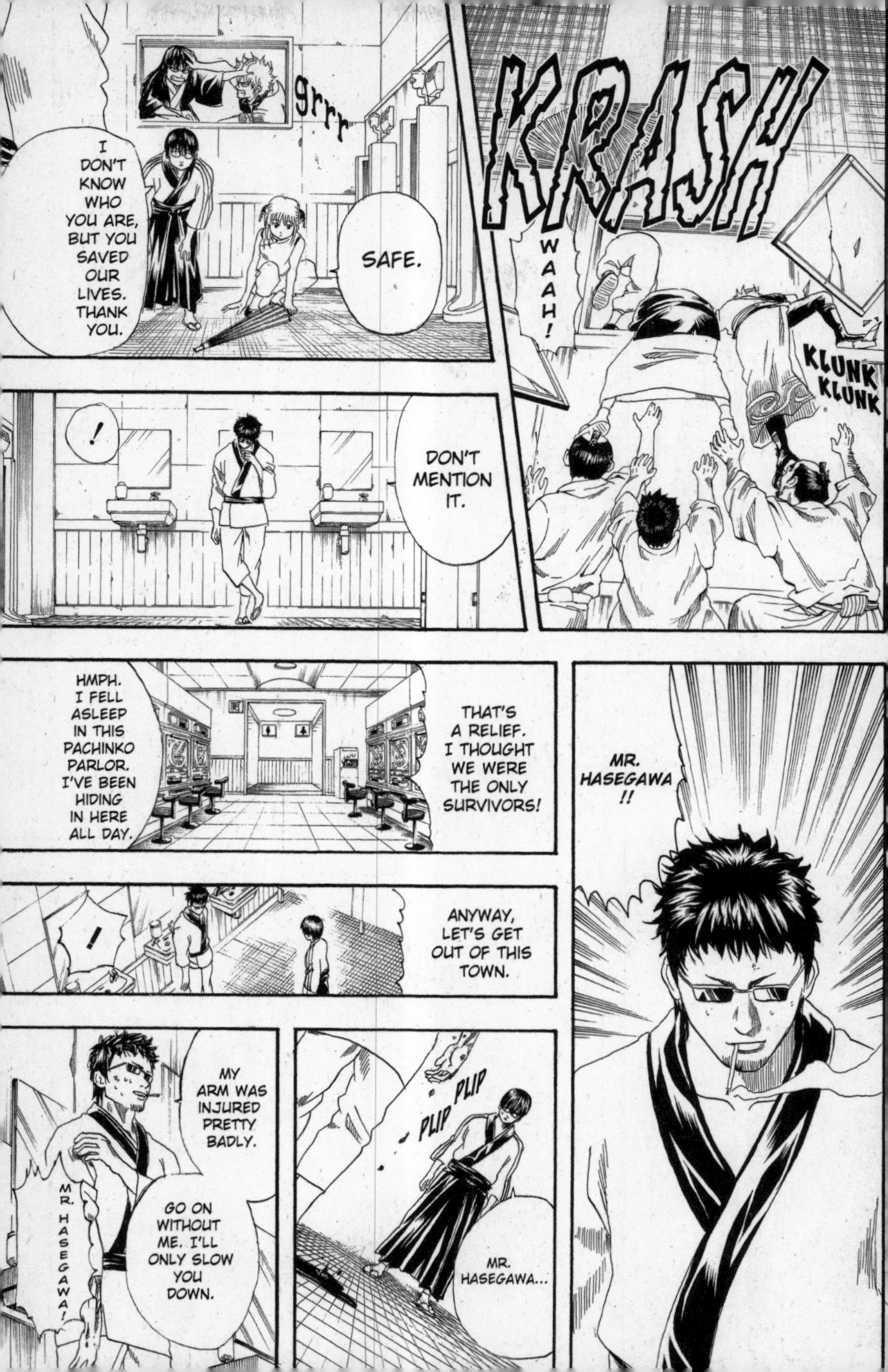
KRASH
WAAAH!
KLUNK KLUNK
grrr
SAFE.
I DON'T KNOW WHO YOU ARE, BUT YOU SAVED OUR LIVES. THANK YOU.
DON'T MENTION IT.
!
MR. HASEGAWA!!
THAT'S A RELIEF. I THOUGHT WE WERE THE ONLY SURVIVORS!
HMPH. I FELL ASLEEP IN THIS PACHINKO PARLOR. I'VE BEEN HIDING IN HERE ALL DAY.
ANYWAY, LET'S GET OUT OF THIS TOWN.
!
PLIP PLIP
MR. HASEGAWA...
MY ARM WAS INJURED PRETTY BADLY.
GO ON WITHOUT ME. I'LL ONLY SLOW YOU DOWN.
MR. HASEGAWA!

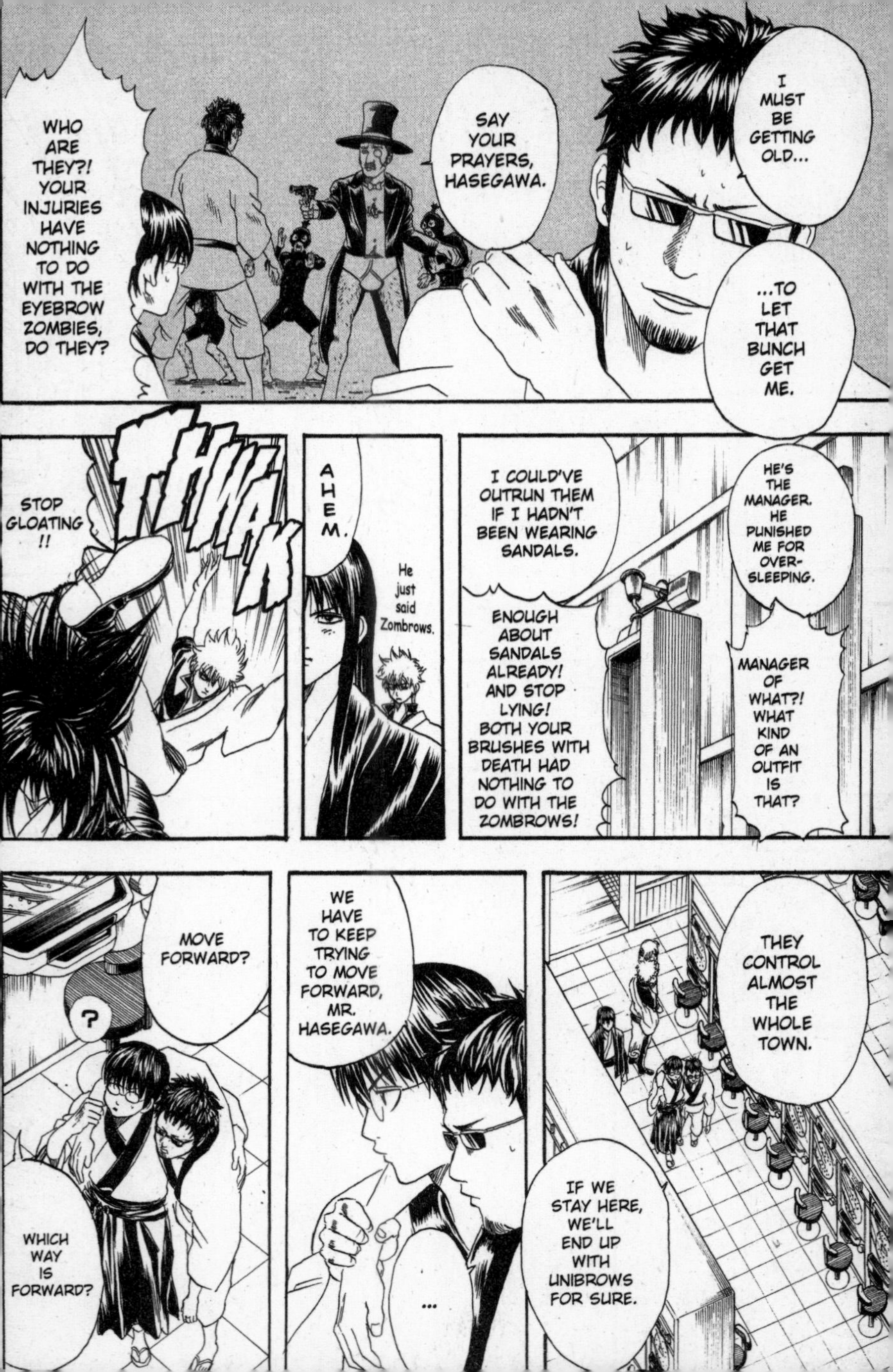
I MUST BE GETTING OLD...
...TO LET THAT BUNCH GET ME.
SAY YOUR PRAYERS, HASEGAWA.
WHO ARE THEY?! YOUR INJURIES HAVE NOTHING TO DO WITH THE EYEBROW ZOMBIES, DO THEY?
HE'S THE MANAGER. HE PUNISHED ME FOR OVER-SLEEPING.
MANAGER OF WHAT?! WHAT KIND OF AN OUTFIT IS THAT?
I COULD'VE OUTRUN THEM IF I HADN'T BEEN WEARING SANDALS.
ENOUGH ABOUT SANDALS ALREADY! AND STOP LYING! BOTH YOUR BRUSHES WITH DEATH HAD NOTHING TO DO WITH THE ZOMBROWS!
AHEM.
He just said Zombrows.
THWAK
STOP GLOATING!!
THEY CONTROL ALMOST THE WHOLE TOWN.
IF WE STAY HERE, WE'LL END UP WITH UNIBROWS FOR SURE.
WE HAVE TO KEEP TRYING TO MOVE FORWARD, MR. HASEGAWA.
...
MOVE FORWARD?
?
WHICH WAY IS FORWARD?

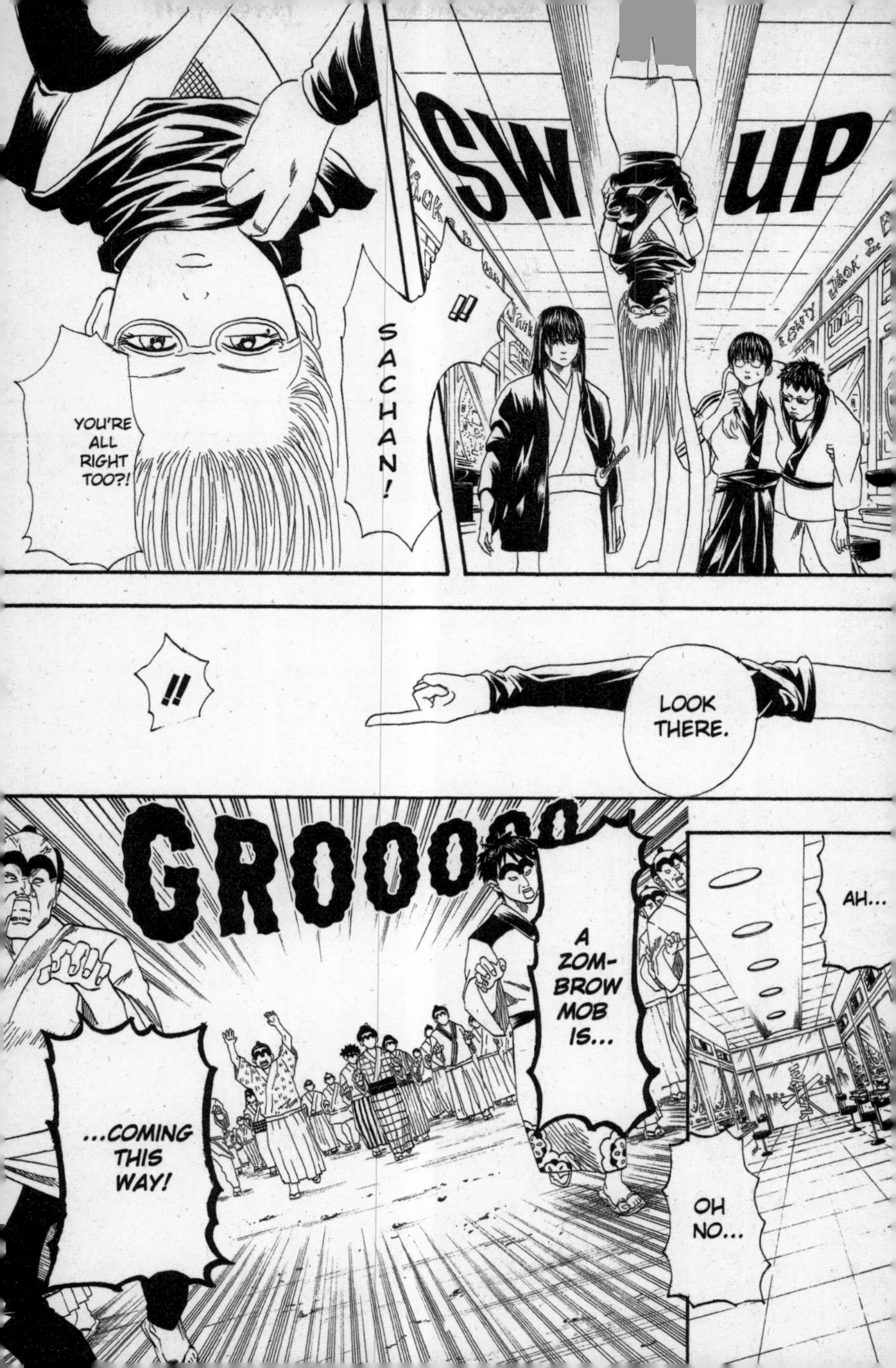
SW UP
!!
SACHAN!
YOU'RE ALL RIGHT TOO?!
LOOK THERE.
!!
AH...
OH NO...
GROOOOO
A ZOM-BROW MOB IS...
...COMING THIS WAY!

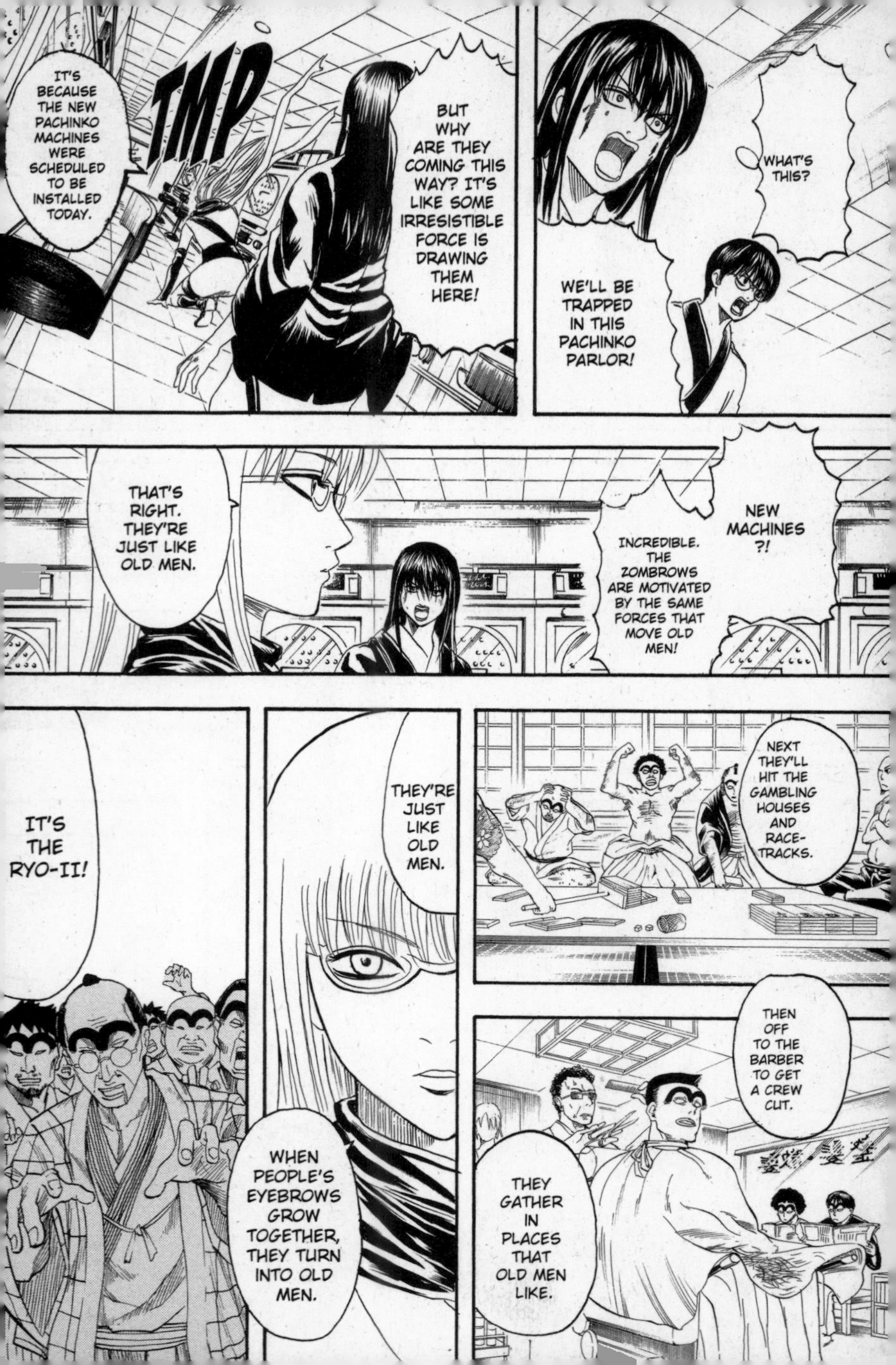
WHAT'S THIS?
WE'LL BE TRAPPED IN THIS PACHINKO PARLOR!
BUT WHY ARE THEY COMING THIS WAY? IT'S LIKE SOME IRRESISTIBLE FORCE IS DRAWING THEM HERE!
TMP
IT'S BECAUSE THE NEW PACHINKO MACHINES WERE SCHEDULED TO BE INSTALLED TODAY.
NEW MACHINES?!
INCREDIBLE. THE ZOMBROWS ARE MOTIVATED BY THE SAME FORCES THAT MOVE OLD MEN!
THAT'S RIGHT. THEY'RE JUST LIKE OLD MEN.
NEXT THEY'LL HIT THE GAMBLING HOUSES AND RACE-TRACKS.
THEN OFF TO THE BARBER TO GET A CREW CUT.
THEY GATHER IN PLACES THAT OLD MEN LIKE.
THEY'RE JUST LIKE OLD MEN.
WHEN PEOPLE'S EYEBROWS GROW TOGETHER, THEY TURN INTO OLD MEN.
IT'S THE RYO-II!

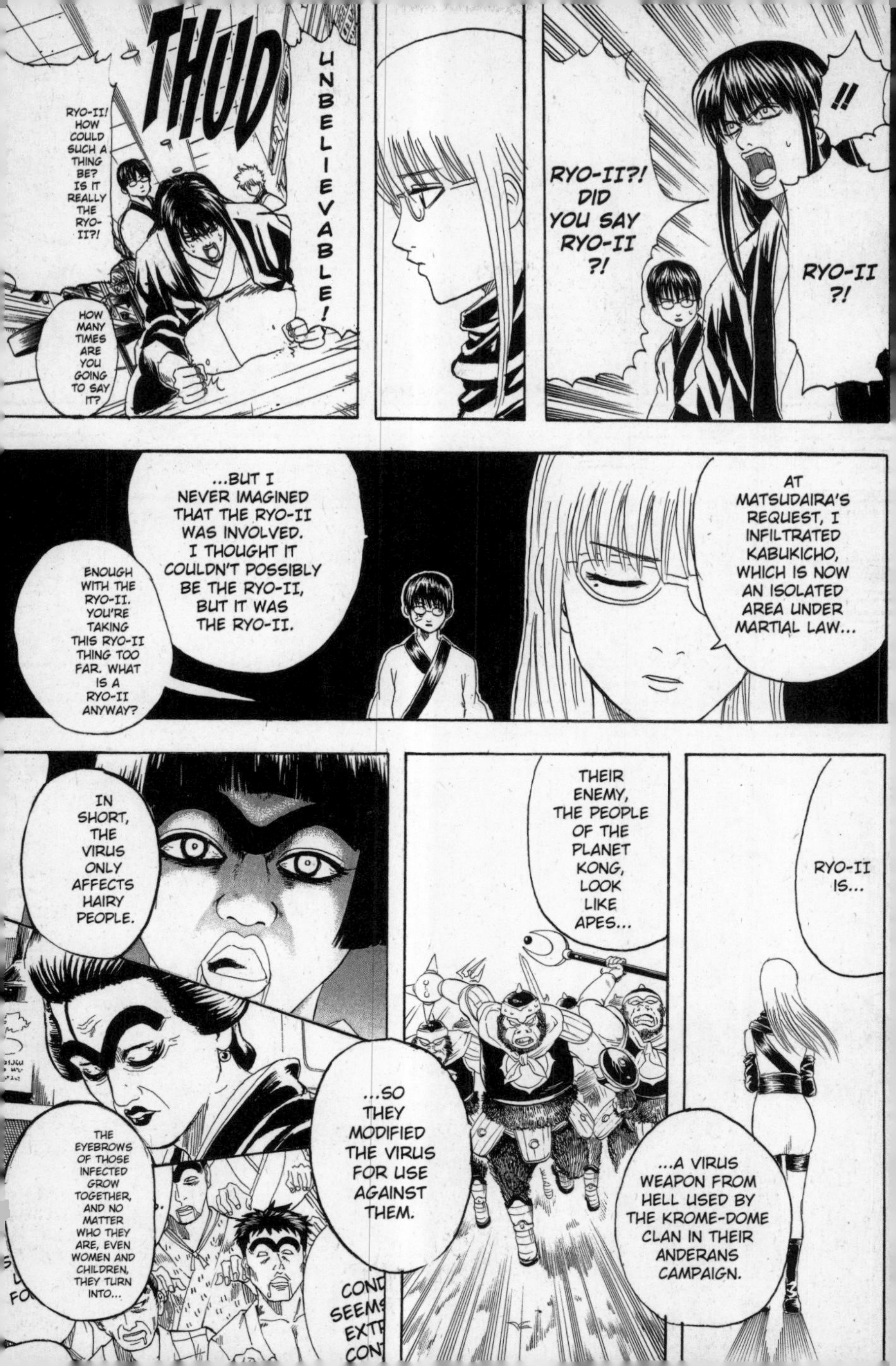
!!
RYO-II ?!
RYO-II?! DID YOU SAY RYO-II ?!
UNBELIEVABLE!
THUD
RYO-II! HOW COULD SUCH A THING BE? IS IT REALLY THE RYO-II?!
HOW MANY TIMES ARE YOU GOING TO SAY IT?
AT MATSUDAIRA'S REQUEST, I INFILTRATED KABUKICHO, WHICH IS NOW AN ISOLATED AREA UNDER MARTIAL LAW...
...BUT I NEVER IMAGINED THAT THE RYO-II WAS INVOLVED. I THOUGHT IT COULDN'T POSSIBLY BE THE RYO-II, BUT IT WAS THE RYO-II.
ENOUGH WITH THE RYO-II. YOU'RE TAKING THIS RYO-II THING TOO FAR. WHAT IS A RYO-II ANYWAY?
RYO-II IS...
...A VIRUS WEAPON FROM HELL USED BY THE KROME-DOME CLAN IN THEIR ANDERANS CAMPAIGN.
THEIR ENEMY, THE PEOPLE OF THE PLANET KONG, LOOK LIKE APES...
...SO THEY MODIFIED THE VIRUS FOR USE AGAINST THEM.
IN SHORT, THE VIRUS ONLY AFFECTS HAIRY PEOPLE.
THE EYEBROWS OF THOSE INFECTED GROW TOGETHER, AND NO MATTER WHO THEY ARE, EVEN WOMEN AND CHILDREN, THEY TURN INTO...

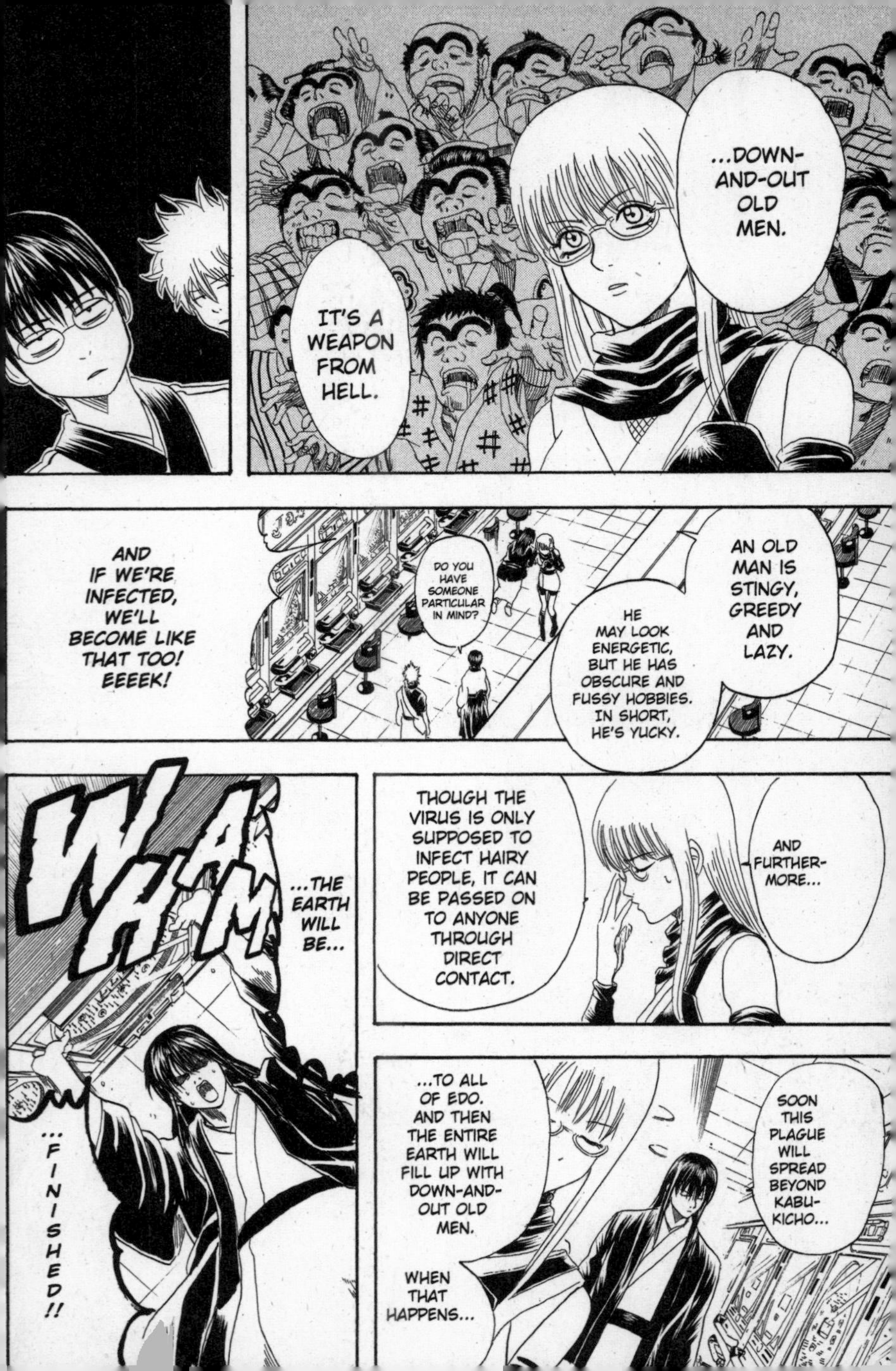
...DOWN-AND-OUT OLD MEN.
IT'S A WEAPON FROM HELL.
AN OLD MAN IS STINGY, GREEDY AND LAZY.
HE MAY LOOK ENERGETIC, BUT HE HAS OBSCURE AND FUSSY HOBBIES. IN SHORT, HE'S YUCKY.
DO YOU HAVE SOMEONE PARTICULAR IN MIND?
AND IF WE'RE INFECTED, WE'LL BECOME LIKE THAT TOO! EEEEK!
AND FURTHER-MORE...
THOUGH THE VIRUS IS ONLY SUPPOSED TO INFECT HAIRY PEOPLE, IT CAN BE PASSED ON TO ANYONE THROUGH DIRECT CONTACT.
SOON THIS PLAGUE WILL SPREAD BEYOND KABU-KICHO...
...TO ALL OF EDO. AND THEN THE ENTIRE EARTH WILL FILL UP WITH DOWN-AND-OUT OLD MEN.
WHEN THAT HAPPENS...
...THE EARTH WILL BE...
WHAM
...FINISHED!!

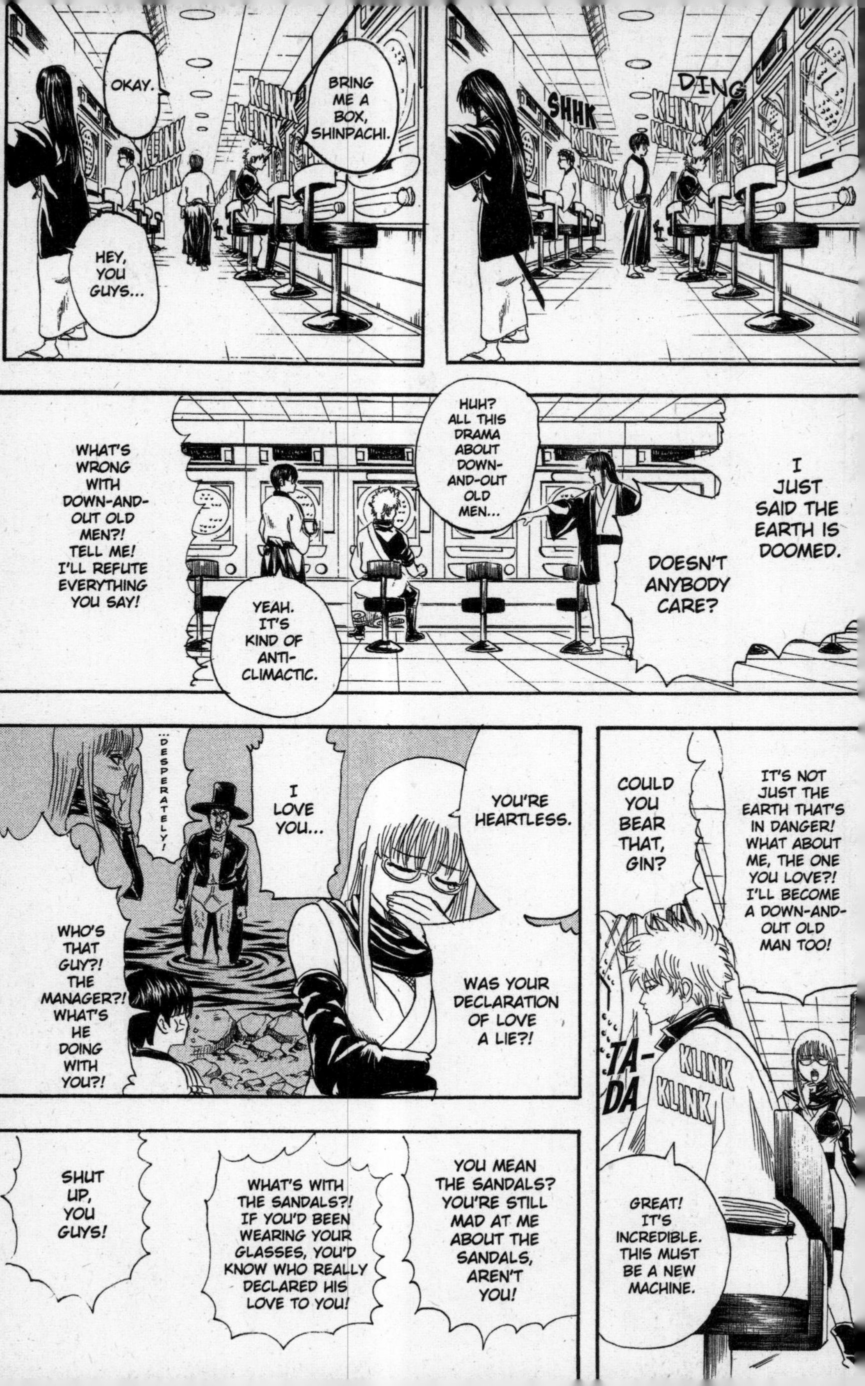
DING
SHHK
KLINK
KLINK
KLINK
KLINK
BRING ME A BOX, SHINPACHI.
OKAY.
KLINK
KLINK
KLINK
KLINK
HEY, YOU GUYS...
I JUST SAID THE EARTH IS DOOMED.
DOESN'T ANYBODY CARE?
HUH? ALL THIS DRAMA ABOUT DOWN-AND-OUT OLD MEN...
YEAH. IT'S KIND OF ANTI-CLIMACTIC.
WHAT'S WRONG WITH DOWN-AND-OUT OLD MEN?! TELL ME! I'LL REFUTE EVERYTHING YOU SAY!
IT'S NOT JUST THE EARTH THAT'S IN DANGER! WHAT ABOUT ME, THE ONE YOU LOVE?! I'LL BECOME A DOWN-AND-OUT OLD MAN TOO!
COULD YOU BEAR THAT, GIN?
TA-DA
KLINK
KLINK
GREAT! IT'S INCREDIBLE. THIS MUST BE A NEW MACHINE.
YOU'RE HEARTLESS.
WAS YOUR DECLARATION OF LOVE A LIE?!
I LOVE YOU...
...DESPERATELY!
WHO'S THAT GUY?! THE MANAGER?! WHAT'S HE DOING WITH YOU?!
YOU MEAN THE SANDALS? YOU'RE STILL MAD AT ME ABOUT THE SANDALS, AREN'T YOU!
WHAT'S WITH THE SANDALS?! IF YOU'D BEEN WEARING YOUR GLASSES, YOU'D KNOW WHO REALLY DECLARED HIS LOVE TO YOU!
SHUT UP, YOU GUYS!

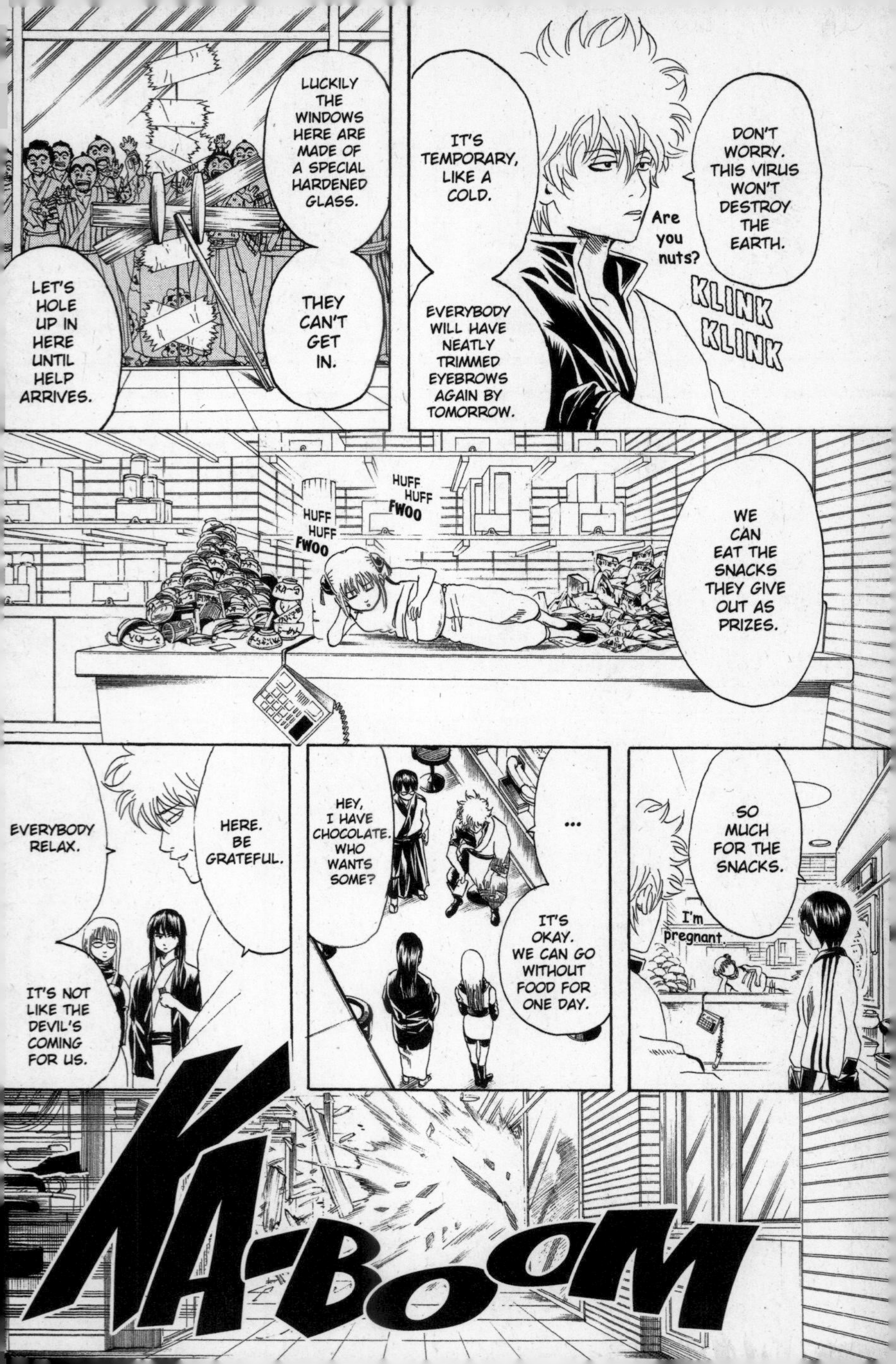
DON'T WORRY. THIS VIRUS WON'T DESTROY THE EARTH.
Are you nuts?
KLINK KLINK
IT'S TEMPORARY, LIKE A COLD.
EVERYBODY WILL HAVE NEATLY TRIMMED EYEBROWS AGAIN BY TOMORROW.
LUCKILY THE WINDOWS HERE ARE MADE OF A SPECIAL HARDENED GLASS.
THEY CAN'T GET IN.
LET'S HOLE UP IN HERE UNTIL HELP ARRIVES.
WE CAN EAT THE SNACKS THEY GIVE OUT AS PRIZES.
HUFF HUFF FWOO
HUFF HUFF FWOO
SO MUCH FOR THE SNACKS.
I'm pregnant.
...
IT'S OKAY. WE CAN GO WITHOUT FOOD FOR ONE DAY.
HEY, I HAVE CHOCOLATE. WHO WANTS SOME?
HERE. BE GRATEFUL.
EVERYBODY RELAX.
IT'S NOT LIKE THE DEVIL'S COMING FOR US.
KA-BOOM

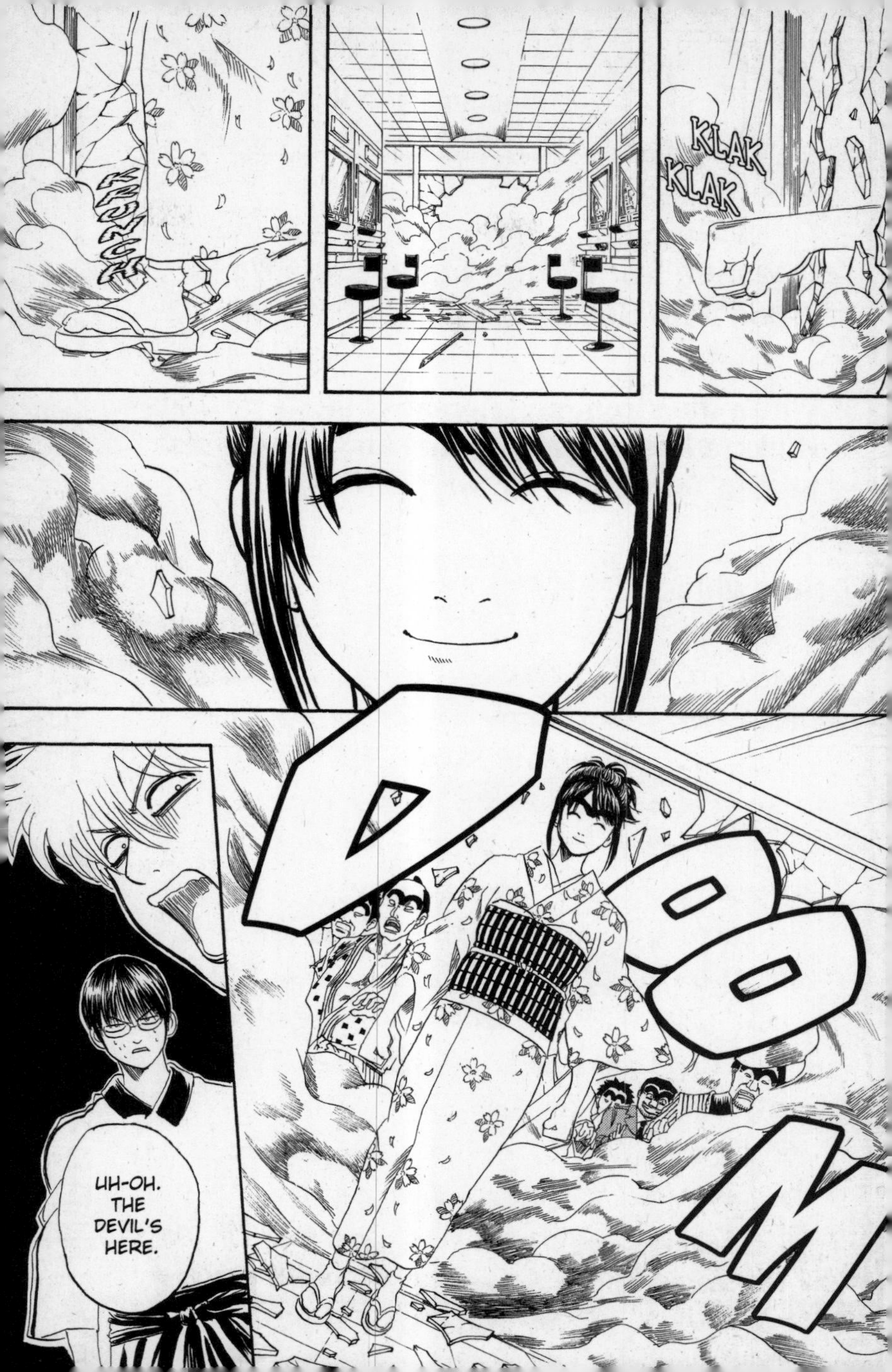
KLAK
KLAK
KRUNCH
DOOM
UH-OH. THE DEVIL'S HERE.

<Question from Mom, Sunny-Side Up Is Good with Soy Sauce>

Who's the strongest: Kondo, Hijikata or Okita? Hijikata has defeated Okita, and Kondo has beaten Tojo, right? So who is it?

<Answer>

Strength is a tricky thing. Between two more or less equally matched opponents, mental conditioning is more important. I suppose a really strong person can use his or her power effectively regardless of mood or attitude, but at the elite level, subtle differences often determine the outcome of a fight. So I can't say who's number one with certainty, but when it comes to swordplay, Okita is the best.

(Q&A #49 is on page 108)

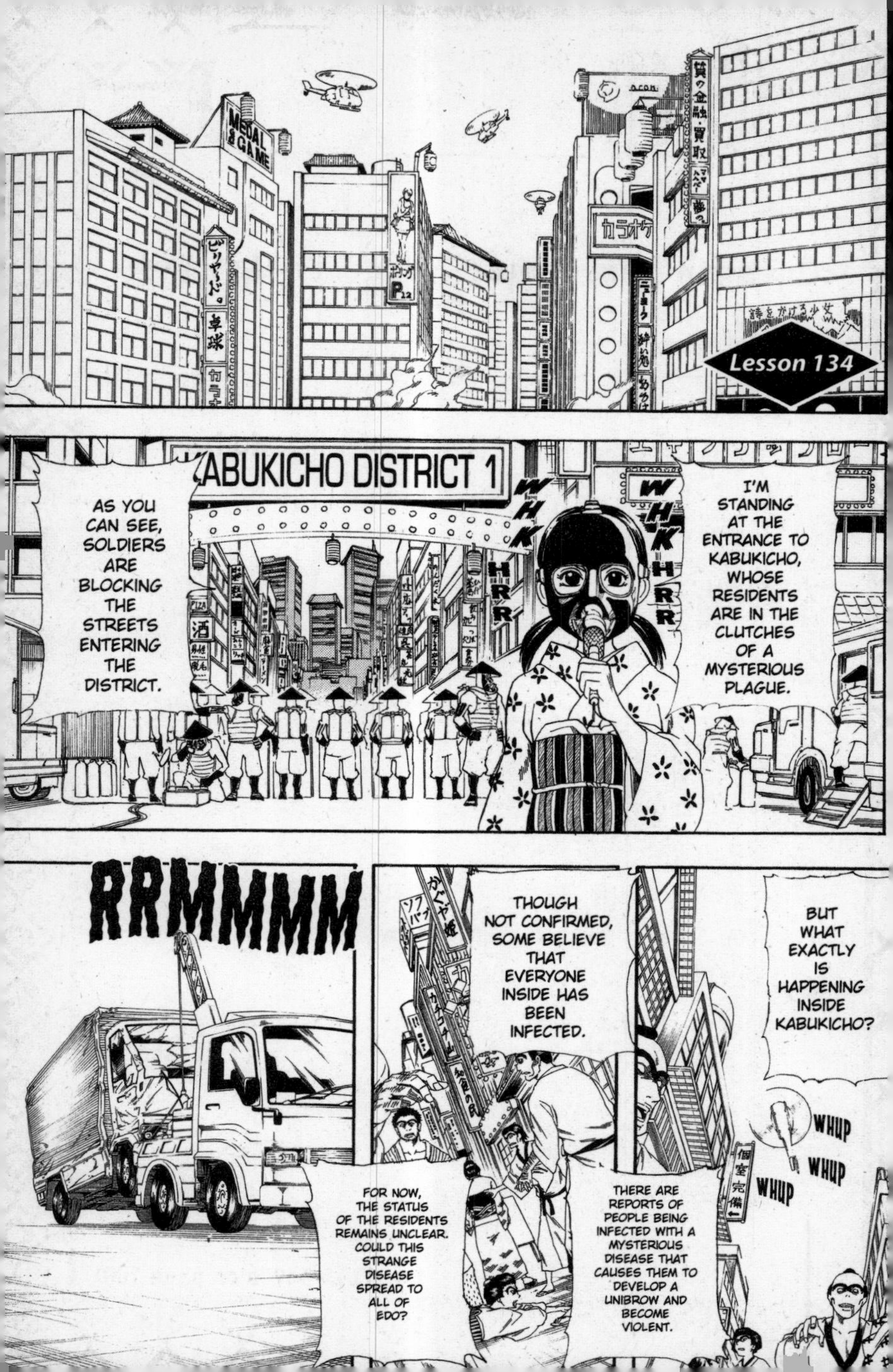
MEDAL & GAME
カラオケ
Lesson 134
KABUKICHO DISTRICT 1
I'M STANDING AT THE ENTRANCE TO KABUKICHO, WHOSE RESIDENTS ARE IN THE CLUTCHES OF A MYSTERIOUS PLAGUE.
WHK HRR
WHK HRR
AS YOU CAN SEE, SOLDIERS ARE BLOCKING THE STREETS ENTERING THE DISTRICT.
BUT WHAT EXACTLY IS HAPPENING INSIDE KABUKICHO?
THOUGH NOT CONFIRMED, SOME BELIEVE THAT EVERYONE INSIDE HAS BEEN INFECTED.
WHUP WHUP WHUP
THERE ARE REPORTS OF PEOPLE BEING INFECTED WITH A MYSTERIOUS DISEASE THAT CAUSES THEM TO DEVELOP A UNIBROW AND BECOME VIOLENT.
FOR NOW, THE STATUS OF THE RESIDENTS REMAINS UNCLEAR. COULD THIS STRANGE DISEASE SPREAD TO ALL OF EDO?
RRMMMM

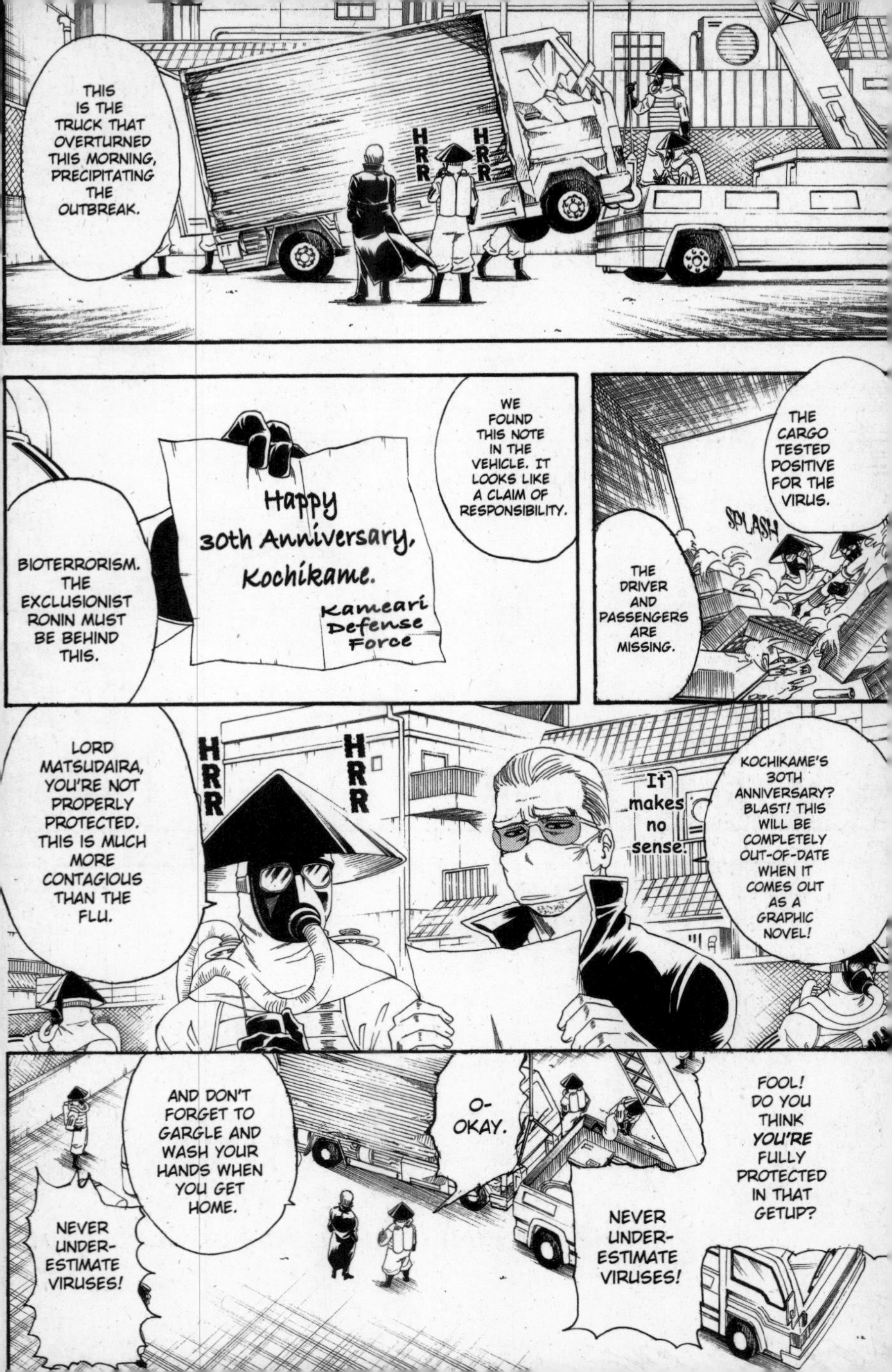
THIS IS THE TRUCK THAT OVERTURNED THIS MORNING, PRECIPITATING THE OUTBREAK.
HRR
HRR
THE CARGO TESTED POSITIVE FOR THE VIRUS.
SPLASH
THE DRIVER AND PASSENGERS ARE MISSING.
WE FOUND THIS NOTE IN THE VEHICLE. IT LOOKS LIKE A CLAIM OF RESPONSIBILITY.
Happy 30th Anniversary, Kochikame.
Kameari Defense Force
BIOTERRORISM. THE EXCLUSIONIST RONIN MUST BE BEHIND THIS.
KOCHIKAME'S 30TH ANNIVERSARY? BLAST! THIS WILL BE COMPLETELY OUT-OF-DATE WHEN IT COMES OUT AS A GRAPHIC NOVEL!
It makes no sense.
HRR
HRR
LORD MATSUDAIRA, YOU'RE NOT PROPERLY PROTECTED. THIS IS MUCH MORE CONTAGIOUS THAN THE FLU.
FOOL! DO YOU THINK *YOU'RE* FULLY PROTECTED IN THAT GETUP?
O-OKAY.
NEVER UNDER-ESTIMATE VIRUSES!
AND DON'T FORGET TO GARGLE AND WASH YOUR HANDS WHEN YOU GET HOME.
NEVER UNDER-ESTIMATE VIRUSES!

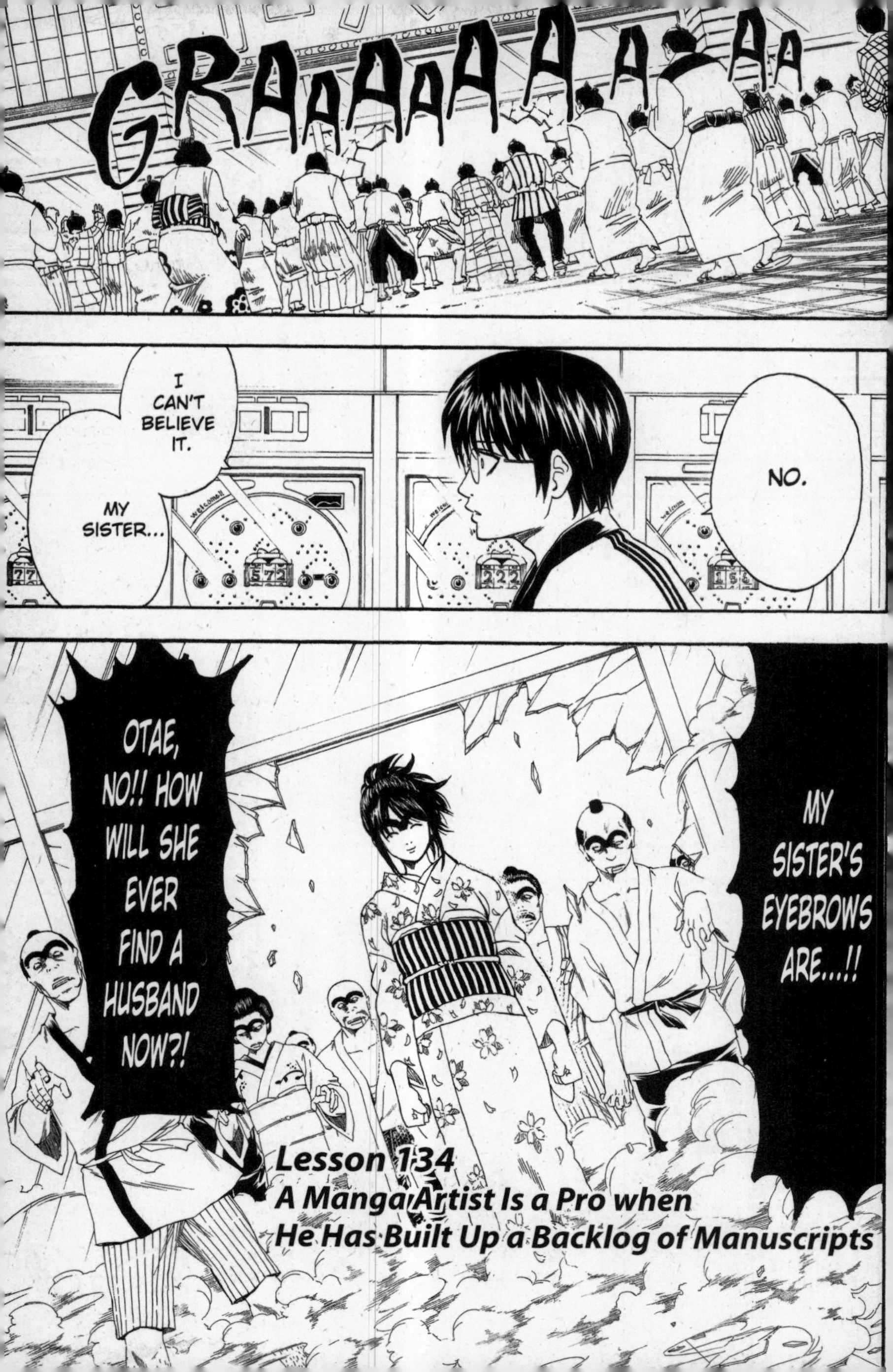
GRAAAAAA A A AA
NO.
I CAN'T BELIEVE IT.
MY SISTER...
MY SISTER'S EYEBROWS ARE...!!
OTAE, NO!! HOW WILL SHE EVER FIND A HUSBAND NOW?!
Lesson 134
A Manga Artist Is a Pro when He Has Built Up a Backlog of Manuscripts

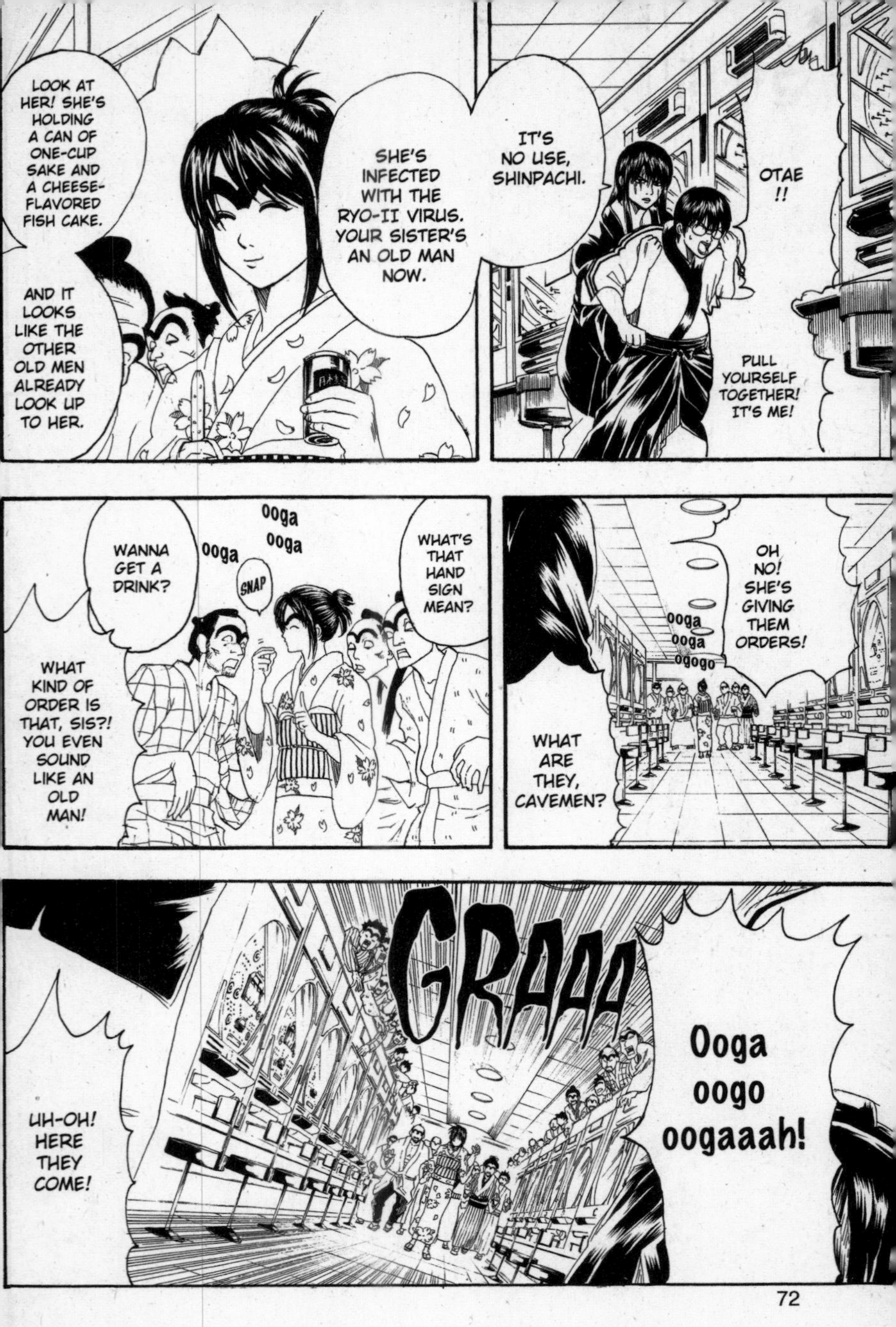
OTAE!!
PULL YOURSELF TOGETHER! IT'S ME!
IT'S NO USE, SHINPACHI.
SHE'S INFECTED WITH THE RYO-II VIRUS. YOUR SISTER'S AN OLD MAN NOW.
LOOK AT HER! SHE'S HOLDING A CAN OF ONE-CUP SAKE AND A CHEESE-FLAVORED FISH CAKE.
AND IT LOOKS LIKE THE OTHER OLD MEN ALREADY LOOK UP TO HER.
OH NO! SHE'S GIVING THEM ORDERS!
ooga ooga ogogo
WHAT ARE THEY, CAVEMEN?
WHAT'S THAT HAND SIGN MEAN?
ooga ooga
ooga
SNAP
WANNA GET A DRINK?
WHAT KIND OF ORDER IS THAT, SIS?! YOU EVEN SOUND LIKE AN OLD MAN!
GRAAA
Ooga oogo oogaaah!
UH-OH! HERE THEY COME!

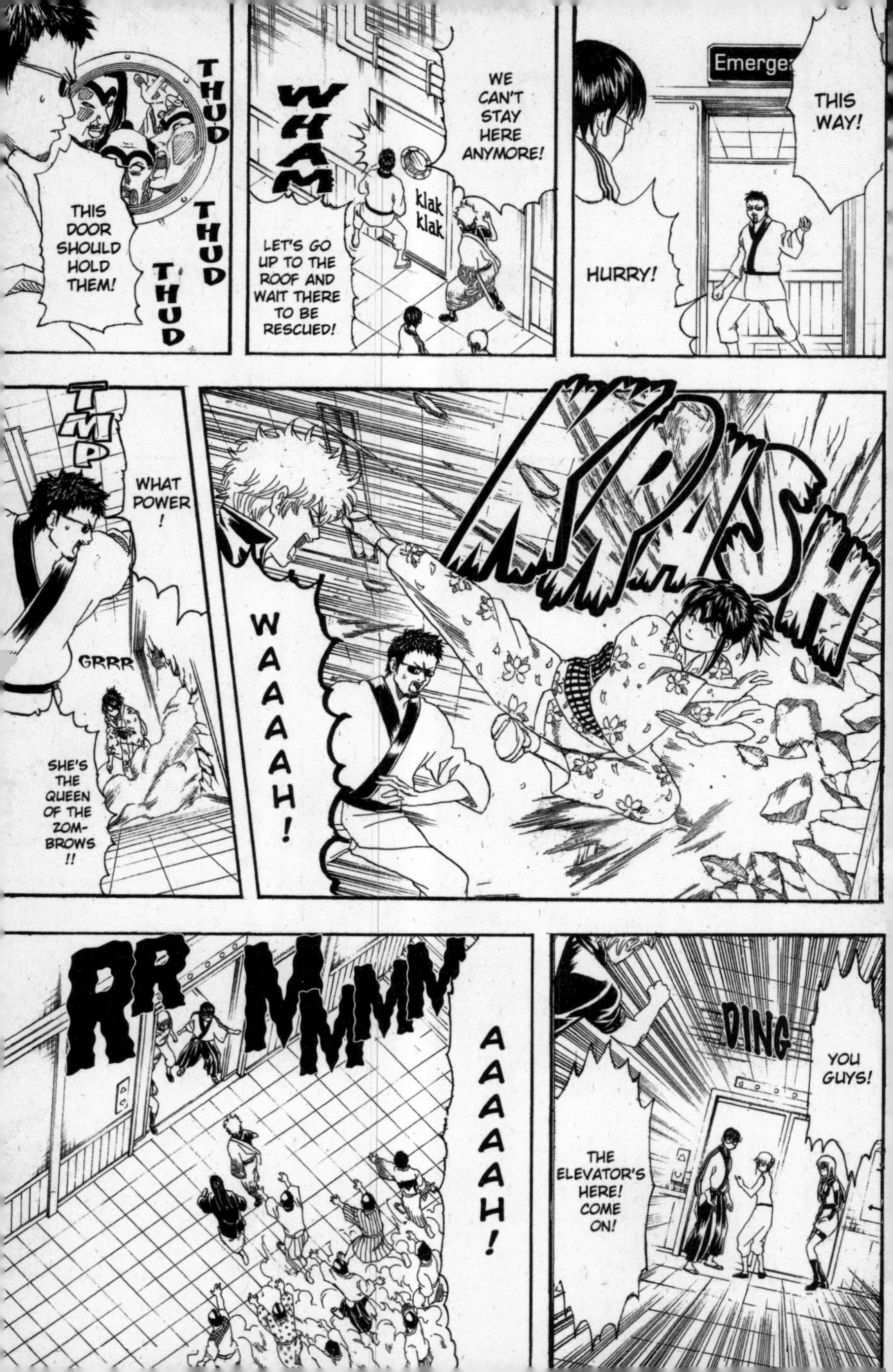

Emerge
THIS WAY!
HURRY!
WE CAN'T STAY HERE ANYMORE!
WHAM
klak klak
LET'S GO UP TO THE ROOF AND WAIT THERE TO BE RESCUED!
THUD
THUD
THUD
THIS DOOR SHOULD HOLD THEM!
KRASH
WAAAAAH!
TMP
WHAT POWER!
GRRR
SHE'S THE QUEEN OF THE ZOM-BROWS!!
DING
YOU GUYS!
THE ELEVATOR'S HERE! COME ON!
RRMMMN
AAAAAAH!

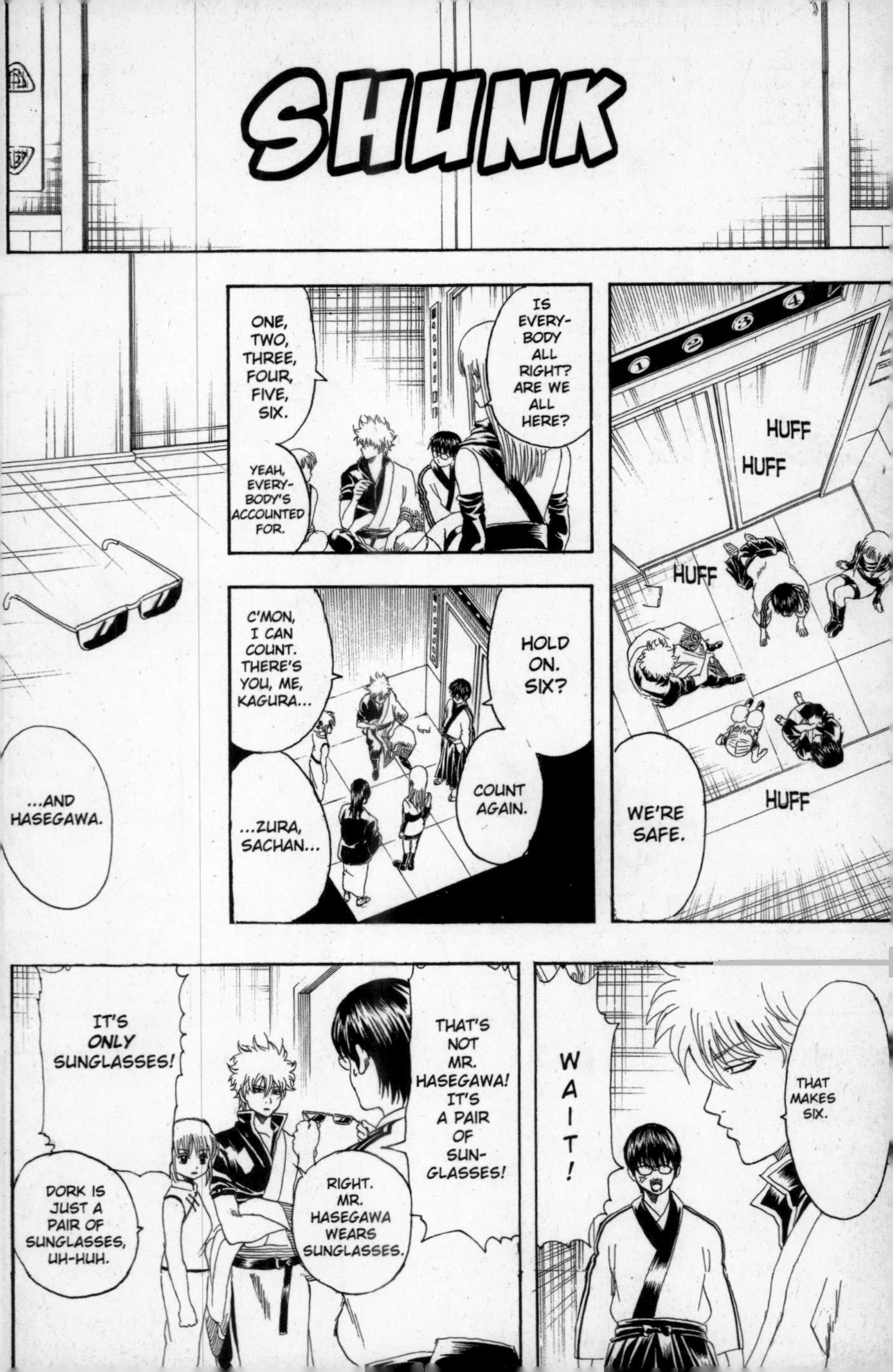
SHUNK
HUFF
HUFF
HUFF
HUFF
WE'RE SAFE.
IS EVERYBODY ALL RIGHT? ARE WE ALL HERE?
ONE, TWO, THREE, FOUR, FIVE, SIX.
YEAH, EVERYBODY'S ACCOUNTED FOR.
HOLD ON. SIX?
C'MON, I CAN COUNT. THERE'S YOU, ME, KAGURA...
COUNT AGAIN.
...ZURA, SACHAN...
...AND HASEGAWA.
THAT MAKES SIX.
WAIT!
THAT'S NOT MR. HASEGAWA! IT'S A PAIR OF SUN-GLASSES!
IT'S ONLY SUNGLASSES!
RIGHT. MR. HASEGAWA WEARS SUNGLASSES.
DORK IS JUST A PAIR OF SUNGLASSES, UH-HUH.

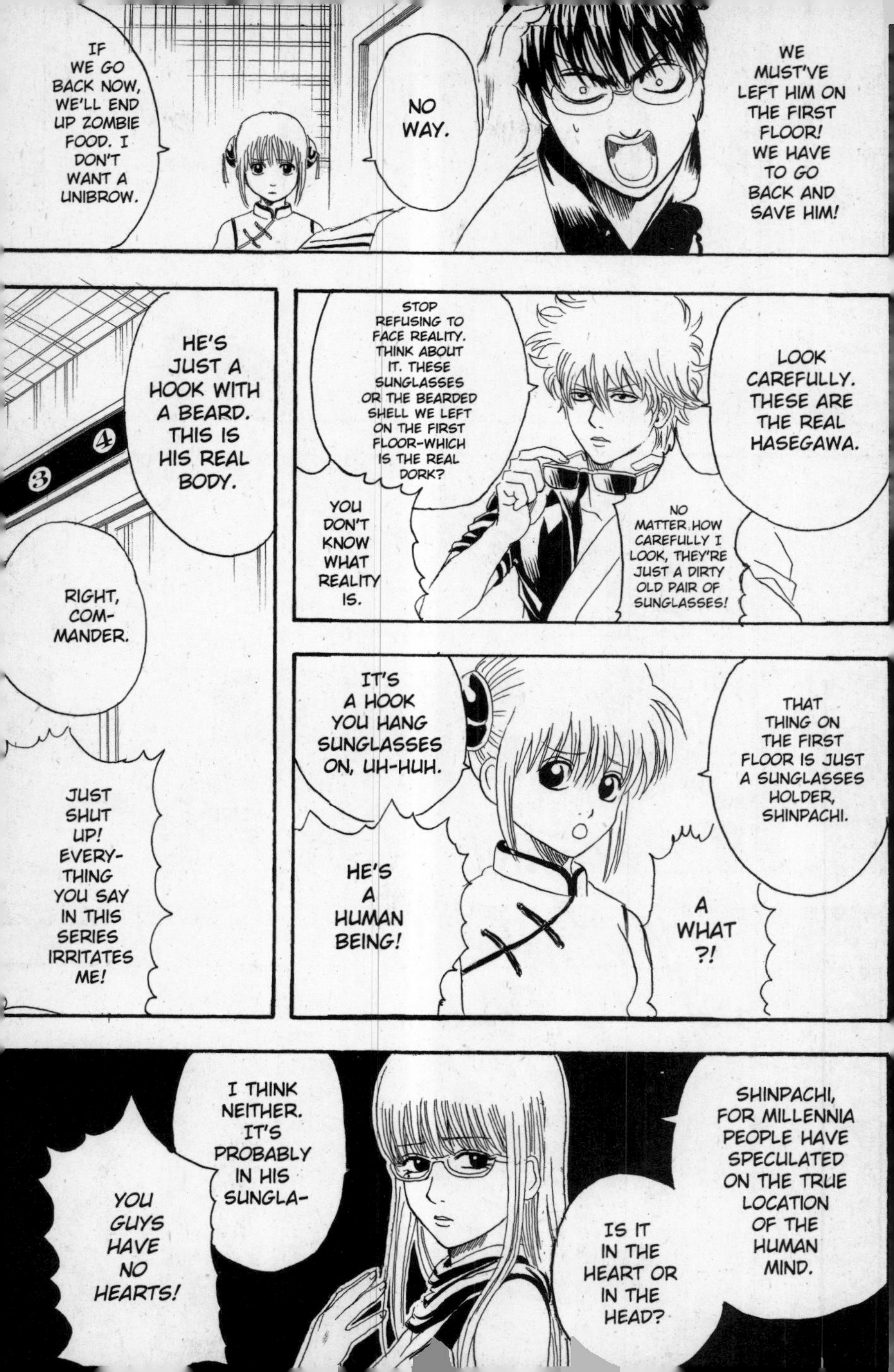
WE MUST'VE LEFT HIM ON THE FIRST FLOOR! WE HAVE TO GO BACK AND SAVE HIM!
NO WAY.
IF WE GO BACK NOW, WE'LL END UP ZOMBIE FOOD. I DON'T WANT A UNIBROW.
LOOK CAREFULLY. THESE ARE THE REAL HASEGAWA.
NO MATTER HOW CAREFULLY I LOOK, THEY'RE JUST A DIRTY OLD PAIR OF SUNGLASSES!
STOP REFUSING TO FACE REALITY. THINK ABOUT IT. THESE SUNGLASSES OR THE BEARDED SHELL WE LEFT ON THE FIRST FLOOR-WHICH IS THE REAL DORK?
YOU DON'T KNOW WHAT REALITY IS.
THAT THING ON THE FIRST FLOOR IS JUST A SUNGLASSES HOLDER, SHINPACHI.
A WHAT?!
IT'S A HOOK YOU HANG SUNGLASSES ON, UH-HUH.
HE'S A HUMAN BEING!
HE'S JUST A HOOK WITH A BEARD. THIS IS HIS REAL BODY.
RIGHT, COM-MANDER.
JUST SHUT UP! EVERY-THING YOU SAY IN THIS SERIES IRRITATES ME!
SHINPACHI, FOR MILLENNIA PEOPLE HAVE SPECULATED ON THE TRUE LOCATION OF THE HUMAN MIND.
IS IT IN THE HEART OR IN THE HEAD?
I THINK NEITHER. IT'S PROBABLY IN HIS SUNGLA-
YOU GUYS HAVE NO HEARTS!

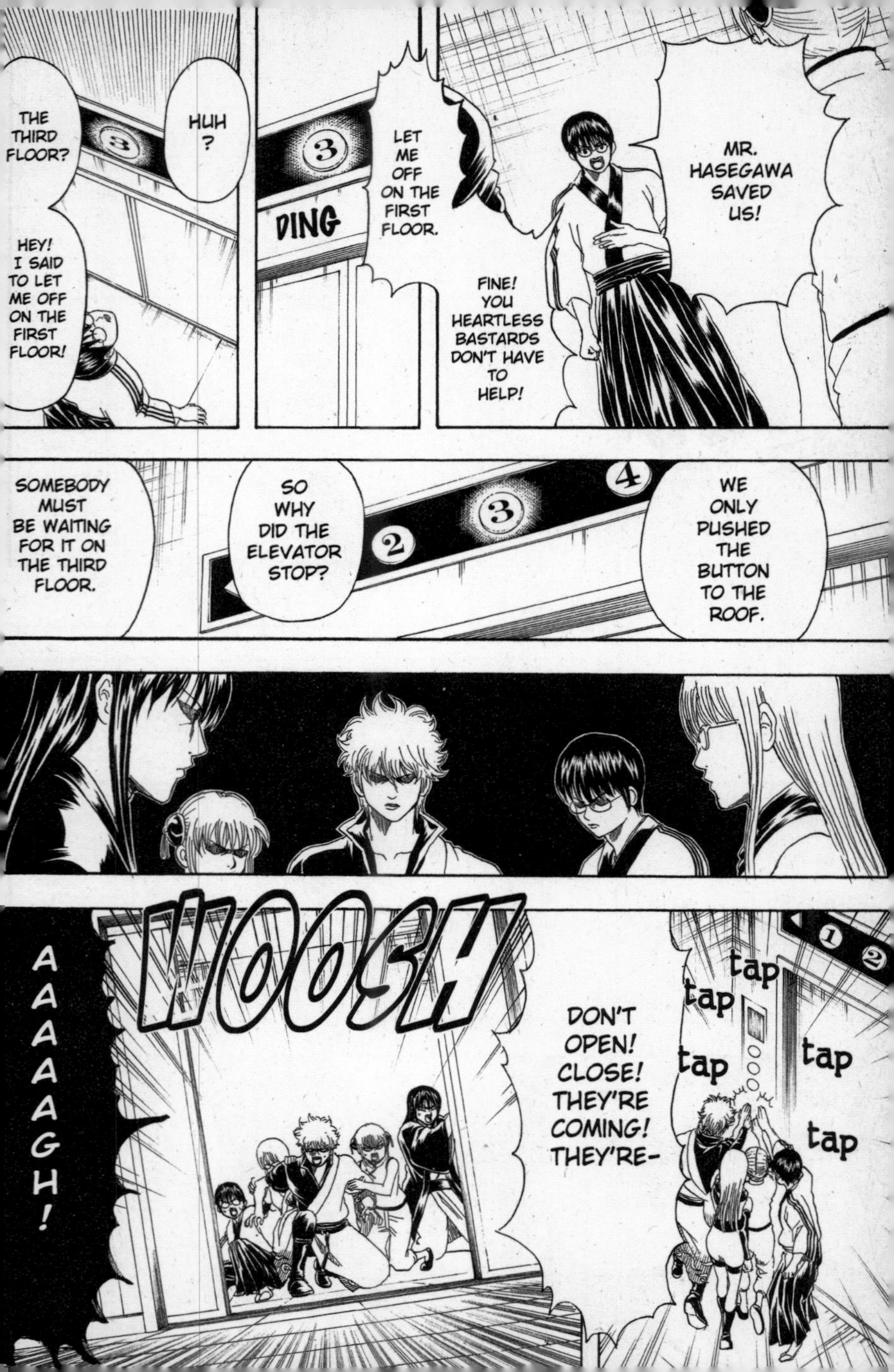
MR. HASEGAWA SAVED US!
FINE! YOU HEARTLESS BASTARDS DON'T HAVE TO HELP!
LET ME OFF ON THE FIRST FLOOR.
DING
HUH ?
THE THIRD FLOOR?
HEY! I SAID TO LET ME OFF ON THE FIRST FLOOR!
WE ONLY PUSHED THE BUTTON TO THE ROOF.
SO WHY DID THE ELEVATOR STOP?
SOMEBODY MUST BE WAITING FOR IT ON THE THIRD FLOOR.
tap tap tap tap tap
DON'T OPEN! CLOSE! THEY'RE COMING! THEY'RE-
WOOSH
AAAAAAAGH!

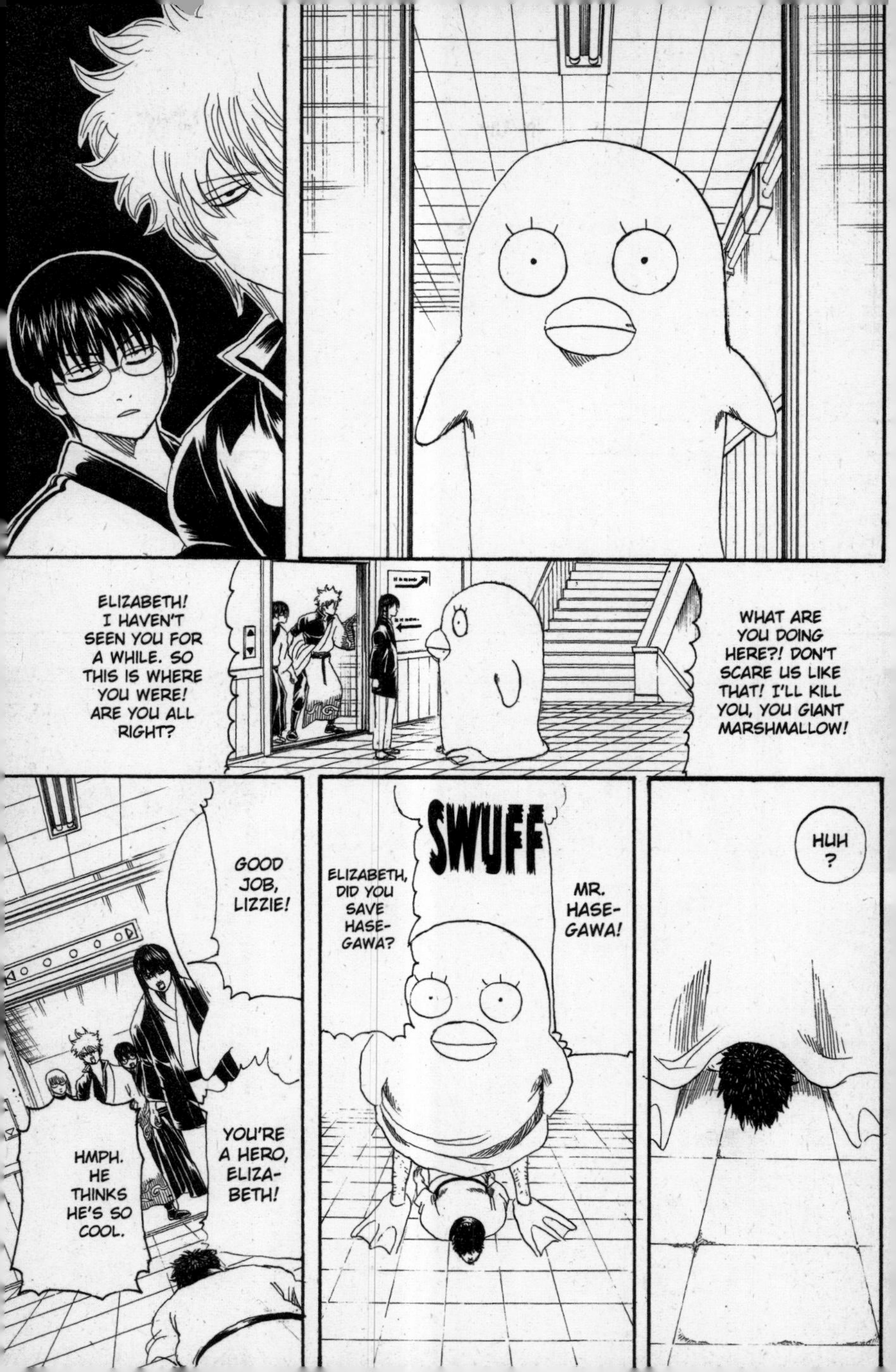

WHAT ARE YOU DOING HERE?! DON'T SCARE US LIKE THAT! I'LL KILL YOU, YOU GIANT MARSHMALLOW!
ELIZABETH! I HAVEN'T SEEN YOU FOR A WHILE. SO THIS IS WHERE YOU WERE! ARE YOU ALL RIGHT?
HUH ?
SWUFF
MR. HASE-GAWA!
ELIZABETH, DID YOU SAVE HASE-GAWA?
GOOD JOB, LIZZIE!
YOU'RE A HERO, ELIZA-BETH!
HMPH. HE THINKS HE'S SO COOL.

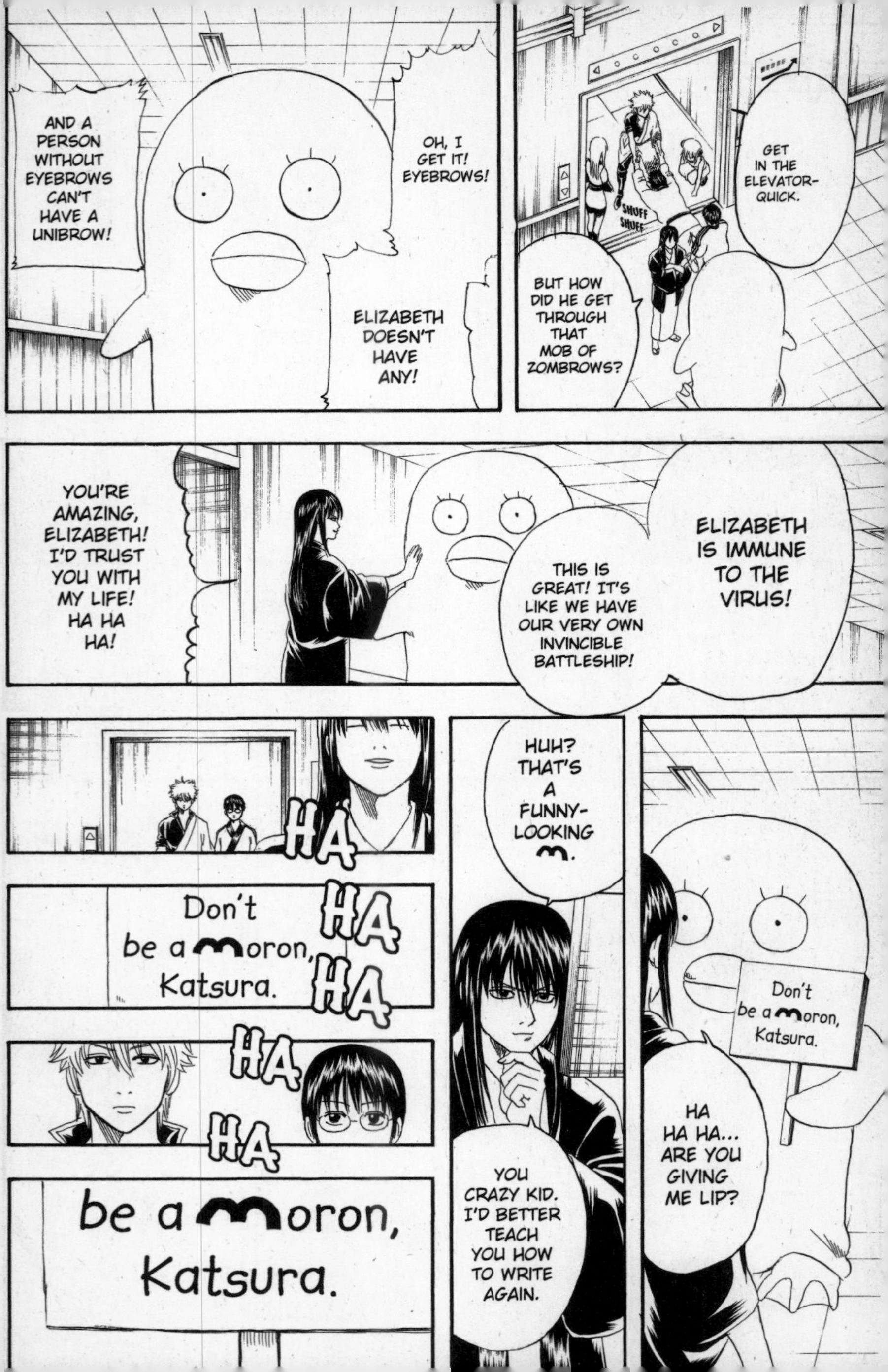
GET IN THE ELEVATOR-QUICK.
SHUFF SHUFF
BUT HOW DID HE GET THROUGH THAT MOB OF ZOMBROWS?
OH, I GET IT! EYEBROWS!
AND A PERSON WITHOUT EYEBROWS CAN'T HAVE A UNIBROW!
ELIZABETH DOESN'T HAVE ANY!
ELIZABETH IS IMMUNE TO THE VIRUS!
THIS IS GREAT! IT'S LIKE WE HAVE OUR VERY OWN INVINCIBLE BATTLESHIP!
YOU'RE AMAZING, ELIZABETH! I'D TRUST YOU WITH MY LIFE! HA HA HA!
Don't be a moron, Katsura.
HA HA HA... ARE YOU GIVING ME LIP?
HUH? THAT'S A FUNNY-LOOKING m.
YOU CRAZY KID. I'D BETTER TEACH YOU HOW TO WRITE AGAIN.
HA
HA
Don't be a moron, Katsura.
HA
HA
HA
be a moron, Katsura.

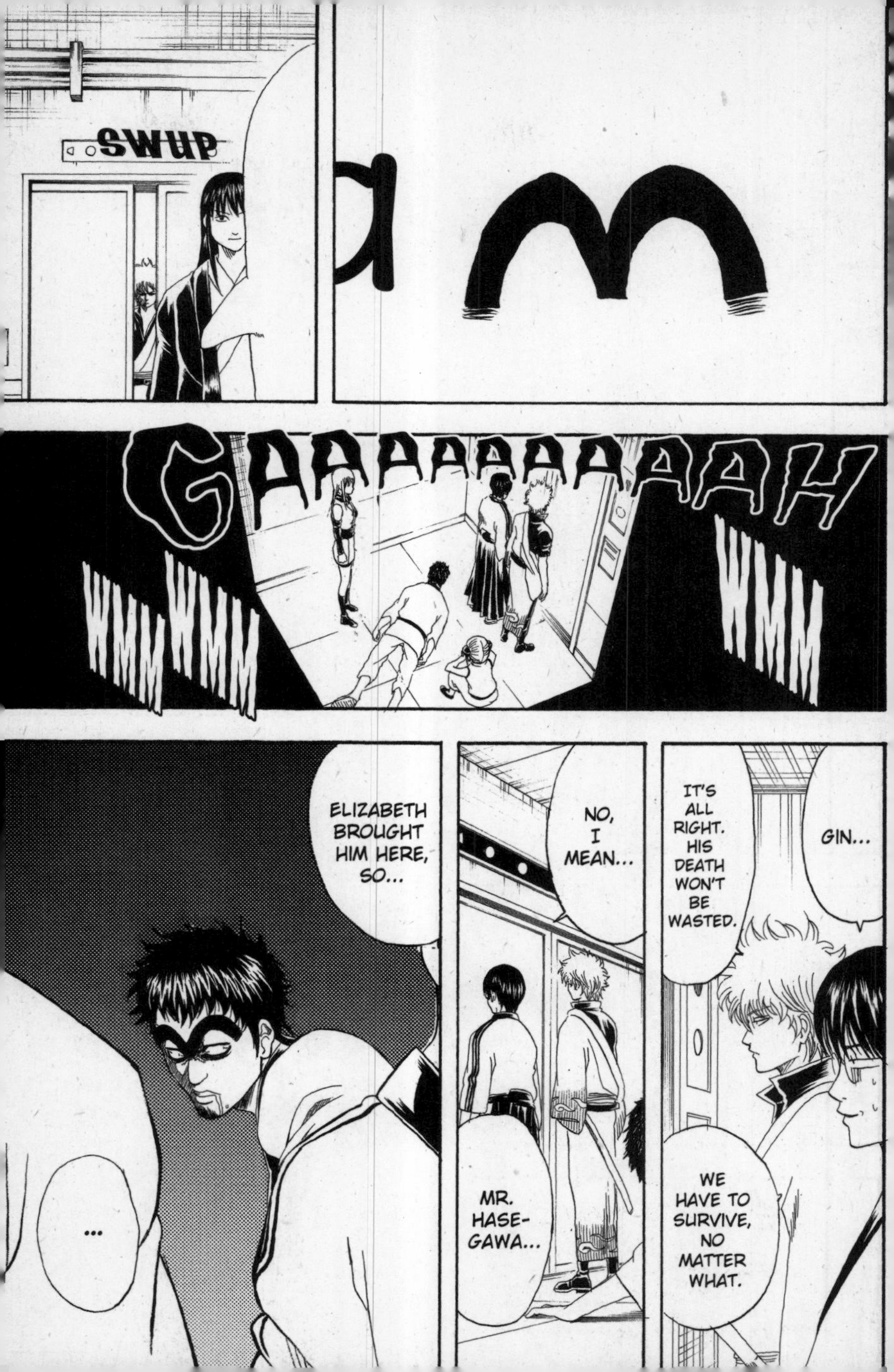
am
SWUP
GAAAAAAAAAAH
WMM
WMM WMM
GIN...
IT'S ALL RIGHT. HIS DEATH WON'T BE WASTED.
WE HAVE TO SURVIVE, NO MATTER WHAT.
NO, I MEAN...
MR. HASE-GAWA...
ELIZABETH BROUGHT HIM HERE, SO...
...

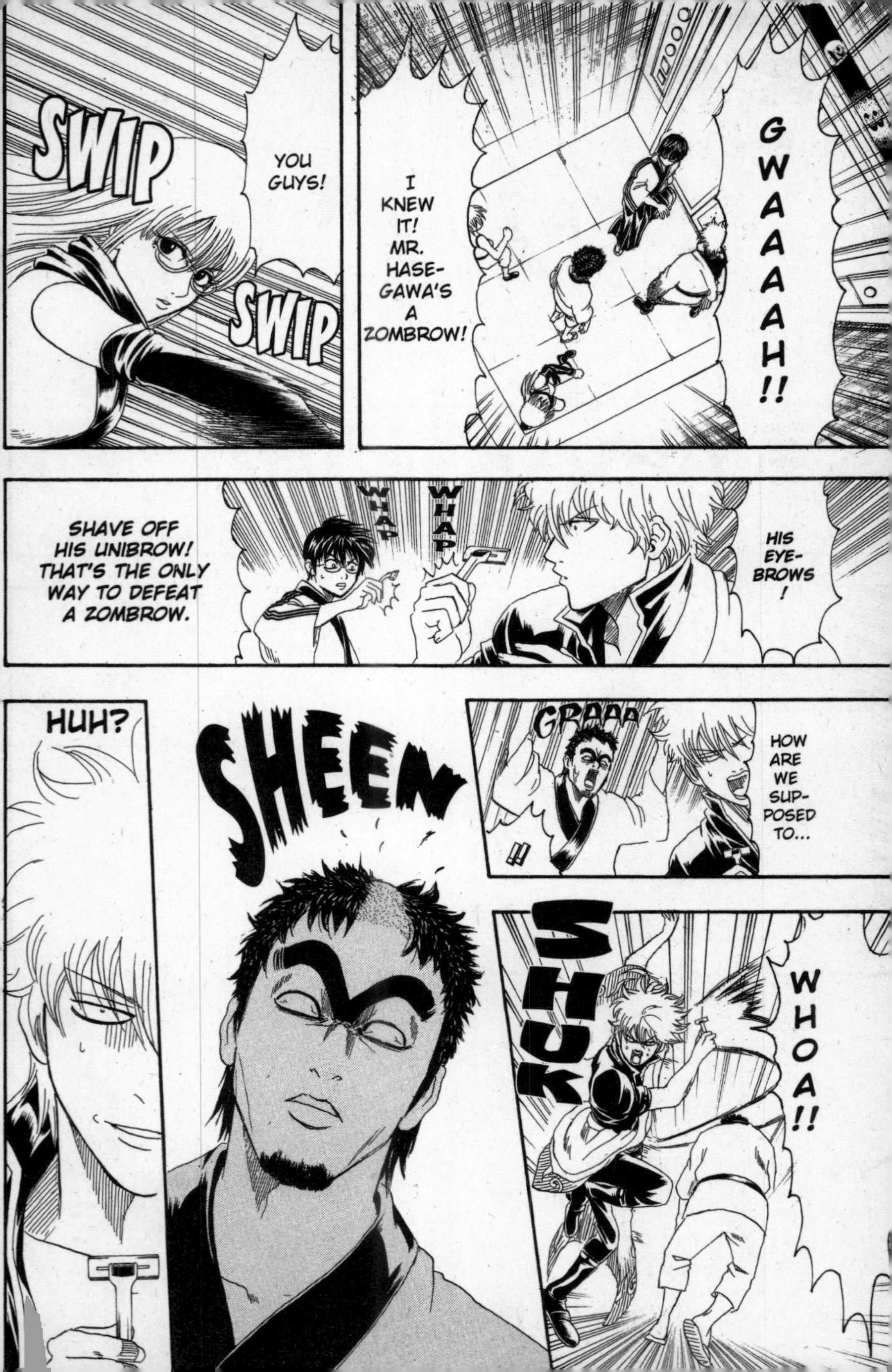
GWAAAAAH!!
I KNEW IT! MR. HASEGAWA'S A ZOMBROW!
YOU GUYS!
SWIP
SWIP
HIS EYEBROWS!
WHAP
WHAP
SHAVE OFF HIS UNIBROW! THAT'S THE ONLY WAY TO DEFEAT A ZOMBROW.
HOW ARE WE SUPPOSED TO...
GRAAA
!!
WHOA!!
SHUK
SHEEN
HUH?

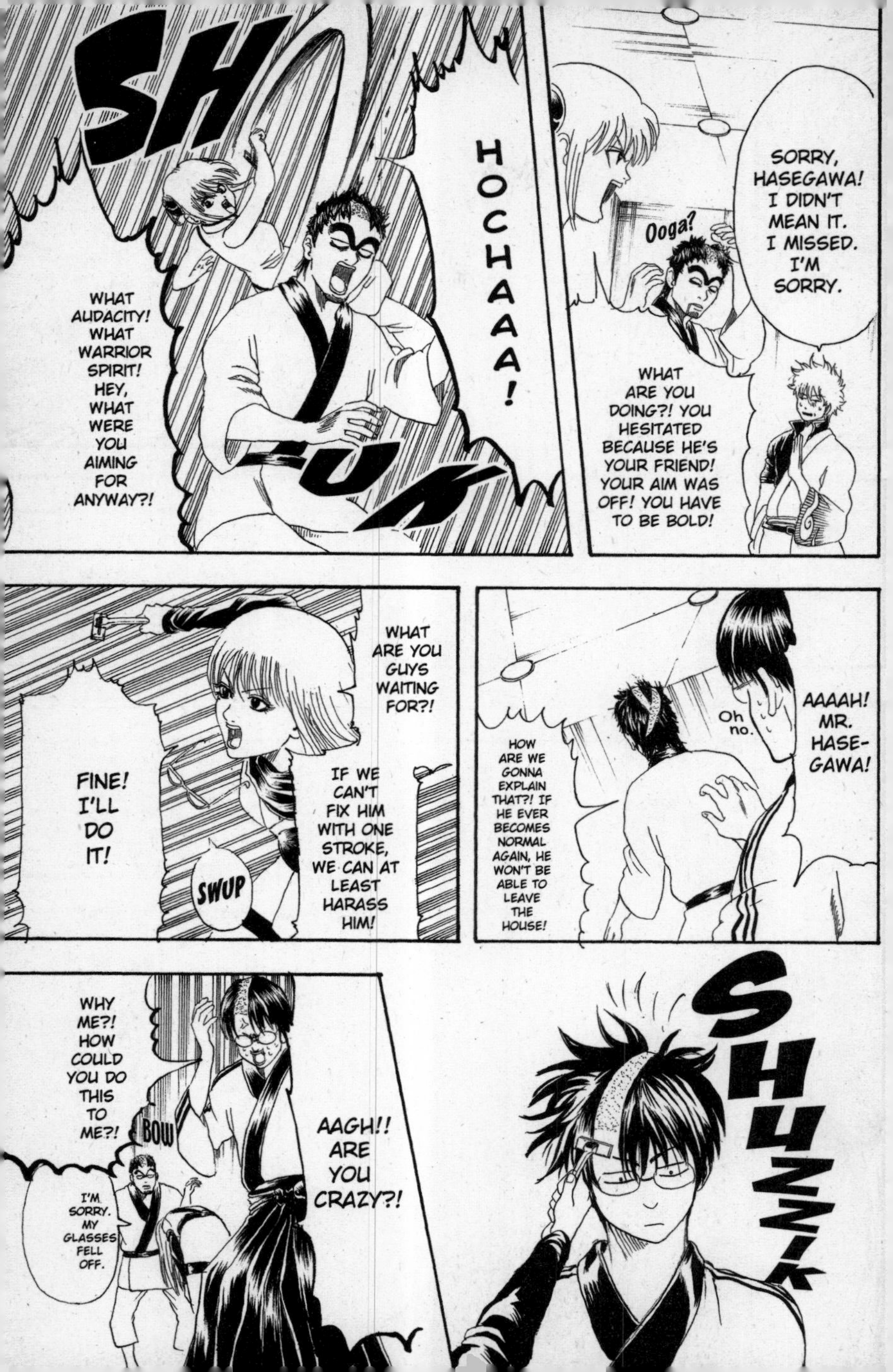
SORRY, HASEGAWA! I DIDN'T MEAN IT. I MISSED. I'M SORRY.
Ooga?
WHAT ARE YOU DOING?! YOU HESITATED BECAUSE HE'S YOUR FRIEND! YOUR AIM WAS OFF! YOU HAVE TO BE BOLD!
SH
HOCHAAA!
WHAT AUDACITY! WHAT WARRIOR SPIRIT! HEY, WHAT WERE YOU AIMING FOR ANYWAY?!
LUK
AAAAH! MR. HASE-GAWA!
Oh no.
HOW ARE WE GONNA EXPLAIN THAT?! IF HE EVER BECOMES NORMAL AGAIN, HE WON'T BE ABLE TO LEAVE THE HOUSE!
WHAT ARE YOU GUYS WAITING FOR?!
IF WE CAN'T FIX HIM WITH ONE STROKE, WE CAN AT LEAST HARASS HIM!
FINE! I'LL DO IT!
SWUP
SHUZIK
AAGH!! ARE YOU CRAZY?!
WHY ME?! HOW COULD YOU DO THIS TO ME?!
BOW
I'M SORRY. MY GLASSES FELL OFF.

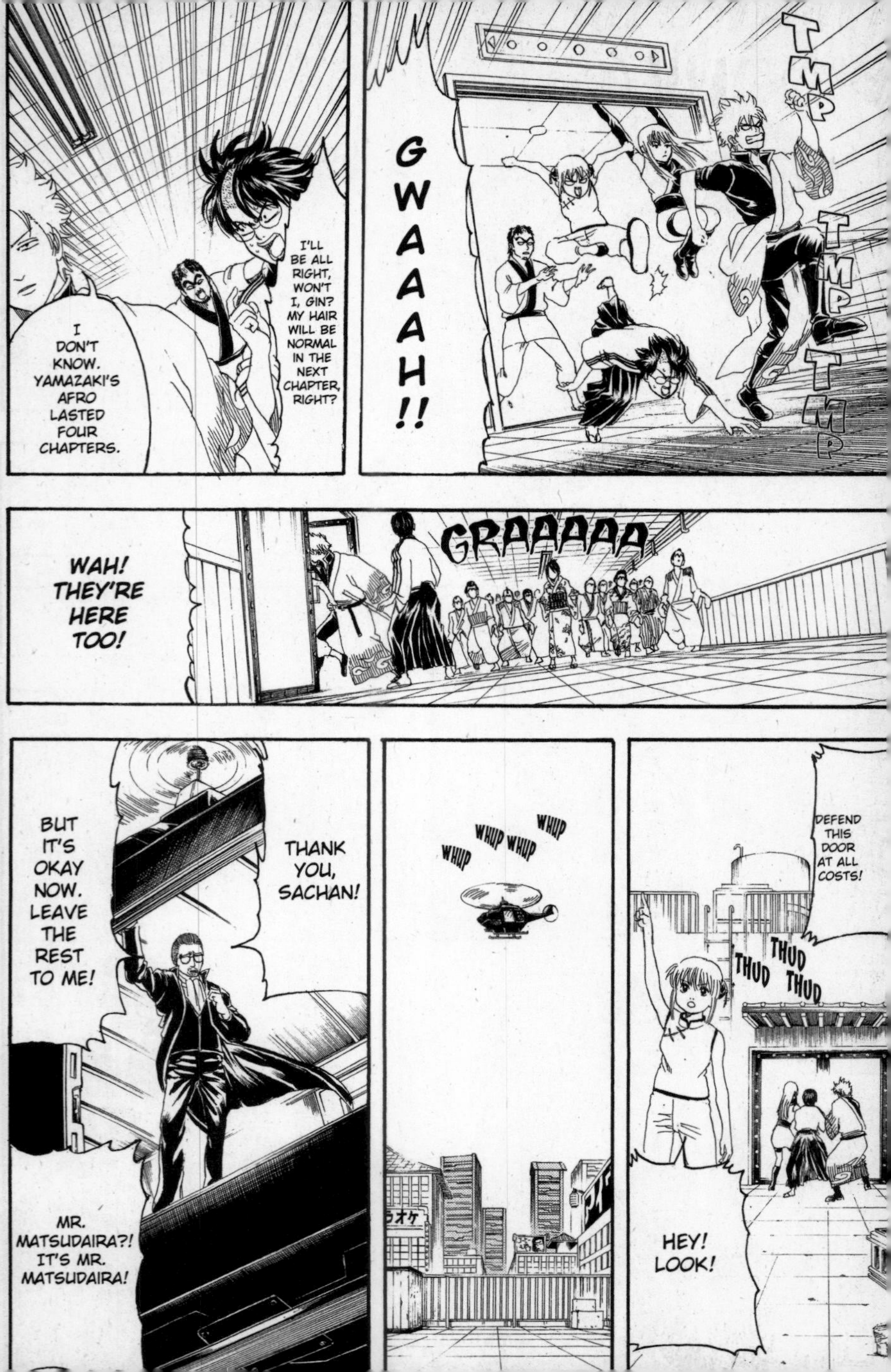

TMP
GWAAAAH!!
TMP TMP
I'LL BE ALL RIGHT, WON'T I, GIN? MY HAIR WILL BE NORMAL IN THE NEXT CHAPTER, RIGHT?
I DON'T KNOW. YAMAZAKI'S AFRO LASTED FOUR CHAPTERS.
GRAAAAAA
WAH! THEY'RE HERE TOO!
DEFEND THIS DOOR AT ALL COSTS!
THUD THUD
THUD THUD
HEY! LOOK!
WHUP
WHUP WHUP
WHUP
THANK YOU, SACHAN!
BUT IT'S OKAY NOW. LEAVE THE REST TO ME!
MR. MATSUDAIRA?! IT'S MR. MATSUDAIRA!

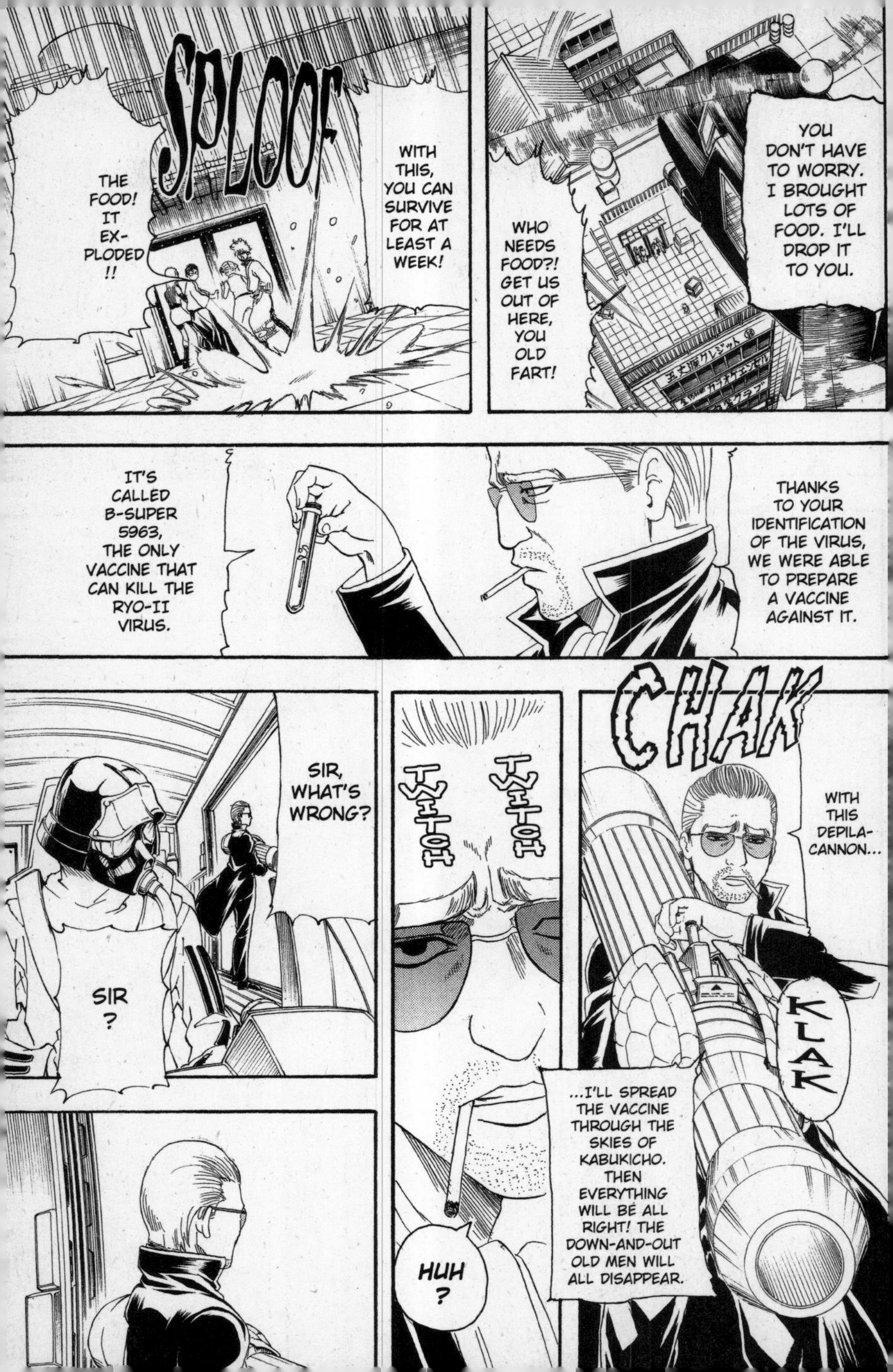
YOU DON'T HAVE TO WORRY. I BROUGHT LOTS OF FOOD. I'LL DROP IT TO YOU.
WHO NEEDS FOOD?! GET US OUT OF HERE, YOU OLD FART!
WITH THIS, YOU CAN SURVIVE FOR AT LEAST A WEEK!
SPLOOF
THE FOOD! IT EXPLODED!!
THANKS TO YOUR IDENTIFICATION OF THE VIRUS, WE WERE ABLE TO PREPARE A VACCINE AGAINST IT.
IT'S CALLED B-SUPER 5963, THE ONLY VACCINE THAT CAN KILL THE RYO-II VIRUS.
CHAK
WITH THIS DEPILA-CANNON...
KLAK
...I'LL SPREAD THE VACCINE THROUGH THE SKIES OF KABUKICHO. THEN EVERYTHING WILL BE ALL RIGHT! THE DOWN-AND-OUT OLD MEN WILL ALL DISAPPEAR.
TWITCH
TWITCH
HUH?
SIR, WHAT'S WRONG?
SIR?

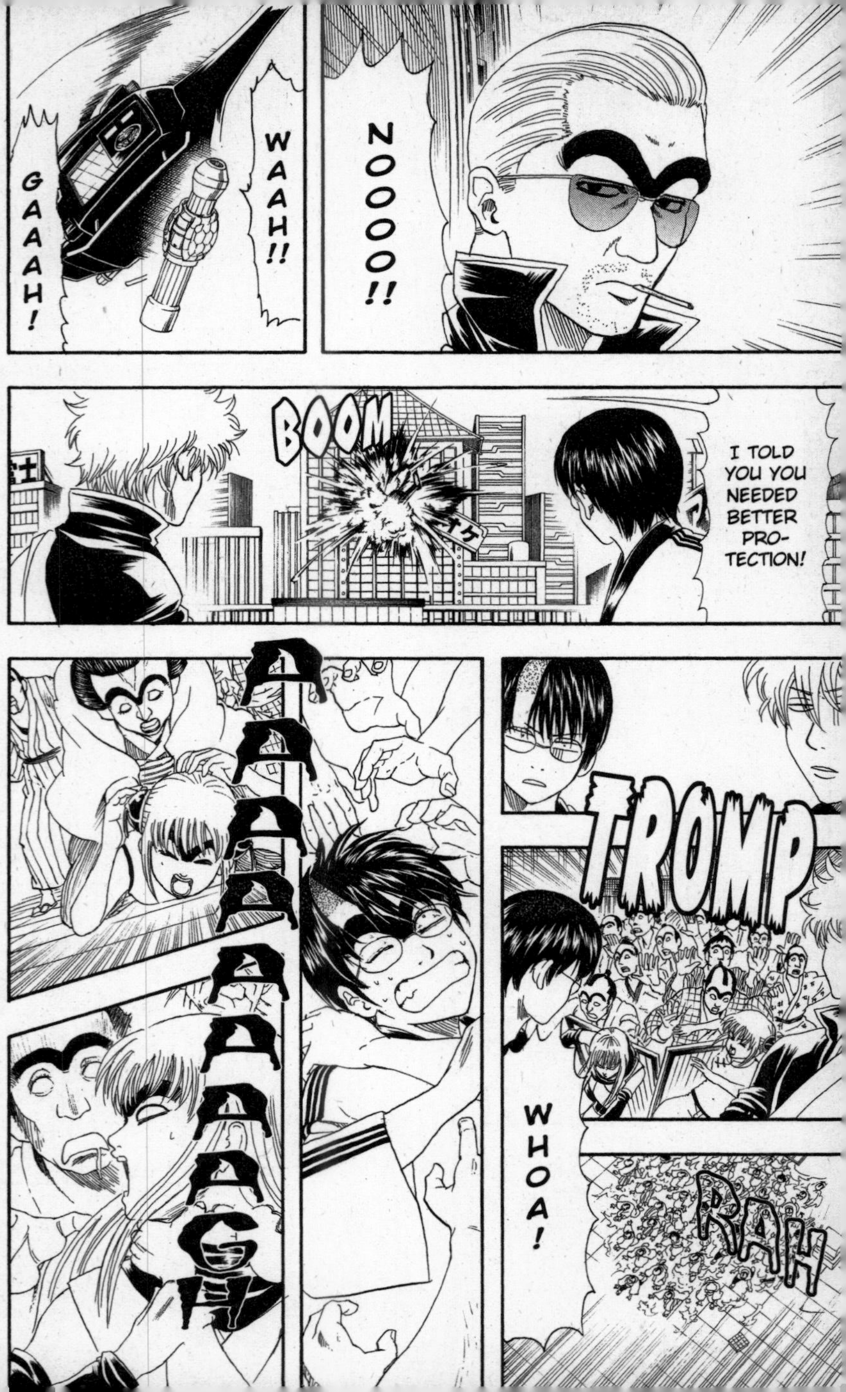
NOOOOO!!
WAAAH!!
GAAAAH!
I TOLD YOU YOU NEEDED BETTER PROTECTION!
BOOM
TROMP
WHOA!
RAH
AAAAAAAAGH

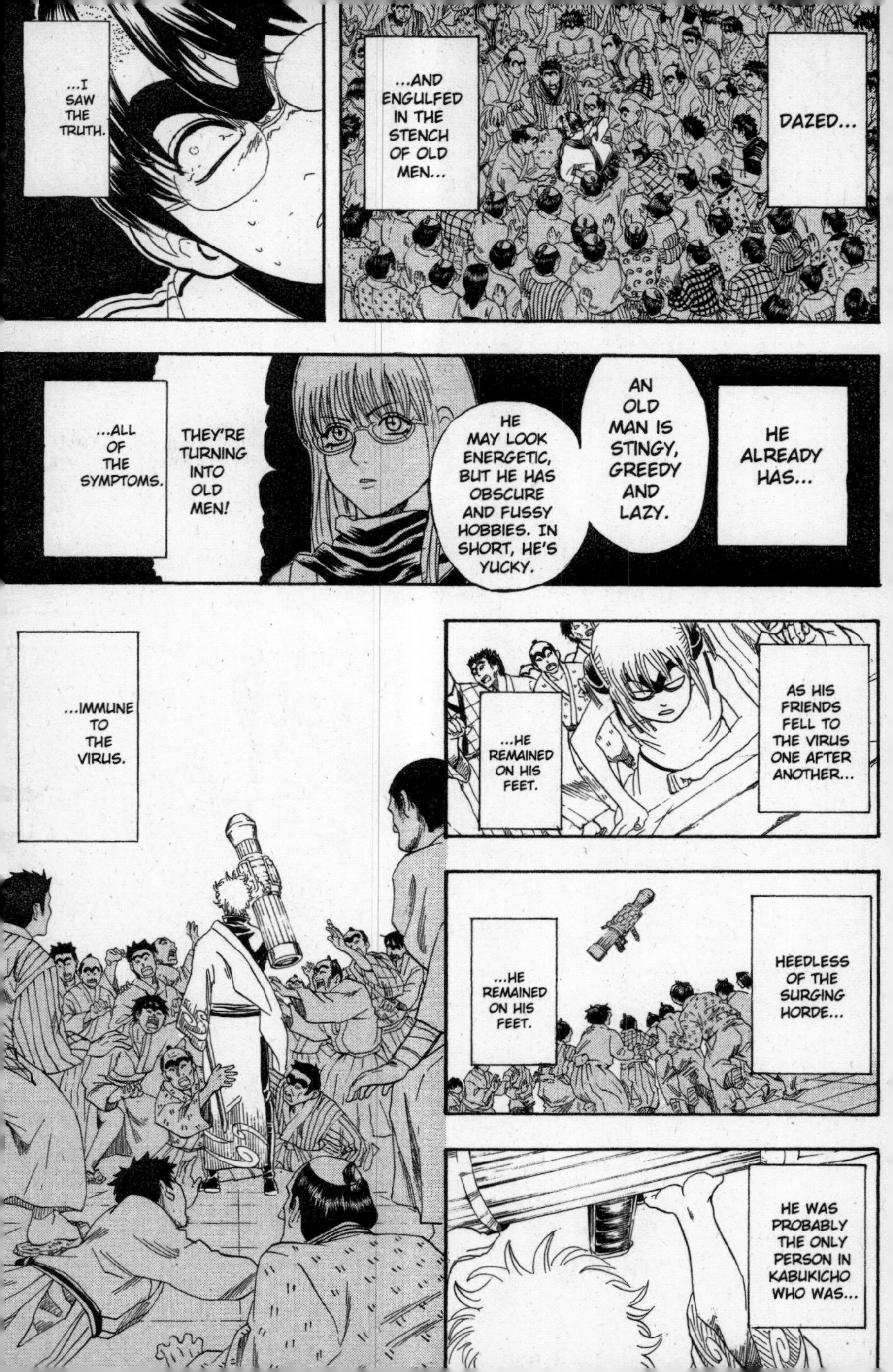
DAZED...
...AND ENGULFED IN THE STENCH OF OLD MEN...
...I SAW THE TRUTH.
HE ALREADY HAS...
AN OLD MAN IS STINGY, GREEDY AND LAZY.
HE MAY LOOK ENERGETIC, BUT HE HAS OBSCURE AND FUSSY HOBBIES. IN SHORT, HE'S YUCKY.
THEY'RE TURNING INTO OLD MEN!
...ALL OF THE SYMPTOMS.
AS HIS FRIENDS FELL TO THE VIRUS ONE AFTER ANOTHER...
...HE REMAINED ON HIS FEET.
HEEDLESS OF THE SURGING HORDE...
...HE REMAINED ON HIS FEET.
HE WAS PROBABLY THE ONLY PERSON IN KABUKICHO WHO WAS...
...IMMUNE TO THE VIRUS.

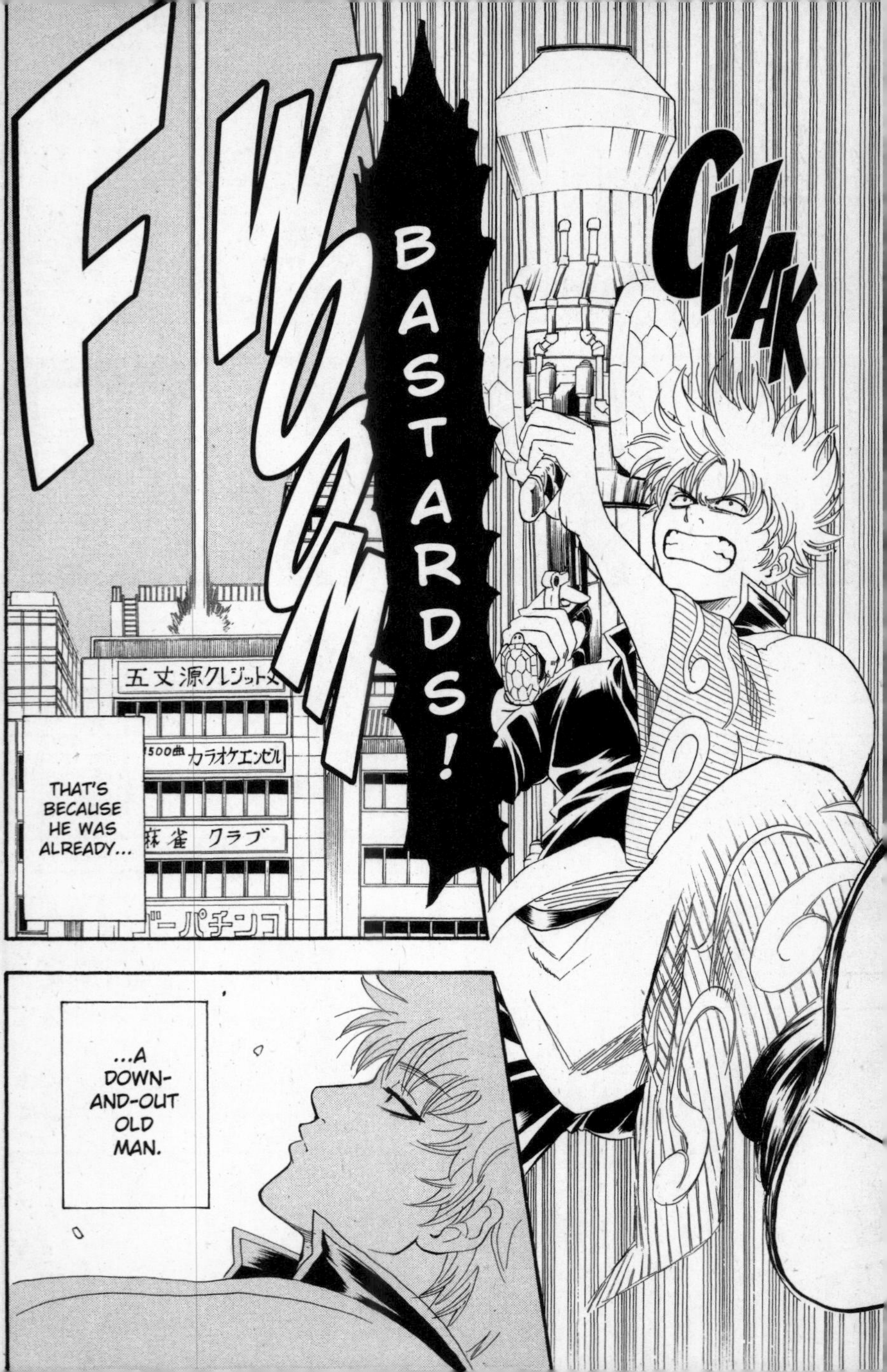
CHAK
BASTARDS!
FWOOM
五丈源クレジット
1500曲 カラオケエンゼル
麻雀 クラブ
パチンコ
THAT'S BECAUSE HE WAS ALREADY...
...A DOWN-AND-OUT OLD MAN.

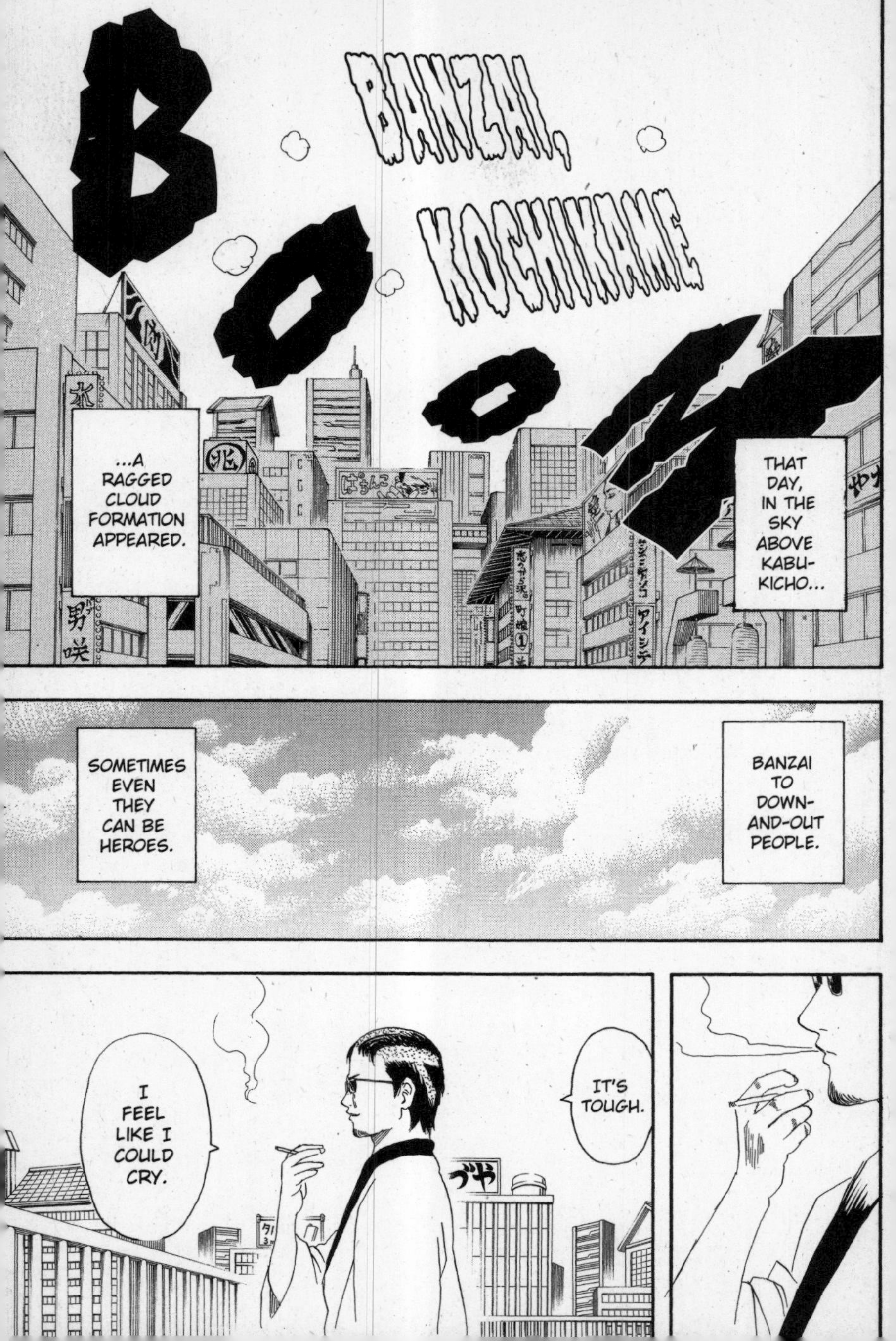
THAT DAY, IN THE SKY ABOVE KABUKICHO...
BANZAI, KOCHIKAME
...A RAGGED CLOUD FORMATION APPEARED.
BANZAI TO DOWN-AND-OUT PEOPLE.
SOMETIMES EVEN THEY CAN BE HEROES.
IT'S TOUGH.
I FEEL LIKE I COULD CRY.

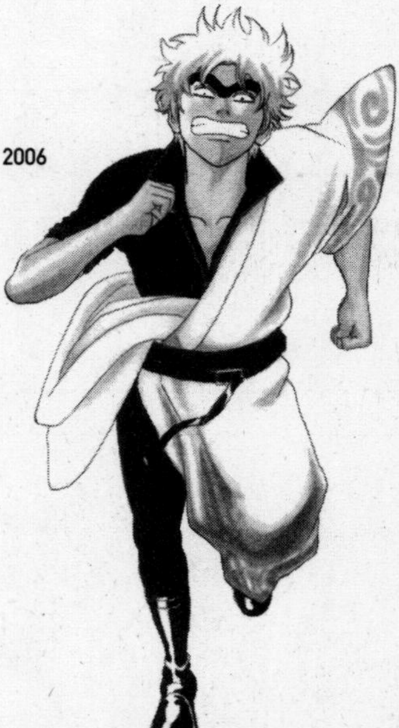

● From the cover of *Weekly Shonen JUMP* Vol. 42, 2006

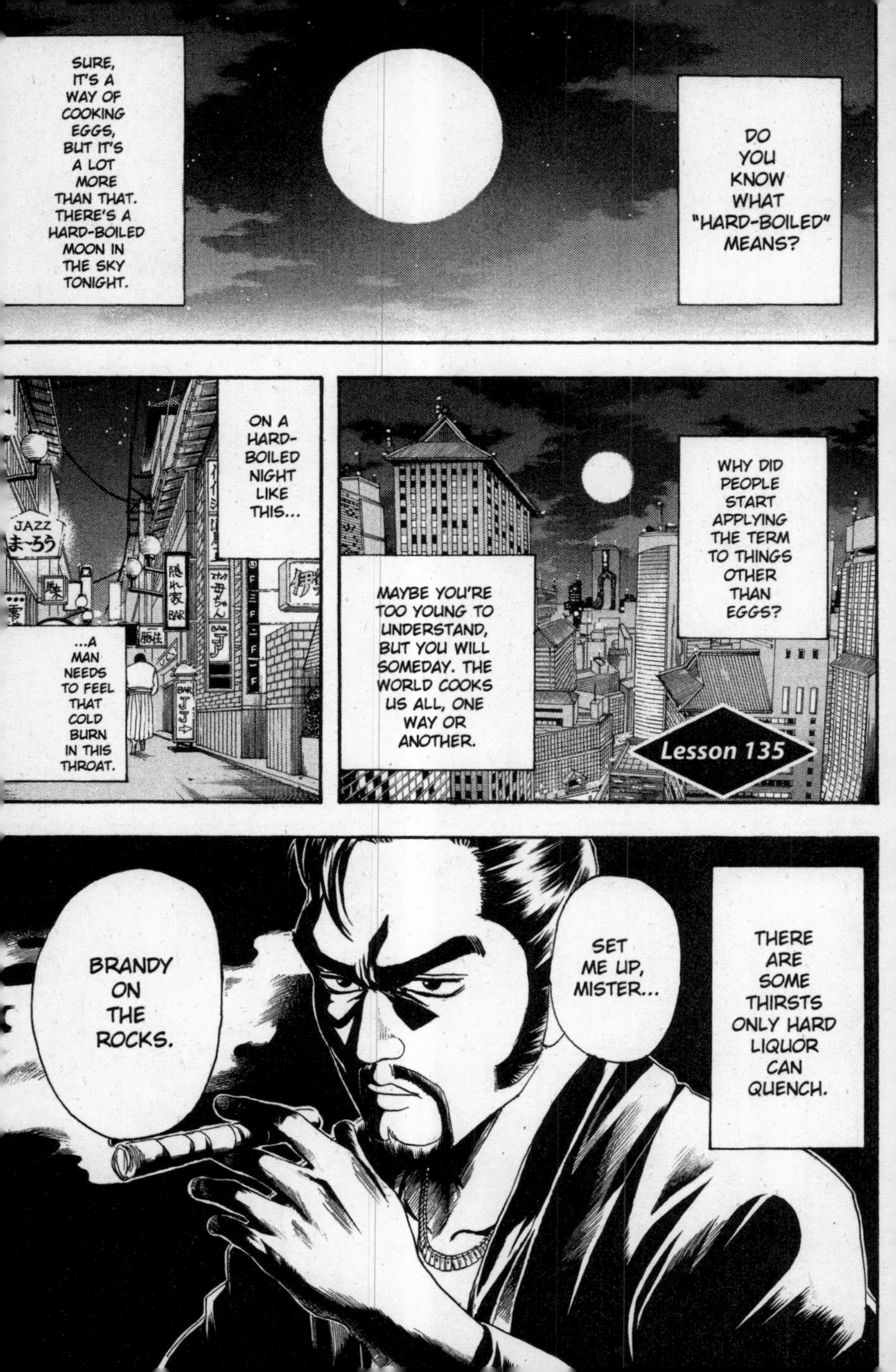
DO YOU KNOW WHAT "HARD-BOILED" MEANS?
SURE, IT'S A WAY OF COOKING EGGS, BUT IT'S A LOT MORE THAN THAT. THERE'S A HARD-BOILED MOON IN THE SKY TONIGHT.
WHY DID PEOPLE START APPLYING THE TERM TO THINGS OTHER THAN EGGS?
MAYBE YOU'RE TOO YOUNG TO UNDERSTAND, BUT YOU WILL SOMEDAY. THE WORLD COOKS US ALL, ONE WAY OR ANOTHER.
Lesson 135
ON A HARD-BOILED NIGHT LIKE THIS...
JAZZ まーろう
隠れ家 BAR
BAR JJ
...A MAN NEEDS TO FEEL THAT COLD BURN IN THIS THROAT.
THERE ARE SOME THIRSTS ONLY HARD LIQUOR CAN QUENCH.
SET ME UP, MISTER...
BRANDY ON THE ROCKS.

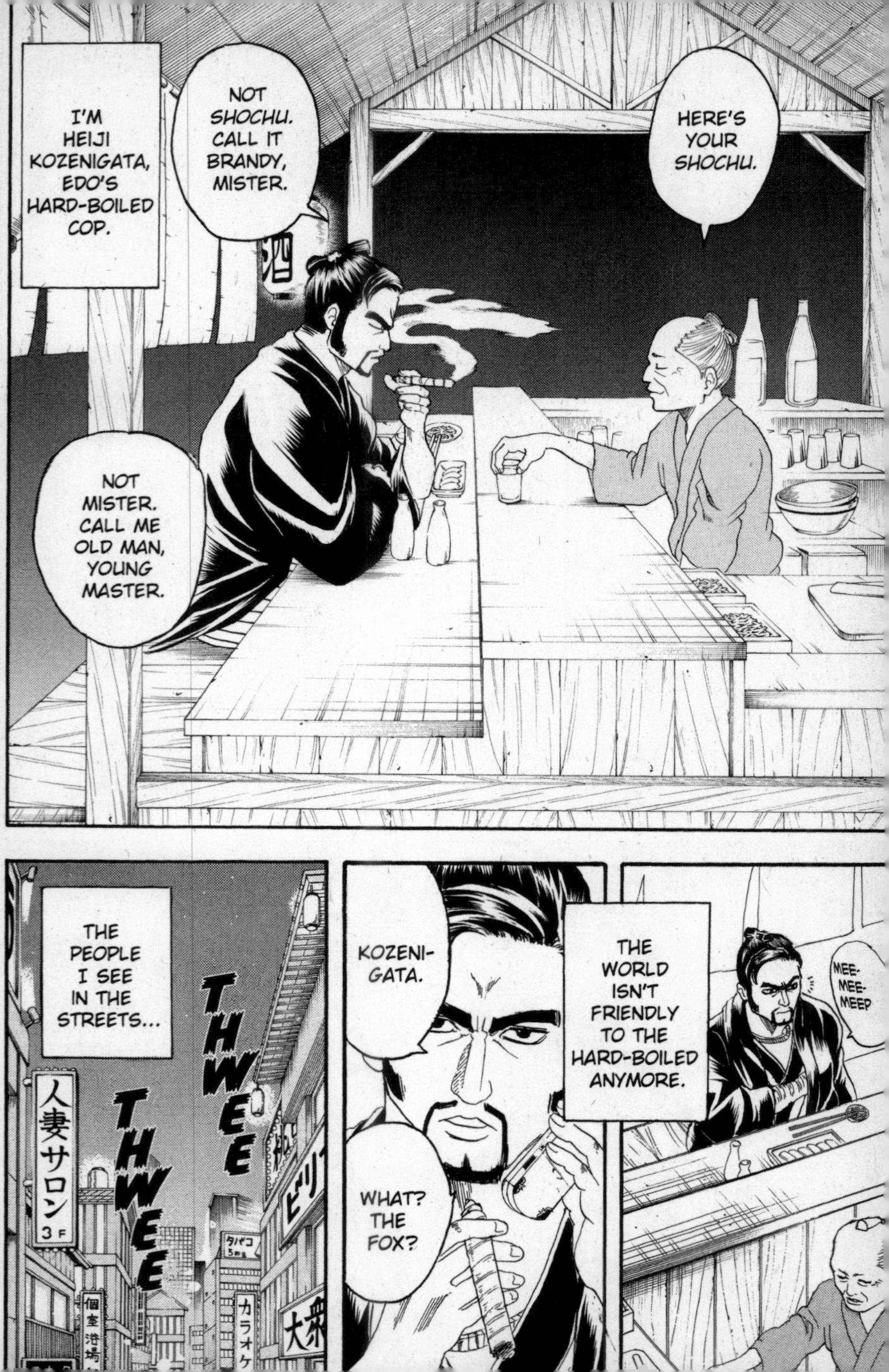
HERE'S YOUR SHOCHU.
NOT SHOCHU. CALL IT BRANDY, MISTER.
I'M HEIJI KOZENIGATA, EDO'S HARD-BOILED COP.
NOT MISTER. CALL ME OLD MAN, YOUNG MASTER.
MEE-MEE-MEEP
THE WORLD ISN'T FRIENDLY TO THE HARD-BOILED ANYMORE.
KOZENI-GATA.
WHAT? THE FOX?
THE PEOPLE I SEE IN THE STREETS...
THWEE
THWEE
人妻サロン 3F
タバコ
個室浴場
カラオケ
大衆

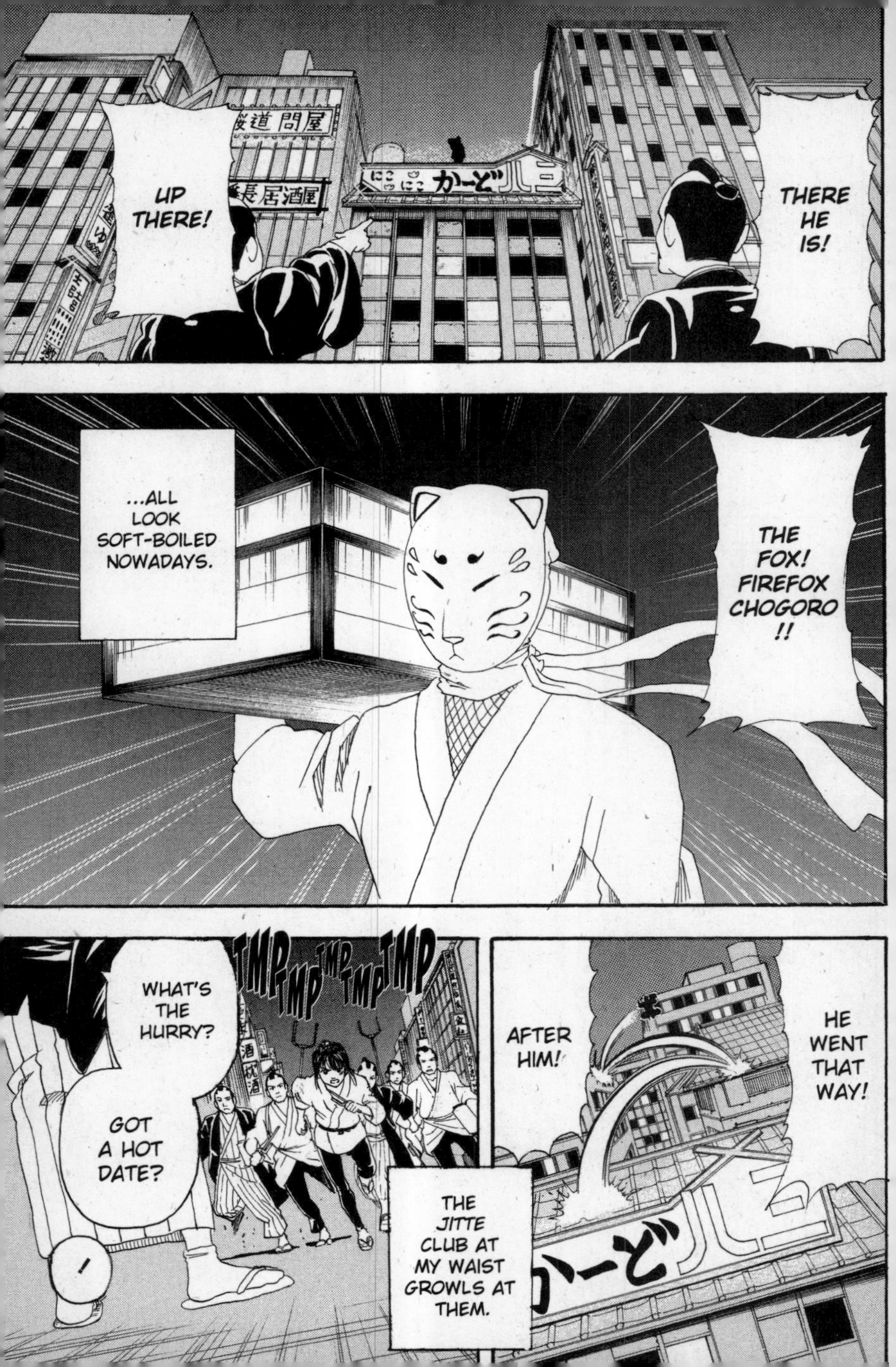
THERE HE IS!
UP THERE!
THE FOX! FIREFOX CHOGORO !!
...ALL LOOK SOFT-BOILED NOWADAYS.
HE WENT THAT WAY!
AFTER HIM!
TMP TMP TMP TMP TMP
WHAT'S THE HURRY?
GOT A HOT DATE?
THE JITTE CLUB AT MY WAIST GROWLS AT THEM.
!

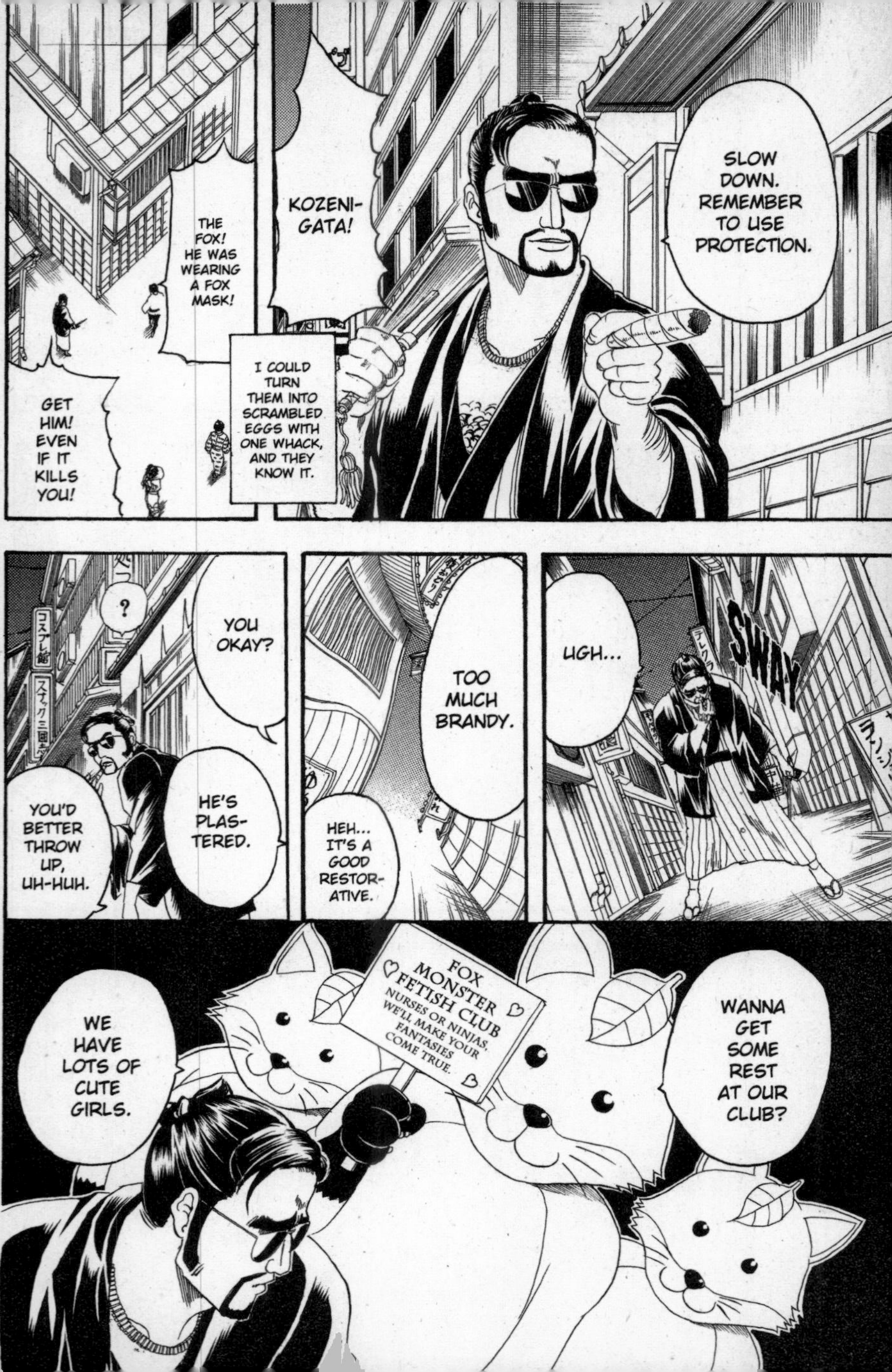

SLOW DOWN. REMEMBER TO USE PROTECTION.
KOZENI-GATA!
I COULD TURN THEM INTO SCRAMBLED EGGS WITH ONE WHACK, AND THEY KNOW IT.
THE FOX! HE WAS WEARING A FOX MASK!
GET HIM! EVEN IF IT KILLS YOU!
SWAY
UGH...
TOO MUCH BRANDY.
HEH... IT'S A GOOD RESTORATIVE.
?
YOU OKAY?
HE'S PLASTERED.
YOU'D BETTER THROW UP, UH-HUH.
WANNA GET SOME REST AT OUR CLUB?
FOX MONSTER FETISH CLUB
NURSES OR NINJAS, WE'LL MAKE YOUR FANTASIES COME TRUE.
WE HAVE LOTS OF CUTE GIRLS.

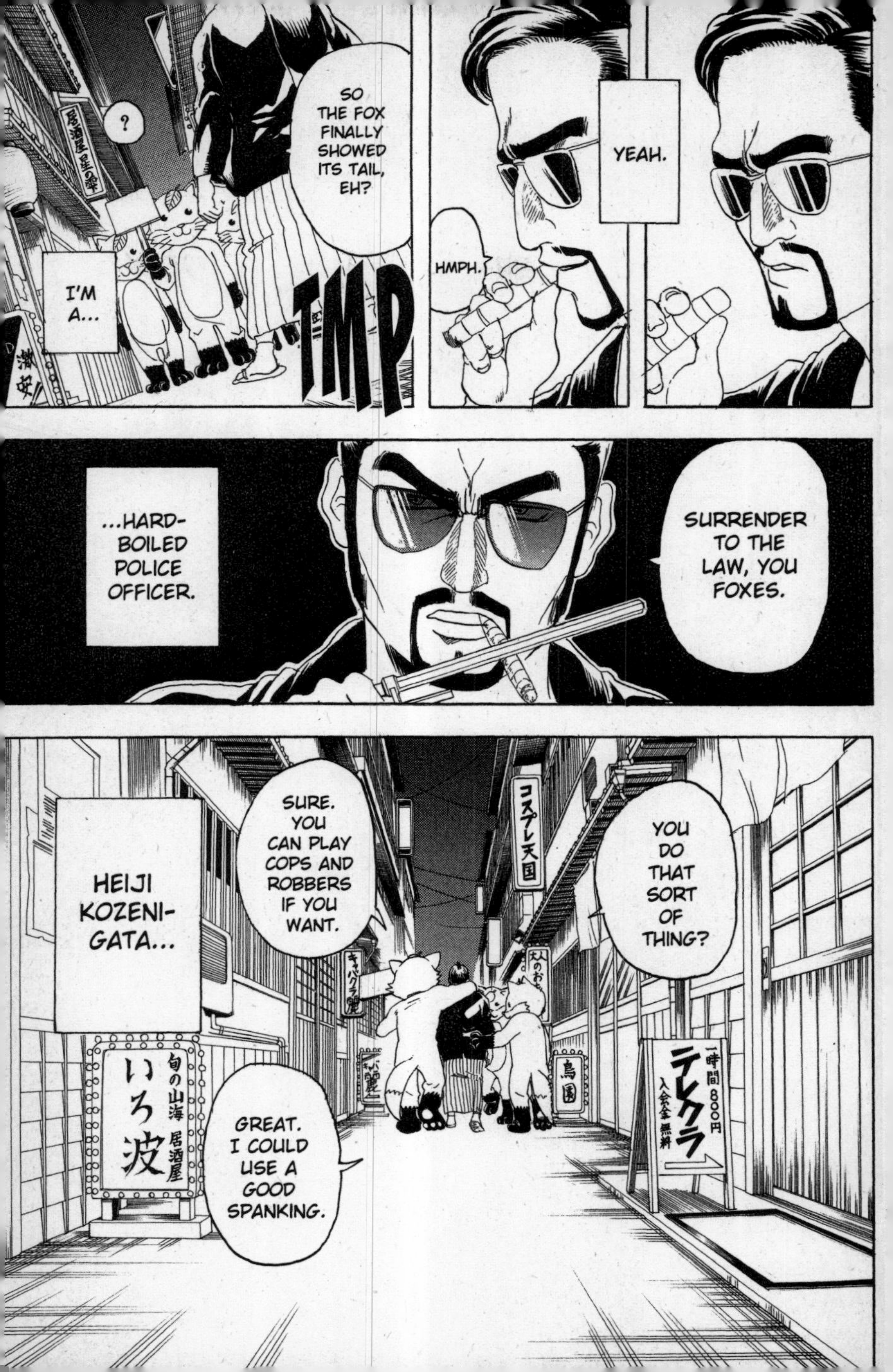
YEAH.
HMPH.
?
SO THE FOX FINALLY SHOWED ITS TAIL, EH?
TMP
I'M A...
SURRENDER TO THE LAW, YOU FOXES.
...HARD-BOILED POLICE OFFICER.
YOU DO THAT SORT OF THING?
コスプレ天国
SURE. YOU CAN PLAY COPS AND ROBBERS IF YOU WANT.
HEIJI KOZENI-GATA...
テレクラ
一時間800円
入会金無料
GREAT. I COULD USE A GOOD SPANKING.
旬の山海 居酒屋
いろ波

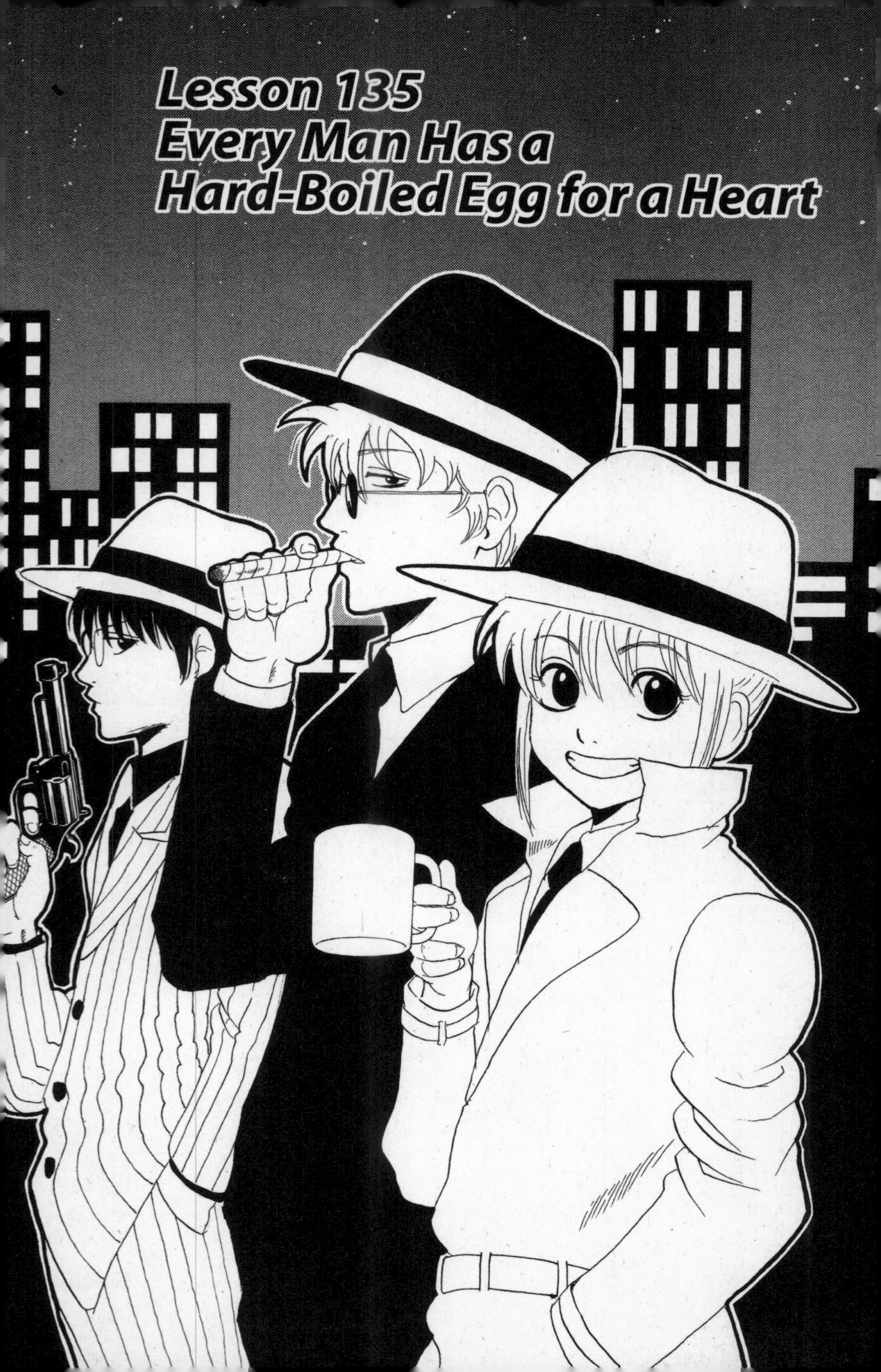
Lesson 135
Every Man Has a
Hard-Boiled Egg for a Heart

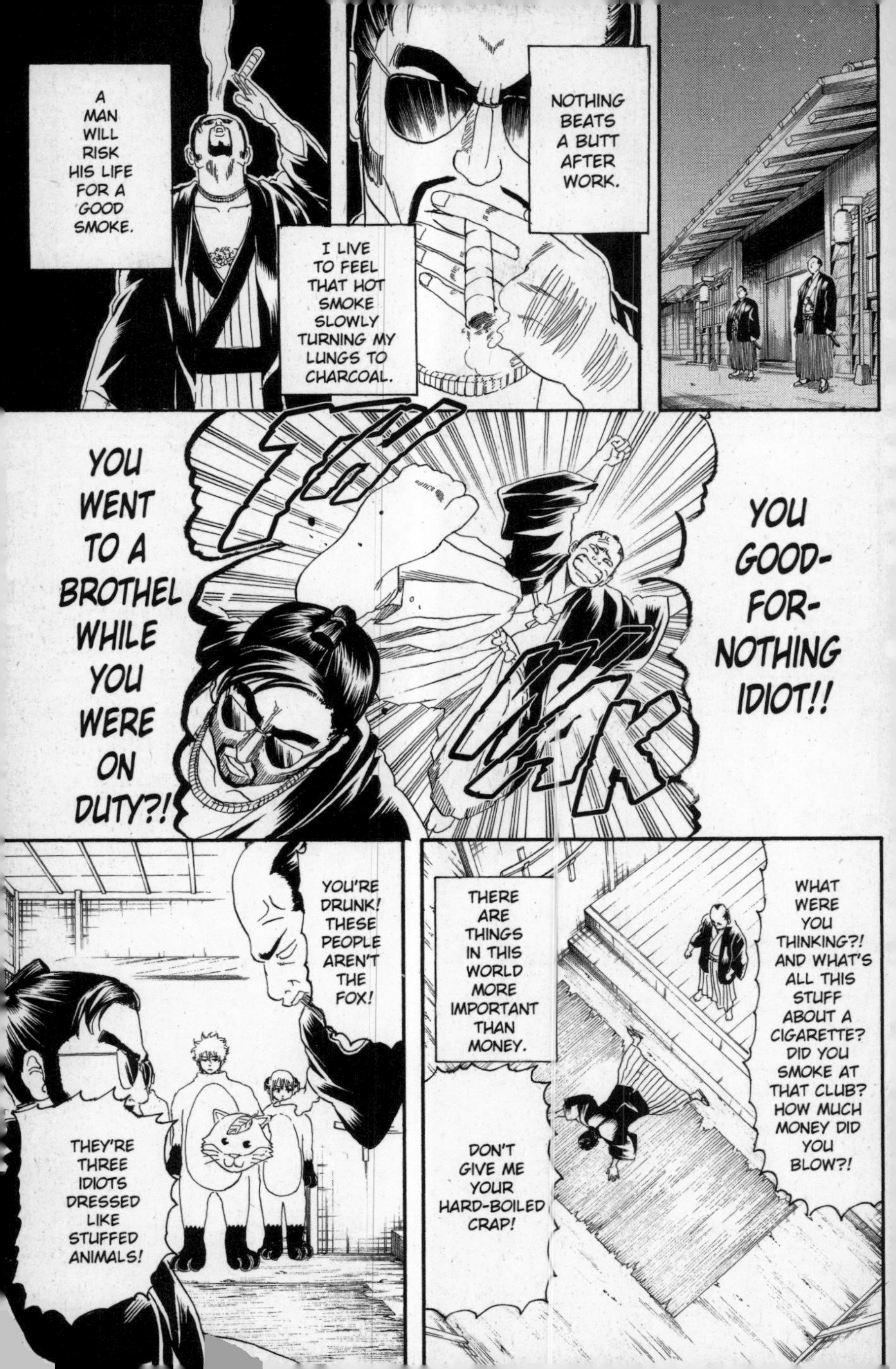
NOTHING BEATS A BUTT AFTER WORK.
I LIVE TO FEEL THAT HOT SMOKE SLOWLY TURNING MY LUNGS TO CHARCOAL.
A MAN WILL RISK HIS LIFE FOR A GOOD SMOKE.
YOU GOOD-FOR-NOTHING IDIOT!!
YOU WENT TO A BROTHEL WHILE YOU WERE ON DUTY?!
WHAT WERE YOU THINKING?! AND WHAT'S ALL THIS STUFF ABOUT A CIGARETTE? DID YOU SMOKE AT THAT CLUB? HOW MUCH MONEY DID YOU BLOW?!
THERE ARE THINGS IN THIS WORLD MORE IMPORTANT THAN MONEY.
DON'T GIVE ME YOUR HARD-BOILED CRAP!
YOU'RE DRUNK! THESE PEOPLE AREN'T THE FOX!
THEY'RE THREE IDIOTS DRESSED LIKE STUFFED ANIMALS!

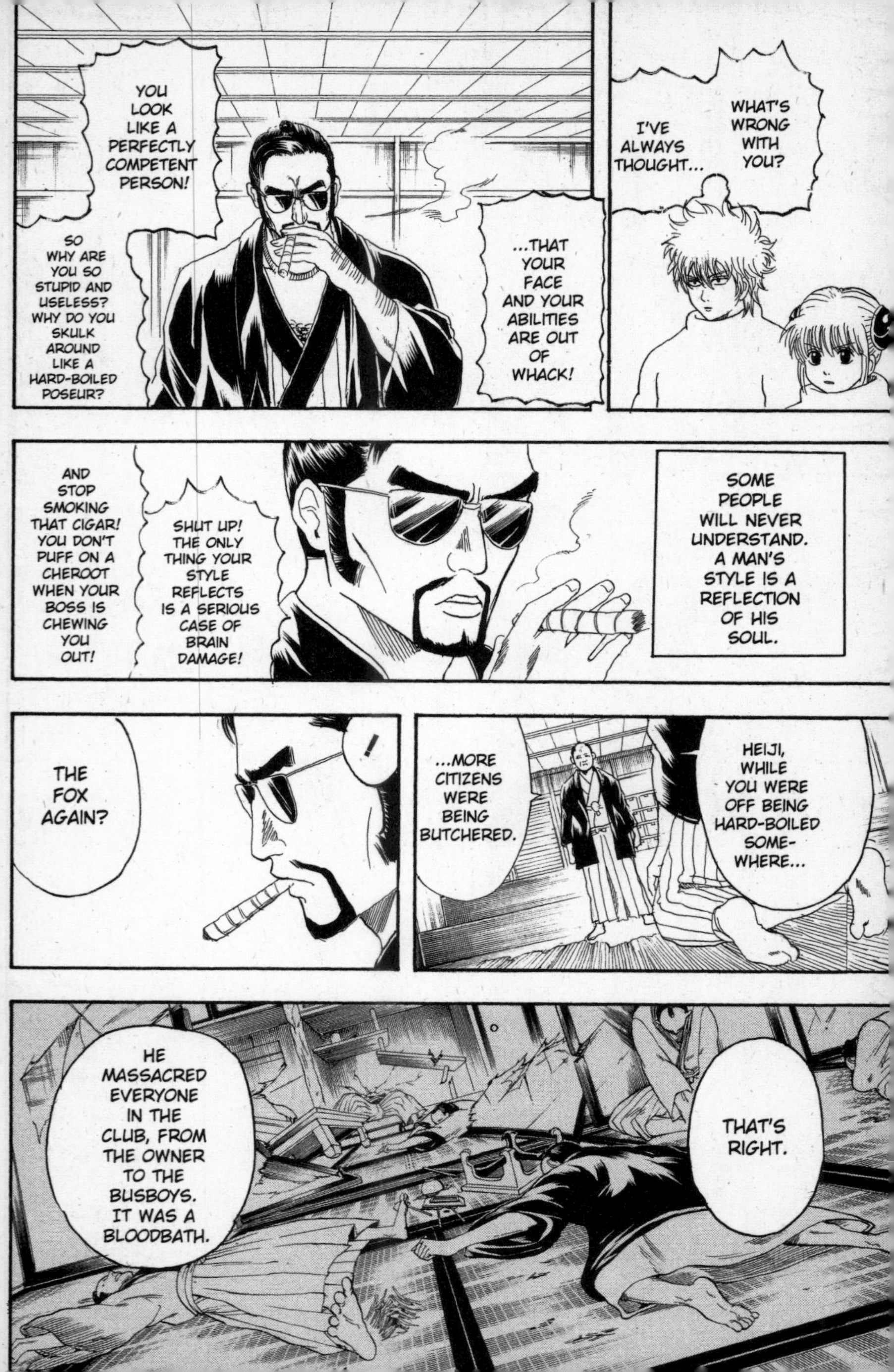
WHAT'S WRONG WITH YOU?
I'VE ALWAYS THOUGHT...
...THAT YOUR FACE AND YOUR ABILITIES ARE OUT OF WHACK!
YOU LOOK LIKE A PERFECTLY COMPETENT PERSON!
SO WHY ARE YOU SO STUPID AND USELESS? WHY DO YOU SKULK AROUND LIKE A HARD-BOILED POSEUR?
SOME PEOPLE WILL NEVER UNDERSTAND. A MAN'S STYLE IS A REFLECTION OF HIS SOUL.
SHUT UP! THE ONLY THING YOUR STYLE REFLECTS IS A SERIOUS CASE OF BRAIN DAMAGE!
AND STOP SMOKING THAT CIGAR! YOU DON'T PUFF ON A CHEROOT WHEN YOUR BOSS IS CHEWING YOU OUT!
HEIJI, WHILE YOU WERE OFF BEING HARD-BOILED SOME-WHERE...
...MORE CITIZENS WERE BEING BUTCHERED.
!
THE FOX AGAIN?
THAT'S RIGHT.
HE MASSACRED EVERYONE IN THE CLUB, FROM THE OWNER TO THE BUSBOYS. IT WAS A BLOODBATH.

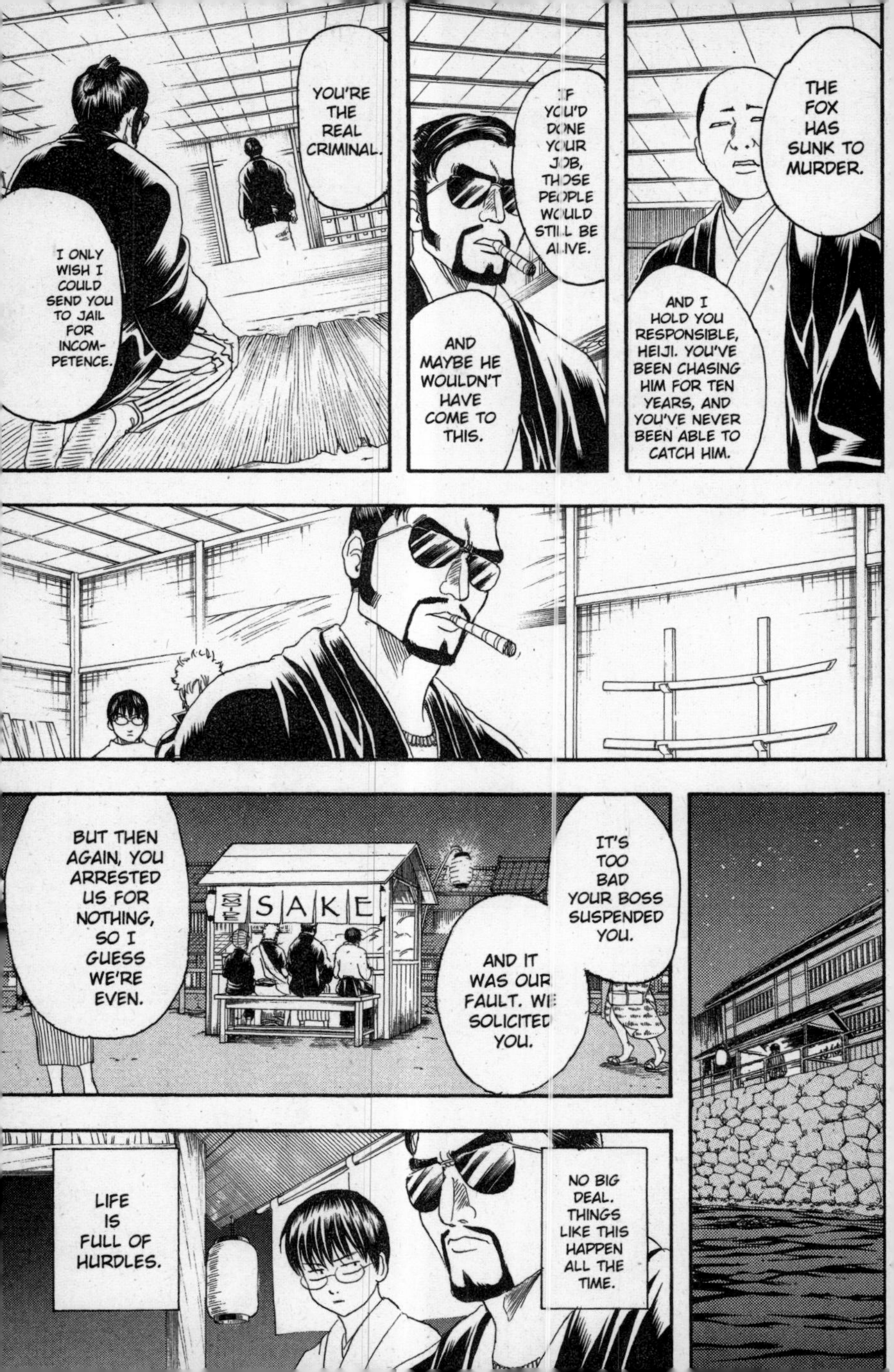
THE FOX HAS SUNK TO MURDER.
AND I HOLD YOU RESPONSIBLE, HEIJI. YOU'VE BEEN CHASING HIM FOR TEN YEARS, AND YOU'VE NEVER BEEN ABLE TO CATCH HIM.
IF YOU'D DONE YOUR JOB, THOSE PEOPLE WOULD STILL BE ALIVE.
AND MAYBE HE WOULDN'T HAVE COME TO THIS.
YOU'RE THE REAL CRIMINAL.
I ONLY WISH I COULD SEND YOU TO JAIL FOR INCOMPETENCE.
IT'S TOO BAD YOUR BOSS SUSPENDED YOU.
AND IT WAS OUR FAULT. WE SOLICITED YOU.
SAKE
BUT THEN AGAIN, YOU ARRESTED US FOR NOTHING, SO I GUESS WE'RE EVEN.
NO BIG DEAL. THINGS LIKE THIS HAPPEN ALL THE TIME.
LIFE IS FULL OF HURDLES.

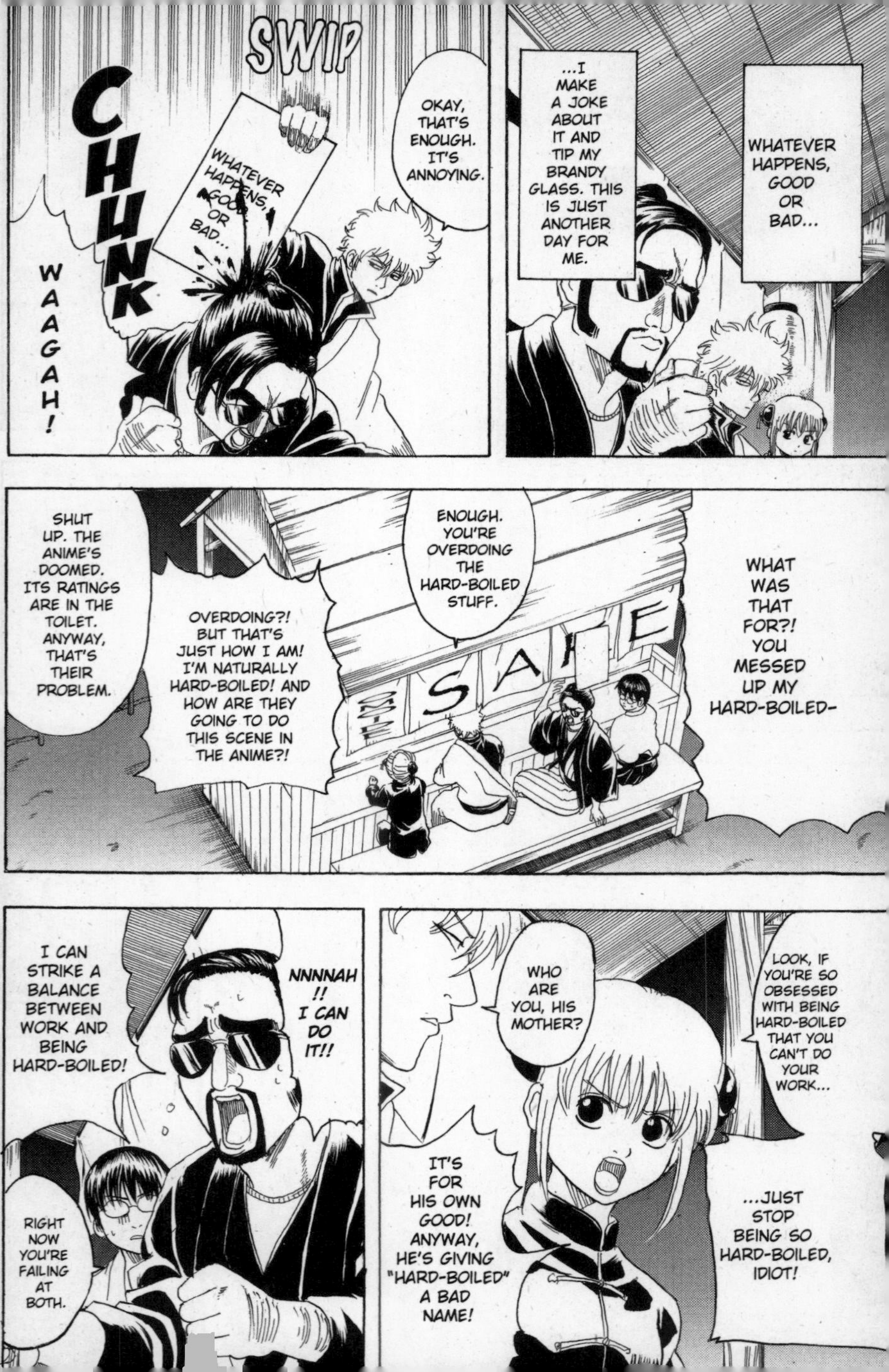
WHATEVER HAPPENS, GOOD OR BAD...
...I MAKE A JOKE ABOUT IT AND TIP MY BRANDY GLASS. THIS IS JUST ANOTHER DAY FOR ME.
SWIP
OKAY, THAT'S ENOUGH. IT'S ANNOYING.
WHATEVER HAPPENS, GOOD OR BAD...
CHUNK
WAAGAH!
WHAT WAS THAT FOR?! YOU MESSED UP MY HARD-BOILED-
ENOUGH. YOU'RE OVERDOING THE HARD-BOILED STUFF.
SAKE
OVERDOING?! BUT THAT'S JUST HOW I AM! I'M NATURALLY HARD-BOILED! AND HOW ARE THEY GOING TO DO THIS SCENE IN THE ANIME?!
SHUT UP. THE ANIME'S DOOMED. ITS RATINGS ARE IN THE TOILET. ANYWAY, THAT'S THEIR PROBLEM.
LOOK, IF YOU'RE SO OBSESSED WITH BEING HARD-BOILED THAT YOU CAN'T DO YOUR WORK...
...JUST STOP BEING SO HARD-BOILED, IDIOT!
WHO ARE YOU, HIS MOTHER?
IT'S FOR HIS OWN GOOD! ANYWAY, HE'S GIVING "HARD-BOILED" A BAD NAME!
NNNNAH!! I CAN DO IT!!
I CAN STRIKE A BALANCE BETWEEN WORK AND BEING HARD-BOILED!
RIGHT NOW YOU'RE FAILING AT BOTH.

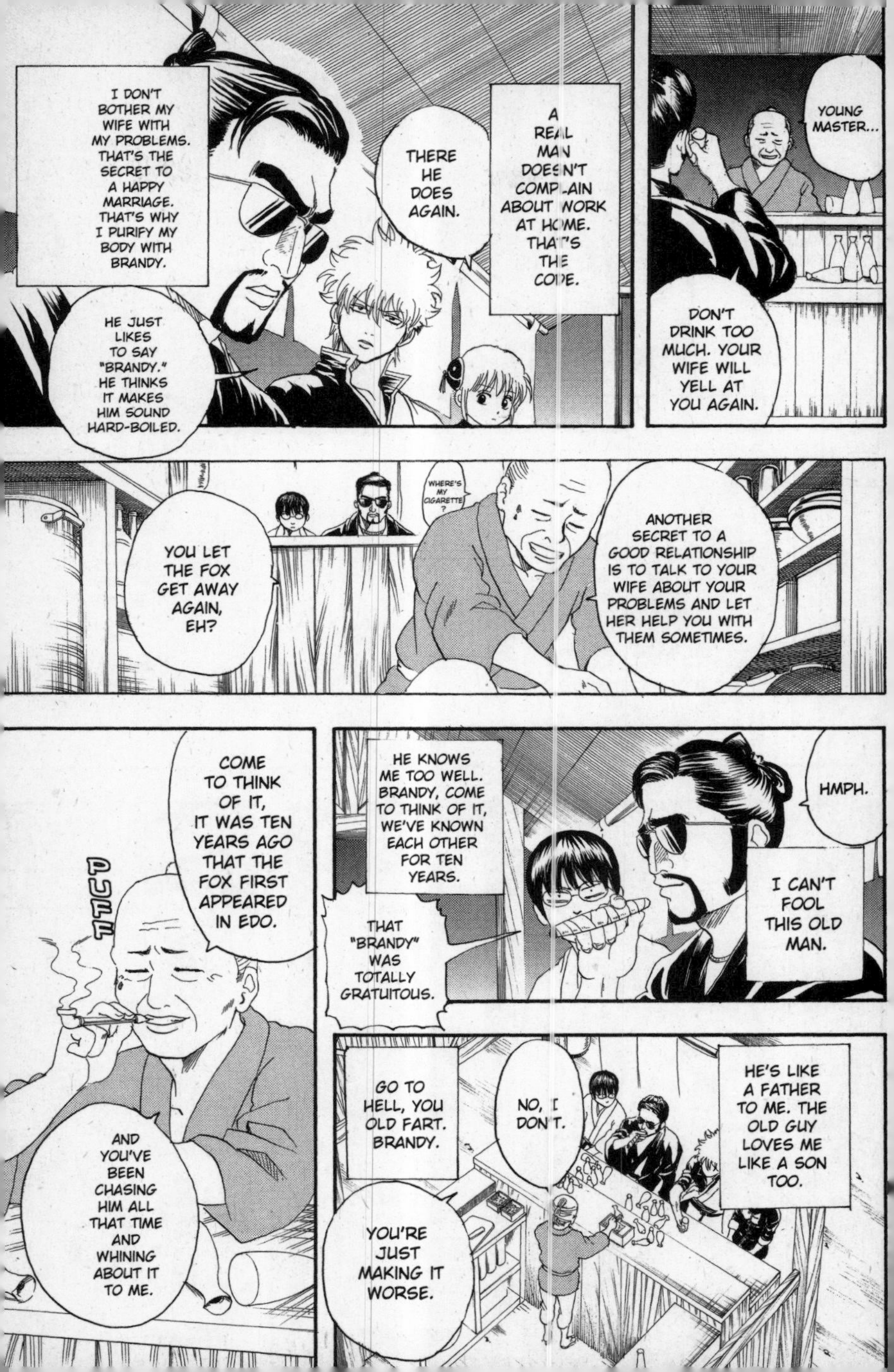
YOUNG MASTER...
DON'T DRINK TOO MUCH. YOUR WIFE WILL YELL AT YOU AGAIN.
A REAL MAN DOESN'T COMPLAIN ABOUT WORK AT HOME. THAT'S THE CODE.
THERE HE DOES AGAIN.
I DON'T BOTHER MY WIFE WITH MY PROBLEMS. THAT'S THE SECRET TO A HAPPY MARRIAGE. THAT'S WHY I PURIFY MY BODY WITH BRANDY.
HE JUST LIKES TO SAY "BRANDY." HE THINKS IT MAKES HIM SOUND HARD-BOILED.
ANOTHER SECRET TO A GOOD RELATIONSHIP IS TO TALK TO YOUR WIFE ABOUT YOUR PROBLEMS AND LET HER HELP YOU WITH THEM SOMETIMES.
WHERE'S MY CIGARETTE?
YOU LET THE FOX GET AWAY AGAIN, EH?
HMPH.
HE KNOWS ME TOO WELL. BRANDY, COME TO THINK OF IT, WE'VE KNOWN EACH OTHER FOR TEN YEARS.
I CAN'T FOOL THIS OLD MAN.
THAT "BRANDY" WAS TOTALLY GRATUITOUS.
HE'S LIKE A FATHER TO ME. THE OLD GUY LOVES ME LIKE A SON TOO.
NO, I DON'T.
GO TO HELL, YOU OLD FART. BRANDY.
YOU'RE JUST MAKING IT WORSE.
COME TO THINK OF IT, IT WAS TEN YEARS AGO THAT THE FOX FIRST APPEARED IN EDO.
PUFF
AND YOU'VE BEEN CHASING HIM ALL THAT TIME AND WHINING ABOUT IT TO ME.

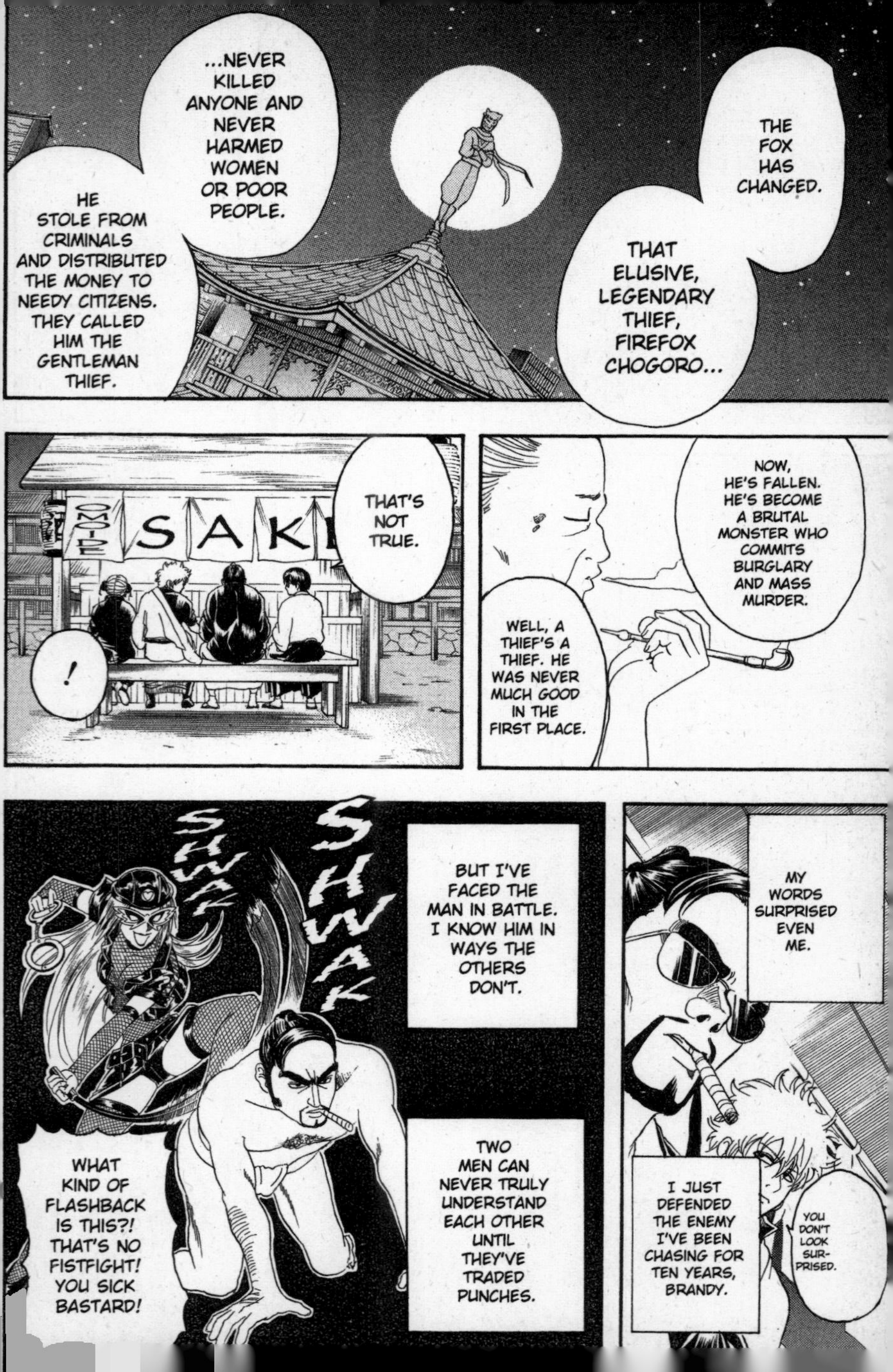
THE FOX HAS CHANGED.
THAT ELUSIVE, LEGENDARY THIEF, FIREFOX CHOGORO...
...NEVER KILLED ANYONE AND NEVER HARMED WOMEN OR POOR PEOPLE.
HE STOLE FROM CRIMINALS AND DISTRIBUTED THE MONEY TO NEEDY CITIZENS. THEY CALLED HIM THE GENTLEMAN THIEF.
NOW, HE'S FALLEN. HE'S BECOME A BRUTAL MONSTER WHO COMMITS BURGLARY AND MASS MURDER.
WELL, A THIEF'S A THIEF. HE WAS NEVER MUCH GOOD IN THE FIRST PLACE.
THAT'S NOT TRUE.
OMOIDE
SAK
!
MY WORDS SURPRISED EVEN ME.
I JUST DEFENDED THE ENEMY I'VE BEEN CHASING FOR TEN YEARS, BRANDY.
YOU DON'T LOOK SUR-PRISED.
BUT I'VE FACED THE MAN IN BATTLE. I KNOW HIM IN WAYS THE OTHERS DON'T.
SHWAK
SHWAK
TWO MEN CAN NEVER TRULY UNDERSTAND EACH OTHER UNTIL THEY'VE TRADED PUNCHES.
WHAT KIND OF FLASHBACK IS THIS?! THAT'S NO FISTFIGHT! YOU SICK BASTARD!

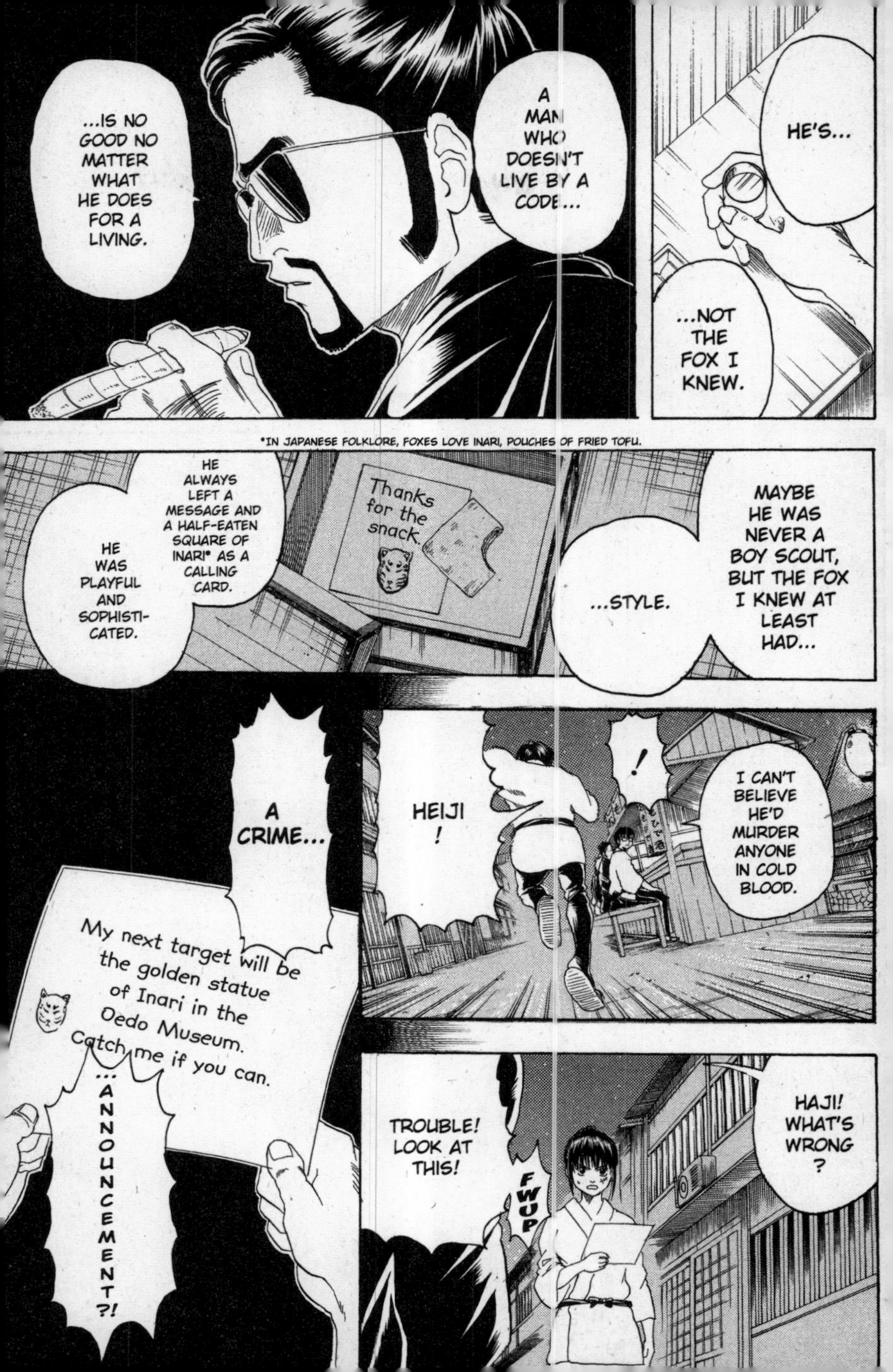
HE'S...
...NOT THE FOX I KNEW.
A MAN WHO DOESN'T LIVE BY A CODE...
...IS NO GOOD NO MATTER WHAT HE DOES FOR A LIVING.
MAYBE HE WAS NEVER A BOY SCOUT, BUT THE FOX I KNEW AT LEAST HAD...
...STYLE.
HE ALWAYS LEFT A MESSAGE AND A HALF-EATEN SQUARE OF INARI* AS A CALLING CARD.
Thanks for the snack.
HE WAS PLAYFUL AND SOPHISTICATED.
I CAN'T BELIEVE HE'D MURDER ANYONE IN COLD BLOOD.
!
HEIJI!
HAJI! WHAT'S WRONG?
TROUBLE! LOOK AT THIS!
FWUP
A CRIME...
My next target will be the golden statue of Inari in the Oedo Museum. Catch me if you can.
...ANNOUNCEMENT?!

*IN JAPANESE FOLKLORE, FOXES LOVE INARI, POUCHES OF FRIED TOFU.

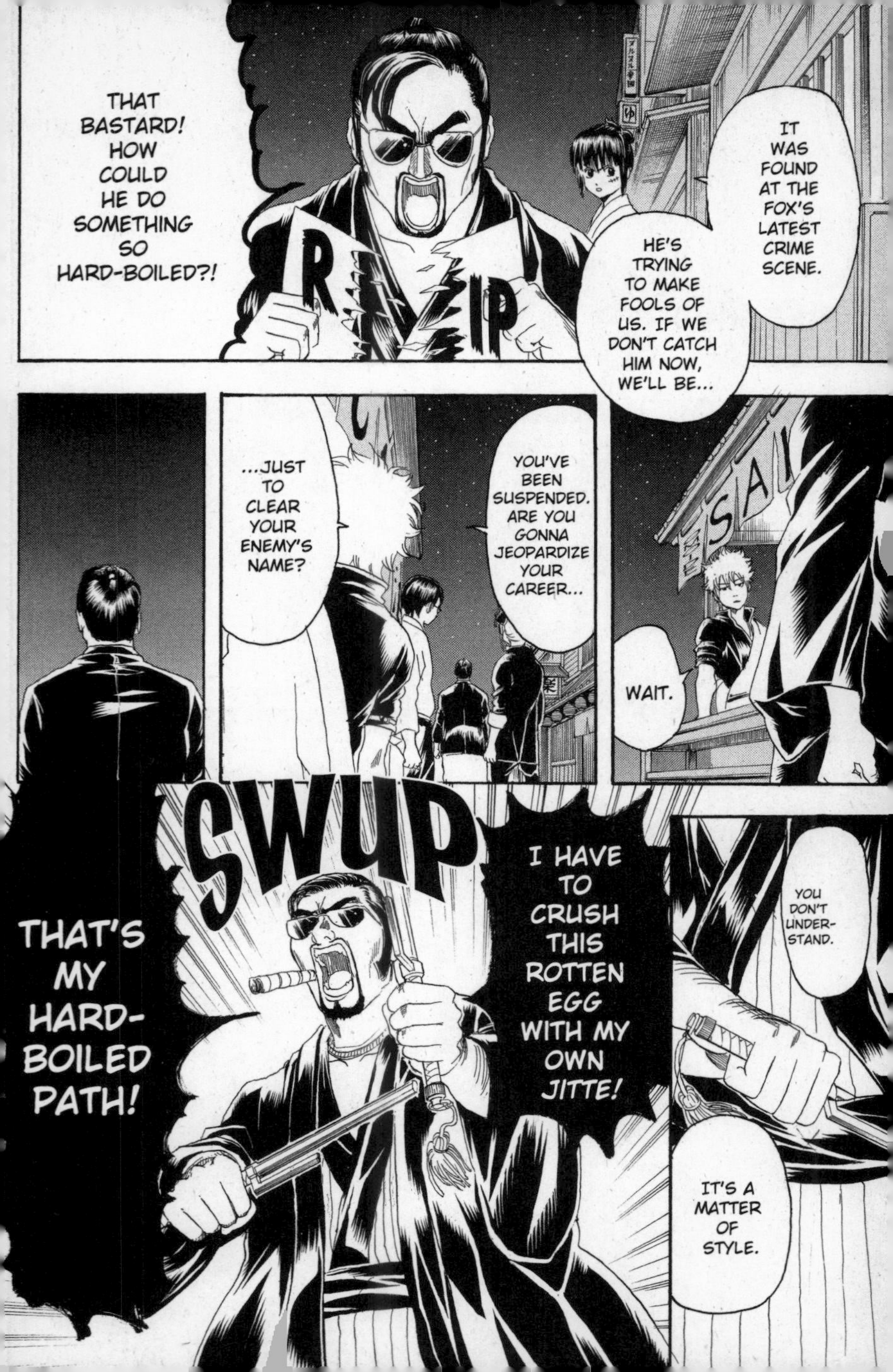
IT WAS FOUND AT THE FOX'S LATEST CRIME SCENE.
HE'S TRYING TO MAKE FOOLS OF US. IF WE DON'T CATCH HIM NOW, WE'LL BE...
THAT BASTARD! HOW COULD HE DO SOMETHING SO HARD-BOILED?!
RIP
WAIT.
YOU'VE BEEN SUSPENDED. ARE YOU GONNA JEOPARDIZE YOUR CAREER...
...JUST TO CLEAR YOUR ENEMY'S NAME?
YOU DON'T UNDER-STAND.
IT'S A MATTER OF STYLE.
SWUP
I HAVE TO CRUSH THIS ROTTEN EGG WITH MY OWN JITTE!
THAT'S MY HARD-BOILED PATH!

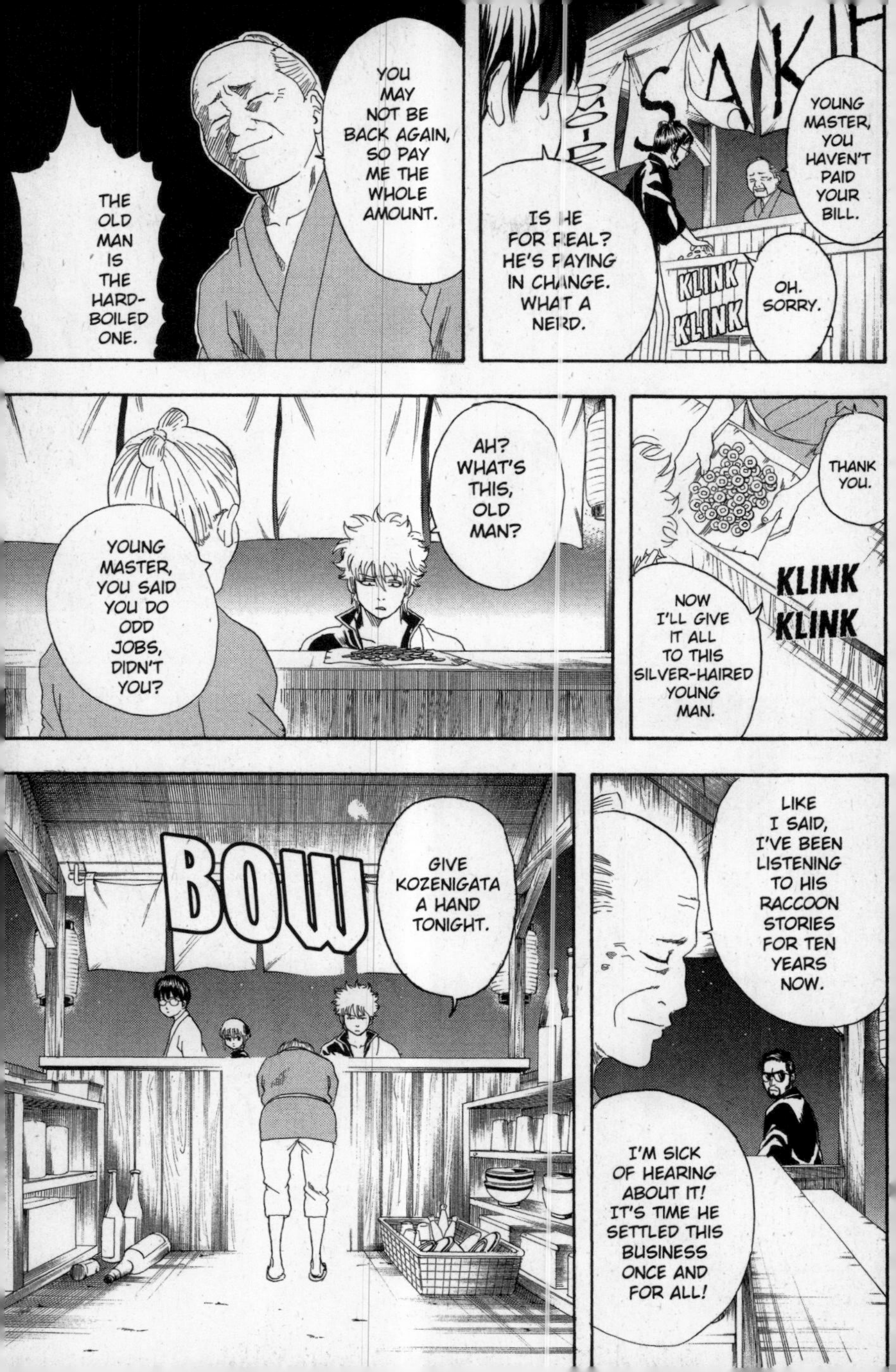
YOUNG MASTER, YOU HAVEN'T PAID YOUR BILL.
OH. SORRY.
KLINK KLINK
IS HE FOR REAL? HE'S PAYING IN CHANGE. WHAT A NERD.
YOU MAY NOT BE BACK AGAIN, SO PAY ME THE WHOLE AMOUNT.
THE OLD MAN IS THE HARD-BOILED ONE.
THANK YOU.
KLINK KLINK
NOW I'LL GIVE IT ALL TO THIS SILVER-HAIRED YOUNG MAN.
AH? WHAT'S THIS, OLD MAN?
YOUNG MASTER, YOU SAID YOU DO ODD JOBS, DIDN'T YOU?
LIKE I SAID, I'VE BEEN LISTENING TO HIS RACCOON STORIES FOR TEN YEARS NOW.
I'M SICK OF HEARING ABOUT IT! IT'S TIME HE SETTLED THIS BUSINESS ONCE AND FOR ALL!
GIVE KOZENIGATA A HAND TONIGHT.
BOW

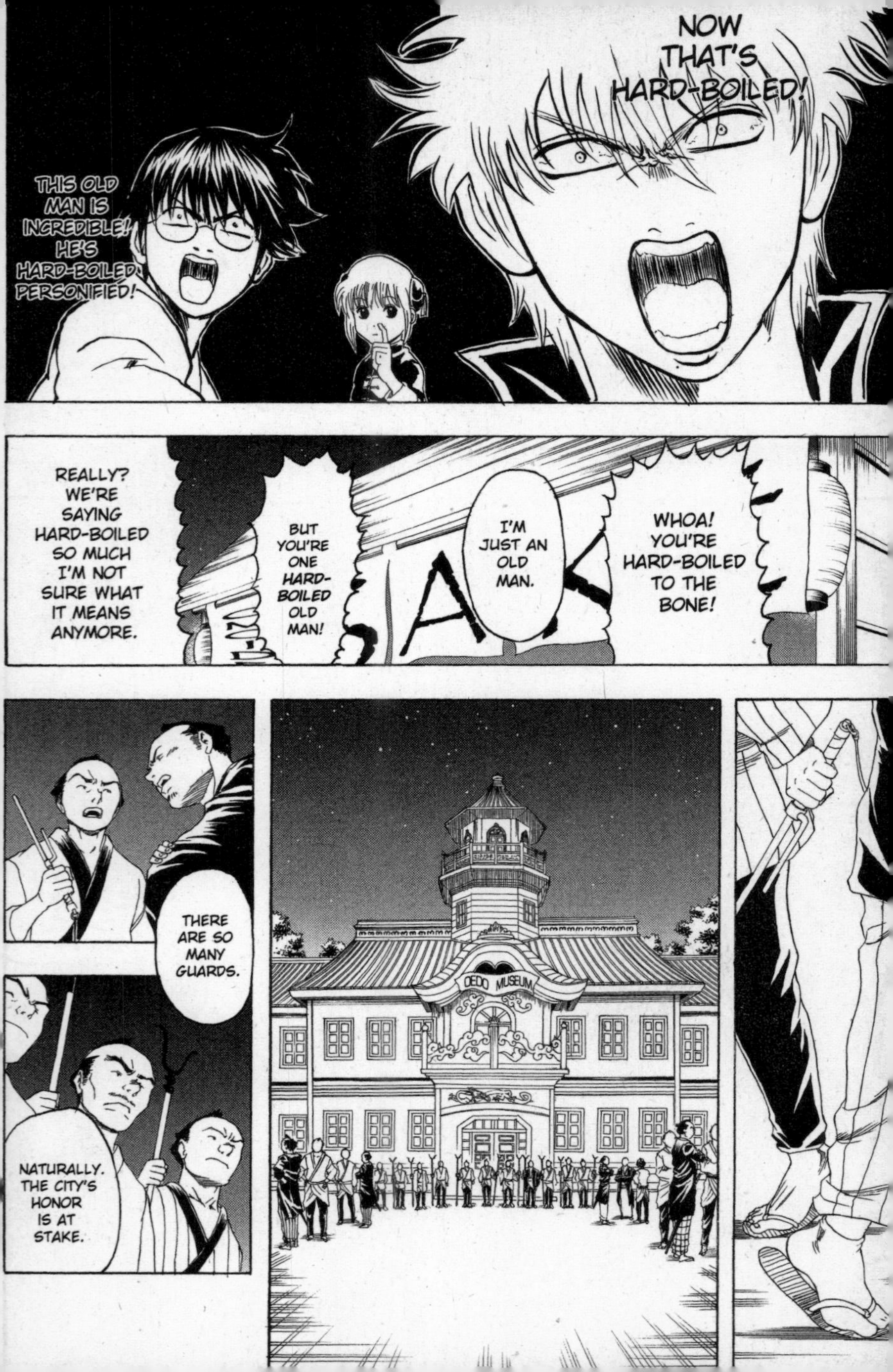
NOW THAT'S HARD-BOILED!
THIS OLD MAN IS INCREDIBLE! HE'S HARD-BOILED PERSONIFIED!
WHOA! YOU'RE HARD-BOILED TO THE BONE!
I'M JUST AN OLD MAN.
BUT YOU'RE ONE HARD-BOILED OLD MAN!
REALLY? WE'RE SAYING HARD-BOILED SO MUCH I'M NOT SURE WHAT IT MEANS ANYMORE.
OEDO MUSEUM
THERE ARE SO MANY GUARDS.
NATURALLY. THE CITY'S HONOR IS AT STAKE.

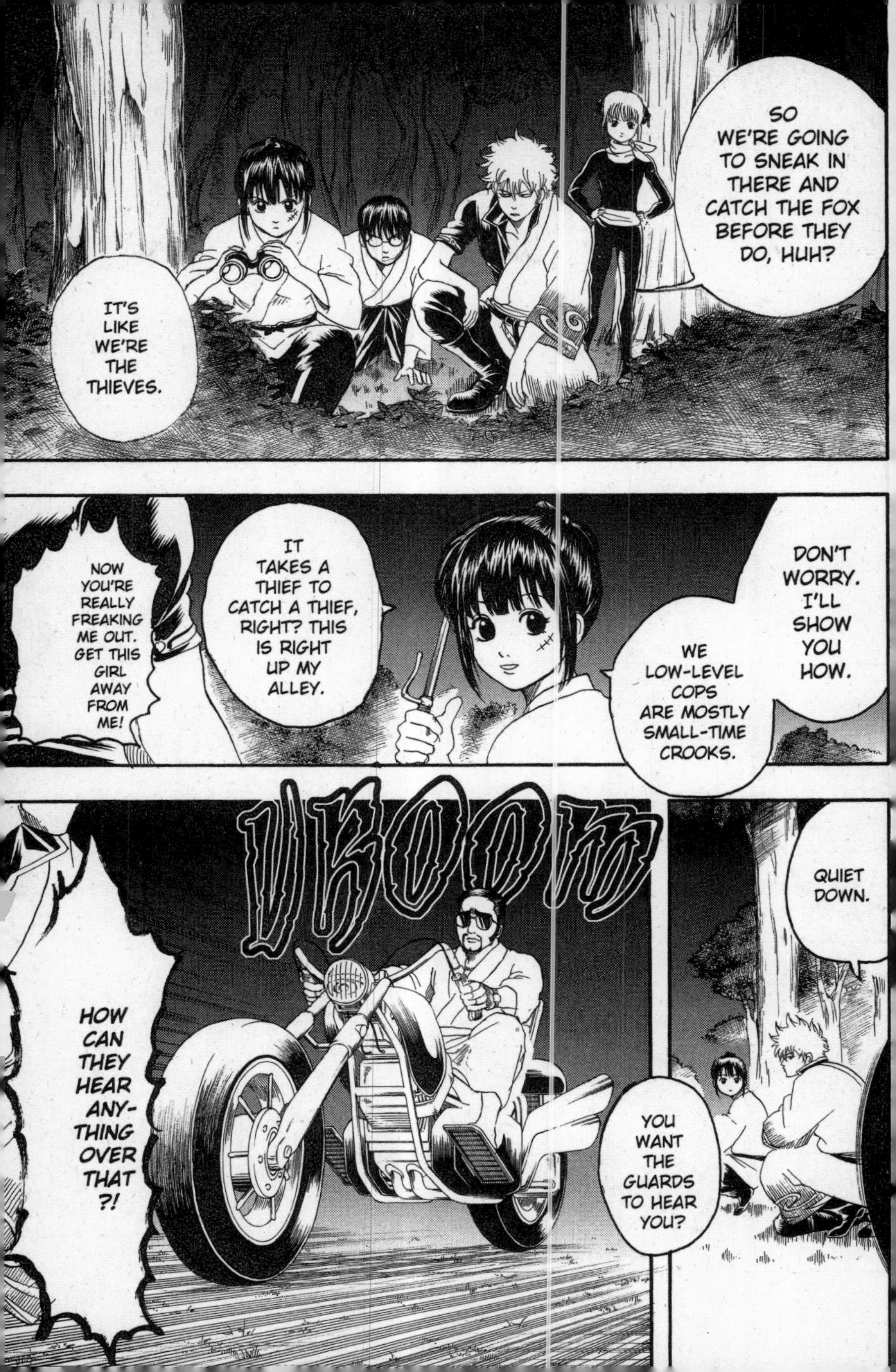
SO WE'RE GOING TO SNEAK IN THERE AND CATCH THE FOX BEFORE THEY DO, HUH?
IT'S LIKE WE'RE THE THIEVES.
DON'T WORRY. I'LL SHOW YOU HOW.
WE LOW-LEVEL COPS ARE MOSTLY SMALL-TIME CROOKS.
IT TAKES A THIEF TO CATCH A THIEF, RIGHT? THIS IS RIGHT UP MY ALLEY.
NOW YOU'RE REALLY FREAKING ME OUT. GET THIS GIRL AWAY FROM ME!
QUIET DOWN.
YOU WANT THE GUARDS TO HEAR YOU?
VROOM
HOW CAN THEY HEAR ANYTHING OVER THAT?!

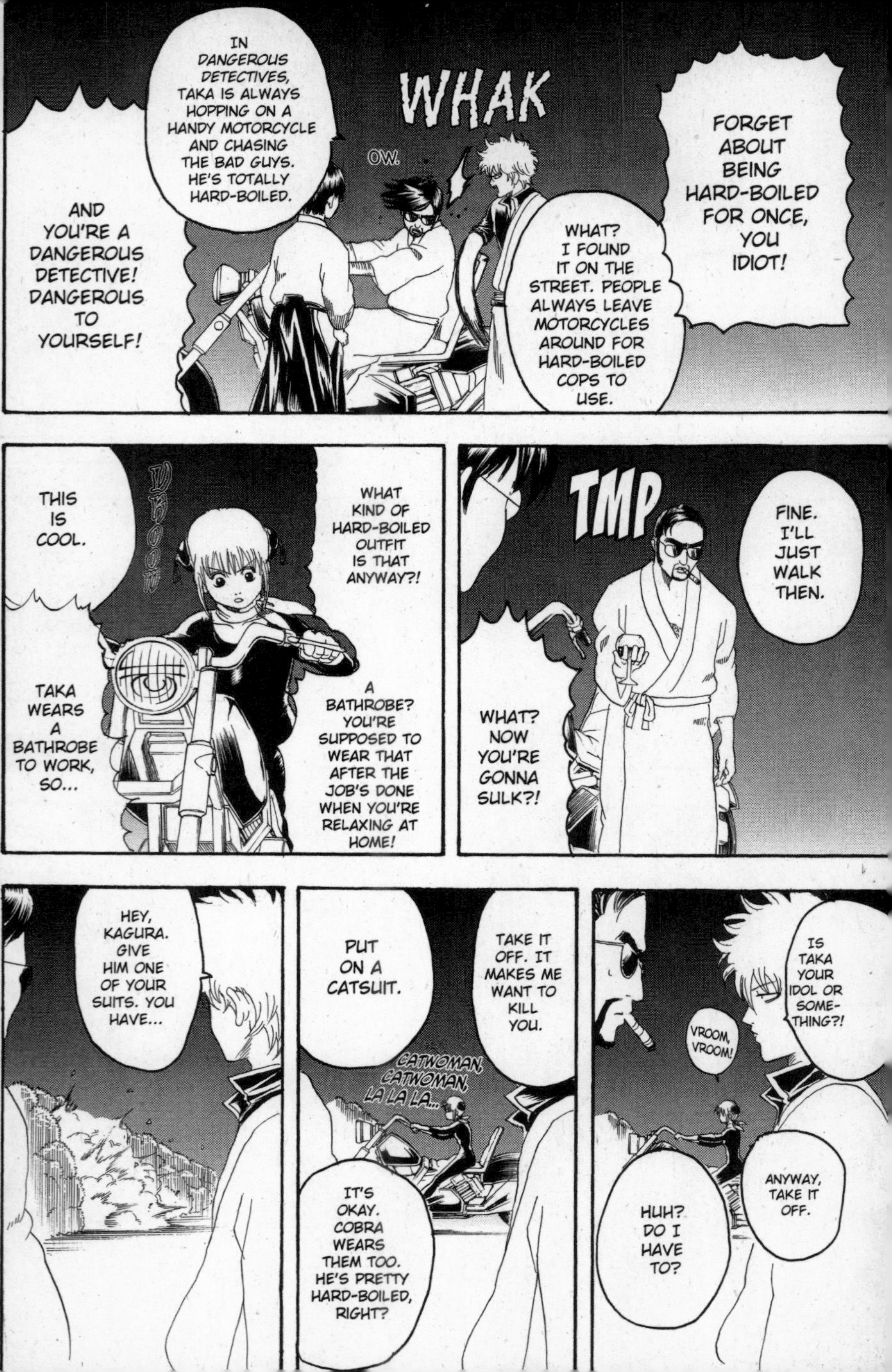
FORGET ABOUT BEING HARD-BOILED FOR ONCE, YOU IDIOT!
WHAK
OW.
WHAT? I FOUND IT ON THE STREET. PEOPLE ALWAYS LEAVE MOTORCYCLES AROUND FOR HARD-BOILED COPS TO USE.
IN DANGEROUS DETECTIVES, TAKA IS ALWAYS HOPPING ON A HANDY MOTORCYCLE AND CHASING THE BAD GUYS. HE'S TOTALLY HARD-BOILED.
AND YOU'RE A DANGEROUS DETECTIVE! DANGEROUS TO YOURSELF!
TMP
FINE. I'LL JUST WALK THEN.
WHAT? NOW YOU'RE GONNA SULK?!
WHAT KIND OF HARD-BOILED OUTFIT IS THAT ANYWAY?!
THIS IS COOL.
A BATHROBE? YOU'RE SUPPOSED TO WEAR THAT AFTER THE JOB'S DONE WHEN YOU'RE RELAXING AT HOME!
TAKA WEARS A BATHROBE TO WORK, SO...
IS TAKA YOUR IDOL OR SOME-THING?!
VROOM, VROOM!
ANYWAY, TAKE IT OFF.
HUH? DO I HAVE TO?
TAKE IT OFF. IT MAKES ME WANT TO KILL YOU.
PUT ON A CATSUIT.
CATWOMAN, CATWOMAN, LA LA LA...
IT'S OKAY. COBRA WEARS THEM TOO. HE'S PRETTY HARD-BOILED, RIGHT?
HEY, KAGURA. GIVE HIM ONE OF YOUR SUITS. YOU HAVE...

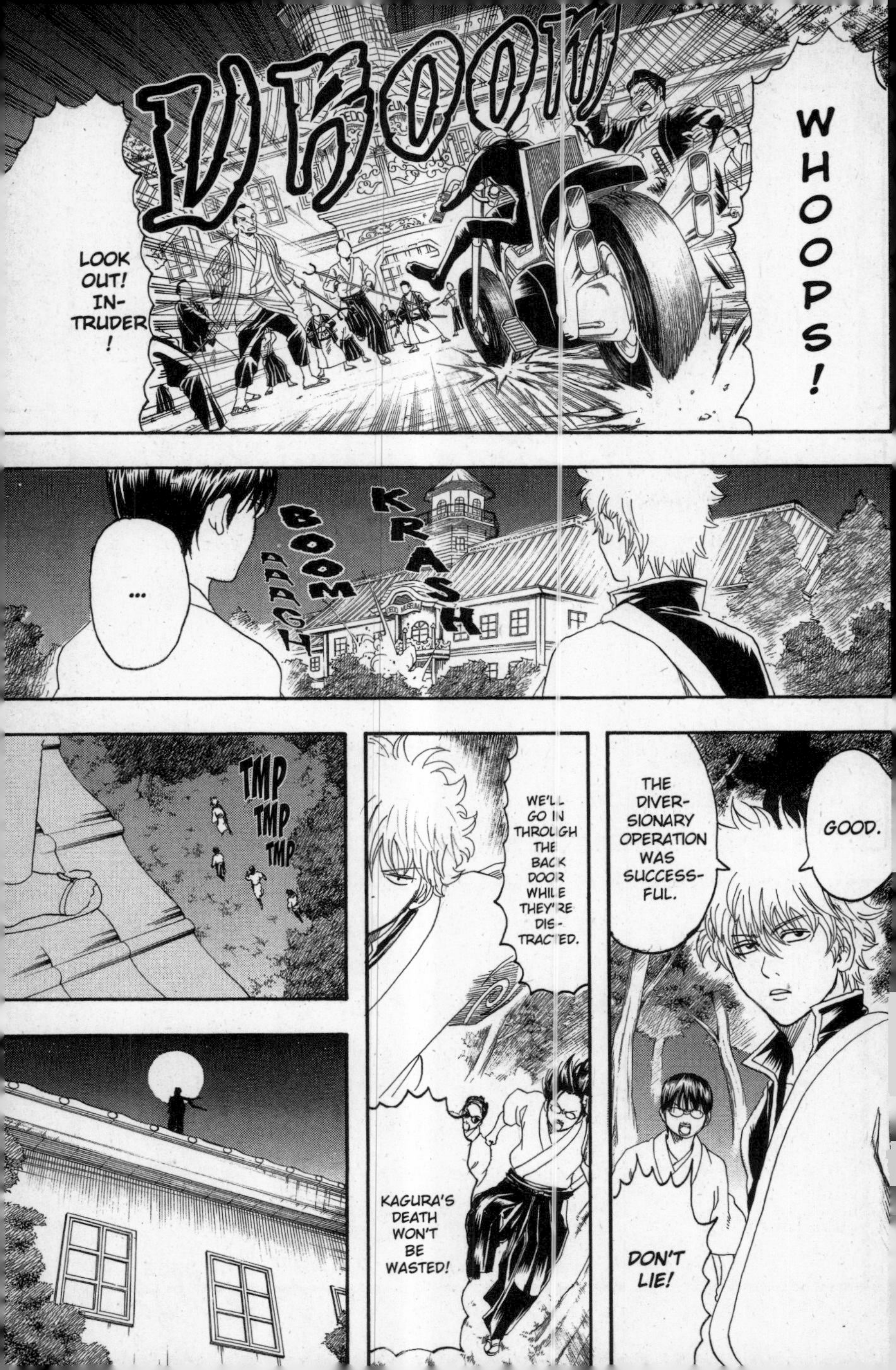
WHOOPS!
VROOOM
LOOK OUT! IN-TRUDER!
KRASH
BOOM
AAAGH
...
GOOD.
THE DIVER-SIONARY OPERATION WAS SUCCESS-FUL.
DON'T LIE!
WE'LL GO IN THROUGH THE BACK DOOR WHILE THEY'RE DIS-TRACTED.
KAGURA'S DEATH WON'T BE WASTED!
TMP TMP TMP

<Question from Lasagna from Kochi Prefecture>

I want to be a manga artist, but will I have to go live in Tokyo? I'd like to stay in Kochi Prefecture or somewhere in the Shikoku area if possible.

<Answer>

You can be a manga artist anywhere you want. Some artists that do girls' manga live and work in rural areas like Hokkaido, but they mostly work for monthly magazines. I've heard that some manga artists who work for **Weekly Shonen Jump** draw their manga in rural areas. But you'll have to be able to manage your schedule yourself. It'd be impossible for a hopeless guy like me who can't meet deadlines.

(Q&A #50 is on page 128)

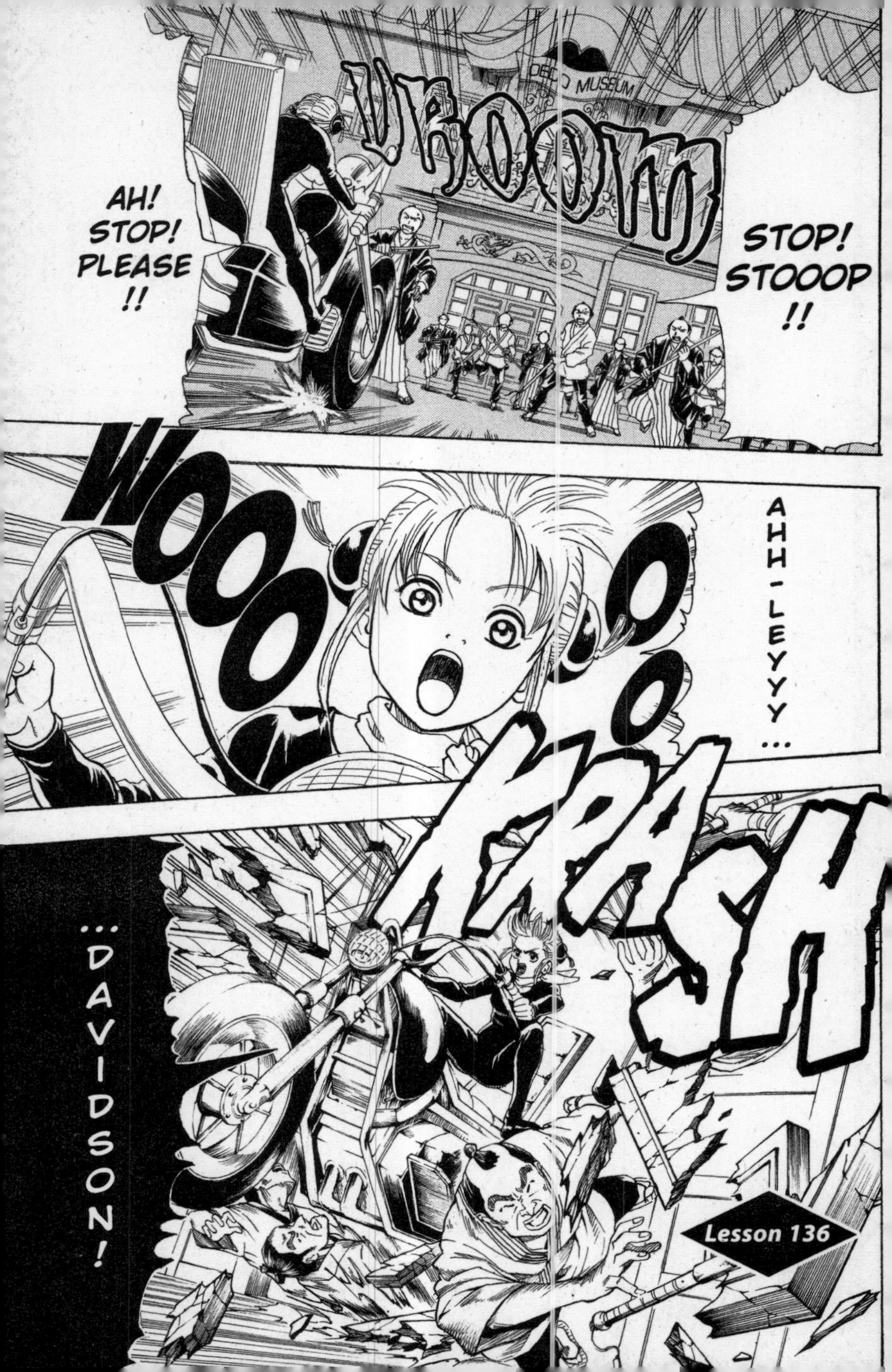
STOP! STOOOP!!
VROOM
AH! STOP! PLEASE!!
AHH-LEYYY...
WOOOOO
...DAVIDSON!
Lesson 136

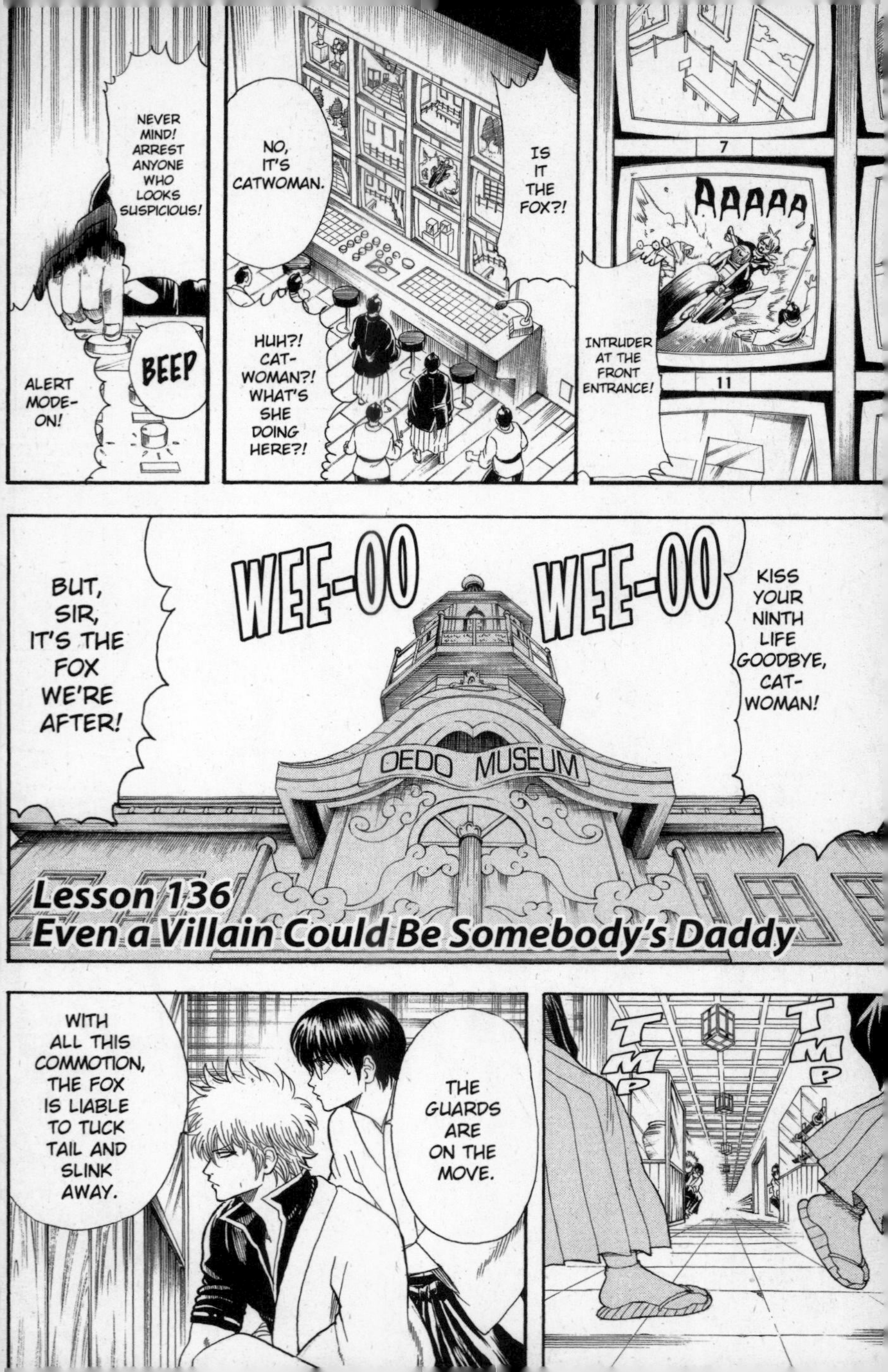
7
AAAAA
11
INTRUDER AT THE FRONT ENTRANCE!
IS IT THE FOX?!
NO, IT'S CATWOMAN.
HUH?! CAT-WOMAN?! WHAT'S SHE DOING HERE?!
NEVER MIND! ARREST ANYONE WHO LOOKS SUSPICIOUS!
BEEP
ALERT MODE-ON!
KISS YOUR NINTH LIFE GOODBYE, CAT-WOMAN!
WEE-OO
WEE-OO
BUT, SIR, IT'S THE FOX WE'RE AFTER!
OEDO MUSEUM
Lesson 136
Even a Villain Could Be Somebody's Daddy
TMP
TMP
THE GUARDS ARE ON THE MOVE.
WITH ALL THIS COMMOTION, THE FOX IS LIABLE TO TUCK TAIL AND SLINK AWAY.

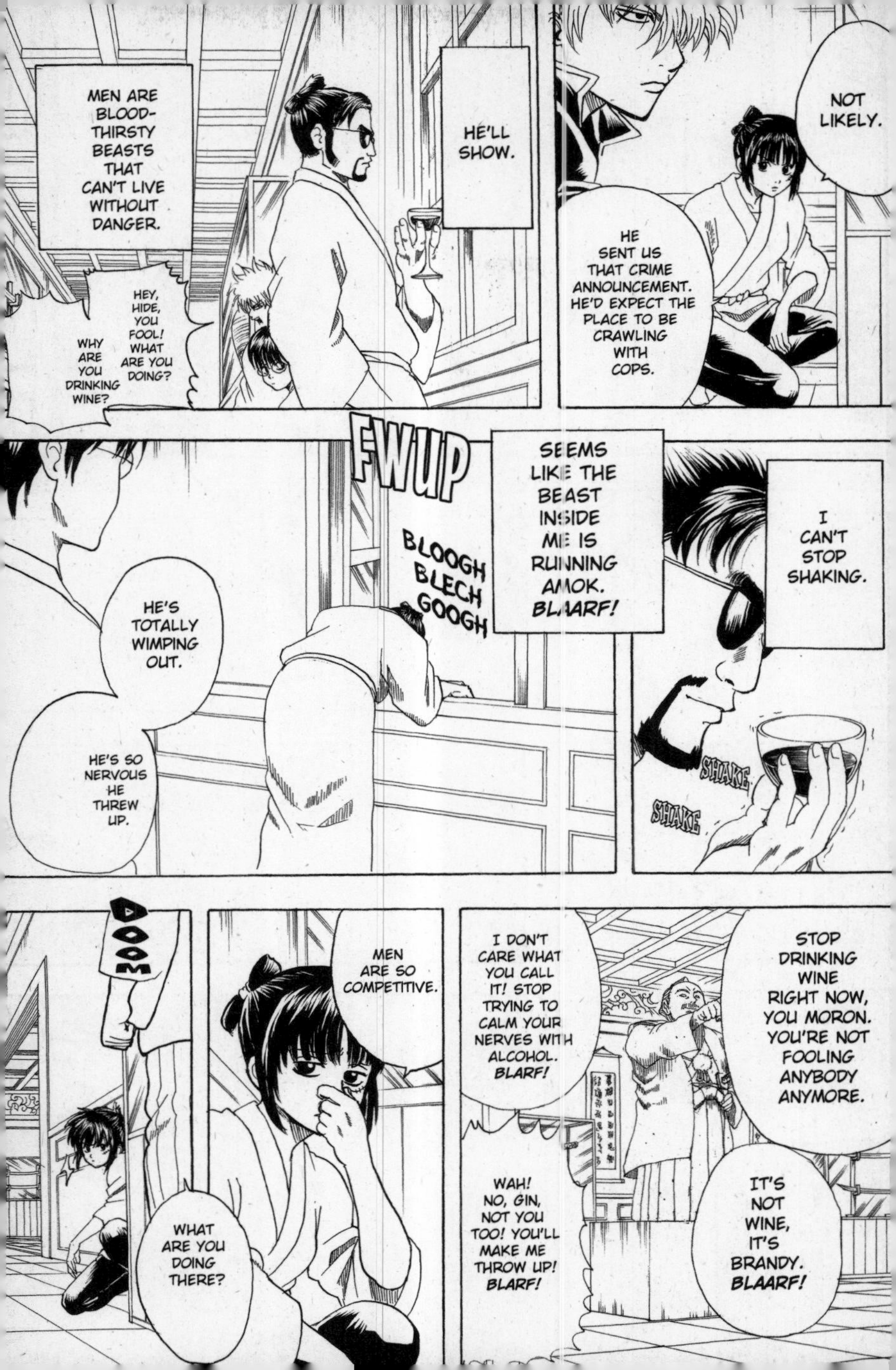
NOT LIKELY.
HE SENT US THAT CRIME ANNOUNCEMENT. HE'D EXPECT THE PLACE TO BE CRAWLING WITH COPS.
HE'LL SHOW.
MEN ARE BLOOD-THIRSTY BEASTS THAT CAN'T LIVE WITHOUT DANGER.
HEY, HIDE, YOU FOOL! WHAT ARE YOU DOING?
WHY ARE YOU DRINKING WINE?
I CAN'T STOP SHAKING.
SHAKE
SHAKE
SEEMS LIKE THE BEAST INSIDE ME IS RUNNING AMOK. *BLAARF!*
FWUP
BLOOGH BLECH GOOGH
HE'S TOTALLY WIMPING OUT.
HE'S SO NERVOUS HE THREW UP.
STOP DRINKING WINE RIGHT NOW, YOU MORON. YOU'RE NOT FOOLING ANYBODY ANYMORE.
IT'S NOT WINE, IT'S BRANDY. *BLAARF!*
I DON'T CARE WHAT YOU CALL IT! STOP TRYING TO CALM YOUR NERVES WITH ALCOHOL. *BLARF!*
WAH! NO, GIN, NOT YOU TOO! YOU'LL MAKE ME THROW UP! *BLARF!*
MEN ARE SO COMPETITIVE.
WHAT ARE YOU DOING THERE?
DOOM

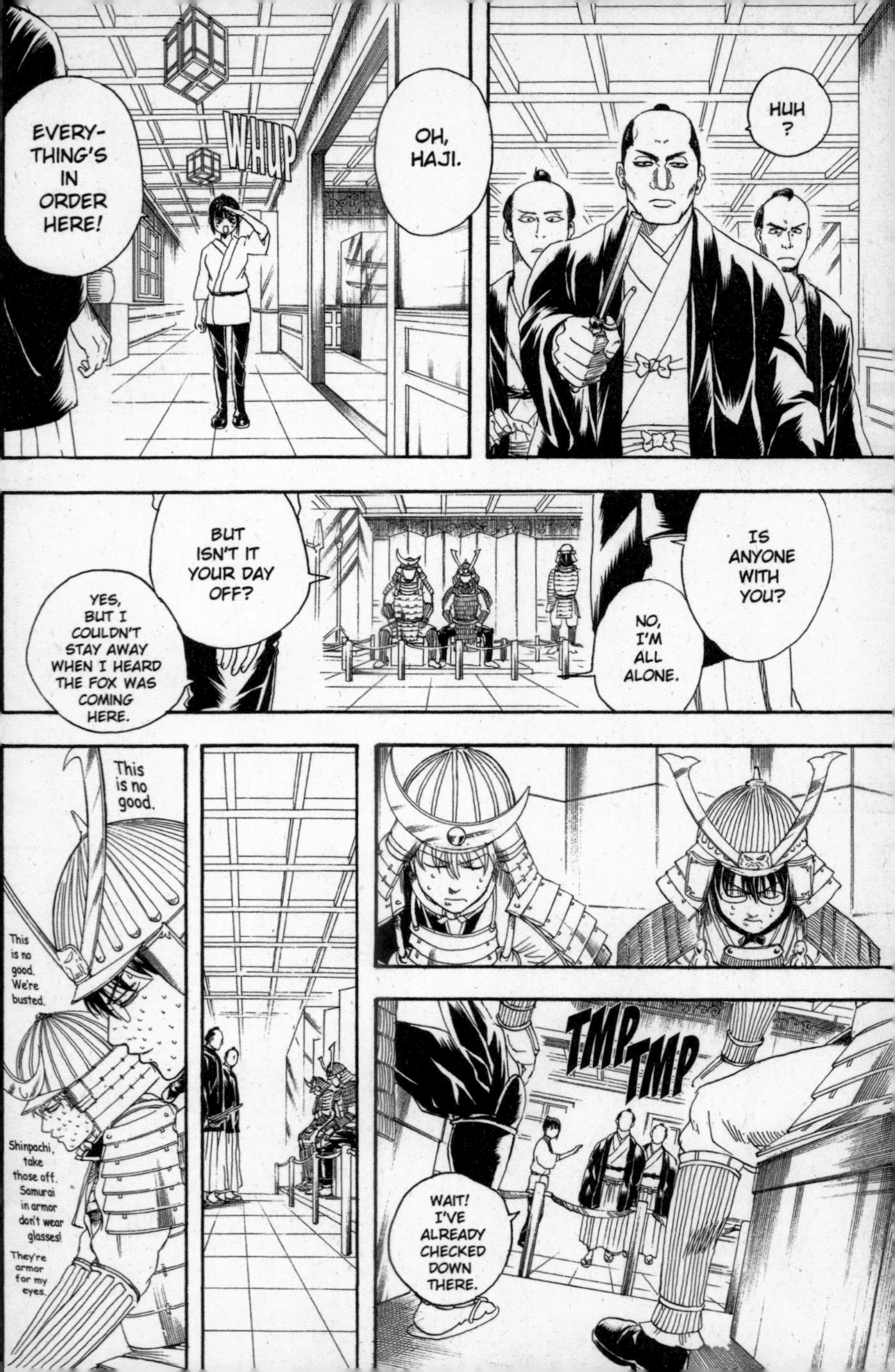
HUH ?
OH, HAJI.
WHUP
EVERY-THING'S IN ORDER HERE!
IS ANYONE WITH YOU?
NO, I'M ALL ALONE.
BUT ISN'T IT YOUR DAY OFF?
YES, BUT I COULDN'T STAY AWAY WHEN I HEARD THE FOX WAS COMING HERE.
TMP TMP
WAIT! I'VE ALREADY CHECKED DOWN THERE.
This is no good.
This is no good. We're busted.
Shinpachi, take those off. Samurai in armor don't wear glasses!
They're armor for my eyes.

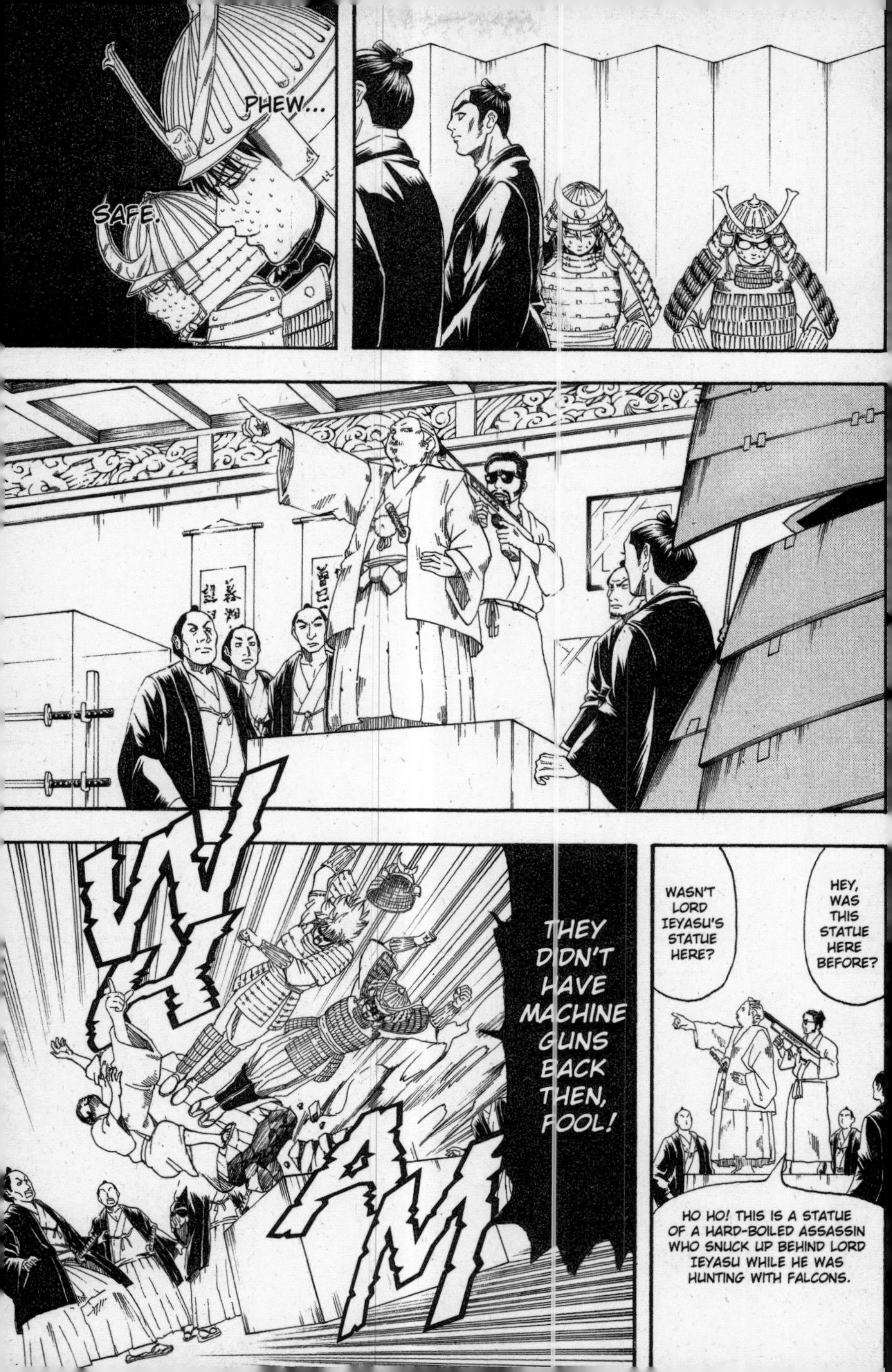
PHEW...
SAFE.
HEY, WAS THIS STATUE HERE BEFORE?
WASN'T LORD IEYASU'S STATUE HERE?
HO HO! THIS IS A STATUE OF A HARD-BOILED ASSASSIN WHO SNUCK UP BEHIND LORD IEYASU WHILE HE WAS HUNTING WITH FALCONS.
THEY DIDN'T HAVE MACHINE GUNS BACK THEN, FOOL!
WHAM

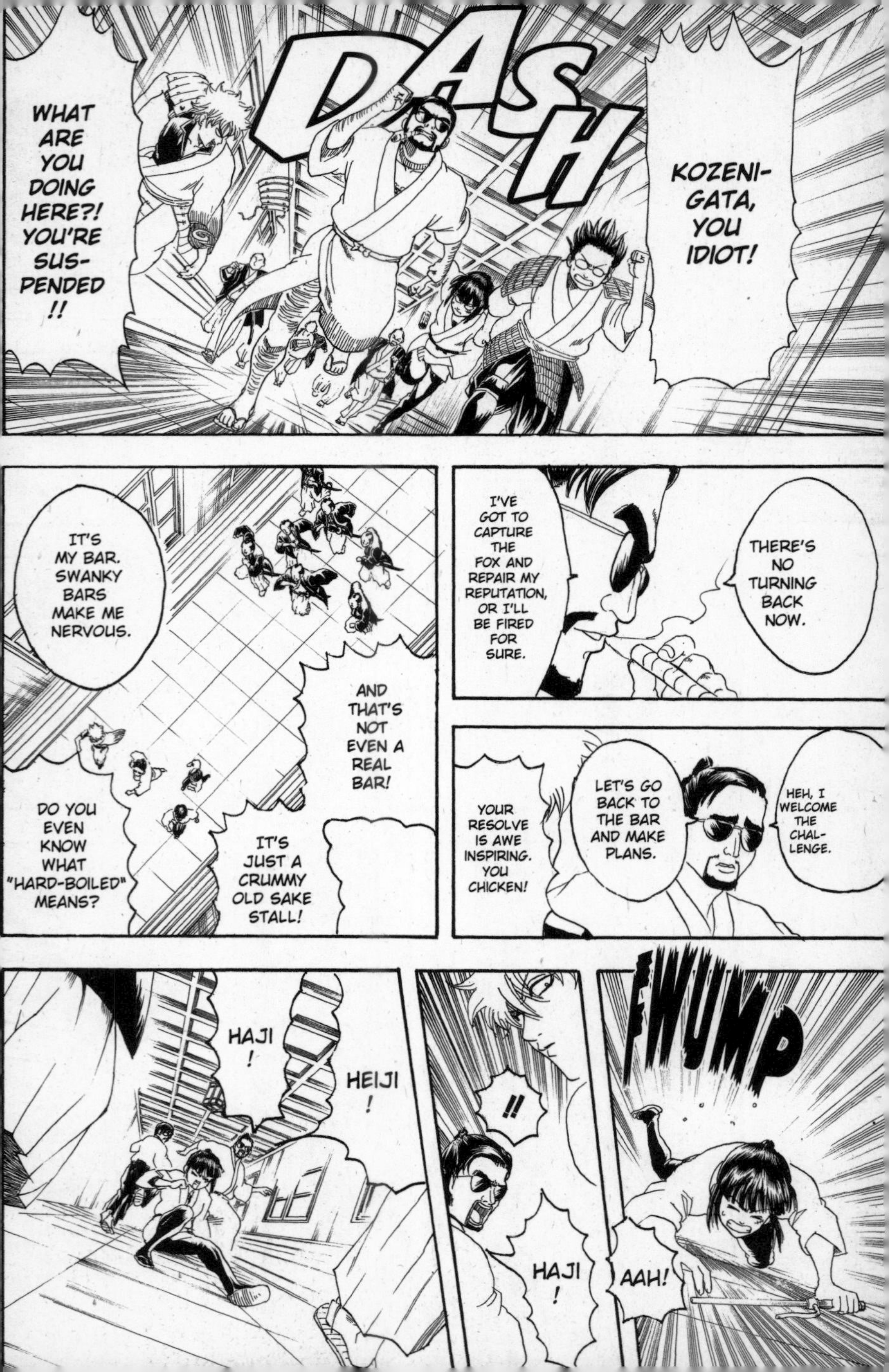
DASH
KOZENI-GATA, YOU IDIOT!
WHAT ARE YOU DOING HERE?! YOU'RE SUS-PENDED!!
THERE'S NO TURNING BACK NOW.
I'VE GOT TO CAPTURE THE FOX AND REPAIR MY REPUTATION, OR I'LL BE FIRED FOR SURE.
HEH, I WELCOME THE CHAL-LENGE.
LET'S GO BACK TO THE BAR AND MAKE PLANS.
YOUR RESOLVE IS AWE INSPIRING. YOU CHICKEN!
AND THAT'S NOT EVEN A REAL BAR!
IT'S JUST A CRUMMY OLD SAKE STALL!
DO YOU EVEN KNOW WHAT "HARD-BOILED" MEANS?
IT'S MY BAR. SWANKY BARS MAKE ME NERVOUS.
FWUMP
AAH!
!!
HAJI!
HEIJI!
HAJI!

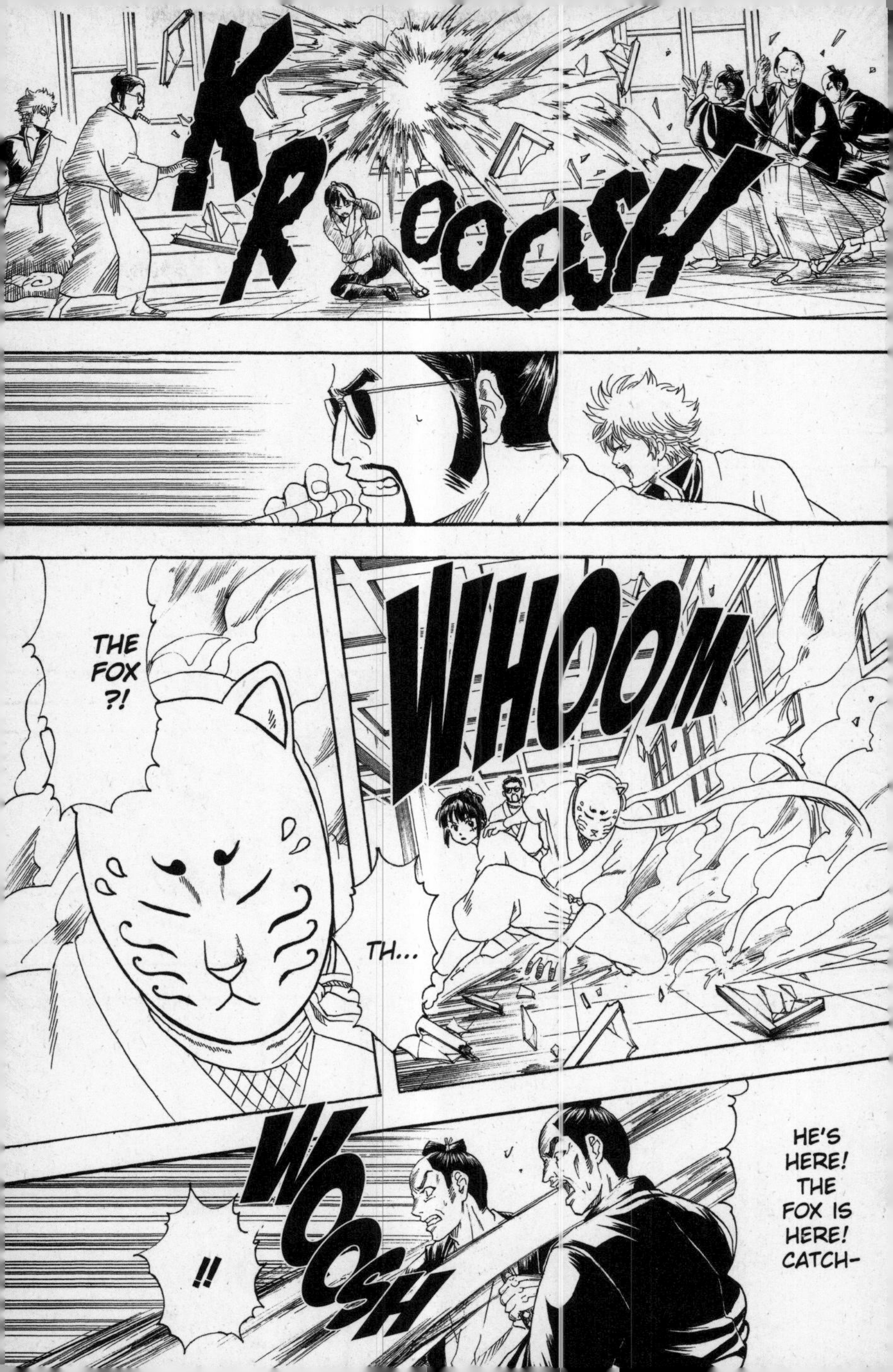
KROOOSH!
WHOOM
TH...
THE FOX ?!
HE'S HERE! THE FOX IS HERE! CATCH-
WOOSH
!!

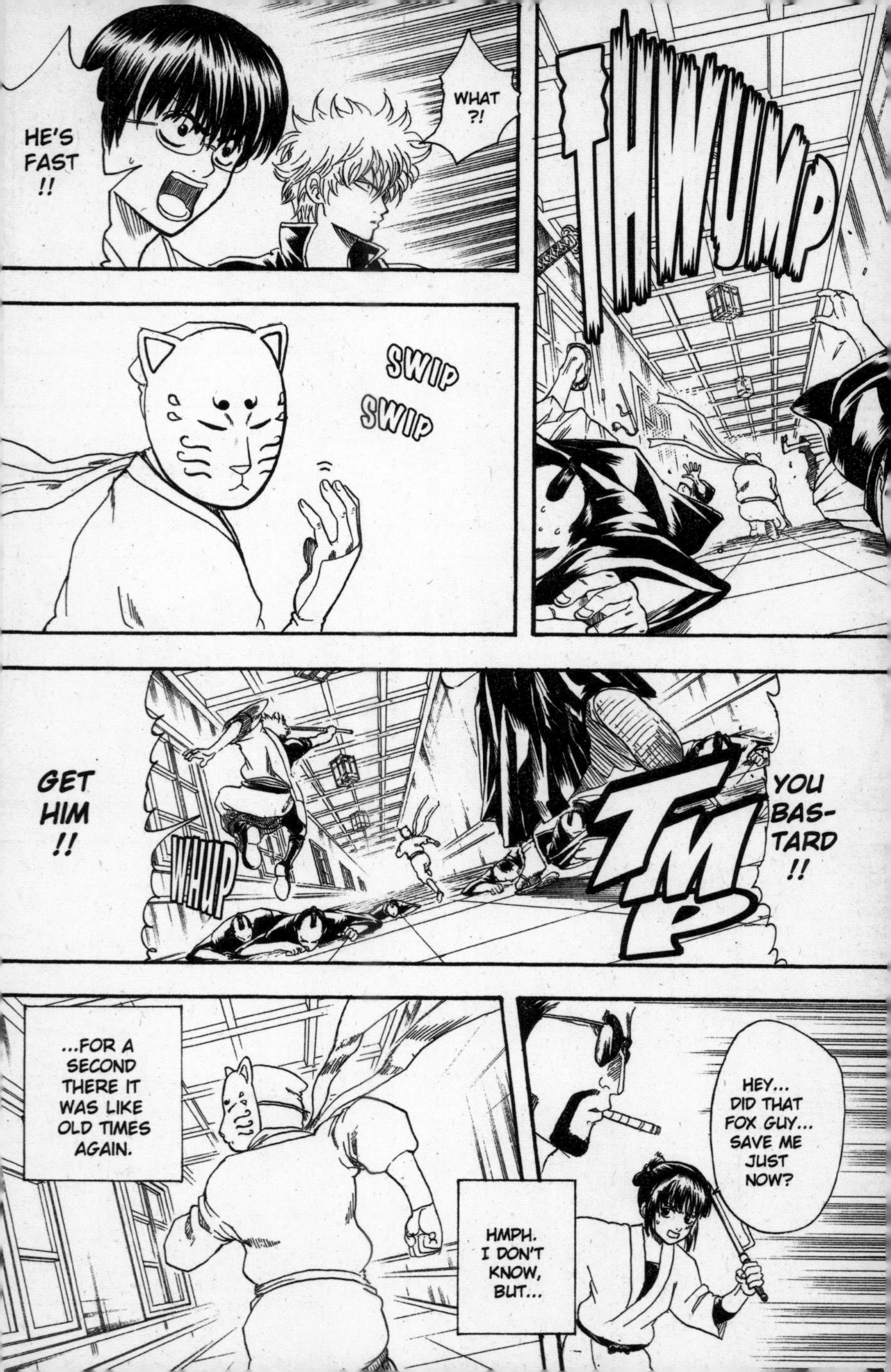
THWUMP
WHAT ?!
HE'S FAST !!
SWIP
SWIP
YOU BASTARD !!
TMP
WHUP
GET HIM !!
HEY... DID THAT FOX GUY... SAVE ME JUST NOW?
HMPH. I DON'T KNOW, BUT...
...FOR A SECOND THERE IT WAS LIKE OLD TIMES AGAIN.

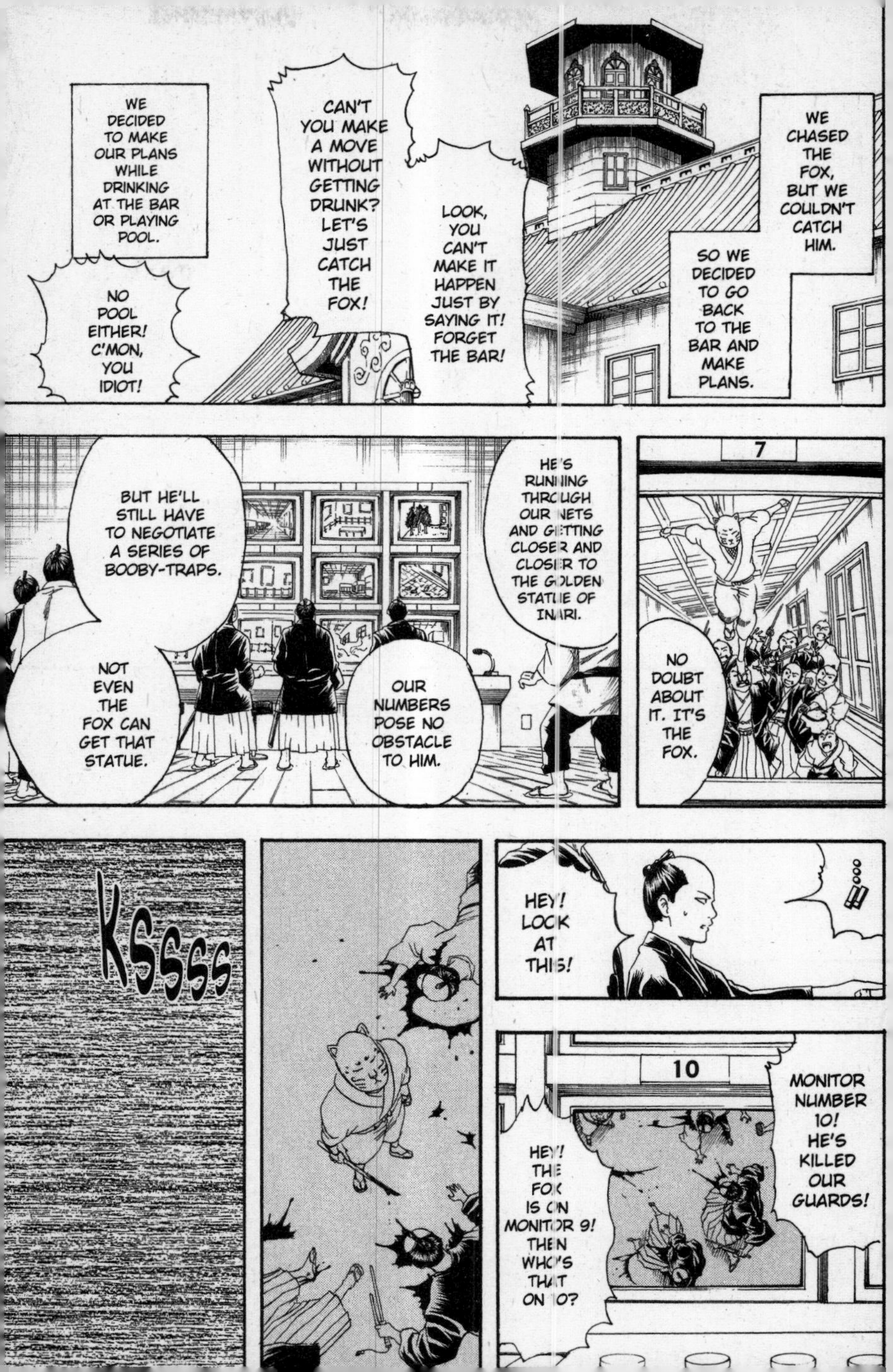
WE CHASED THE FOX, BUT WE COULDN'T CATCH HIM.
SO WE DECIDED TO GO BACK TO THE BAR AND MAKE PLANS.
LOOK, YOU CAN'T MAKE IT HAPPEN JUST BY SAYING IT! FORGET THE BAR!
CAN'T YOU MAKE A MOVE WITHOUT GETTING DRUNK? LET'S JUST CATCH THE FOX!
WE DECIDED TO MAKE OUR PLANS WHILE DRINKING AT THE BAR OR PLAYING POOL.
NO POOL EITHER! C'MON, YOU IDIOT!
7
NO DOUBT ABOUT IT. IT'S THE FOX.
HE'S RUNNING THROUGH OUR NETS AND GETTING CLOSER AND CLOSER TO THE GOLDEN STATUE OF INARI.
OUR NUMBERS POSE NO OBSTACLE TO HIM.
BUT HE'LL STILL HAVE TO NEGOTIATE A SERIES OF BOOBY-TRAPS.
NOT EVEN THE FOX CAN GET THAT STATUE.
HEY! LOOK AT THIS!
10
MONITOR NUMBER 10! HE'S KILLED OUR GUARDS!
HEY! THE FOX IS ON MONITOR 9! THEN WHO'S THAT ON 10?
KSSSS

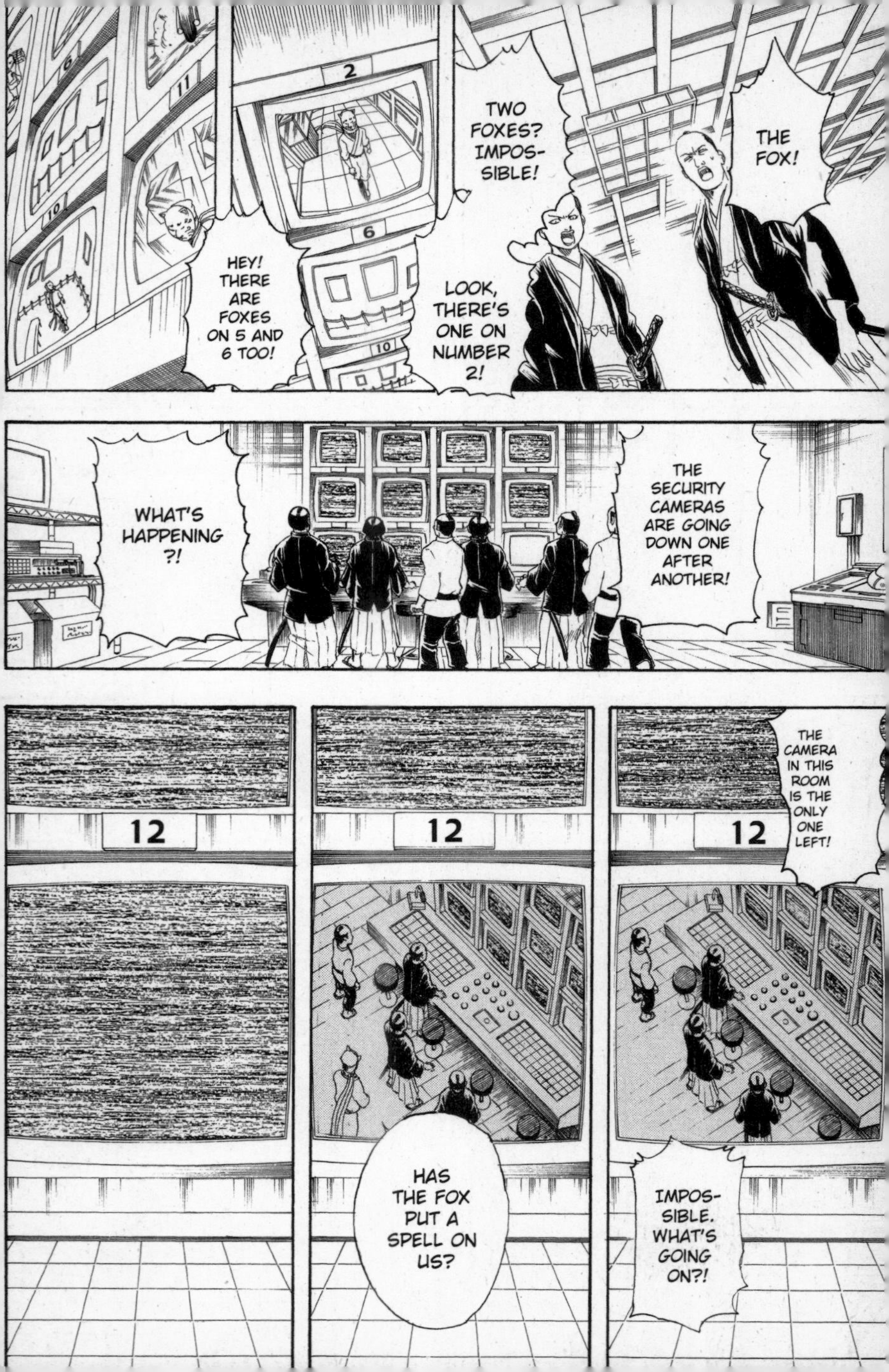
THE FOX!
TWO FOXES? IMPOSSIBLE!
LOOK, THERE'S ONE ON NUMBER 2!
HEY! THERE ARE FOXES ON 5 AND 6 TOO!
THE SECURITY CAMERAS ARE GOING DOWN ONE AFTER ANOTHER!
WHAT'S HAPPENING?!
THE CAMERA IN THIS ROOM IS THE ONLY ONE LEFT!
IMPOSSIBLE. WHAT'S GOING ON?!
HAS THE FOX PUT A SPELL ON US?

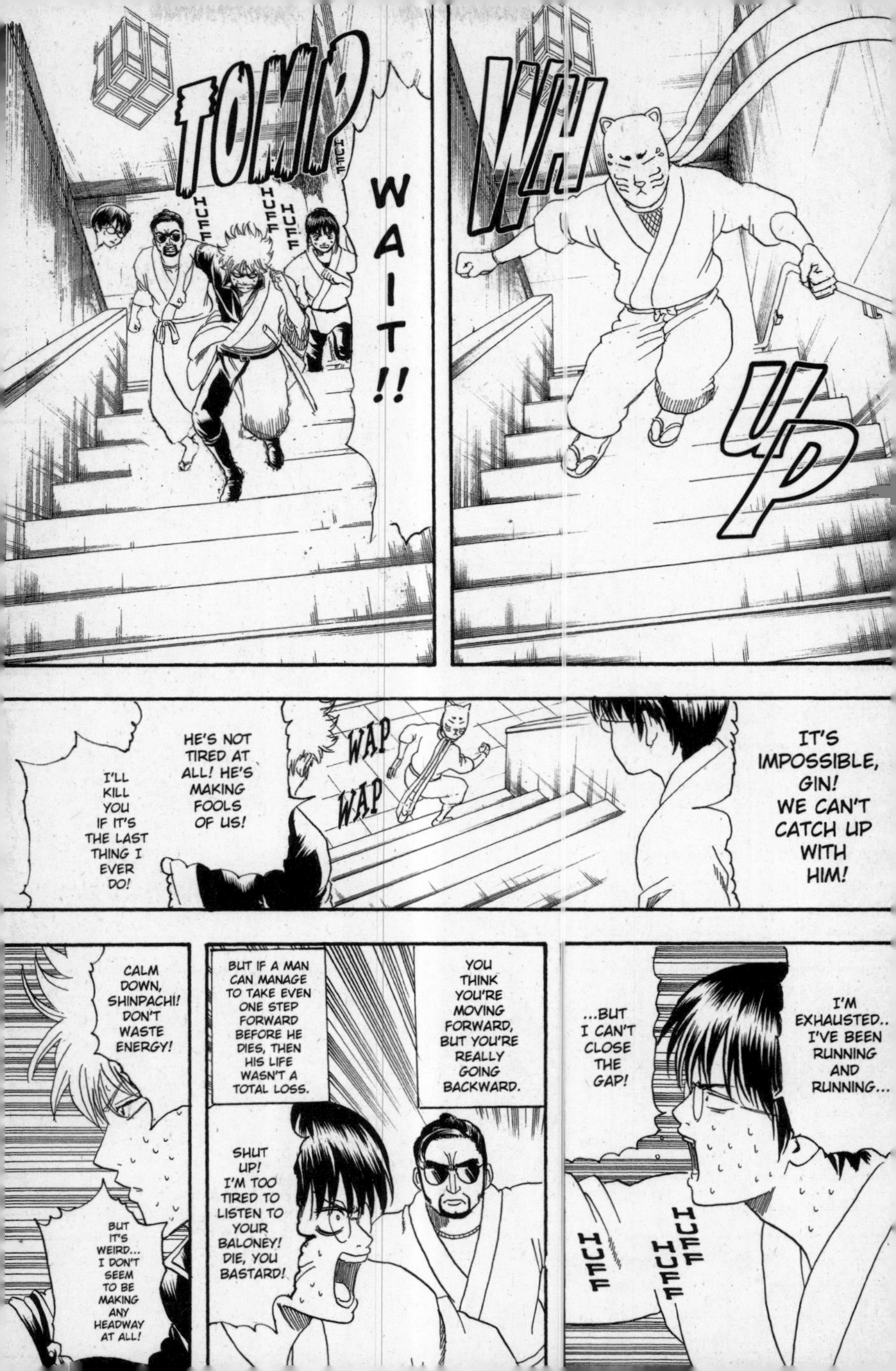

WH
UP
TOMP
HUFF HUFF HUFF HUFF
WAIT!!
IT'S IMPOSSIBLE, GIN! WE CAN'T CATCH UP WITH HIM!
WAP WAP
HE'S NOT TIRED AT ALL! HE'S MAKING FOOLS OF US!
I'LL KILL YOU IF IT'S THE LAST THING I EVER DO!
I'M EXHAUSTED.. I'VE BEEN RUNNING AND RUNNING...
...BUT I CAN'T CLOSE THE GAP!
HUFF HUFF HUFF
YOU THINK YOU'RE MOVING FORWARD, BUT YOU'RE REALLY GOING BACKWARD.
BUT IF A MAN CAN MANAGE TO TAKE EVEN ONE STEP FORWARD BEFORE HE DIES, THEN HIS LIFE WASN'T A TOTAL LOSS.
SHUT UP! I'M TOO TIRED TO LISTEN TO YOUR BALONEY! DIE, YOU BASTARD!
CALM DOWN, SHINPACHI! DON'T WASTE ENERGY!
BUT IT'S WEIRD... I DON'T SEEM TO BE MAKING ANY HEADWAY AT ALL!

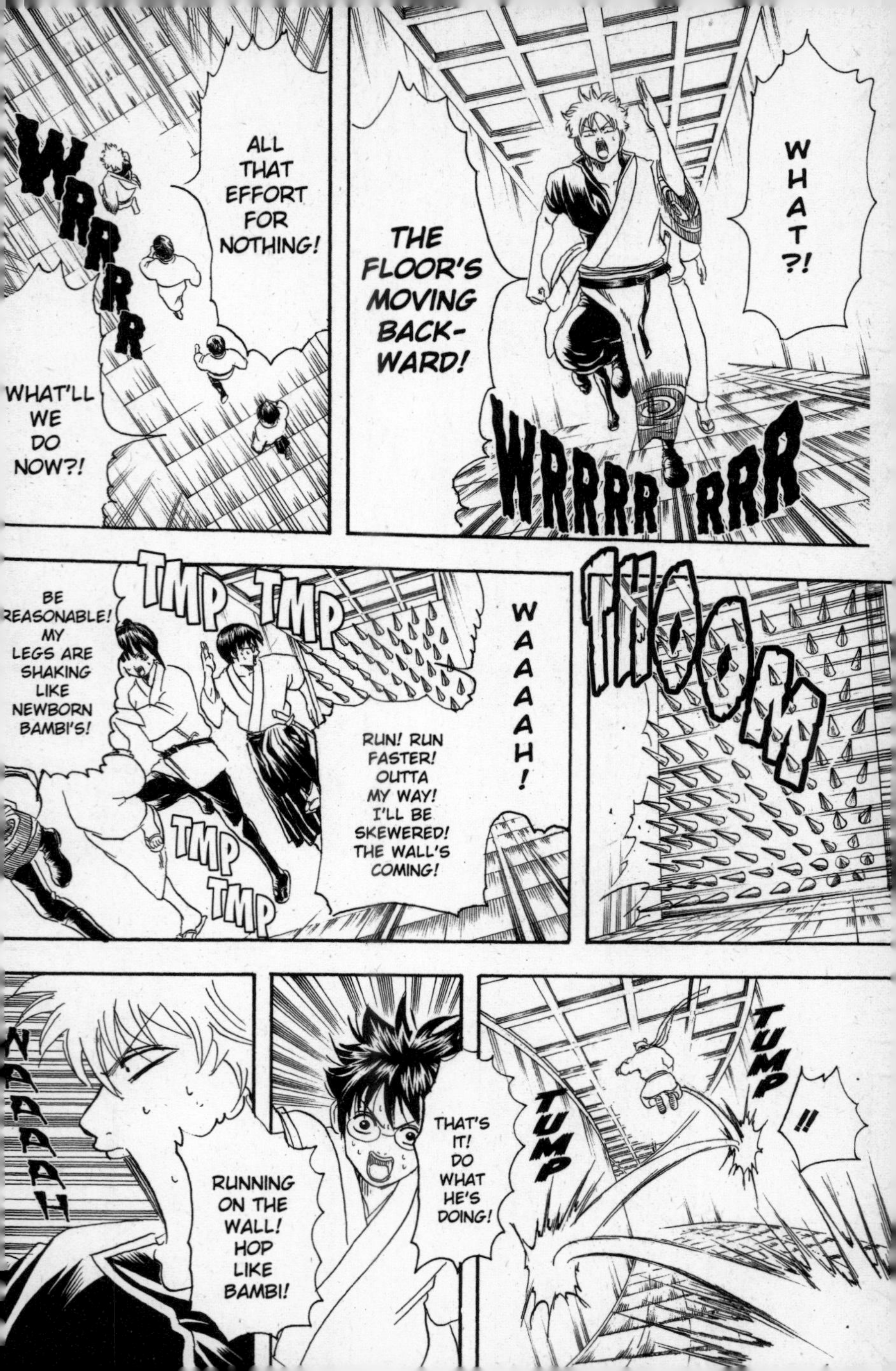
WHAT?!
THE FLOOR'S MOVING BACKWARD!
WRRRRR RRR
ALL THAT EFFORT FOR NOTHING!
WRRRR
WHAT'LL WE DO NOW?!
THOOM
WAAAAAH!
TMP TMP
RUN! RUN FASTER! OUTTA MY WAY! I'LL BE SKEWERED! THE WALL'S COMING!
BE REASONABLE! MY LEGS ARE SHAKING LIKE NEWBORN BAMBI'S!
TMP TMP
TUMP!!
TUMP
THAT'S IT! DO WHAT HE'S DOING!
RUNNING ON THE WALL! HOP LIKE BAMBI!
NAAAAH

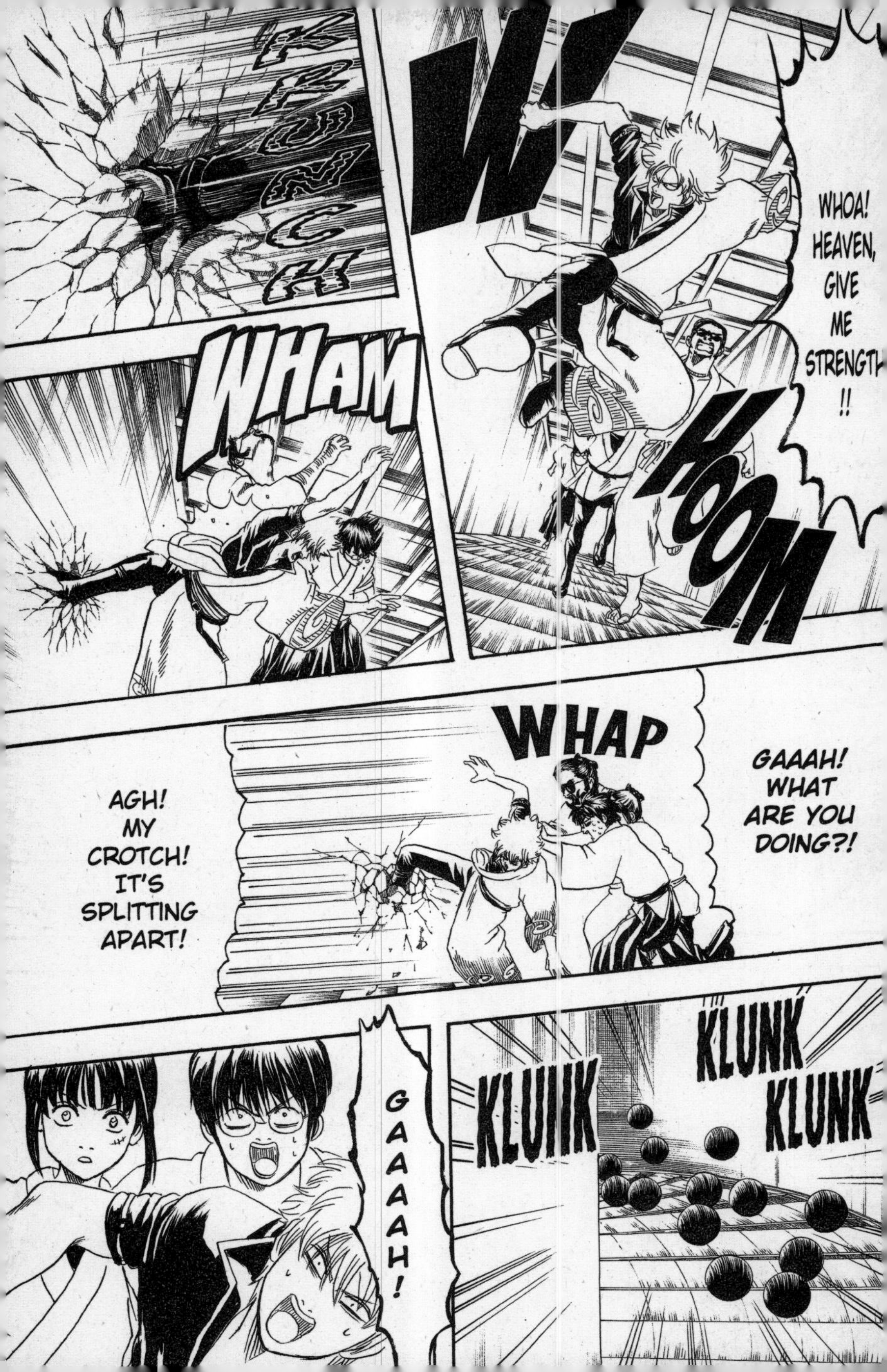
WHOA! HEAVEN, GIVE ME STRENGTH!!
WHOOM
KRUNCH
WHAM
WHAP
GAAAH! WHAT ARE YOU DOING?!
AGH! MY CROTCH! IT'S SPLITTING APART!
KLUNK
KLUNK
KLUNK
KLUNK
GAAAAAH!

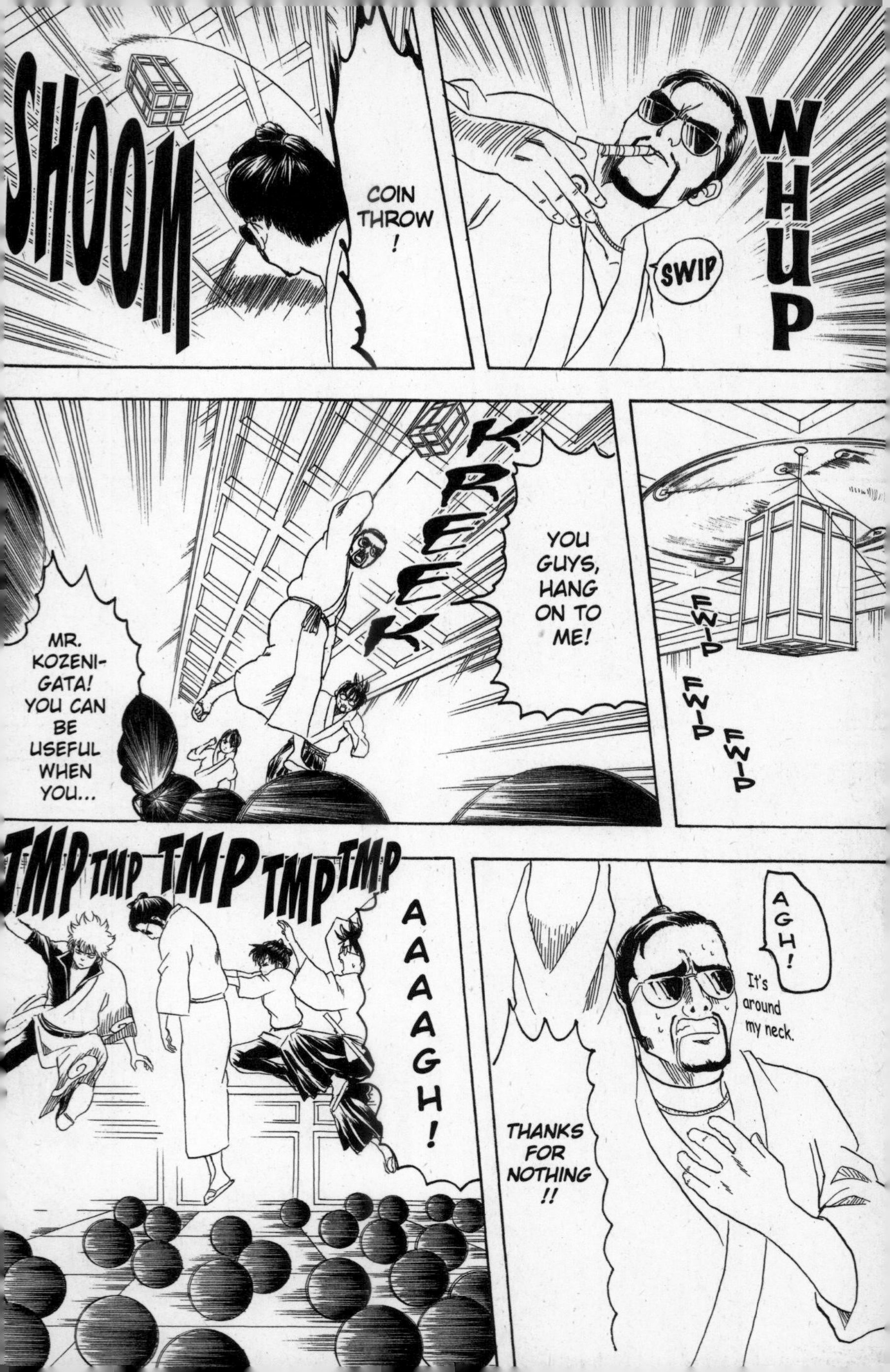
WHUP
SWIP
COIN THROW!
SHOOM
FWIP
FWIP
FWIP
KREEK
YOU GUYS, HANG ON TO ME!
MR. KOZENIGATA! YOU CAN BE USEFUL WHEN YOU...
AGH!
It's around my neck.
THANKS FOR NOTHING!!
TMP TMP TMP TMP TMP
AAAAAGH!

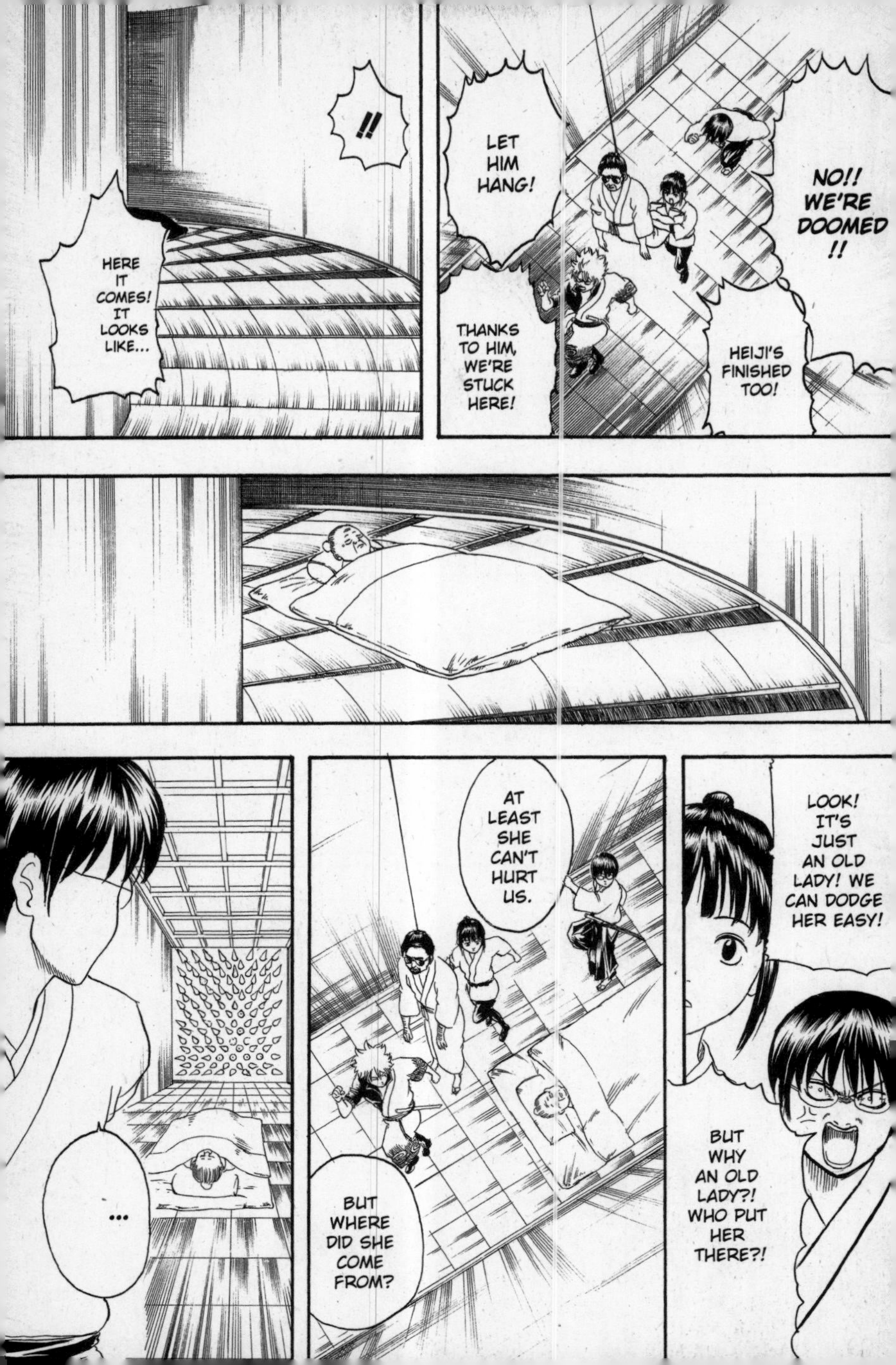
NO!! WE'RE DOOMED!!
LET HIM HANG!
HEIJI'S FINISHED TOO!
THANKS TO HIM, WE'RE STUCK HERE!
!!
HERE IT COMES! IT LOOKS LIKE...
LOOK! IT'S JUST AN OLD LADY! WE CAN DODGE HER EASY!
BUT WHY AN OLD LADY?! WHO PUT HER THERE?!
AT LEAST SHE CAN'T HURT US.
BUT WHERE DID SHE COME FROM?
...

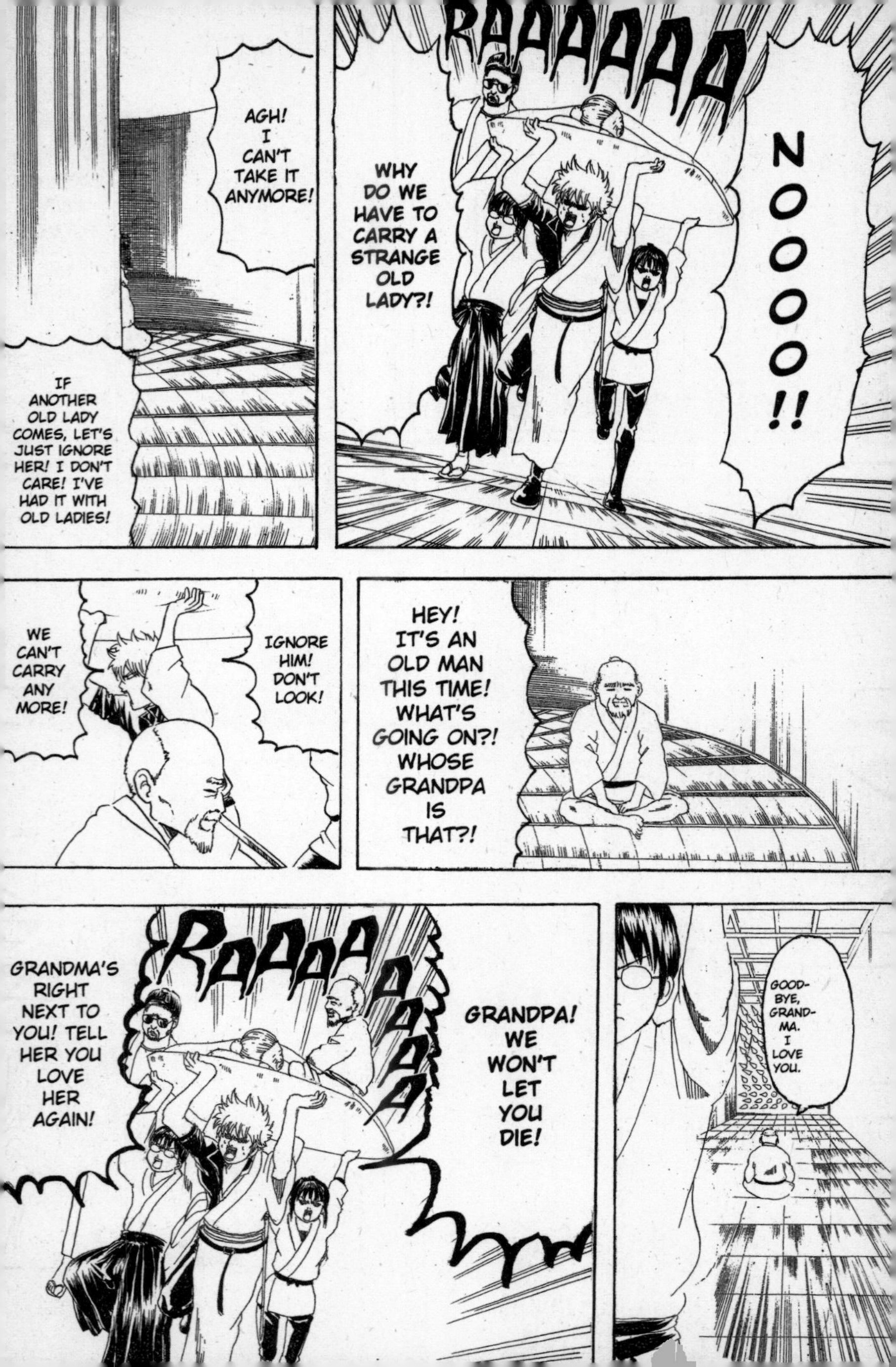

RAAAAAA
NOOOOO!!
WHY DO WE HAVE TO CARRY A STRANGE OLD LADY?!
AGH! I CAN'T TAKE IT ANYMORE!
IF ANOTHER OLD LADY COMES, LET'S JUST IGNORE HER! I DON'T CARE! I'VE HAD IT WITH OLD LADIES!
HEY! IT'S AN OLD MAN THIS TIME! WHAT'S GOING ON?! WHOSE GRANDPA IS THAT?!
IGNORE HIM! DON'T LOOK!
WE CAN'T CARRY ANY MORE!
GOOD-BYE, GRANDMA. I LOVE YOU.
GRANDPA! WE WON'T LET YOU DIE!
RAAAAAAAA
GRANDMA'S RIGHT NEXT TO YOU! TELL HER YOU LOVE HER AGAIN!

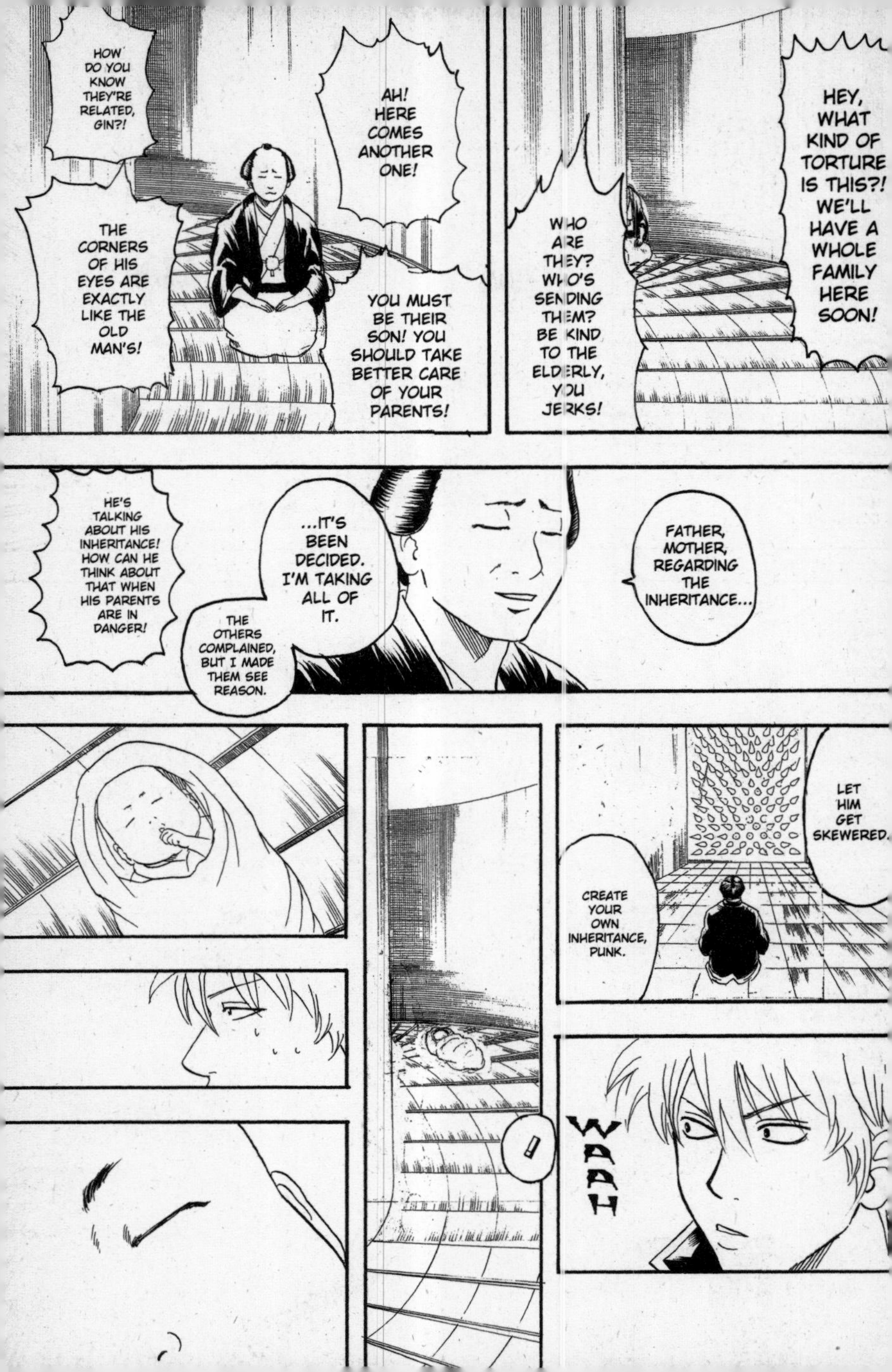
HEY, WHAT KIND OF TORTURE IS THIS?! WE'LL HAVE A WHOLE FAMILY HERE SOON!
WHO ARE THEY? WHO'S SENDING THEM? BE KIND TO THE ELDERLY, YOU JERKS!
AH! HERE COMES ANOTHER ONE!
YOU MUST BE THEIR SON! YOU SHOULD TAKE BETTER CARE OF YOUR PARENTS!
HOW DO YOU KNOW THEY'RE RELATED, GIN?!
THE CORNERS OF HIS EYES ARE EXACTLY LIKE THE OLD MAN'S!
FATHER, MOTHER, REGARDING THE INHERITANCE...
...IT'S BEEN DECIDED. I'M TAKING ALL OF IT.
THE OTHERS COMPLAINED, BUT I MADE THEM SEE REASON.
HE'S TALKING ABOUT HIS INHERITANCE! HOW CAN HE THINK ABOUT THAT WHEN HIS PARENTS ARE IN DANGER!
LET HIM GET SKEWERED.
CREATE YOUR OWN INHERITANCE, PUNK.
WAAH
!

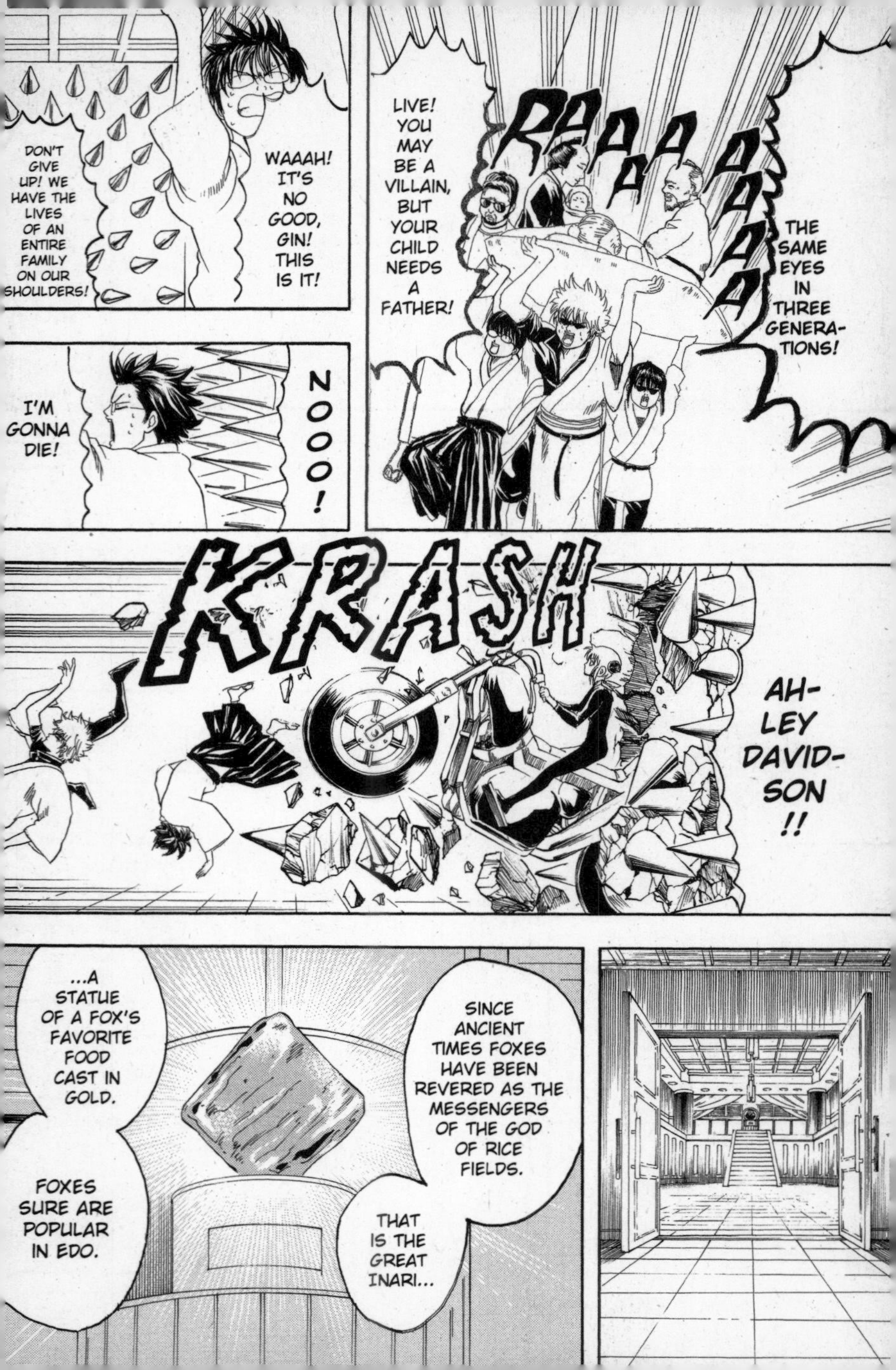
THE SAME EYES IN THREE GENERATIONS!
RAAAAAAAAAA
LIVE! YOU MAY BE A VILLAIN, BUT YOUR CHILD NEEDS A FATHER!
WAAAH! IT'S NO GOOD, GIN! THIS IS IT!
DON'T GIVE UP! WE HAVE THE LIVES OF AN ENTIRE FAMILY ON OUR SHOULDERS!
NOOOO!
I'M GONNA DIE!
AH-LEY DAVIDSON!!
KRASH
SINCE ANCIENT TIMES FOXES HAVE BEEN REVERED AS THE MESSENGERS OF THE GOD OF RICE FIELDS.
THAT IS THE GREAT INARI...
...A STATUE OF A FOX'S FAVORITE FOOD CAST IN GOLD.
FOXES SURE ARE POPULAR IN EDO.

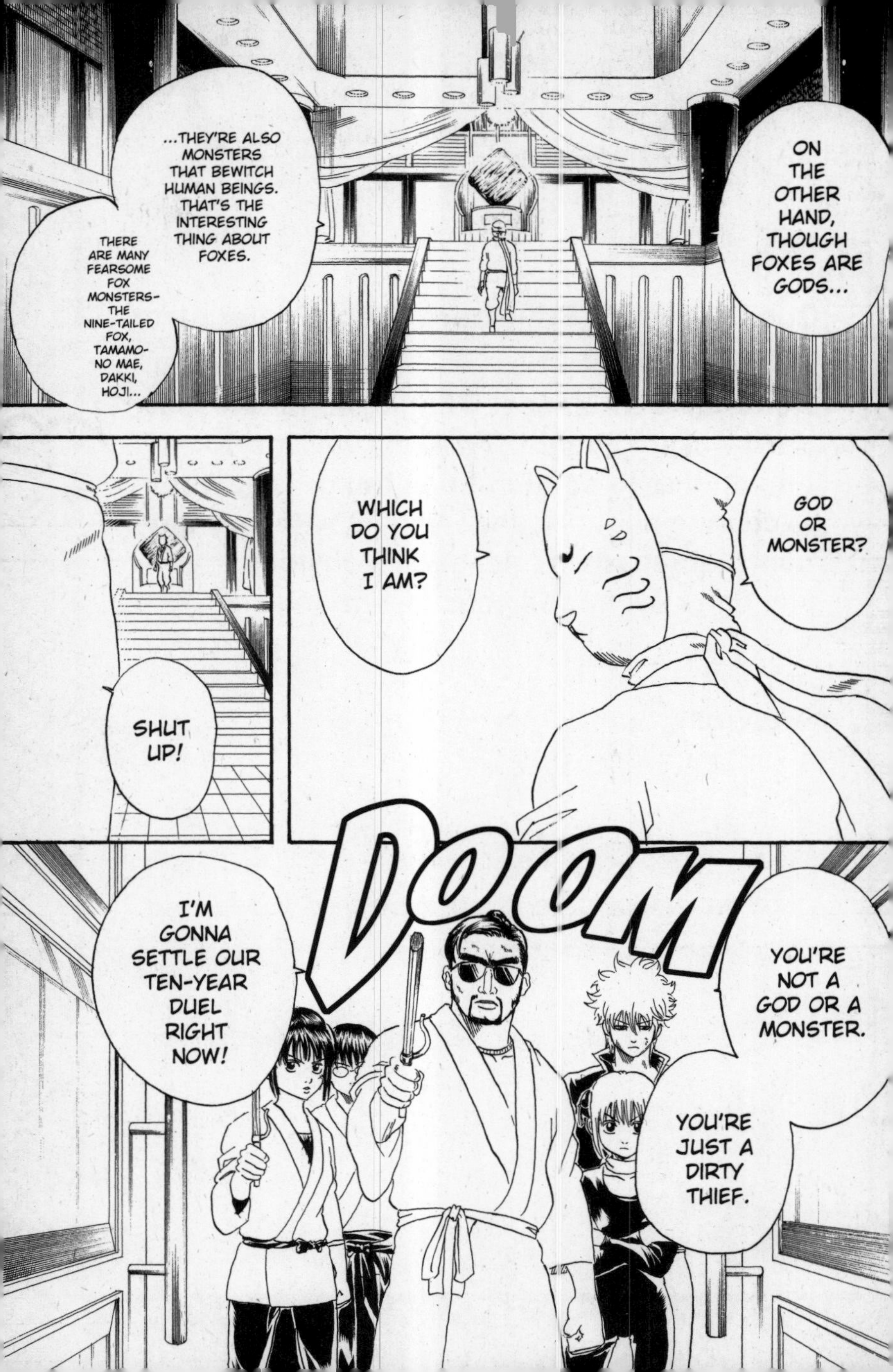
ON THE OTHER HAND, THOUGH FOXES ARE GODS...
...THEY'RE ALSO MONSTERS THAT BEWITCH HUMAN BEINGS. THAT'S THE INTERESTING THING ABOUT FOXES.
THERE ARE MANY FEARSOME FOX MONSTERS- THE NINE-TAILED FOX, TAMAMO-NO MAE, DAKKI, HOJI...
GOD OR MONSTER?
WHICH DO YOU THINK I AM?
SHUT UP!
DOOM
YOU'RE NOT A GOD OR A MONSTER.
YOU'RE JUST A DIRTY THIEF.
I'M GONNA SETTLE OUR TEN-YEAR DUEL RIGHT NOW!

<Question from Fujii from Aichi Prefecture>

Hello, Sorachi Sensei. Thank you for all your hard work. I bought *Gin Tama* volume 15. I'd just like to point out one thing. That whole exchange about Hasegawa, his wife and the doorplate made no sense. It's obvious that you don't even read your own manga.

<Answer>

I'm sorry.
You're absolutely right.
Sometimes I get confused and mix up things like that.

I'll try to do better in the future.

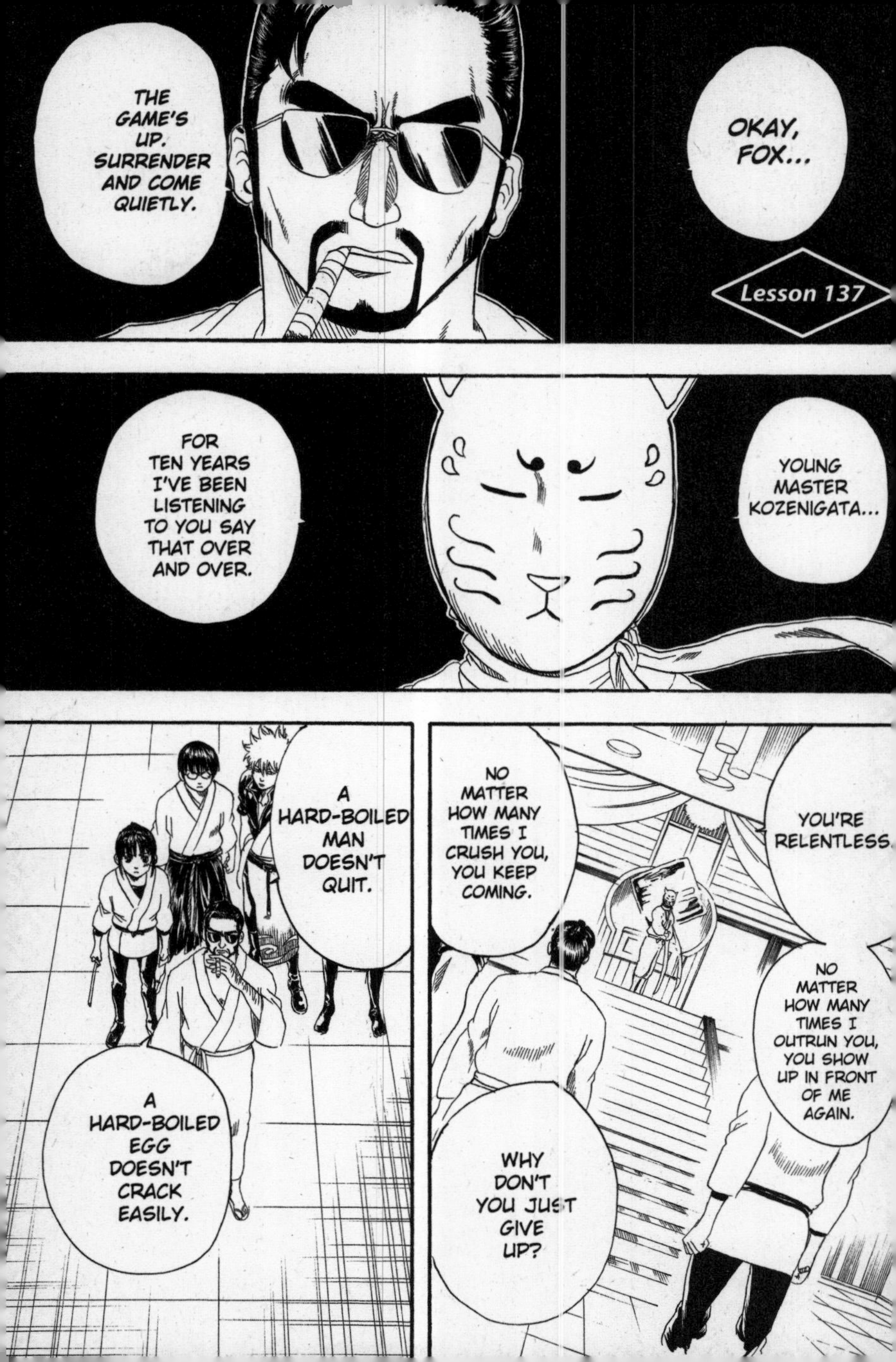
OKAY, FOX...
Lesson 137
THE GAME'S UP. SURRENDER AND COME QUIETLY.
YOUNG MASTER KOZENIGATA...
FOR TEN YEARS I'VE BEEN LISTENING TO YOU SAY THAT OVER AND OVER.
YOU'RE RELENTLESS.
NO MATTER HOW MANY TIMES I OUTRUN YOU, YOU SHOW UP IN FRONT OF ME AGAIN.
NO MATTER HOW MANY TIMES I CRUSH YOU, YOU KEEP COMING.
WHY DON'T YOU JUST GIVE UP?
A HARD-BOILED MAN DOESN'T QUIT.
A HARD-BOILED EGG DOESN'T CRACK EASILY.

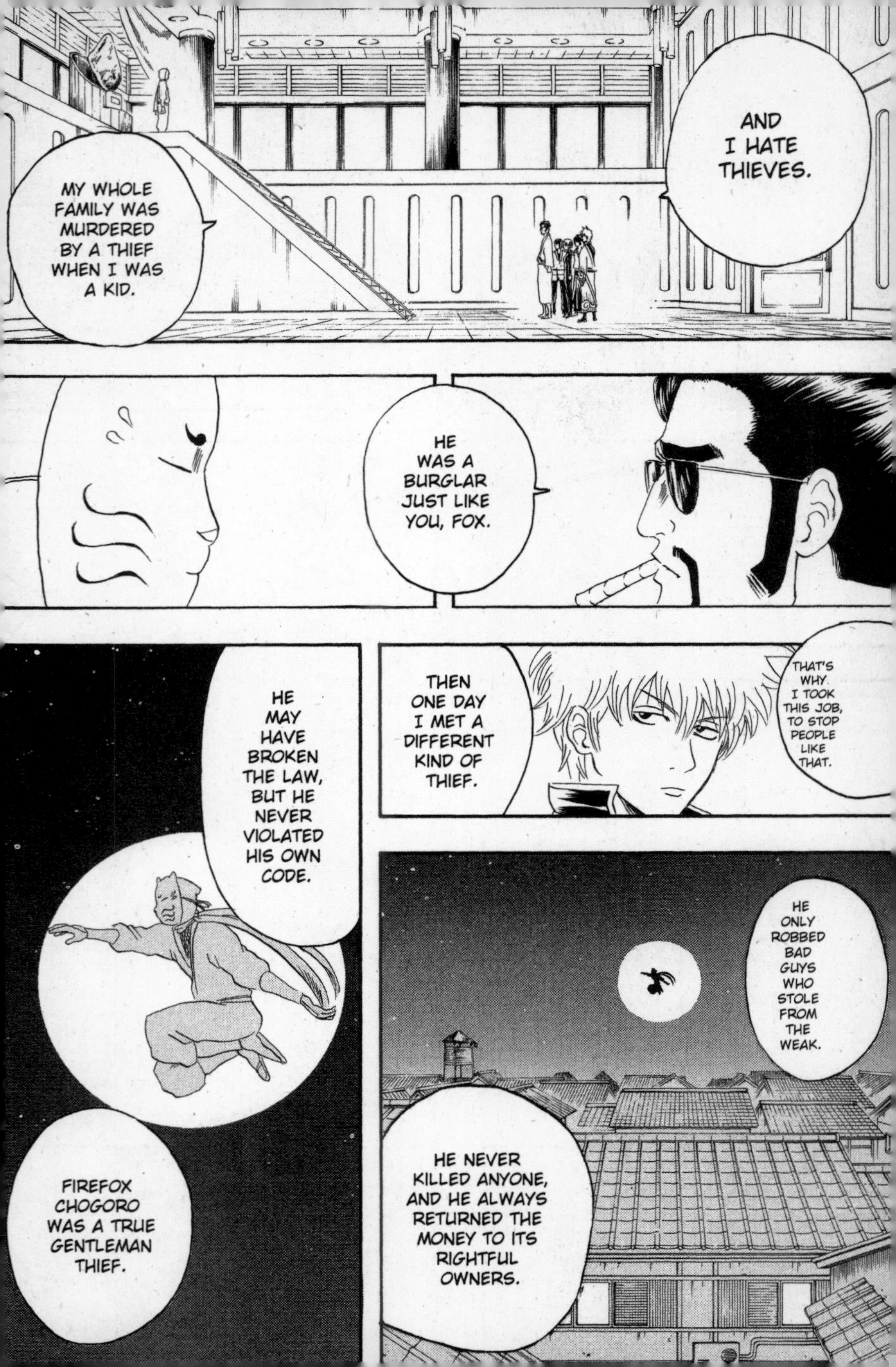
AND I HATE THIEVES.
MY WHOLE FAMILY WAS MURDERED BY A THIEF WHEN I WAS A KID.
HE WAS A BURGLAR JUST LIKE YOU, FOX.
THAT'S WHY. I TOOK THIS JOB, TO STOP PEOPLE LIKE THAT.
THEN ONE DAY I MET A DIFFERENT KIND OF THIEF.
HE ONLY ROBBED BAD GUYS WHO STOLE FROM THE WEAK.
HE NEVER KILLED ANYONE, AND HE ALWAYS RETURNED THE MONEY TO ITS RIGHTFUL OWNERS.
HE MAY HAVE BROKEN THE LAW, BUT HE NEVER VIOLATED HIS OWN CODE.
FIREFOX CHOGORO WAS A TRUE GENTLEMAN THIEF.

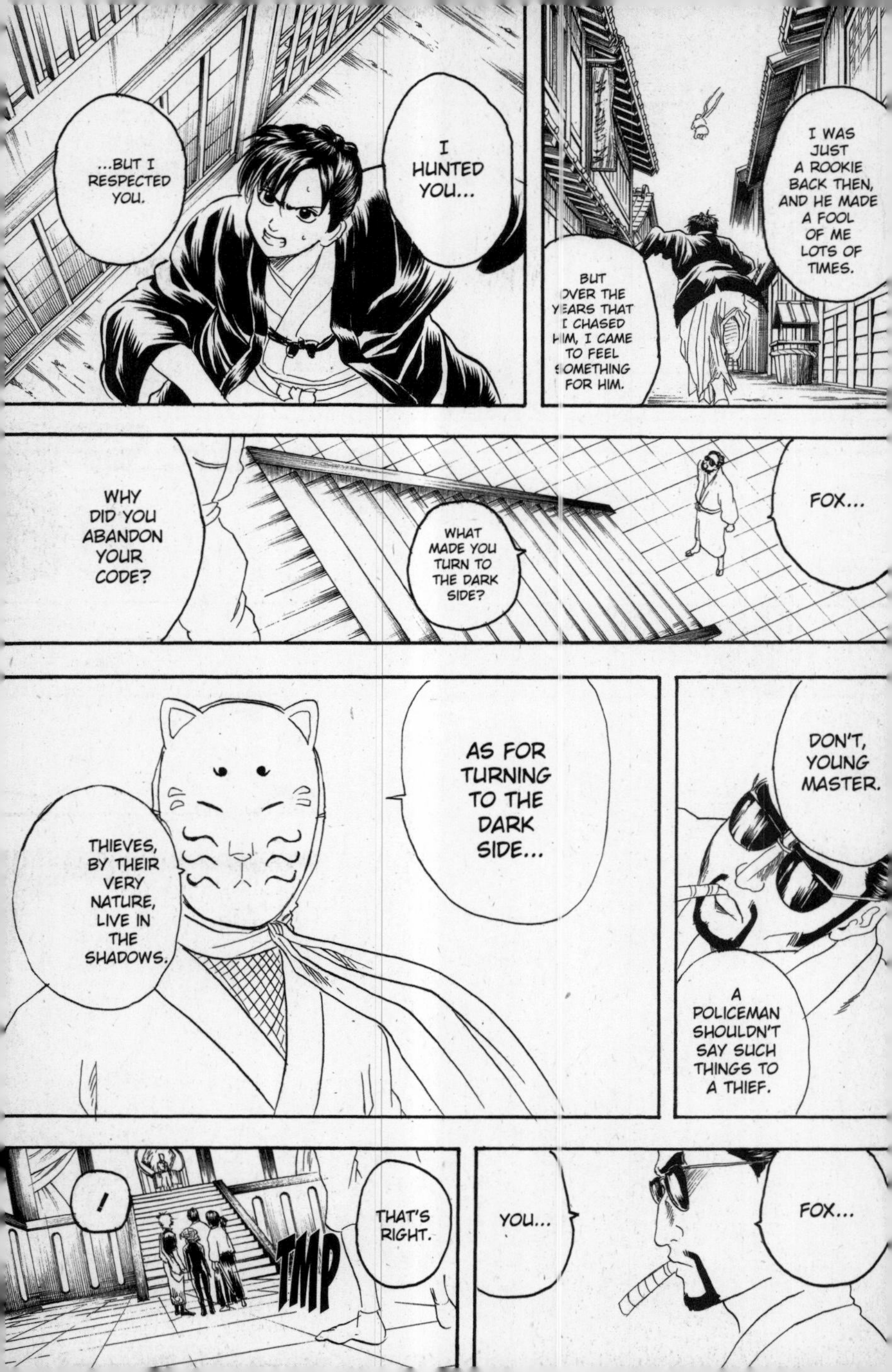
I WAS JUST A ROOKIE BACK THEN, AND HE MADE A FOOL OF ME LOTS OF TIMES.
BUT OVER THE YEARS THAT I CHASED HIM, I CAME TO FEEL SOMETHING FOR HIM.
I HUNTED YOU...
...BUT I RESPECTED YOU.
FOX...
WHAT MADE YOU TURN TO THE DARK SIDE?
WHY DID YOU ABANDON YOUR CODE?
DON'T, YOUNG MASTER.
A POLICEMAN SHOULDN'T SAY SUCH THINGS TO A THIEF.
AS FOR TURNING TO THE DARK SIDE...
THIEVES, BY THEIR VERY NATURE, LIVE IN THE SHADOWS.
FOX...
YOU...
THAT'S RIGHT.
TMP
!

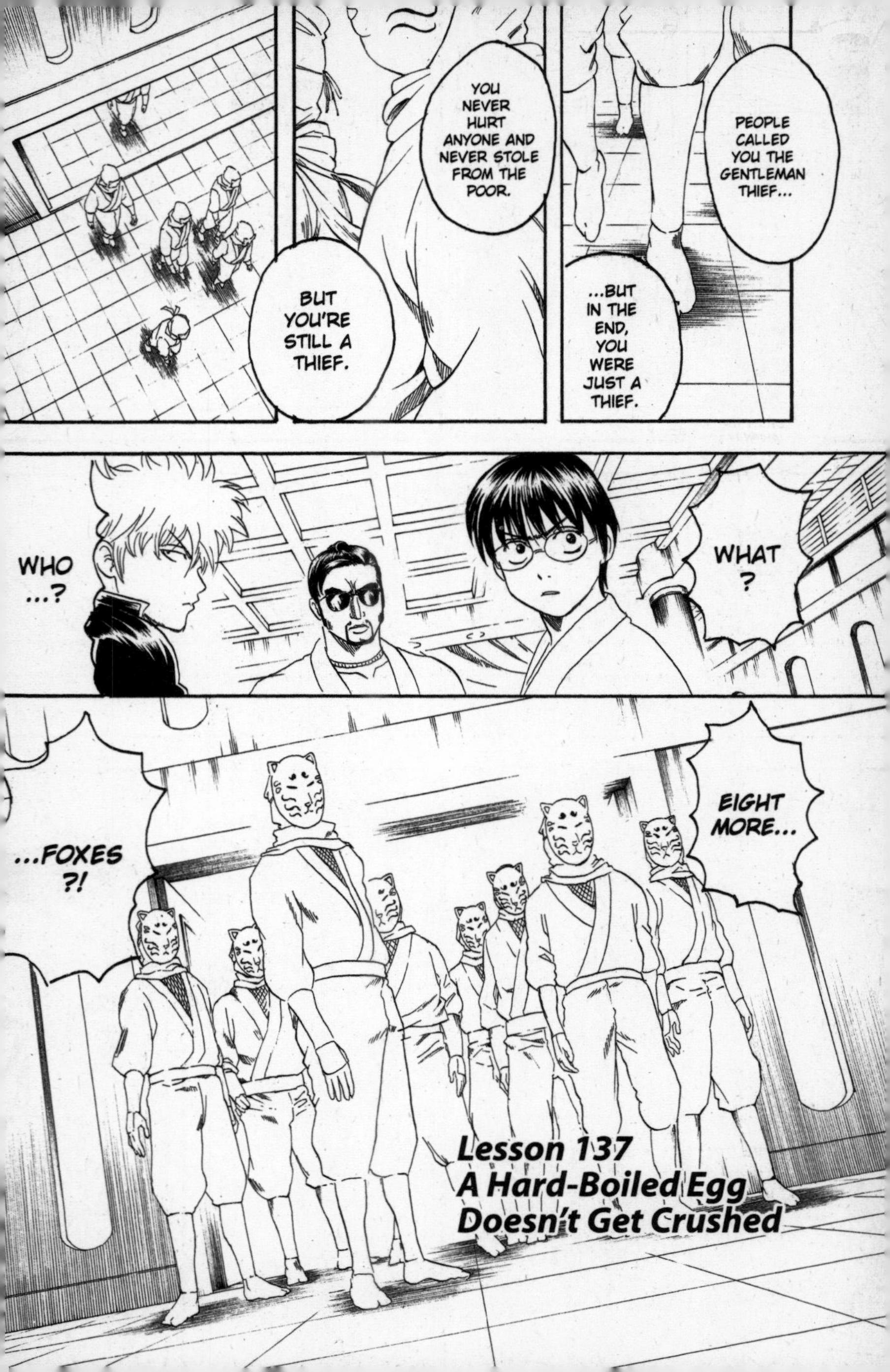
PEOPLE CALLED YOU THE GENTLEMAN THIEF...
...BUT IN THE END, YOU WERE JUST A THIEF.
YOU NEVER HURT ANYONE AND NEVER STOLE FROM THE POOR.
BUT YOU'RE STILL A THIEF.
WHAT ?
WHO ...?
EIGHT MORE...
...FOXES ?!
Lesson 137
A Hard-Boiled Egg Doesn't Get Crushed

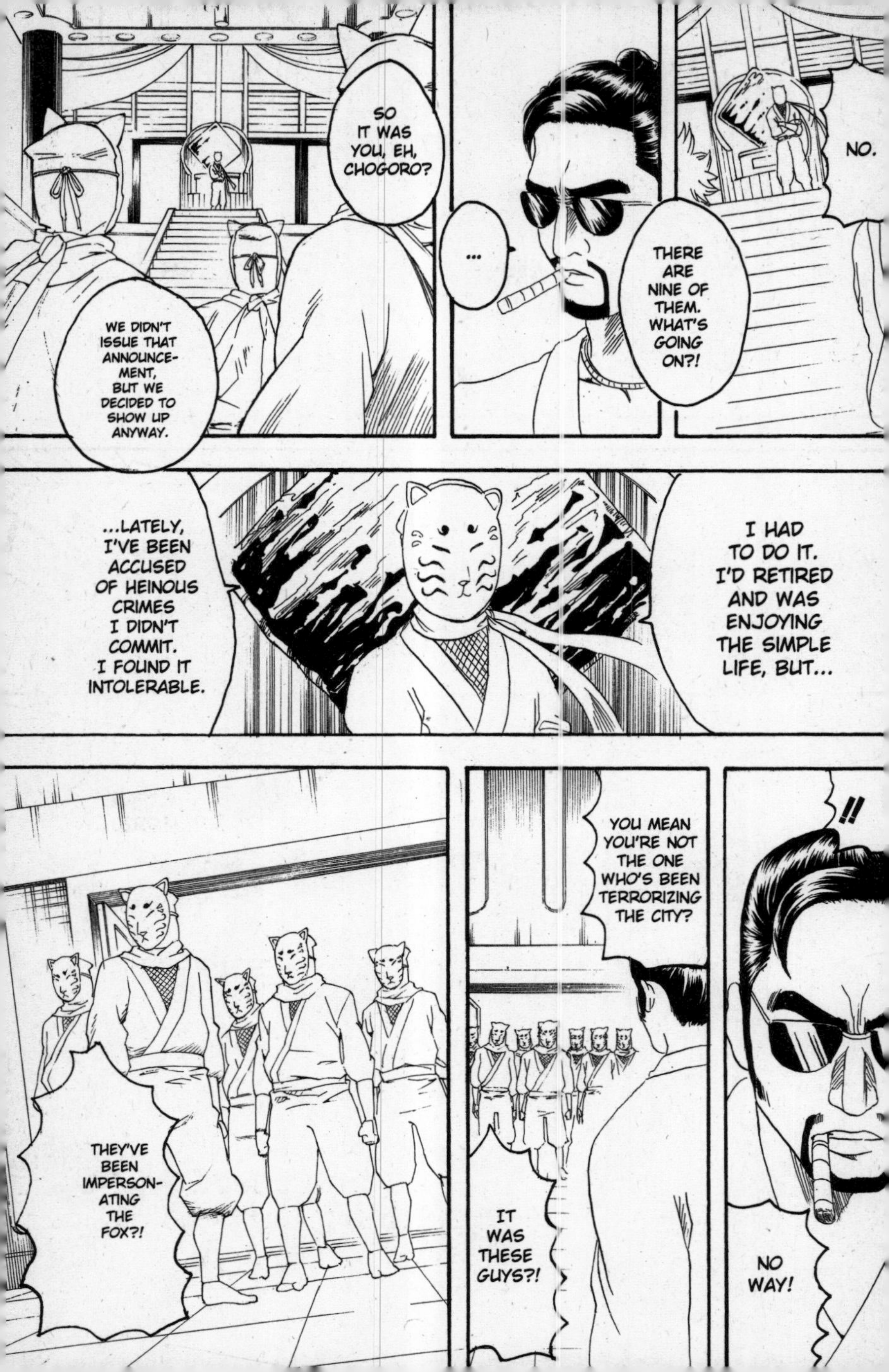
NO.
THERE ARE NINE OF THEM. WHAT'S GOING ON?!
...
SO IT WAS YOU, EH, CHOGORO?
WE DIDN'T ISSUE THAT ANNOUNCEMENT, BUT WE DECIDED TO SHOW UP ANYWAY.
I HAD TO DO IT. I'D RETIRED AND WAS ENJOYING THE SIMPLE LIFE, BUT...
...LATELY, I'VE BEEN ACCUSED OF HEINOUS CRIMES I DIDN'T COMMIT. I FOUND IT INTOLERABLE.
!!
NO WAY!
YOU MEAN YOU'RE NOT THE ONE WHO'S BEEN TERRORIZING THE CITY?
IT WAS THESE GUYS?!
THEY'VE BEEN IMPERSONATING THE FOX?!

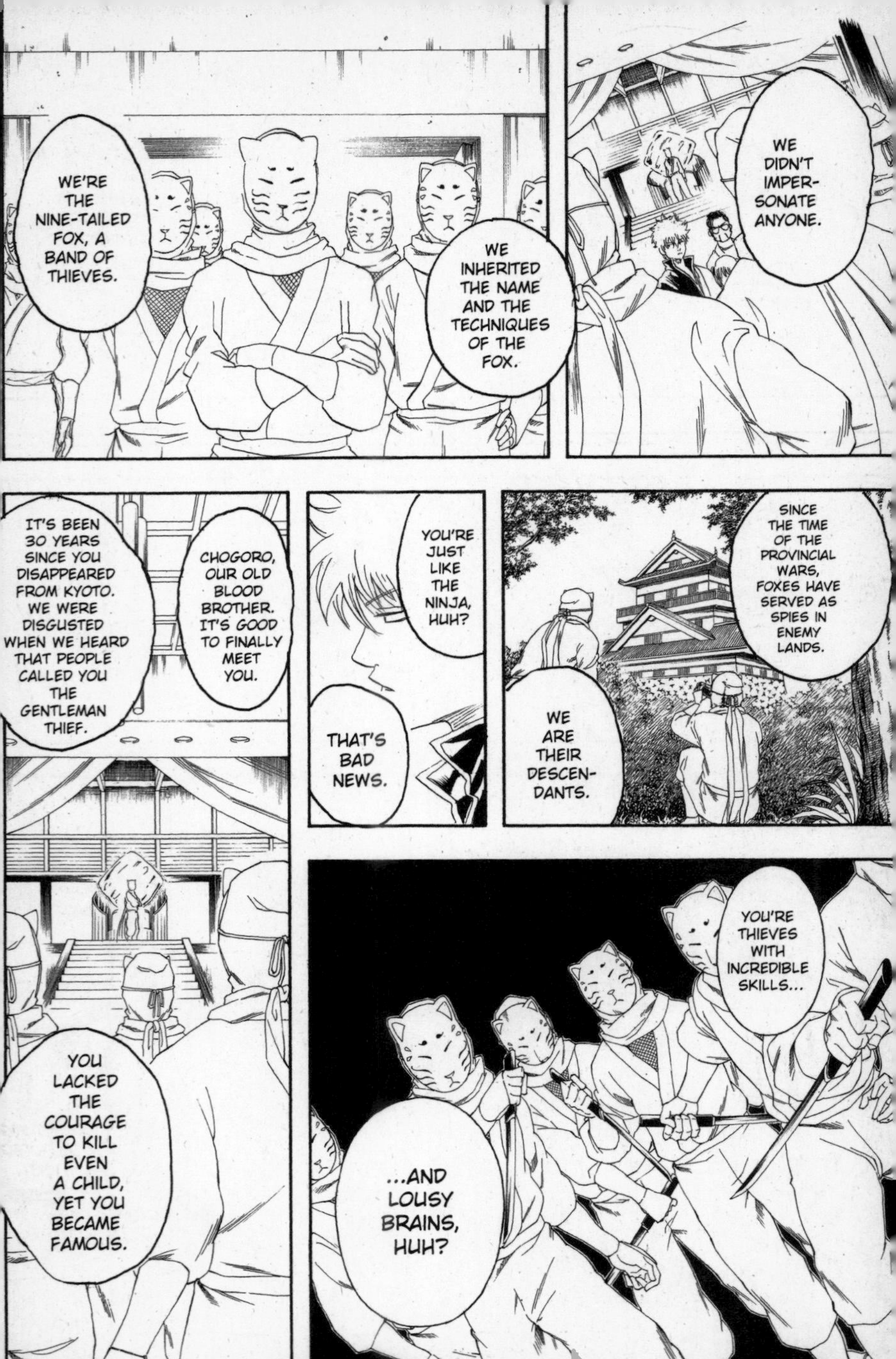
WE DIDN'T IMPERSONATE ANYONE.
WE'RE THE NINE-TAILED FOX, A BAND OF THIEVES.
WE INHERITED THE NAME AND THE TECHNIQUES OF THE FOX.
SINCE THE TIME OF THE PROVINCIAL WARS, FOXES HAVE SERVED AS SPIES IN ENEMY LANDS.
WE ARE THEIR DESCENDANTS.
YOU'RE JUST LIKE THE NINJA, HUH?
THAT'S BAD NEWS.
CHOGORO, OUR OLD BLOOD BROTHER. IT'S GOOD TO FINALLY MEET YOU.
IT'S BEEN 30 YEARS SINCE YOU DISAPPEARED FROM KYOTO. WE WERE DISGUSTED WHEN WE HEARD THAT PEOPLE CALLED YOU THE GENTLEMAN THIEF.
YOU LACKED THE COURAGE TO KILL EVEN A CHILD, YET YOU BECAME FAMOUS.
YOU'RE THIEVES WITH INCREDIBLE SKILLS...
...AND LOUSY BRAINS, HUH?

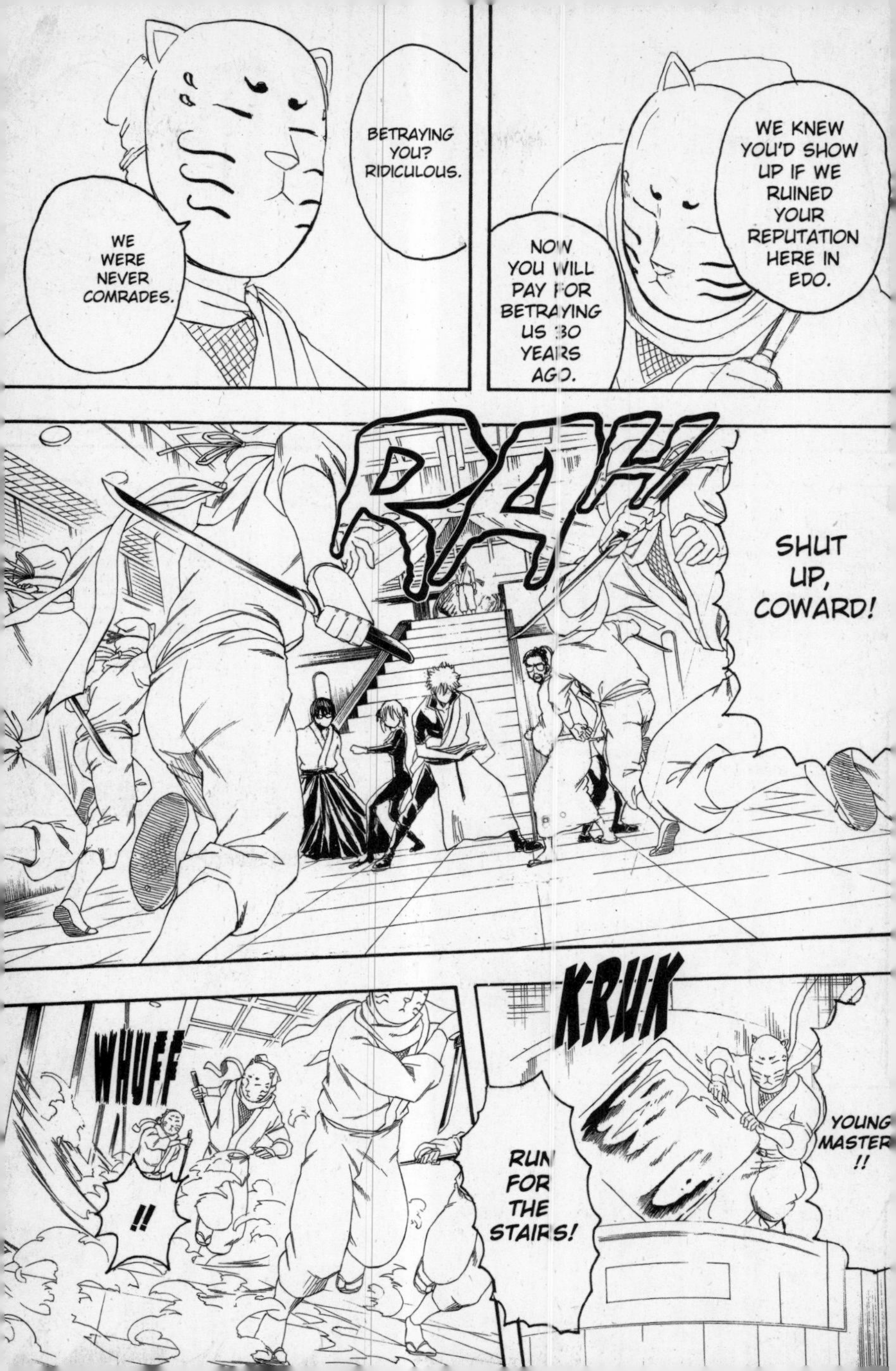
WE KNEW YOU'D SHOW UP IF WE RUINED YOUR REPUTATION HERE IN EDO.
NOW YOU WILL PAY FOR BETRAYING US 30 YEARS AGO.
BETRAYING YOU? RIDICULOUS.
WE WERE NEVER COMRADES.
RAH
SHUT UP, COWARD!
KRUK
YOUNG MASTER!!
RUN FOR THE STAIRS!
WHUFF
!!

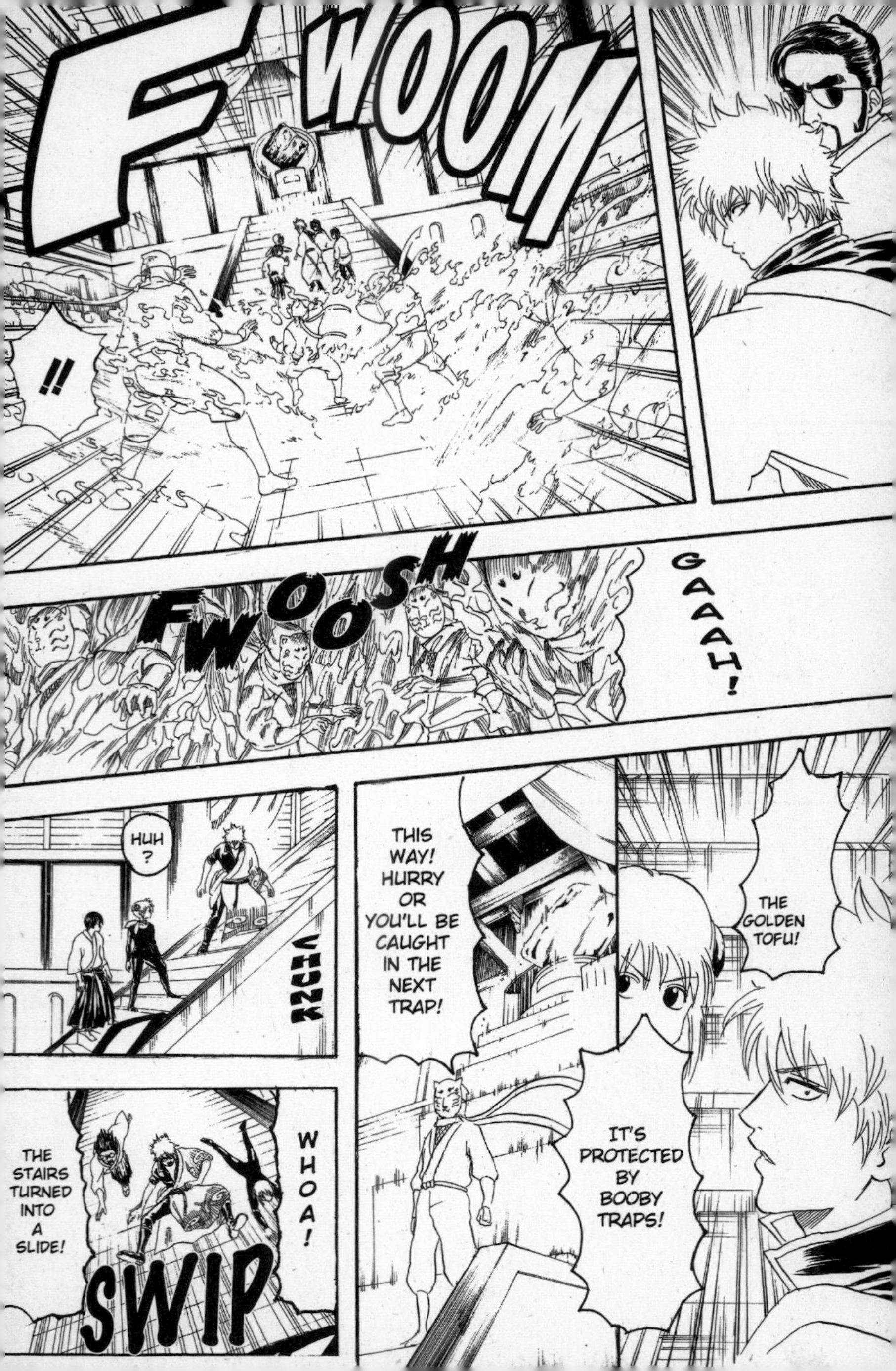
FWOOM
!!
FWOOSH
GAAAH!
THE GOLDEN TOFU!
IT'S PROTECTED BY BOOBY TRAPS!
THIS WAY! HURRY OR YOU'LL BE CAUGHT IN THE NEXT TRAP!
HUH?
CHUNK
WHOA!
THE STAIRS TURNED INTO A SLIDE!
SWIP

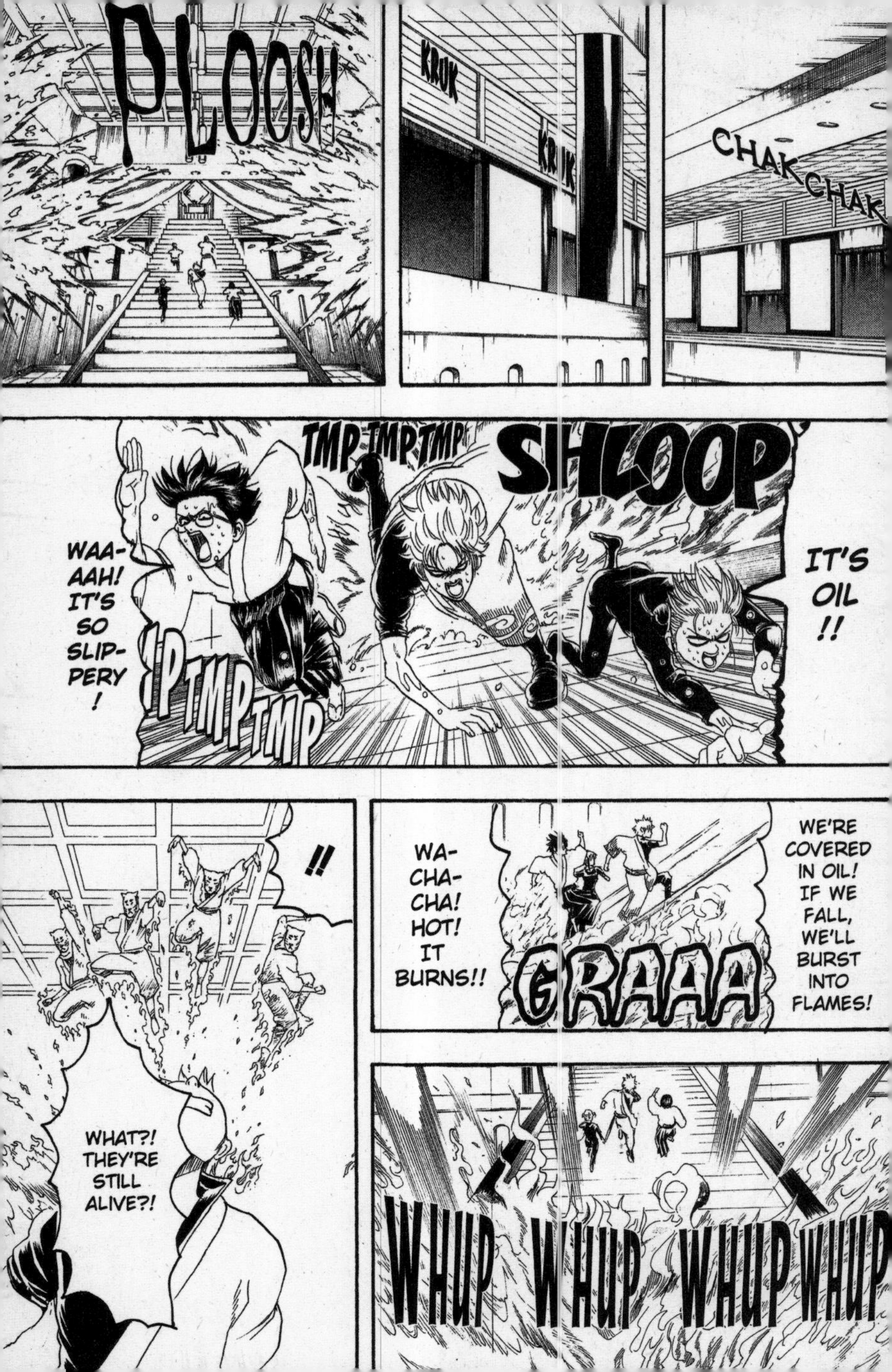
CHAKCHAK
KRUK
KRUK
PLOOSH
IT'S OIL!!
SHLOOP
TMP TMP TMP
WAA-AAH! IT'S SO SLIPPERY!
TMP TMP TMP
WE'RE COVERED IN OIL! IF WE FALL, WE'LL BURST INTO FLAMES!
GRAAA
WA-CHA-CHA! HOT! IT BURNS!!
WHUP WHUP WHUP WHUP
!!
WHAT?! THEY'RE STILL ALIVE?!

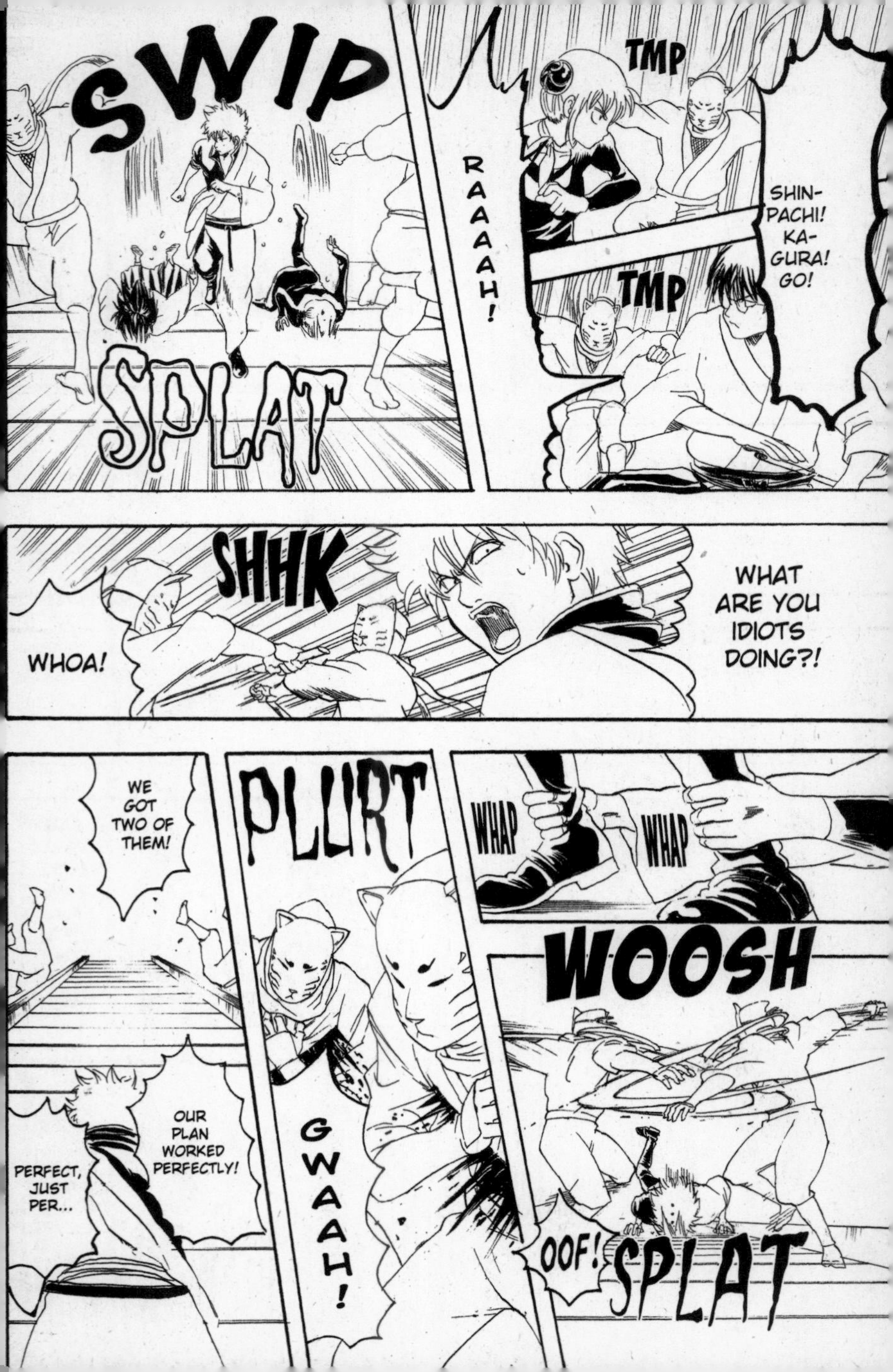
TMP
SHIN-PACHI! KA-GURA! GO!
TMP
RAAAAAH!
SWIP
SPLAT
WHAT ARE YOU IDIOTS DOING?!
SHHK
WHOA!
WHAP
WHAP
WOOSH
OOF!
SPLAT
PLURT
GWAAH!
WE GOT TWO OF THEM!
OUR PLAN WORKED PERFECTLY!
PERFECT, JUST PER...

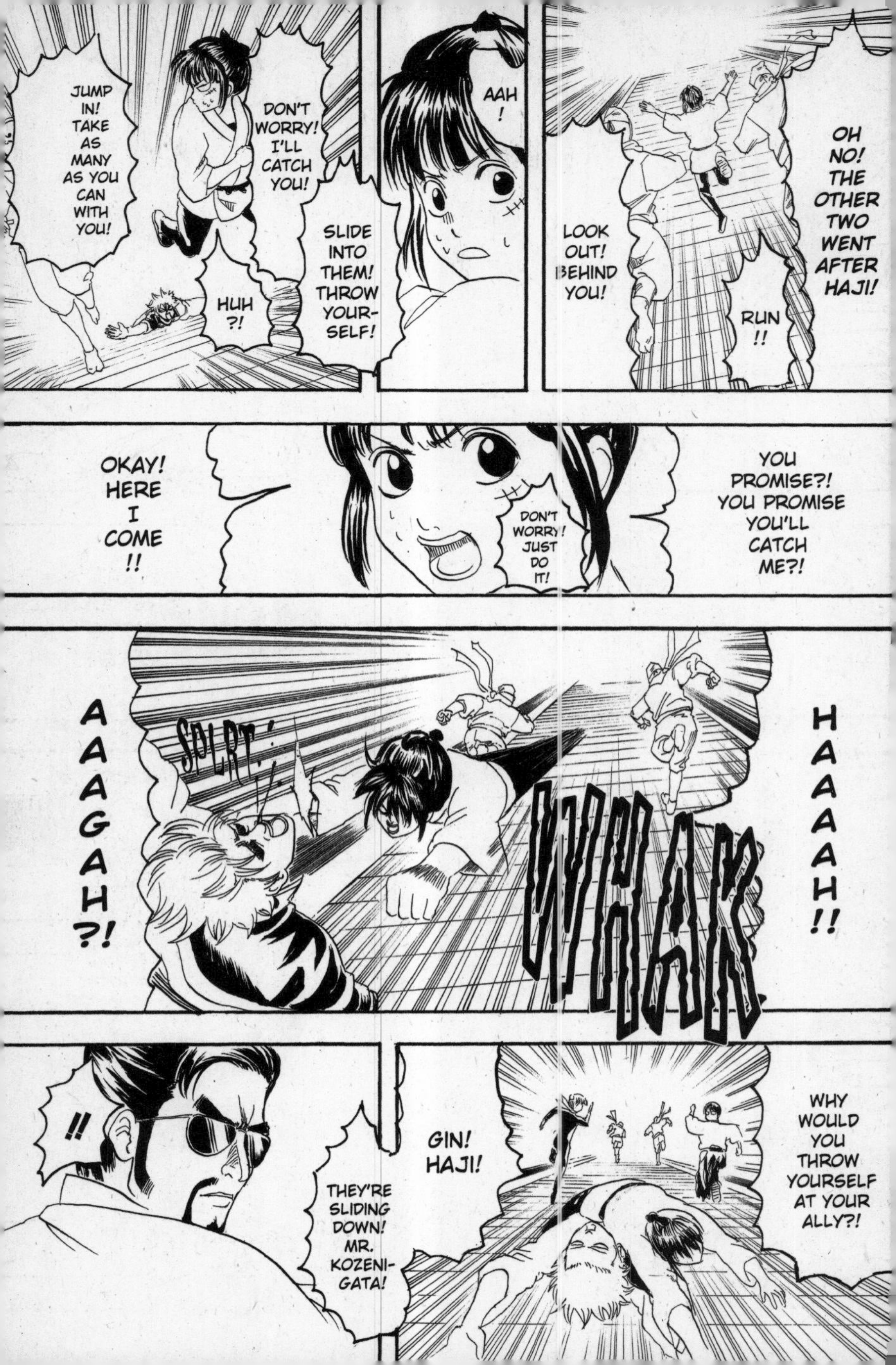
OH NO! THE OTHER TWO WENT AFTER HAJI!
RUN!!
LOOK OUT! BEHIND YOU!
AAH!
SLIDE INTO THEM! THROW YOURSELF!
DON'T WORRY! I'LL CATCH YOU!
JUMP IN! TAKE AS MANY AS YOU CAN WITH YOU!
HUH?!
YOU PROMISE?! YOU PROMISE YOU'LL CATCH ME?!
DON'T WORRY! JUST DO IT!
OKAY! HERE I COME!!
HAAAAAH!!
WHAK
SPLRT
AAAAGAH?!
WHY WOULD YOU THROW YOURSELF AT YOUR ALLY?!
GIN! HAJI!
THEY'RE SLIDING DOWN! MR. KOZENIGATA!
!!

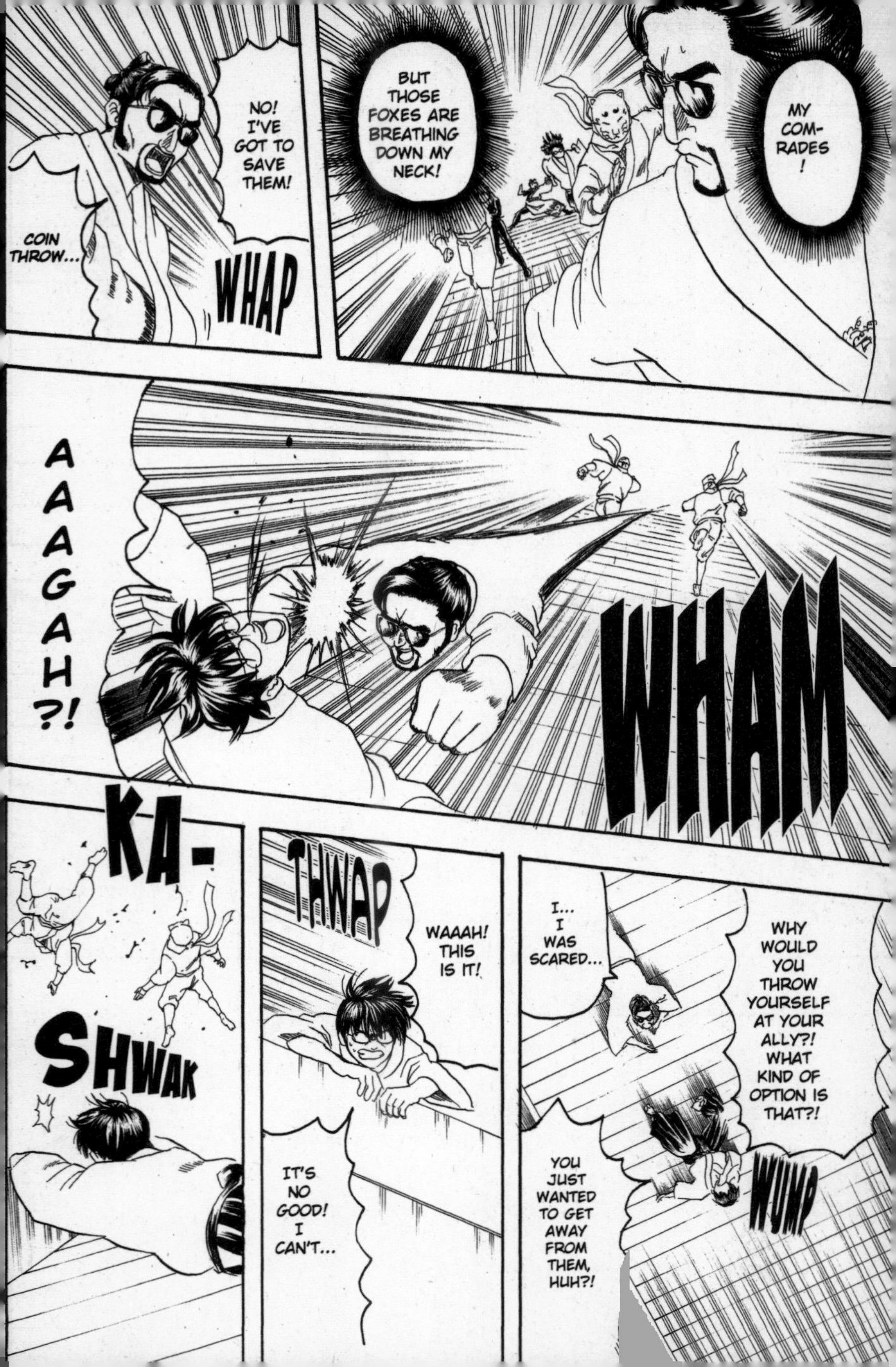
MY COM-RADES!
BUT THOSE FOXES ARE BREATHING DOWN MY NECK!
NO! I'VE GOT TO SAVE THEM!
COIN THROW...
WHAP
WHAM
AAAAGAH?!
WHY WOULD YOU THROW YOURSELF AT YOUR ALLY?! WHAT KIND OF OPTION IS THAT?!
I... I WAS SCARED...
WUMP
YOU JUST WANTED TO GET AWAY FROM THEM, HUH?!
THWAP
WAAAH! THIS IS IT!
IT'S NO GOOD! I CAN'T...
KA-SHWAK

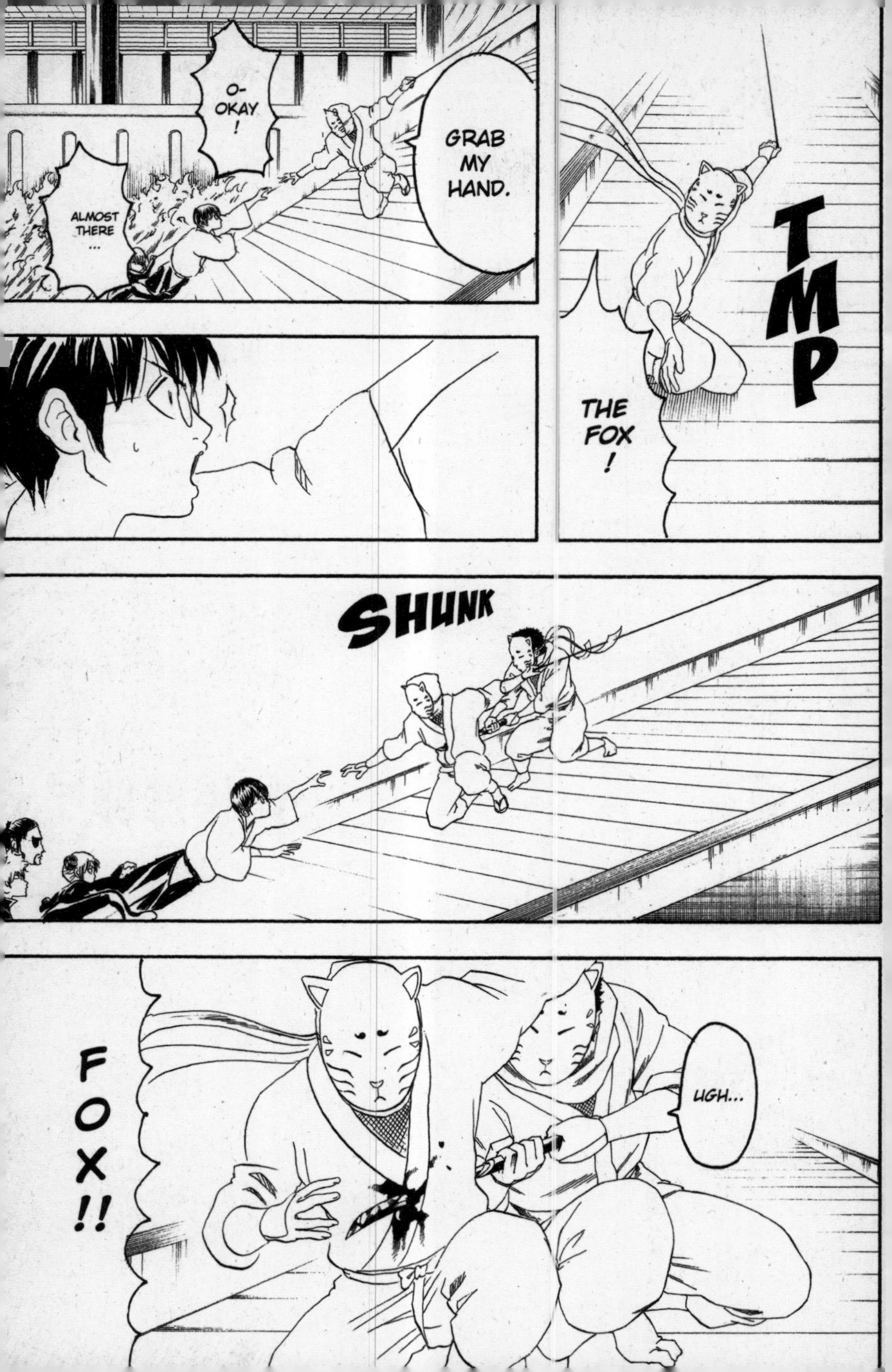
TMP
THE FOX!
GRAB MY HAND.
O-OKAY!
ALMOST THERE...
SHUNK
UGH...
FOX!!

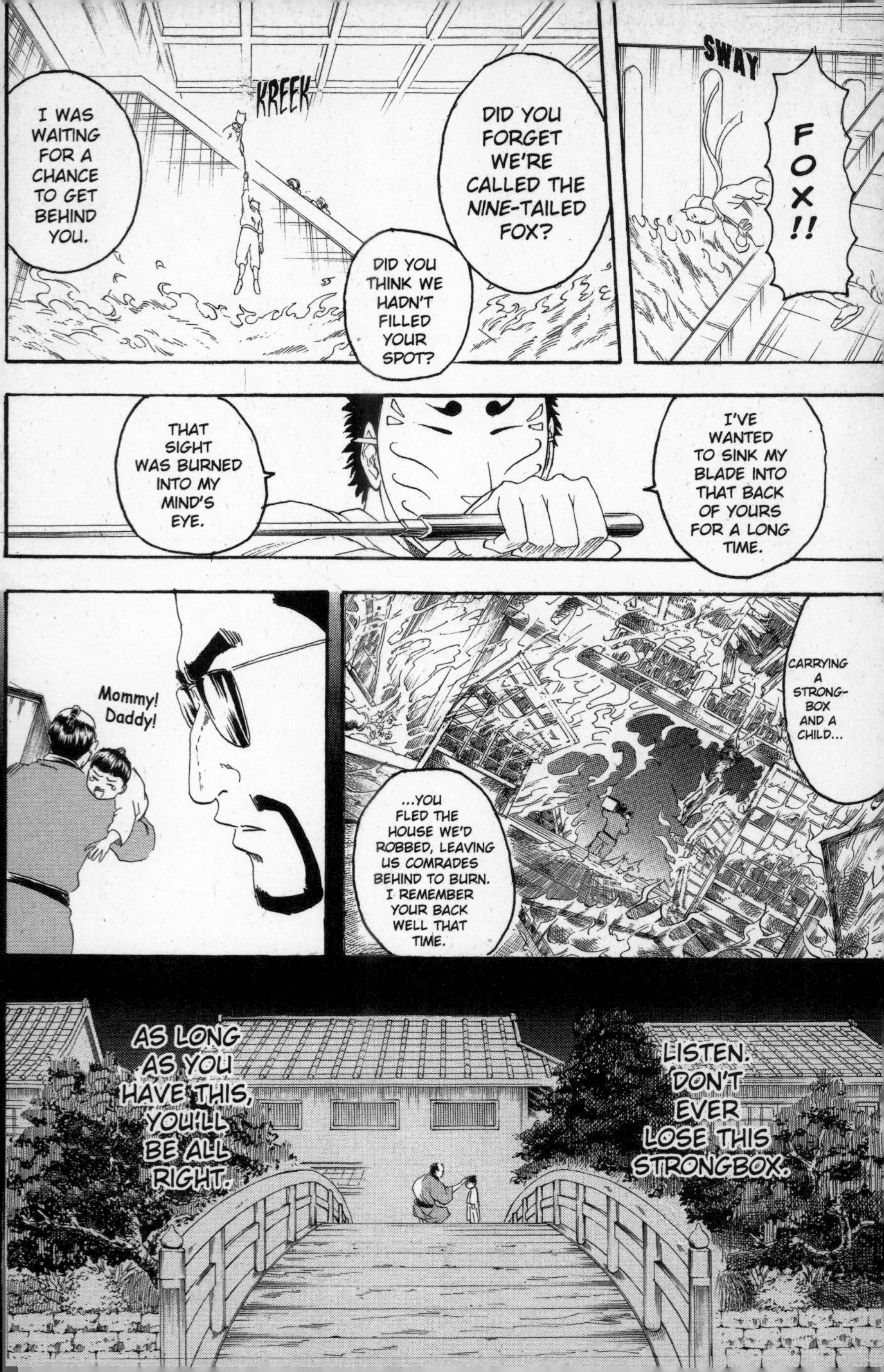
SWAY
FOX!!
DID YOU FORGET WE'RE CALLED THE NINE-TAILED FOX?
DID YOU THINK WE HADN'T FILLED YOUR SPOT?
KREEK
I WAS WAITING FOR A CHANCE TO GET BEHIND YOU.
I'VE WANTED TO SINK MY BLADE INTO THAT BACK OF YOURS FOR A LONG TIME.
THAT SIGHT WAS BURNED INTO MY MIND'S EYE.
CARRYING A STRONG-BOX AND A CHILD...
...YOU FLED THE HOUSE WE'D ROBBED, LEAVING US COMRADES BEHIND TO BURN. I REMEMBER YOUR BACK WELL THAT TIME.
Mommy! Daddy!
LISTEN. DON'T EVER LOSE THIS STRONGBOX.
AS LONG AS YOU HAVE THIS, YOU'LL BE ALL RIGHT.

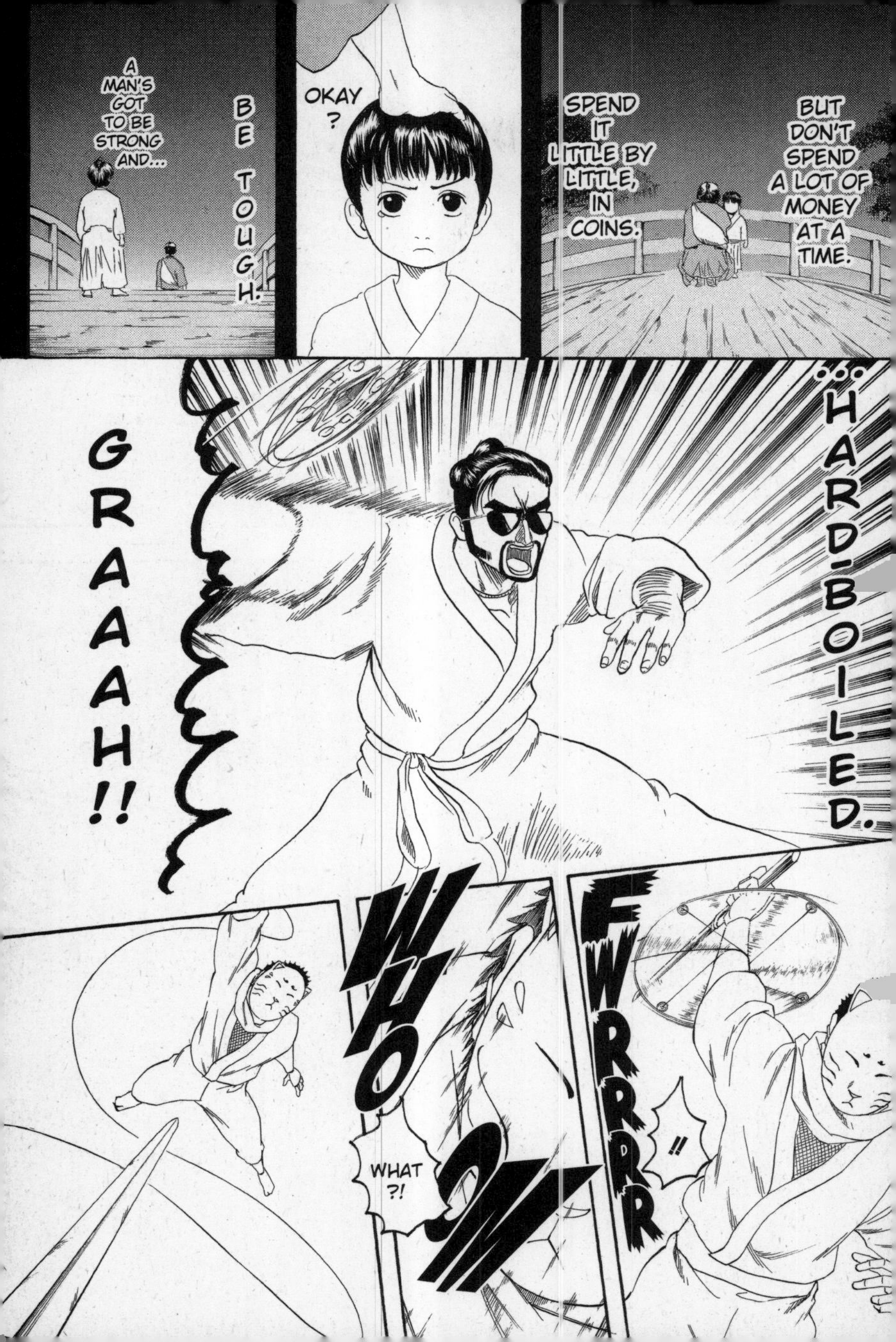

BUT DON'T SPEND A LOT OF MONEY AT A TIME.
SPEND IT LITTLE BY LITTLE, IN COINS.
OKAY ?
BE TOUGH.
A MAN'S GOT TO BE STRONG AND...
...HARD-BOILED.
GRAAAH!!
FWRRRR
!!
WHOOSH
WHAT ?!

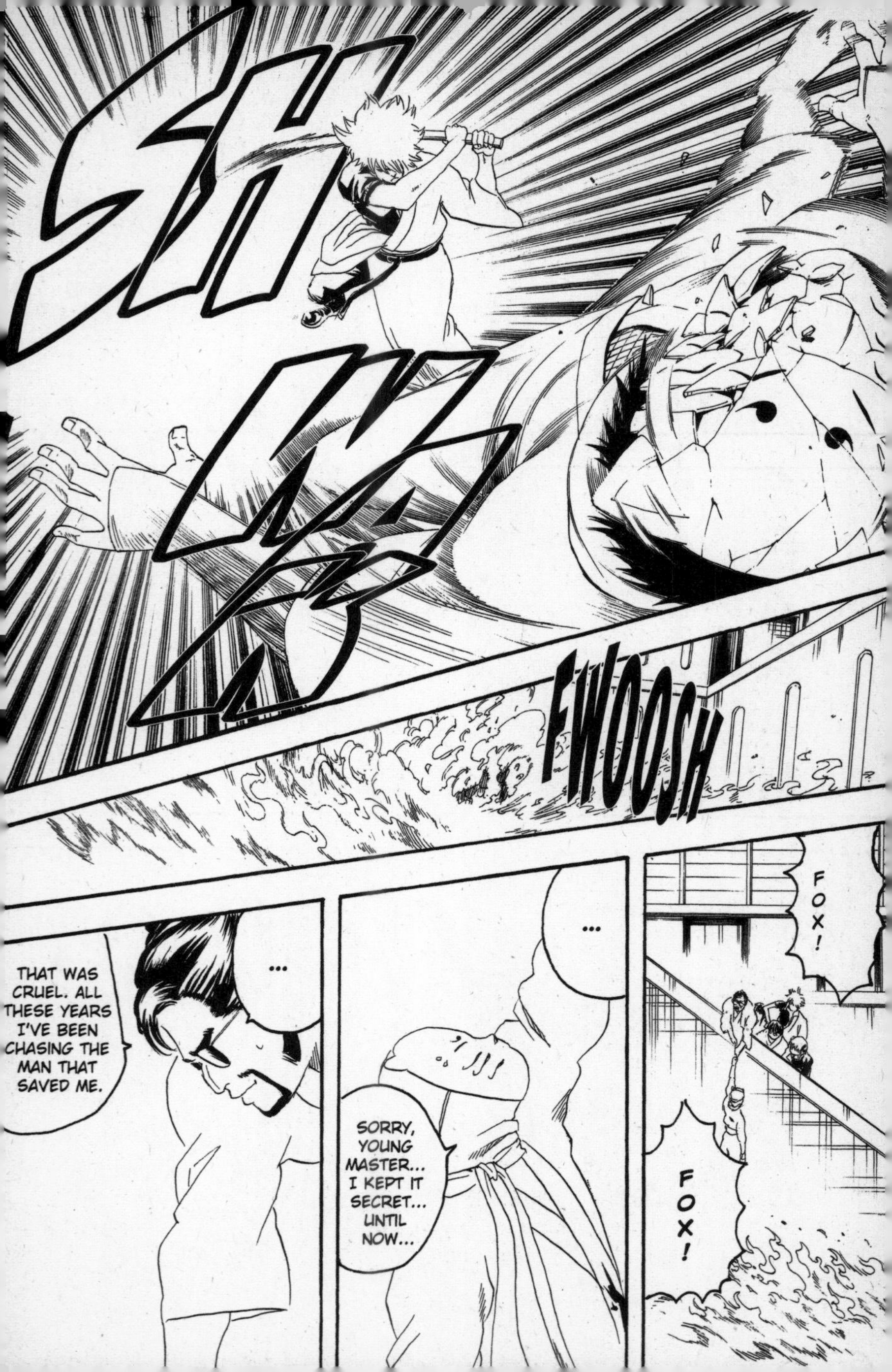
FWOOSH
FOX!
FOX!
...
SORRY, YOUNG MASTER... I KEPT IT SECRET... UNTIL NOW...
...
THAT WAS CRUEL. ALL THESE YEARS I'VE BEEN CHASING THE MAN THAT SAVED ME.

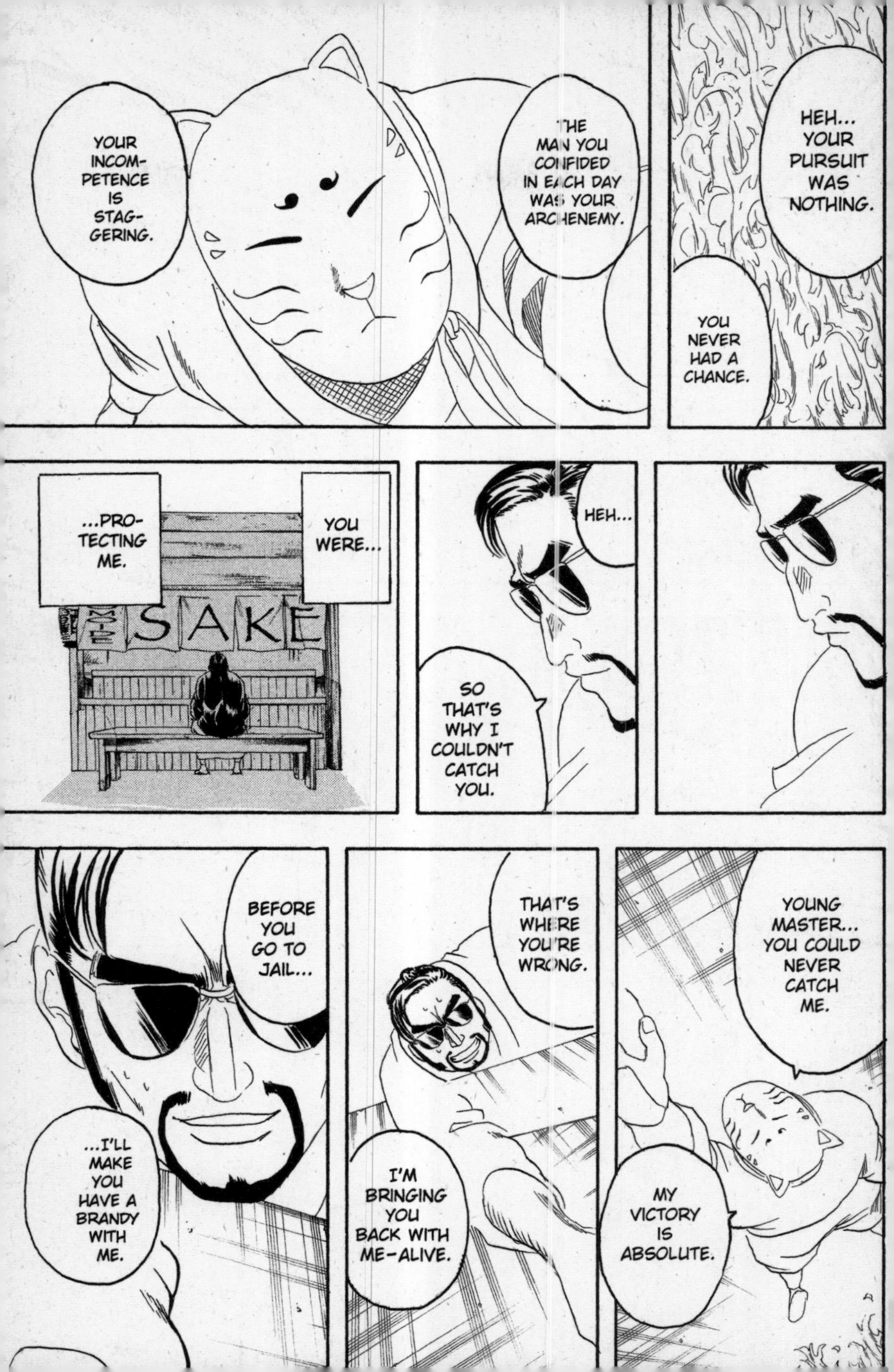
HEH... YOUR PURSUIT WAS NOTHING.
YOU NEVER HAD A CHANCE.
THE MAN YOU CONFIDED IN EACH DAY WAS YOUR ARCHENEMY.
YOUR INCOMPETENCE IS STAGGERING.
HEH...
SO THAT'S WHY I COULDN'T CATCH YOU.
YOU WERE...
...PROTECTING ME.
SAKE
YOUNG MASTER... YOU COULD NEVER CATCH ME.
MY VICTORY IS ABSOLUTE.
THAT'S WHERE YOU'RE WRONG.
I'M BRINGING YOU BACK WITH ME—ALIVE.
BEFORE YOU GO TO JAIL...
...I'LL MAKE YOU HAVE A BRANDY WITH ME.

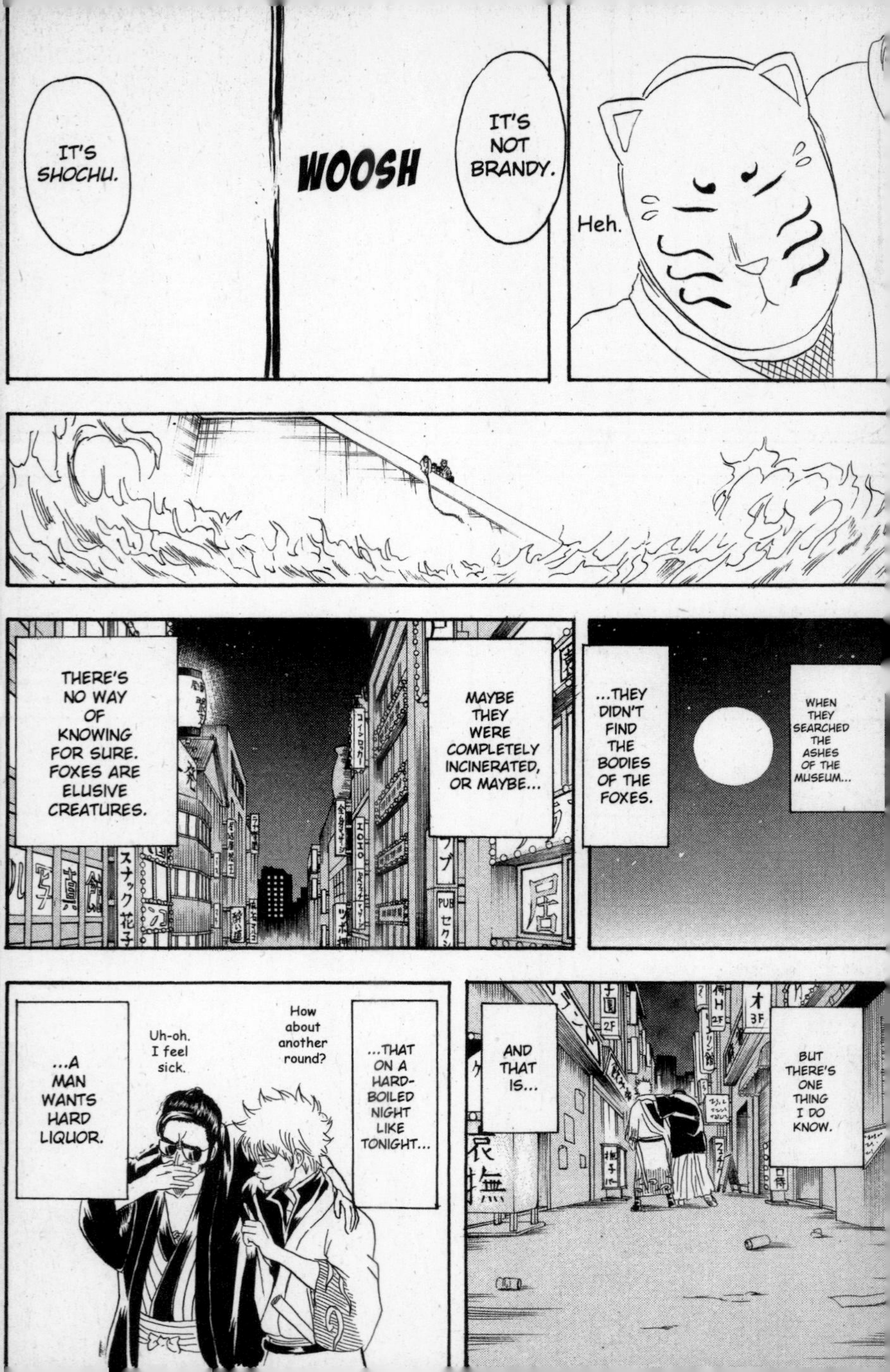

Heh.
IT'S NOT BRANDY.
WOOSH
IT'S SHOCHU.
WHEN THEY SEARCHED THE ASHES OF THE MUSEUM...
...THEY DIDN'T FIND THE BODIES OF THE FOXES.
MAYBE THEY WERE COMPLETELY INCINERATED, OR MAYBE...
THERE'S NO WAY OF KNOWING FOR SURE. FOXES ARE ELUSIVE CREATURES.
BUT THERE'S ONE THING I DO KNOW.
AND THAT IS...
...THAT ON A HARD-BOILED NIGHT LIKE TONIGHT...
How about another round?
Uh-oh. I feel sick.
...A MAN WANTS HARD LIQUOR.

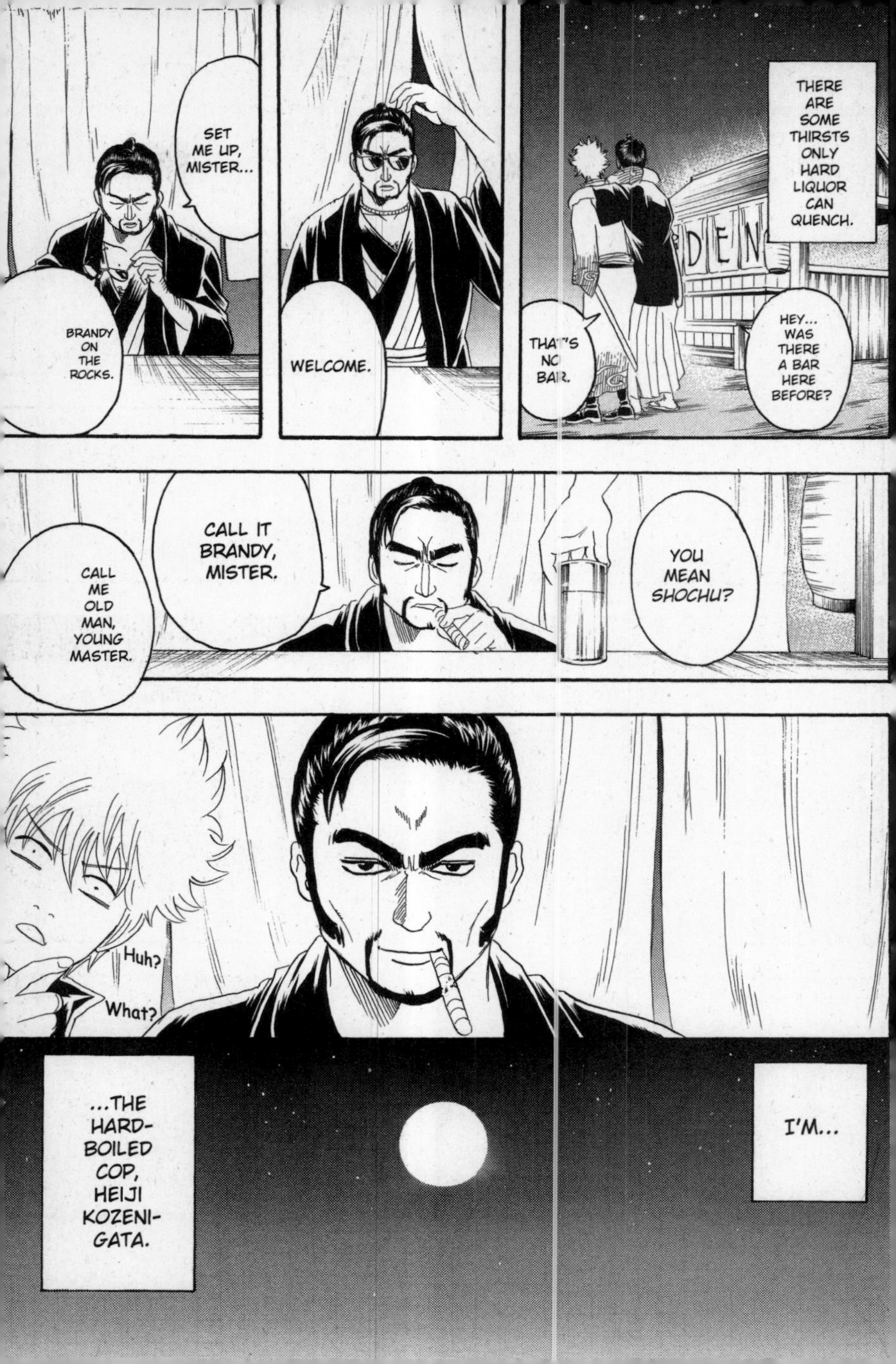
THERE ARE SOME THIRSTS ONLY HARD LIQUOR CAN QUENCH.
HEY... WAS THERE A BAR HERE BEFORE?
THAT'S NO BAR.
WELCOME.
SET ME UP, MISTER...
BRANDY ON THE ROCKS.
YOU MEAN SHOCHU?
CALL IT BRANDY, MISTER.
CALL ME OLD MAN, YOUNG MASTER.
Huh?
What?
I'M...
...THE HARD-BOILED COP, HEIJI KOZENIGATA.

Gin Tama Fan Art!

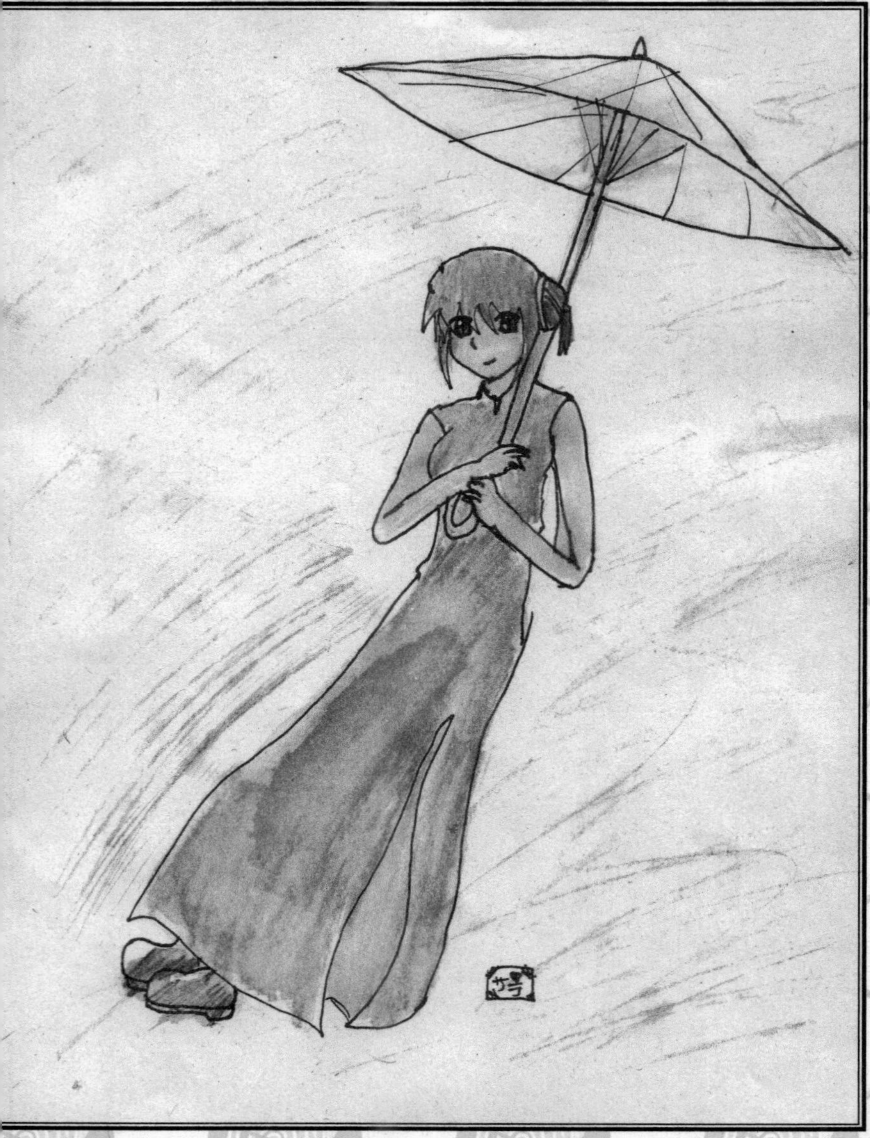

By Sarah Cimaglio

Thanks to all those who submitted! Keep them coming!

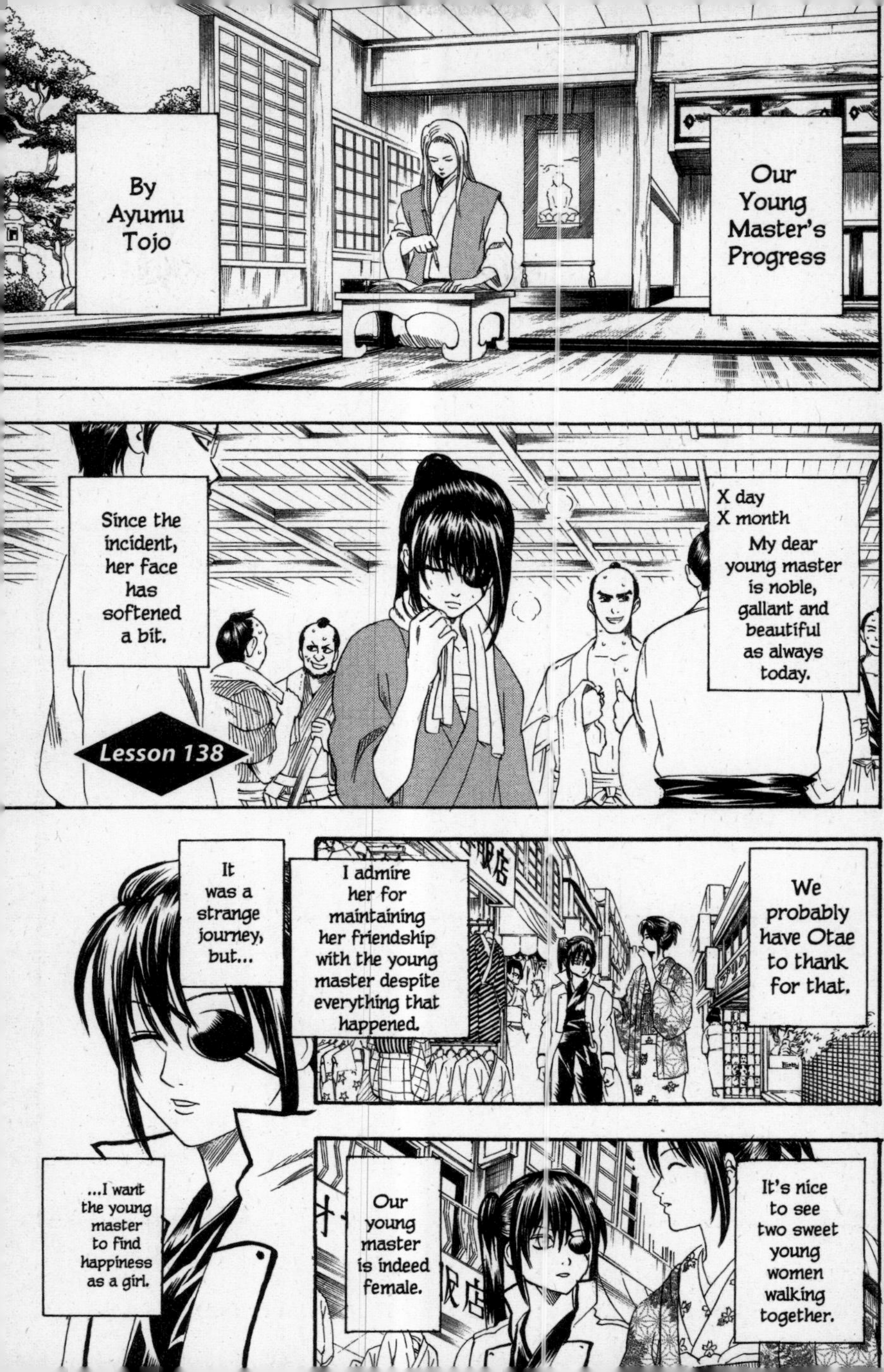
Our Young Master's Progress
By Ayumu Tojo
X day
X month
My dear young master is noble, gallant and beautiful as always today.
Since the incident, her face has softened a bit.
Lesson 138
We probably have Otae to thank for that.
I admire her for maintaining her friendship with the young master despite everything that happened.
It's nice to see two sweet young women walking together.
Our young master is indeed female.
It was a strange journey, but...
...I want the young master to find happiness as a girl.

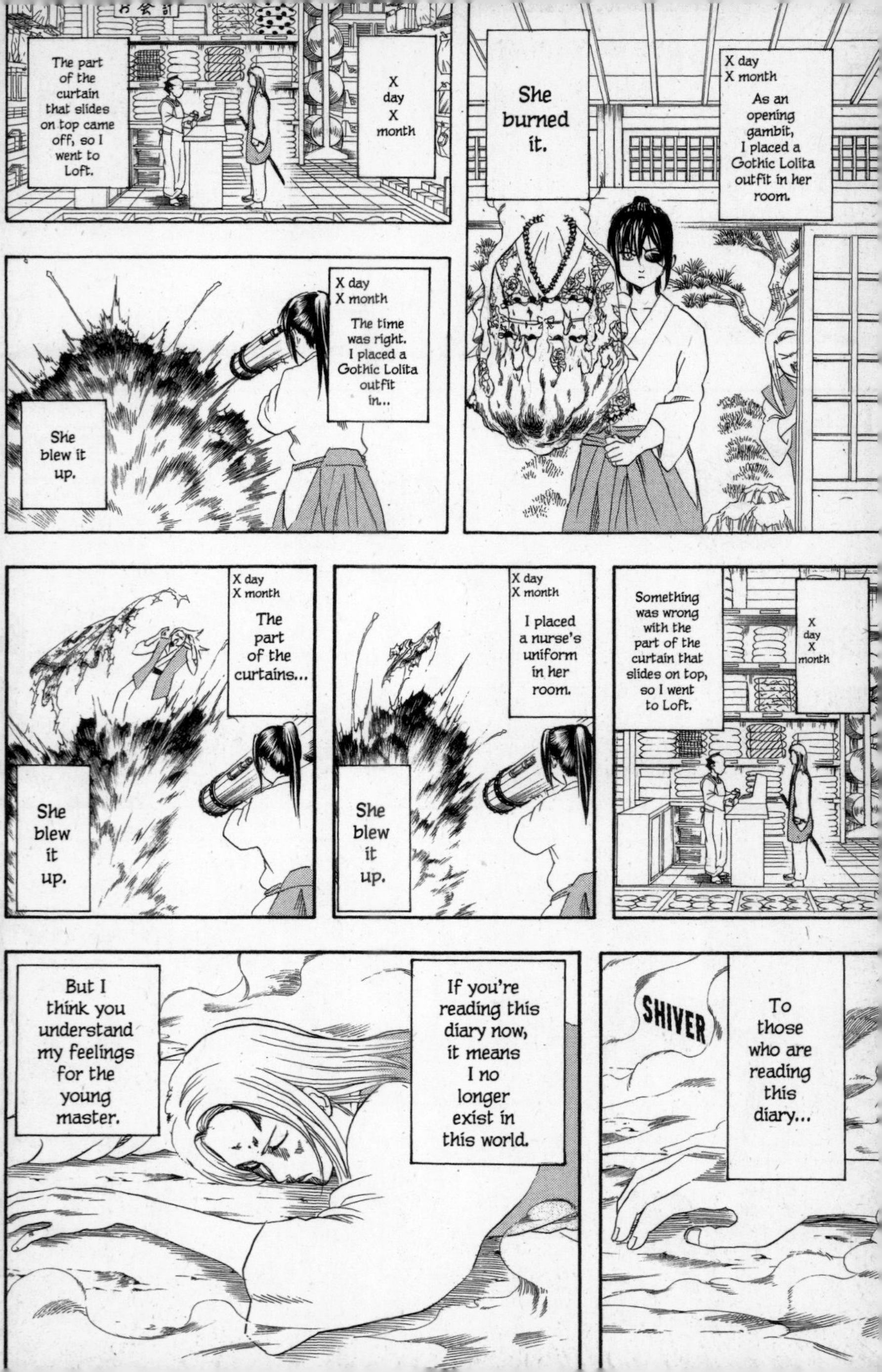
X day
X month
As an opening gambit, I placed a Gothic Lolita outfit in her room.
She burned it.
X day X month
The part of the curtain that slides on top came off, so I went to Loft.
X day
X month
The time was right. I placed a Gothic Lolita outfit in...
She blew it up.
X day X month
Something was wrong with the part of the curtain that slides on top, so I went to Loft.
X day
X month
I placed a nurse's uniform in her room.
She blew it up.
X day
X month
The part of the curtains...
She blew it up.
To those who are reading this diary...
SHIVER
If you're reading this diary now, it means I no longer exist in this world.
But I think you understand my feelings for the young master.

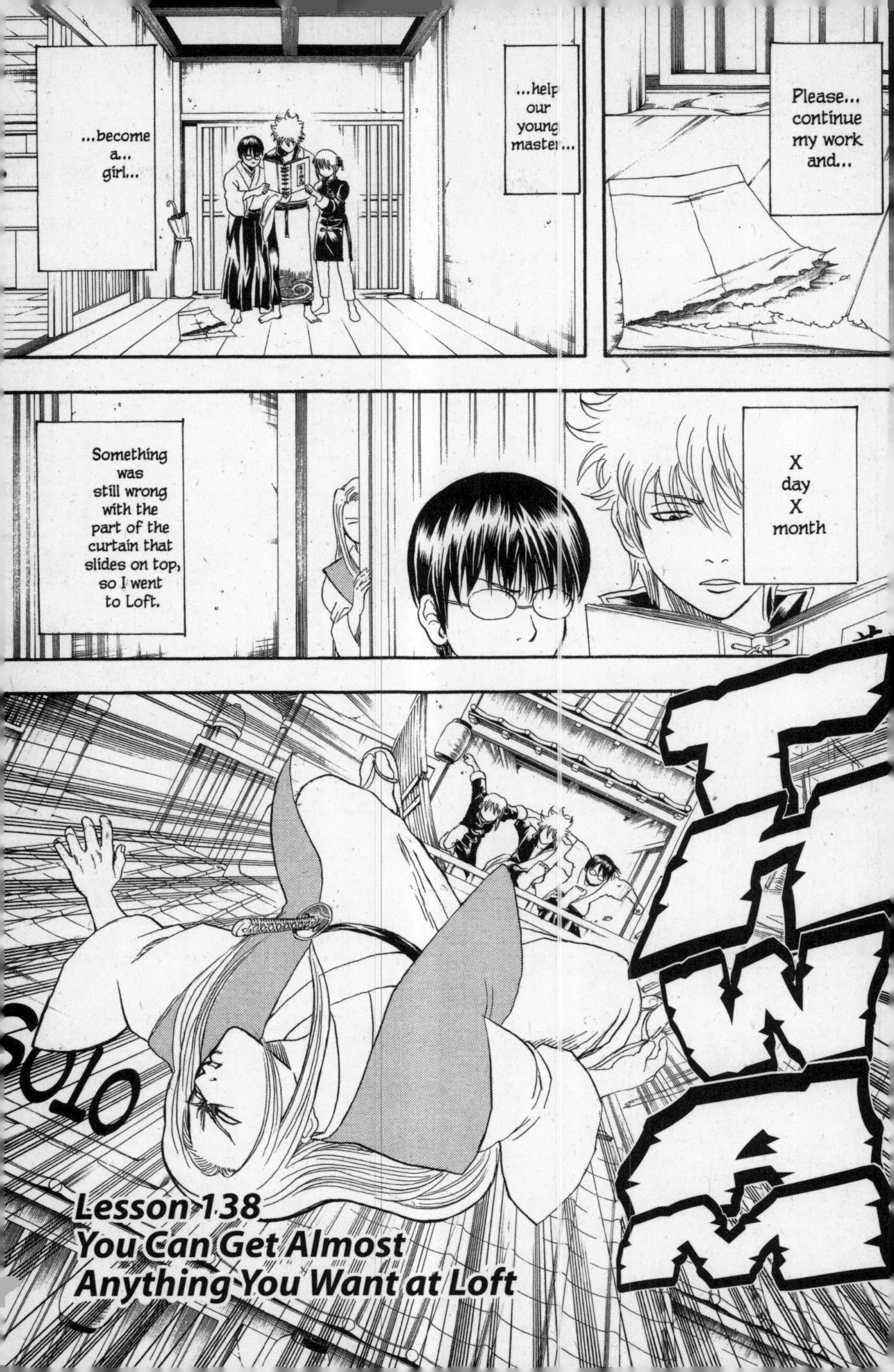
Please... continue my work and...
...help our young master...
...become a... girl...
X day X month
Something was still wrong with the part of the curtain that slides on top, so I went to Loft.
Lesson 138
You Can Get Almost Anything You Want at Loft

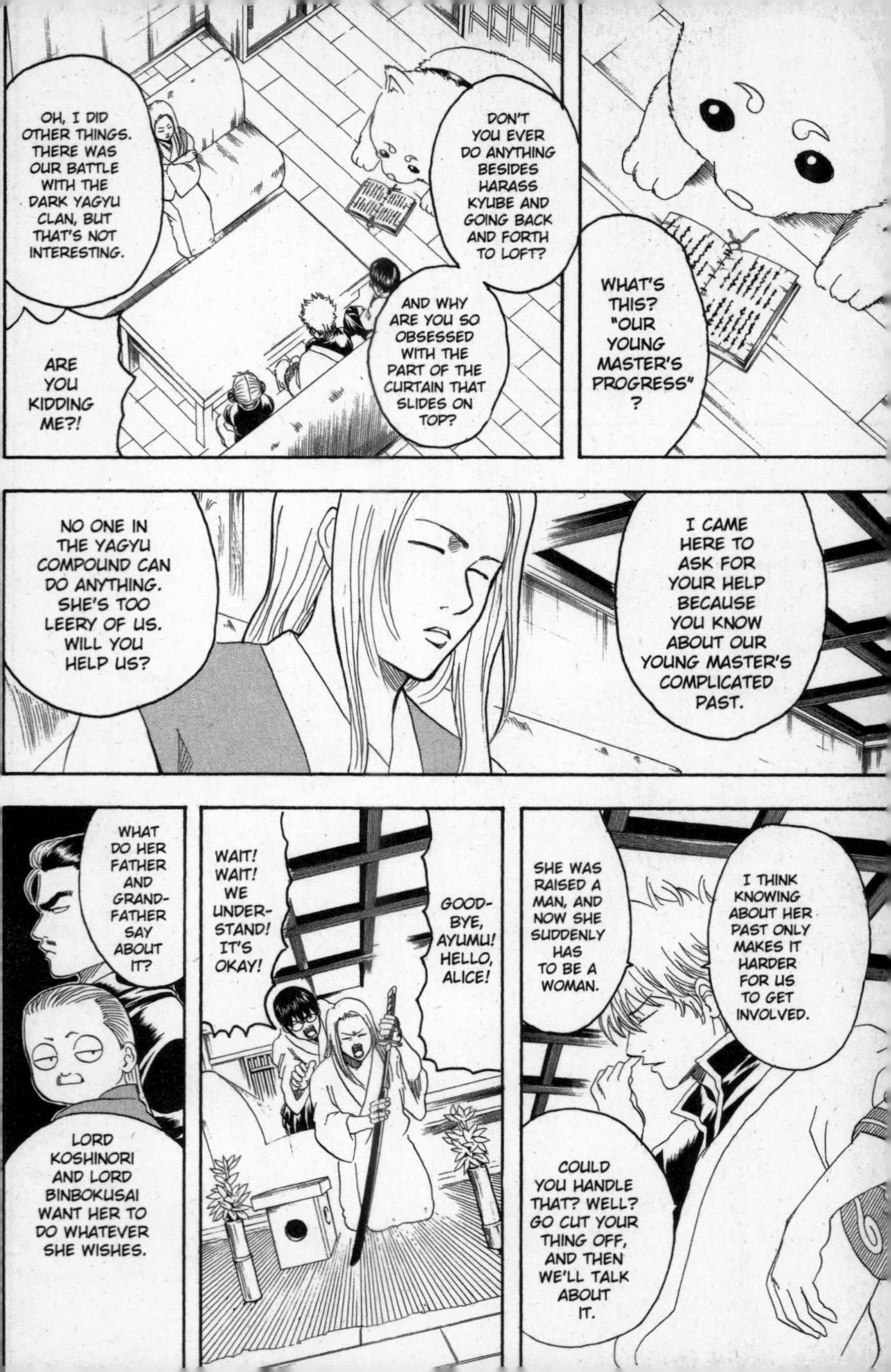

WHAT'S THIS? "OUR YOUNG MASTER'S PROGRESS"?
DON'T YOU EVER DO ANYTHING BESIDES HARASS KYUBE AND GOING BACK AND FORTH TO LOFT?
AND WHY ARE YOU SO OBSESSED WITH THE PART OF THE CURTAIN THAT SLIDES ON TOP?
OH, I DID OTHER THINGS. THERE WAS OUR BATTLE WITH THE DARK YAGYU CLAN, BUT THAT'S NOT INTERESTING.
ARE YOU KIDDING ME?!
I CAME HERE TO ASK FOR YOUR HELP BECAUSE YOU KNOW ABOUT OUR YOUNG MASTER'S COMPLICATED PAST.
NO ONE IN THE YAGYU COMPOUND CAN DO ANYTHING. SHE'S TOO LEERY OF US. WILL YOU HELP US?
I THINK KNOWING ABOUT HER PAST ONLY MAKES IT HARDER FOR US TO GET INVOLVED.
SHE WAS RAISED A MAN, AND NOW SHE SUDDENLY HAS TO BE A WOMAN.
COULD YOU HANDLE THAT? WELL? GO CUT YOUR THING OFF, AND THEN WE'LL TALK ABOUT IT.
GOOD-BYE, AYUMU! HELLO, ALICE!
WAIT! WAIT! WE UNDER-STAND! IT'S OKAY!
WHAT DO HER FATHER AND GRAND-FATHER SAY ABOUT IT?
LORD KOSHINORI AND LORD BINBOKUSAI WANT HER TO DO WHATEVER SHE WISHES.

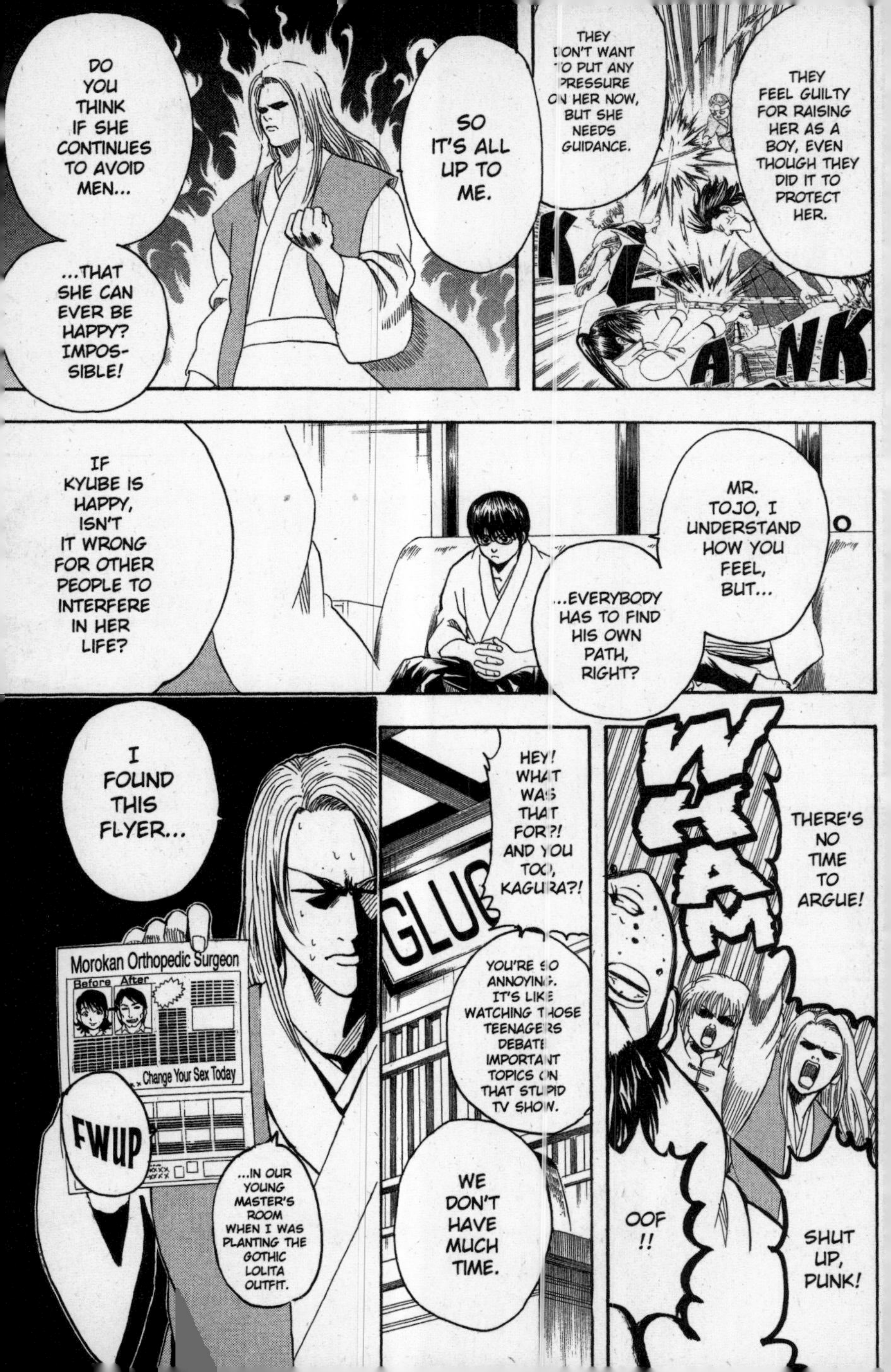
KLANK
THEY FEEL GUILTY FOR RAISING HER AS A BOY, EVEN THOUGH THEY DID IT TO PROTECT HER.
THEY DON'T WANT TO PUT ANY PRESSURE ON HER NOW, BUT SHE NEEDS GUIDANCE.
SO IT'S ALL UP TO ME.
DO YOU THINK IF SHE CONTINUES TO AVOID MEN...
...THAT SHE CAN EVER BE HAPPY? IMPOSSIBLE!
MR. TOJO, I UNDERSTAND HOW YOU FEEL, BUT...
...EVERYBODY HAS TO FIND HIS OWN PATH, RIGHT?
IF KYUBE IS HAPPY, ISN'T IT WRONG FOR OTHER PEOPLE TO INTERFERE IN HER LIFE?
WHAM
THERE'S NO TIME TO ARGUE!
OOF !!
SHUT UP, PUNK!
HEY! WHAT WAS THAT FOR?! AND YOU TOO, KAGURA?!
YOU'RE SO ANNOYING. IT'S LIKE WATCHING THOSE TEENAGERS DEBATE IMPORTANT TOPICS ON THAT STUPID TV SHOW.
WE DON'T HAVE MUCH TIME.
I FOUND THIS FLYER...
Morokan Orthopedic Surgeon
Before
After
Change Your Sex Today
FWUP
...IN OUR YOUNG MASTER'S ROOM WHEN I WAS PLANTING THE GOTHIC LOLITA OUTFIT.

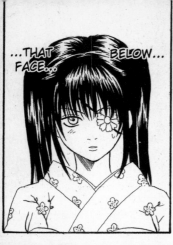

okan Orthopedic Surge
fore
After
SURPRISE YOUR FRIENDS
誰でも!!
WHAA ?!
hange Your Sex Toda
A TOWER ?!
NO WAY.
BELOW...
...THAT FACE...
...IS SHE GOING TO CONSTRUCT...
...A DIRTY TOWER OF BABEL?!
RRMMMMMMMMM
THEY'RE DIRTY ALL RIGHT, BUT YOU GUYS ALL HAVE THEM.
I'LL PAY YOU WHATEVER YOU WANT.
I'M ASKING YOU ONE MORE TIME... MAN TO MAN...
WILL YOU HELP ME STOP THE CONSTRUCTION OF THE TOWER OF BABEL?

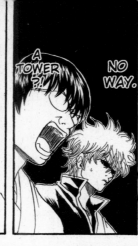

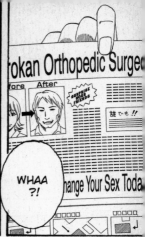

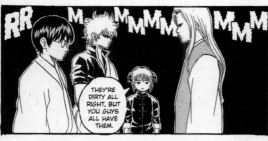

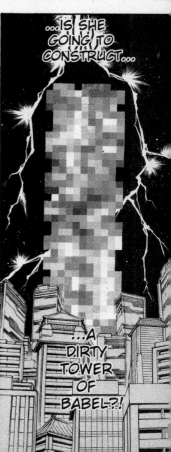

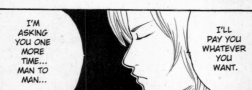

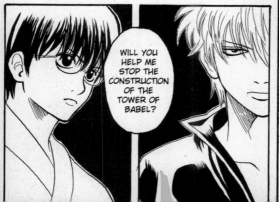

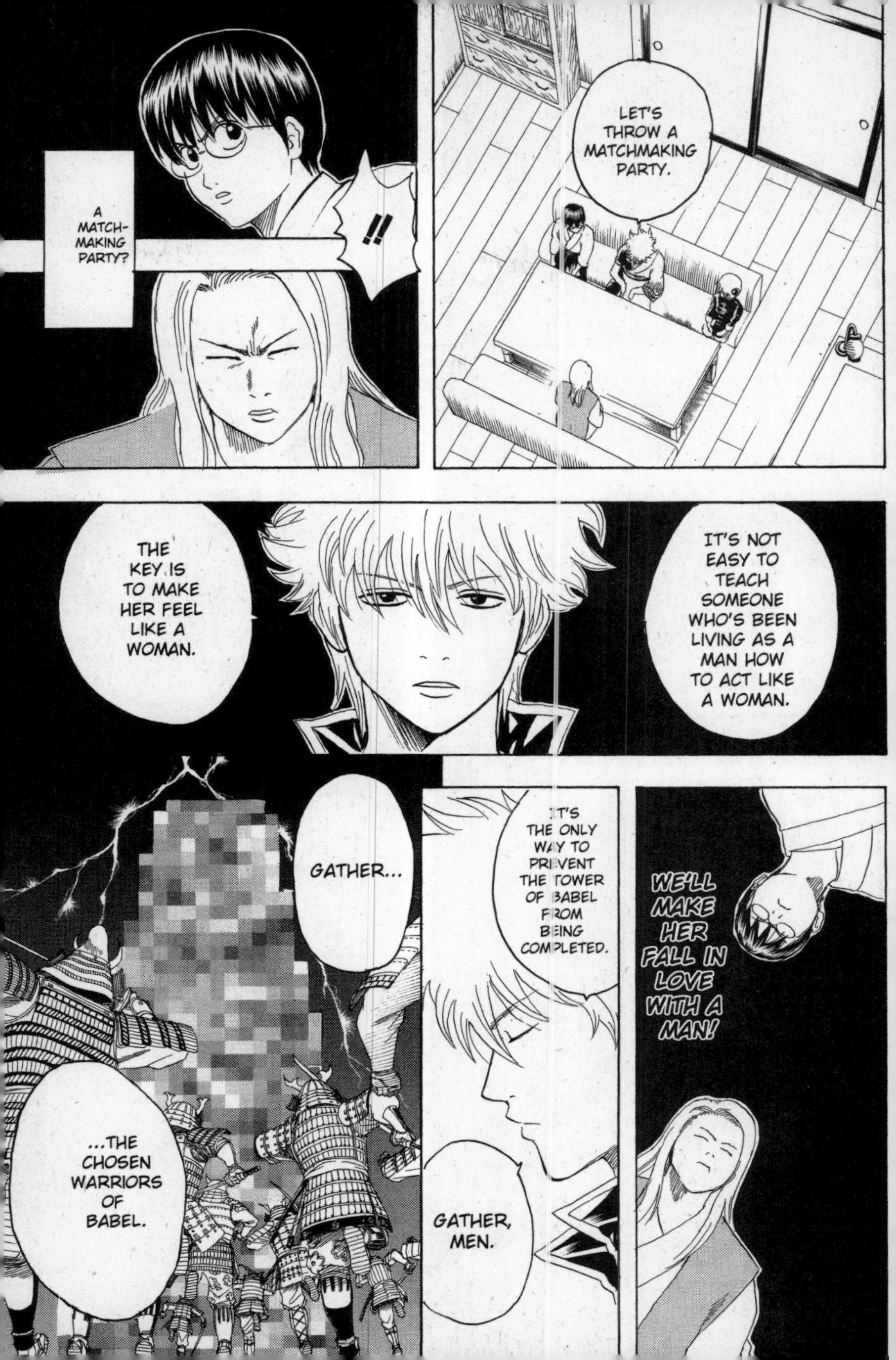
LET'S THROW A MATCHMAKING PARTY.
!!
A MATCH-MAKING PARTY?
IT'S NOT EASY TO TEACH SOMEONE WHO'S BEEN LIVING AS A MAN HOW TO ACT LIKE A WOMAN.
THE KEY IS TO MAKE HER FEEL LIKE A WOMAN.
WE'LL MAKE HER FALL IN LOVE WITH A MAN!
IT'S THE ONLY WAY TO PREVENT THE TOWER OF BABEL FROM BEING COMPLETED.
GATHER, MEN.
GATHER...
...THE CHOSEN WARRIORS OF BABEL.

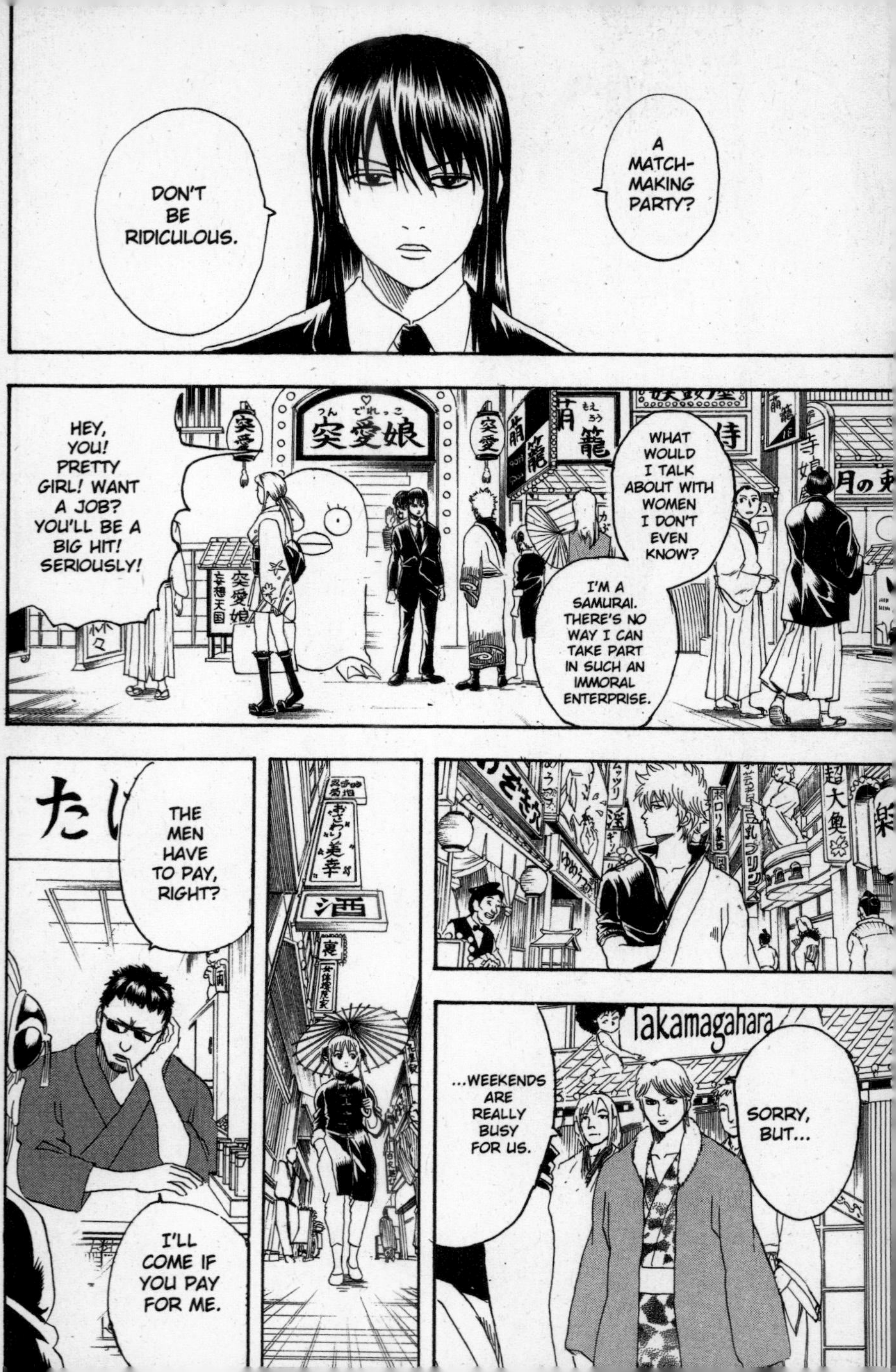
A MATCH-MAKING PARTY?
DON'T BE RIDICULOUS.
WHAT WOULD I TALK ABOUT WITH WOMEN I DON'T EVEN KNOW?
I'M A SAMURAI. THERE'S NO WAY I CAN TAKE PART IN SUCH AN IMMORAL ENTERPRISE.
突愛娘
HEY, YOU! PRETTY GIRL! WANT A JOB? YOU'LL BE A BIG HIT! SERIOUSLY!
Takamagahara
SORRY, BUT...
...WEEKENDS ARE REALLY BUSY FOR US.
酒
THE MEN HAVE TO PAY, RIGHT?
I'LL COME IF YOU PAY FOR ME.

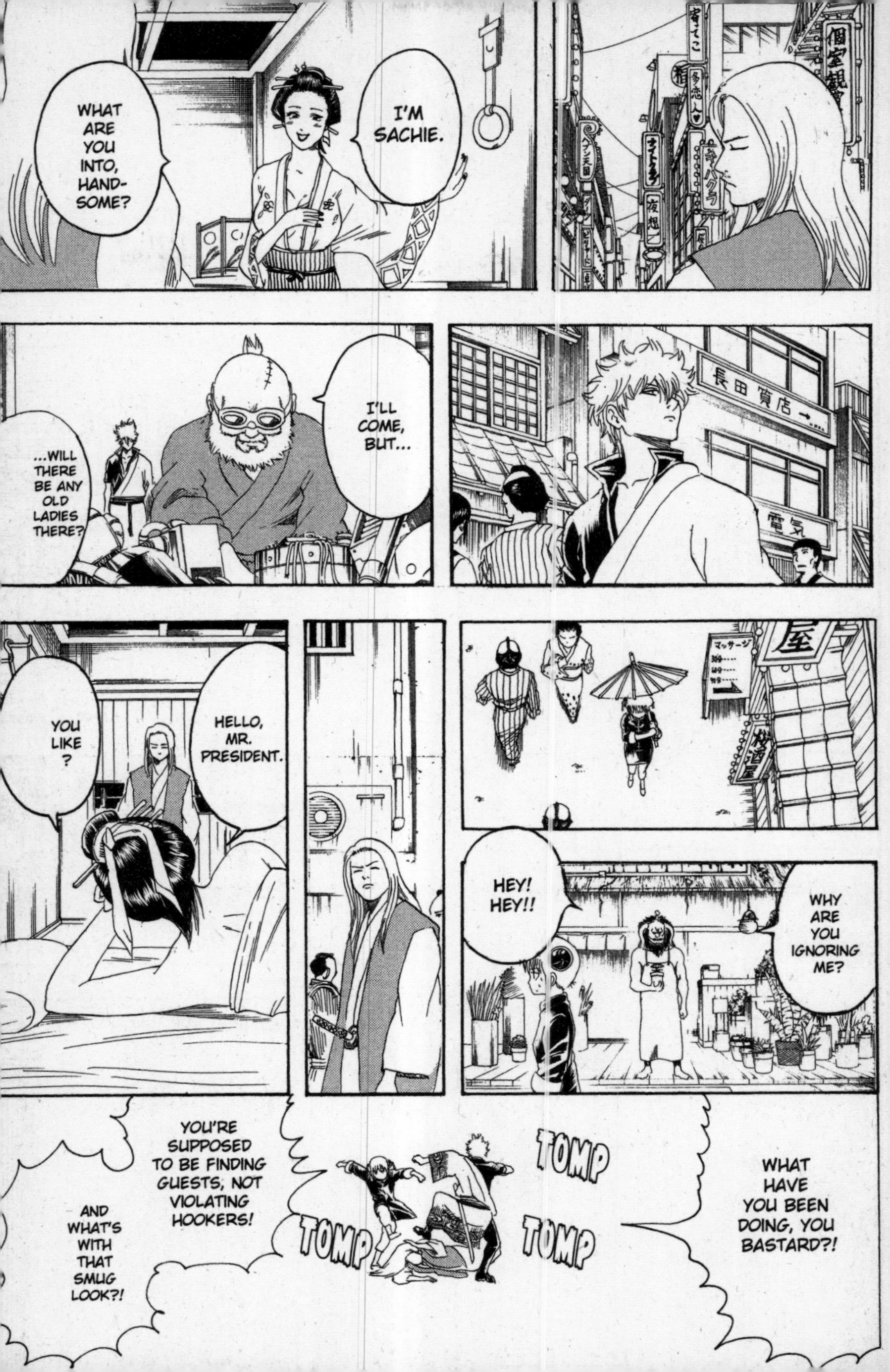
I'M SACHIE.
WHAT ARE YOU INTO, HAND-SOME?
長田質店
電気
I'LL COME, BUT...
...WILL THERE BE ANY OLD LADIES THERE?
WHY ARE YOU IGNORING ME?
HEY! HEY!!
HELLO, MR. PRESIDENT.
YOU LIKE ?
WHAT HAVE YOU BEEN DOING, YOU BASTARD?!
TOMP
TOMP
TOMP
YOU'RE SUPPOSED TO BE FINDING GUESTS, NOT VIOLATING HOOKERS!
AND WHAT'S WITH THAT SMUG LOOK?!

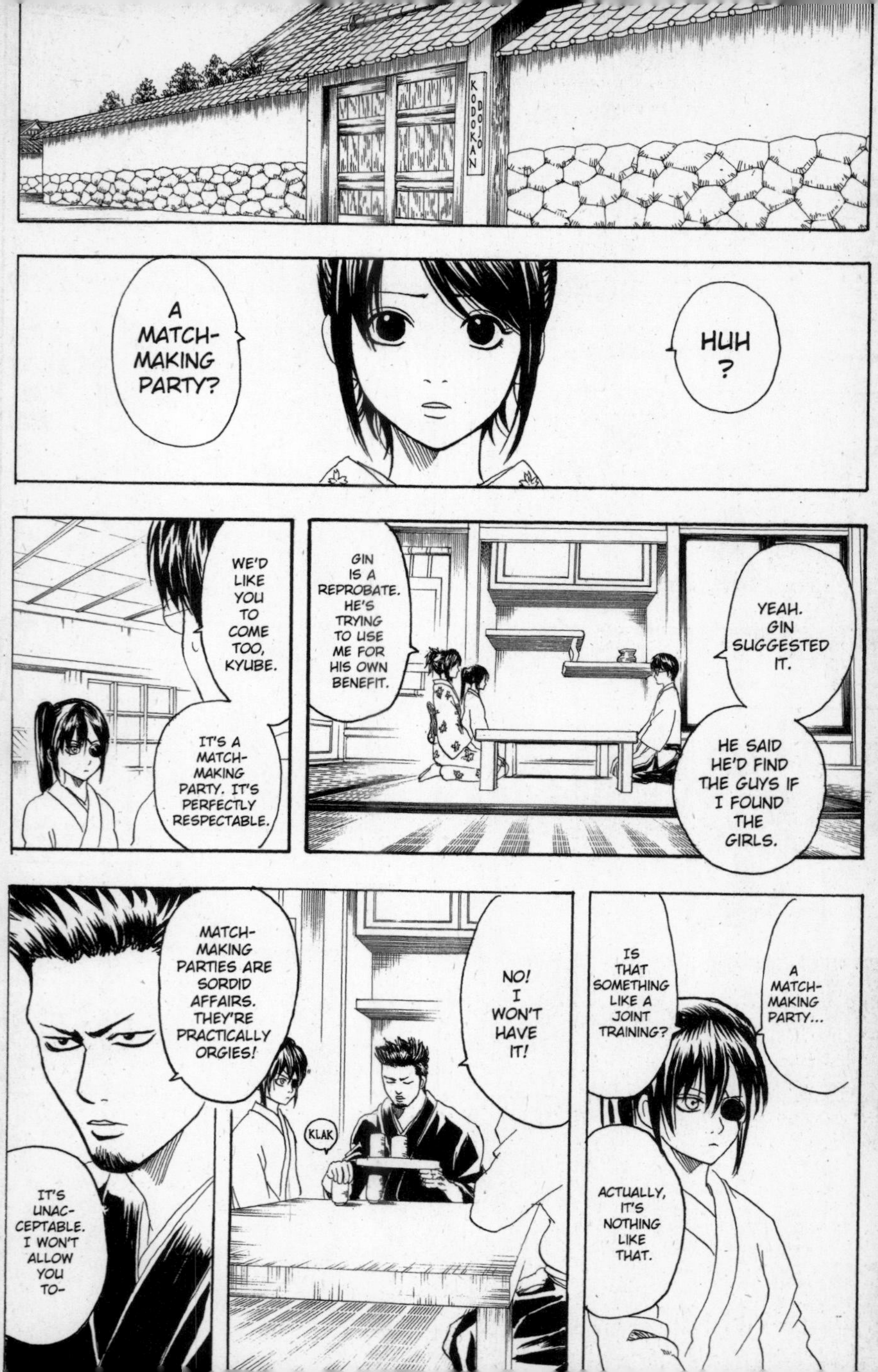
KODOKAN DOJO
HUH?
A MATCH-MAKING PARTY?
YEAH. GIN SUGGESTED IT.
HE SAID HE'D FIND THE GUYS IF I FOUND THE GIRLS.
GIN IS A REPROBATE. HE'S TRYING TO USE ME FOR HIS OWN BENEFIT.
WE'D LIKE YOU TO COME TOO, KYUBE.
IT'S A MATCH-MAKING PARTY. IT'S PERFECTLY RESPECTABLE.
A MATCH-MAKING PARTY...
IS THAT SOMETHING LIKE A JOINT TRAINING?
ACTUALLY, IT'S NOTHING LIKE THAT.
NO! I WON'T HAVE IT!
KLAK
MATCH-MAKING PARTIES ARE SORDID AFFAIRS. THEY'RE PRACTICALLY ORGIES!
IT'S UNACCEPTABLE. I WON'T ALLOW YOU TO-

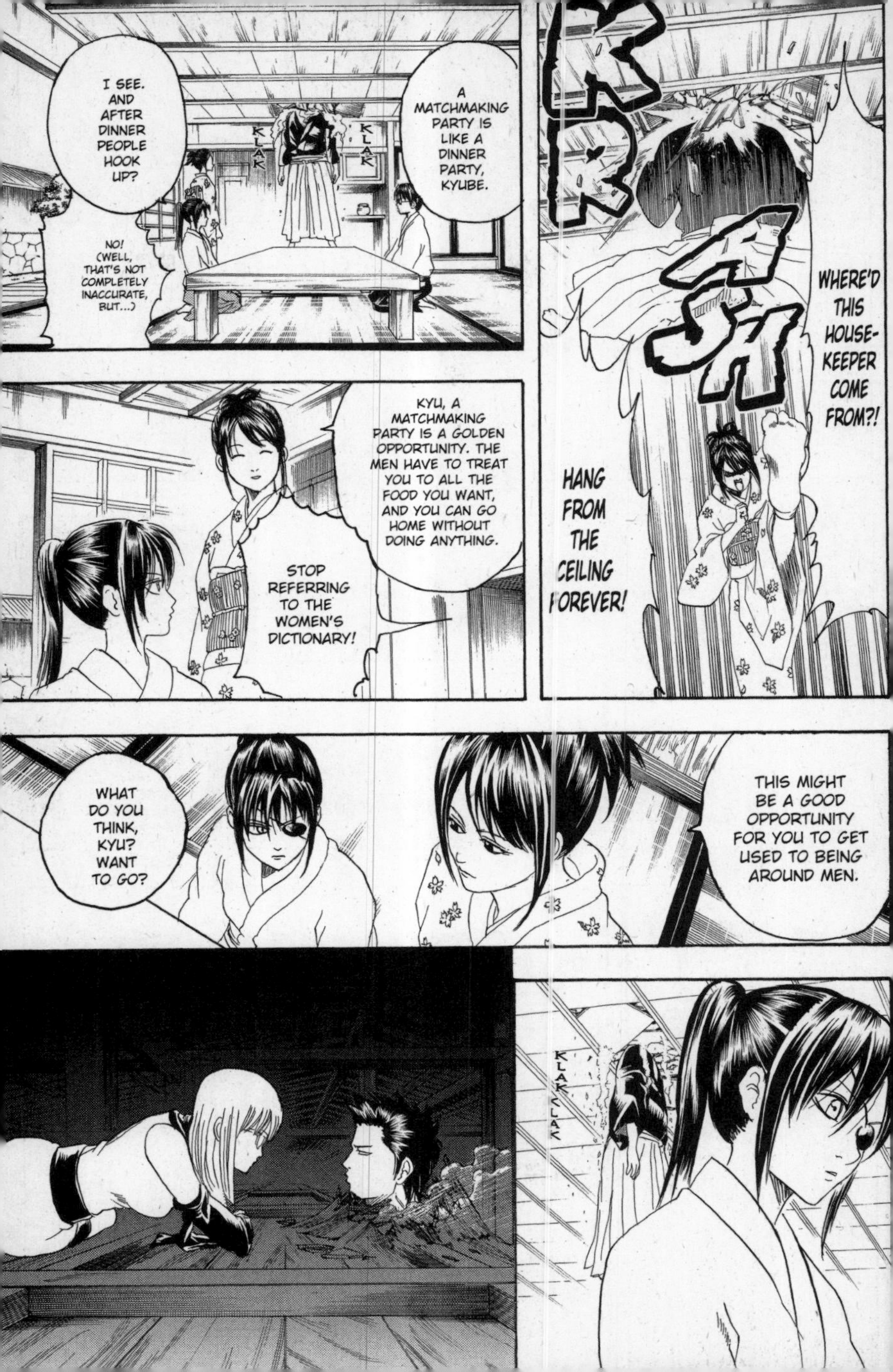
WHERE'D THIS HOUSE-KEEPER COME FROM?!
HANG FROM THE CEILING FOREVER!
A MATCHMAKING PARTY IS LIKE A DINNER PARTY, KYUBE.
KLAK
KLAK
I SEE. AND AFTER DINNER PEOPLE HOOK UP?
NO! (WELL, THAT'S NOT COMPLETELY INACCURATE, BUT...)
KYU, A MATCHMAKING PARTY IS A GOLDEN OPPORTUNITY. THE MEN HAVE TO TREAT YOU TO ALL THE FOOD YOU WANT, AND YOU CAN GO HOME WITHOUT DOING ANYTHING.
STOP REFERRING TO THE WOMEN'S DICTIONARY!
THIS MIGHT BE A GOOD OPPORTUNITY FOR YOU TO GET USED TO BEING AROUND MEN.
WHAT DO YOU THINK, KYU? WANT TO GO?
KLAK
CLAK

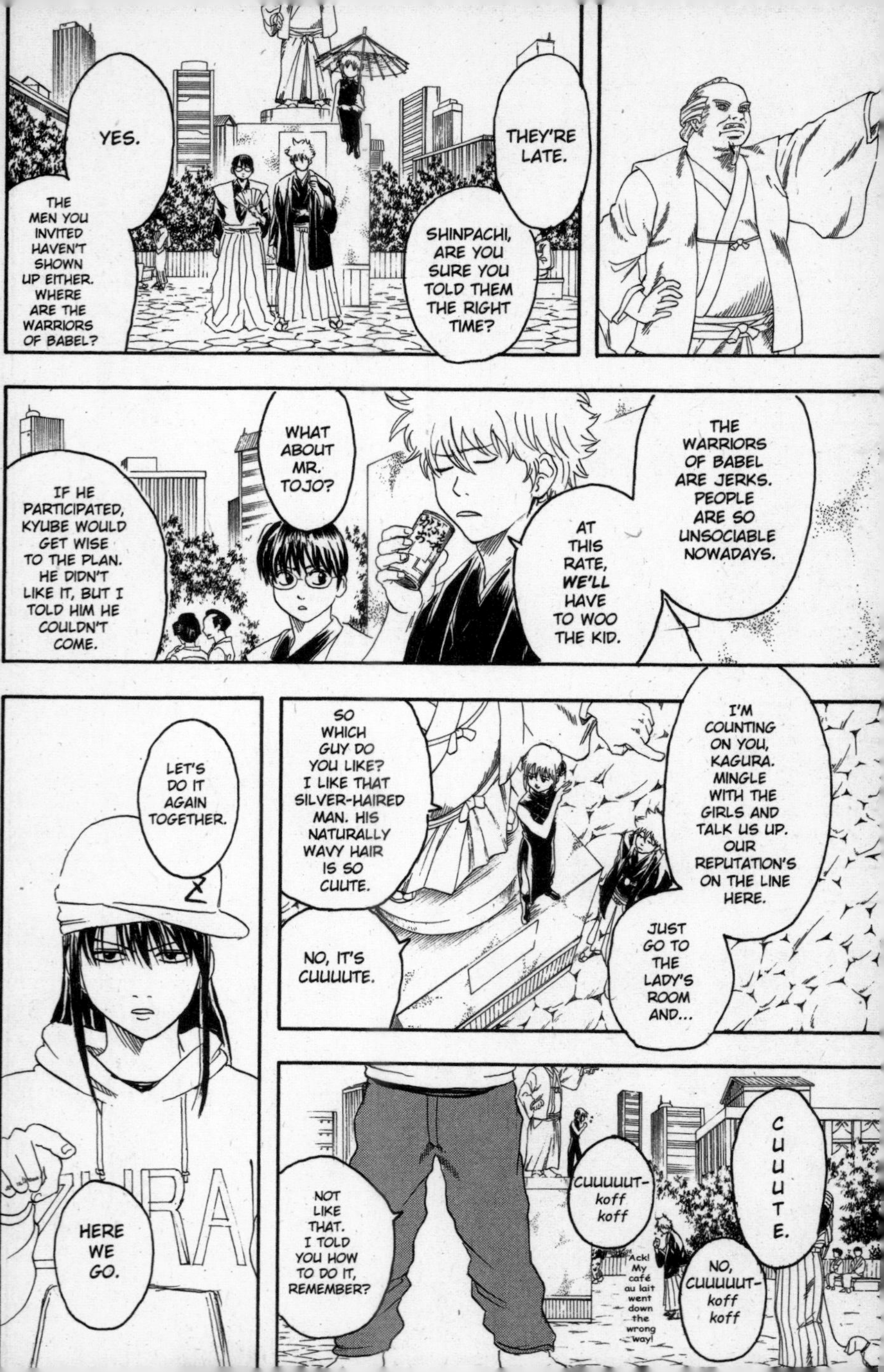

THEY'RE LATE.
SHINPACHI, ARE YOU SURE YOU TOLD THEM THE RIGHT TIME?
YES.
THE MEN YOU INVITED HAVEN'T SHOWN UP EITHER. WHERE ARE THE WARRIORS OF BABEL?
THE WARRIORS OF BABEL ARE JERKS. PEOPLE ARE SO UNSOCIABLE NOWADAYS.
AT THIS RATE, WE'LL HAVE TO WOO THE KID.
WHAT ABOUT MR. TOJO?
IF HE PARTICIPATED, KYUBE WOULD GET WISE TO THE PLAN. HE DIDN'T LIKE IT, BUT I TOLD HIM HE COULDN'T COME.
I'M COUNTING ON YOU, KAGURA. MINGLE WITH THE GIRLS AND TALK US UP. OUR REPUTATION'S ON THE LINE HERE.
JUST GO TO THE LADY'S ROOM AND...
SO WHICH GUY DO YOU LIKE? I LIKE THAT SILVER-HAIRED MAN. HIS NATURALLY WAVY HAIR IS SO CUUTE.
NO, IT'S CUUUUTE.
CUUUTE.
NO, CUUUUUT- koff koff
Ack! My café au lait went down the wrong way!
CUUUUUT- koff koff
NOT LIKE THAT. I TOLD YOU HOW TO DO IT, REMEMBER?
LET'S DO IT AGAIN TOGETHER.
HERE WE GO.

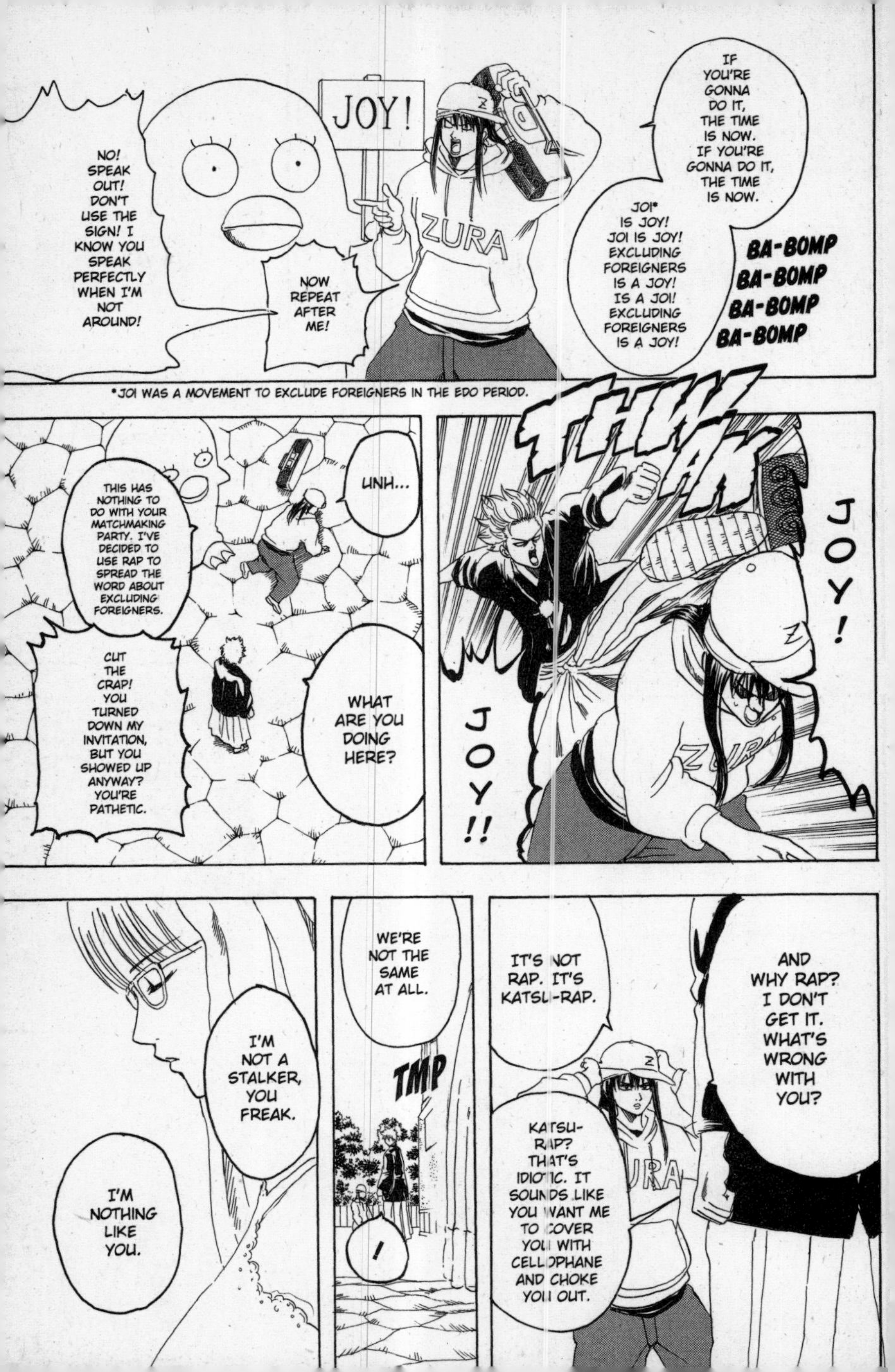
IF YOU'RE GONNA DO IT, THE TIME IS NOW. IF YOU'RE GONNA DO IT, THE TIME IS NOW.
BA-BOMP BA-BOMP BA-BOMP BA-BOMP
JOI* IS JOY! JOI IS JOY! EXCLUDING FOREIGNERS IS A JOY! IS A JOI! EXCLUDING FOREIGNERS IS A JOY!
JOY!
NO! SPEAK OUT! DON'T USE THE SIGN! I KNOW YOU SPEAK PERFECTLY WHEN I'M NOT AROUND!
ZURA
NOW REPEAT AFTER ME!
THWACK
JOY!
JOY!!
UNH...
THIS HAS NOTHING TO DO WITH YOUR MATCHMAKING PARTY. I'VE DECIDED TO USE RAP TO SPREAD THE WORD ABOUT EXCLUDING FOREIGNERS.
WHAT ARE YOU DOING HERE?
CUT THE CRAP! YOU TURNED DOWN MY INVITATION, BUT YOU SHOWED UP ANYWAY? YOU'RE PATHETIC.
AND WHY RAP? I DON'T GET IT. WHAT'S WRONG WITH YOU?
IT'S NOT RAP. IT'S KATSU-RAP.
KATSU-RAP? THAT'S IDIOTIC. IT SOUNDS LIKE YOU WANT ME TO COVER YOU WITH CELLOPHANE AND CHOKE YOU OUT.
WE'RE NOT THE SAME AT ALL.
TMP
!
I'M NOT A STALKER, YOU FREAK.
I'M NOTHING LIKE YOU.

*JOI WAS A MOVEMENT TO EXCLUDE FOREIGNERS IN THE EDO PERIOD.

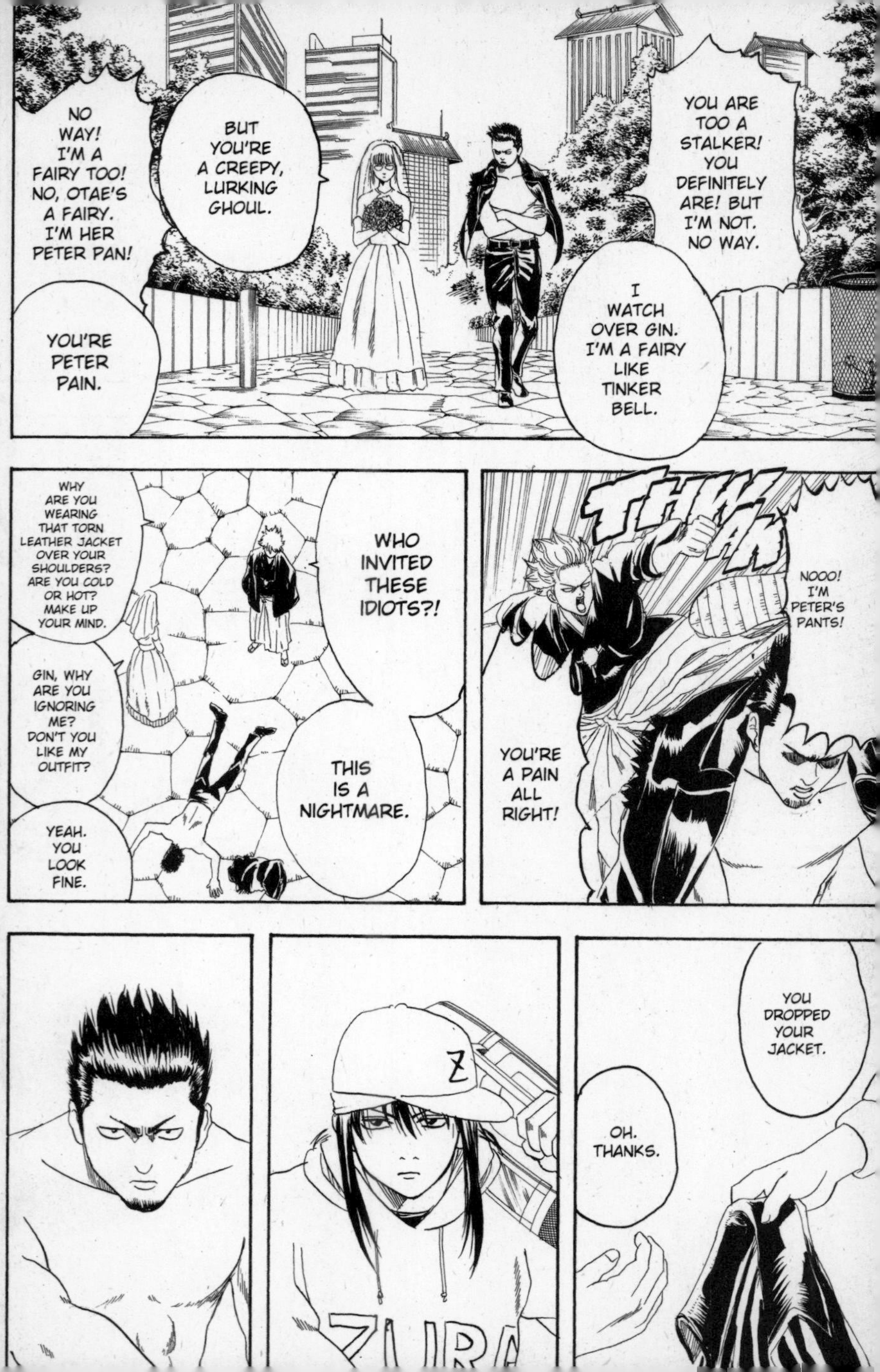
YOU ARE TOO A STALKER! YOU DEFINITELY ARE! BUT I'M NOT. NO WAY.
I WATCH OVER GIN. I'M A FAIRY LIKE TINKER BELL.
BUT YOU'RE A CREEPY, LURKING GHOUL.
NO WAY! I'M A FAIRY TOO! NO, OTAE'S A FAIRY. I'M HER PETER PAN!
YOU'RE PETER PAIN.
THWAK
NOOO! I'M PETER'S PANTS!
YOU'RE A PAIN ALL RIGHT!
WHO INVITED THESE IDIOTS?!
THIS IS A NIGHTMARE.
WHY ARE YOU WEARING THAT TORN LEATHER JACKET OVER YOUR SHOULDERS? ARE YOU COLD OR HOT? MAKE UP YOUR MIND.
GIN, WHY ARE YOU IGNORING ME? DON'T YOU LIKE MY OUTFIT?
YEAH. YOU LOOK FINE.
YOU DROPPED YOUR JACKET.
OH. THANKS.

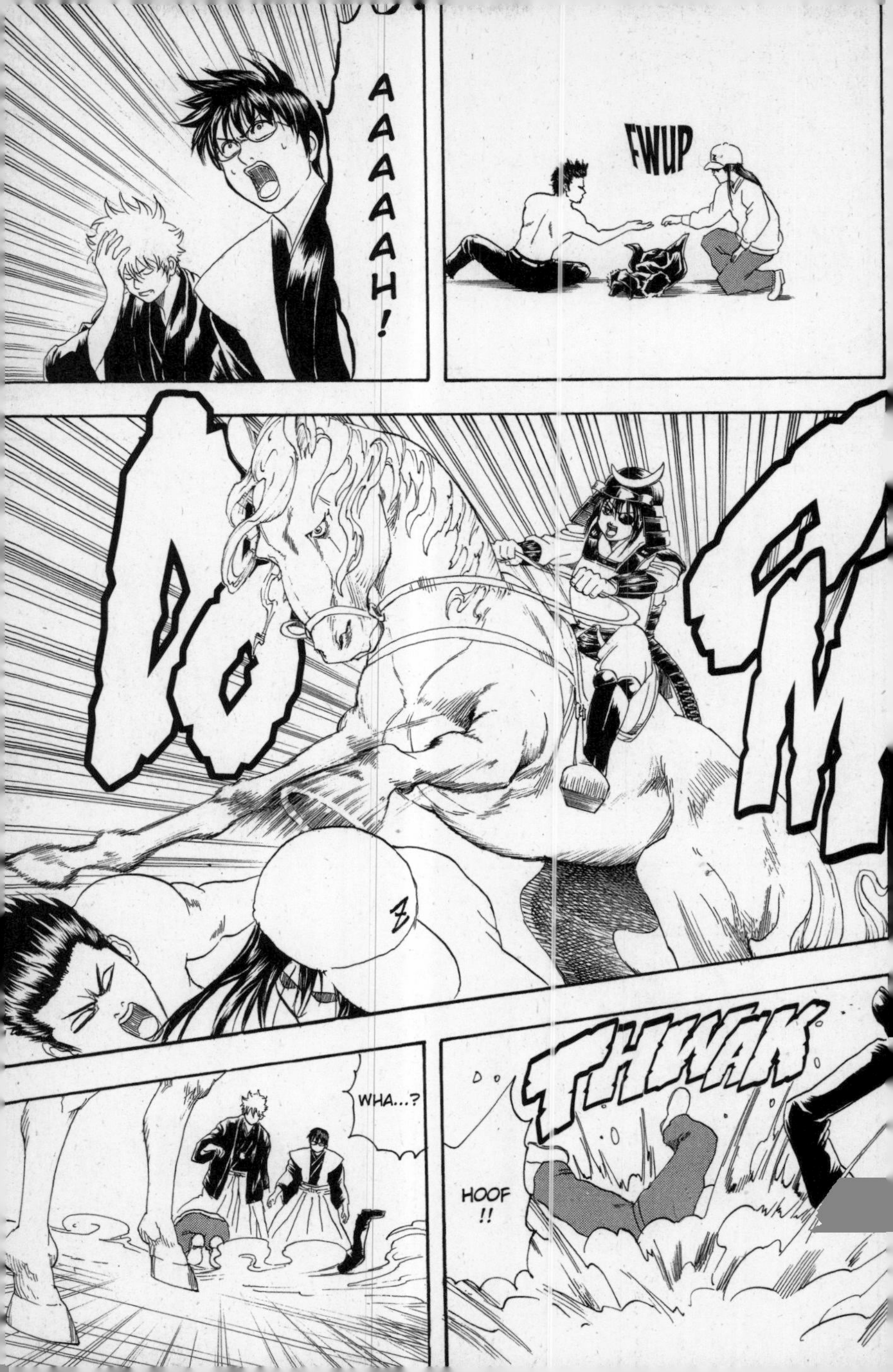

FWUP
AAAAAH!
DOM
THWAK
HOOF !!
WHA...?

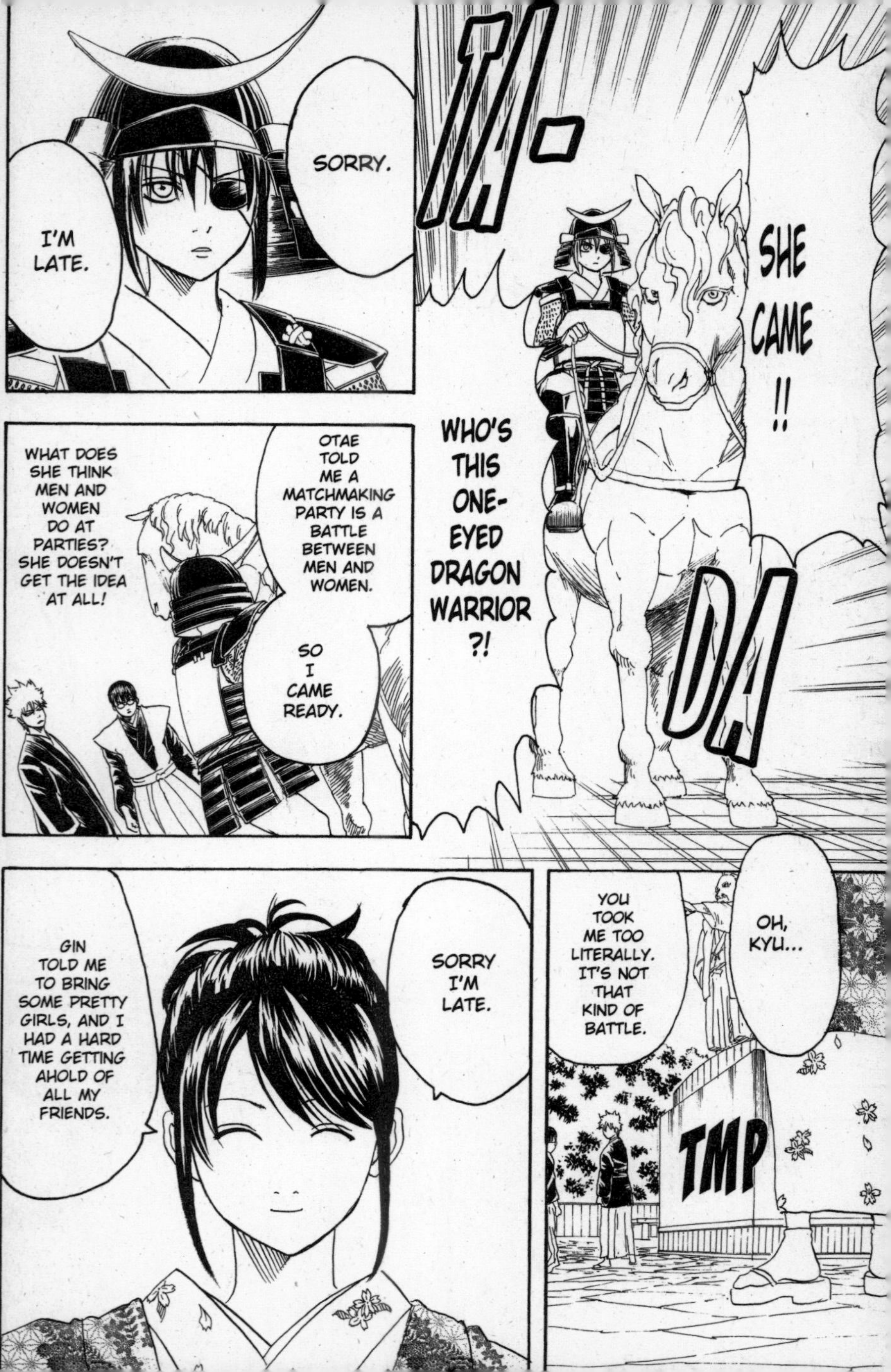
SHE CAME !!
TA-
WHO'S THIS ONE-EYED DRAGON WARRIOR ?!
DA
SORRY.
I'M LATE.
OTAE TOLD ME A MATCHMAKING PARTY IS A BATTLE BETWEEN MEN AND WOMEN.
SO I CAME READY.
WHAT DOES SHE THINK MEN AND WOMEN DO AT PARTIES? SHE DOESN'T GET THE IDEA AT ALL!
OH, KYU...
YOU TOOK ME TOO LITERALLY. IT'S NOT THAT KIND OF BATTLE.
TMP
SORRY I'M LATE.
GIN TOLD ME TO BRING SOME PRETTY GIRLS, AND I HAD A HARD TIME GETTING AHOLD OF ALL MY FRIENDS.

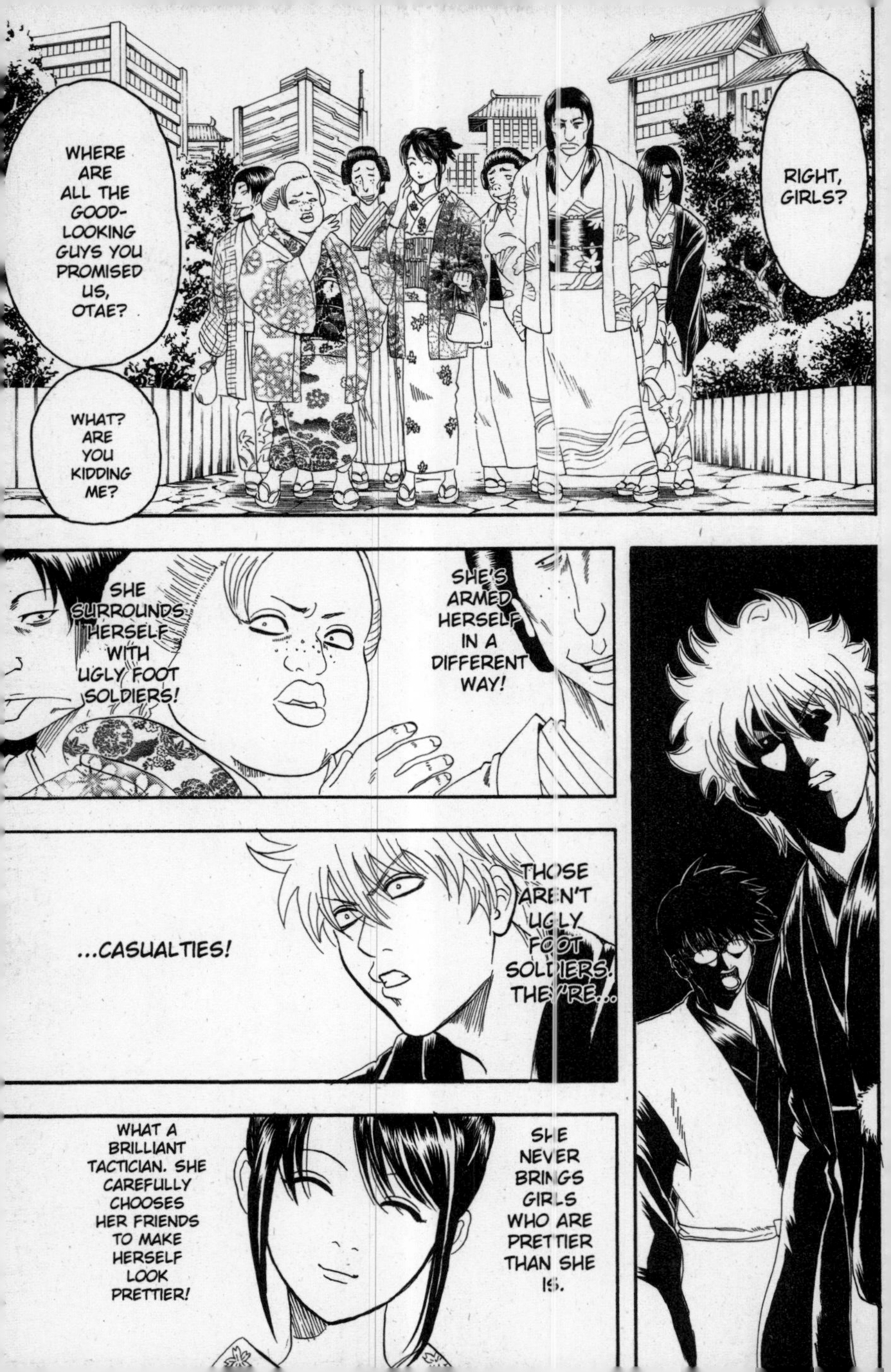
RIGHT, GIRLS?
WHERE ARE ALL THE GOOD-LOOKING GUYS YOU PROMISED US, OTAE?
WHAT? ARE YOU KIDDING ME?
SHE'S ARMED HERSELF IN A DIFFERENT WAY!
SHE SURROUNDS HERSELF WITH UGLY FOOT SOLDIERS!
THOSE AREN'T UGLY FOOT SOLDIERS. THEY'RE...
...CASUALTIES!
SHE NEVER BRINGS GIRLS WHO ARE PRETTIER THAN SHE IS.
WHAT A BRILLIANT TACTICIAN. SHE CAREFULLY CHOOSES HER FRIENDS TO MAKE HERSELF LOOK PRETTIER!

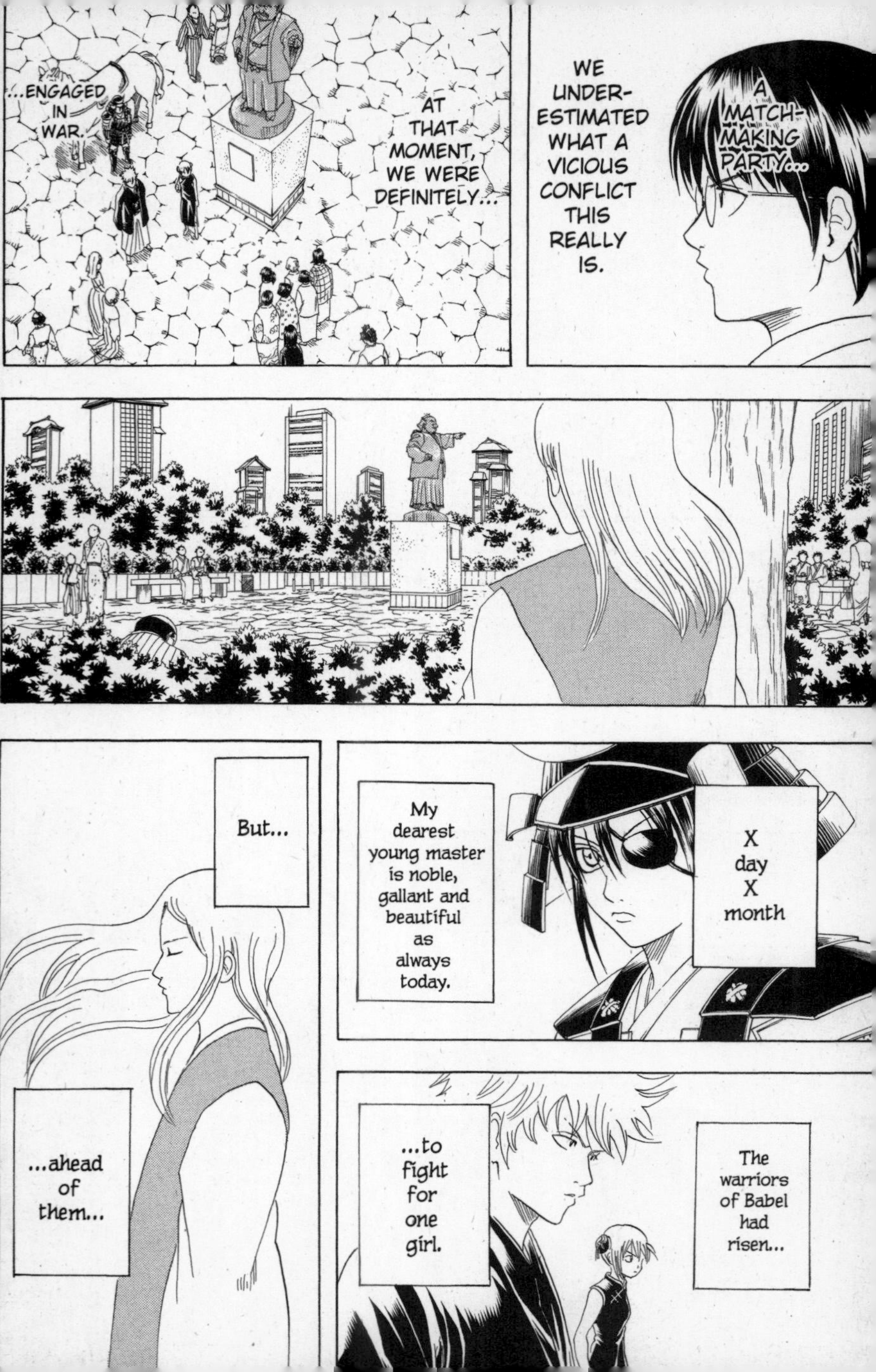
A MATCH-MAKING PARTY...
WE UNDER-ESTIMATED WHAT A VICIOUS CONFLICT THIS REALLY IS.
AT THAT MOMENT, WE WERE DEFINITELY...
...ENGAGED IN WAR.
X day X month
My dearest young master is noble, gallant and beautiful as always today.
The warriors of Babel had risen...
...to fight for one girl.
But...
...ahead of them...

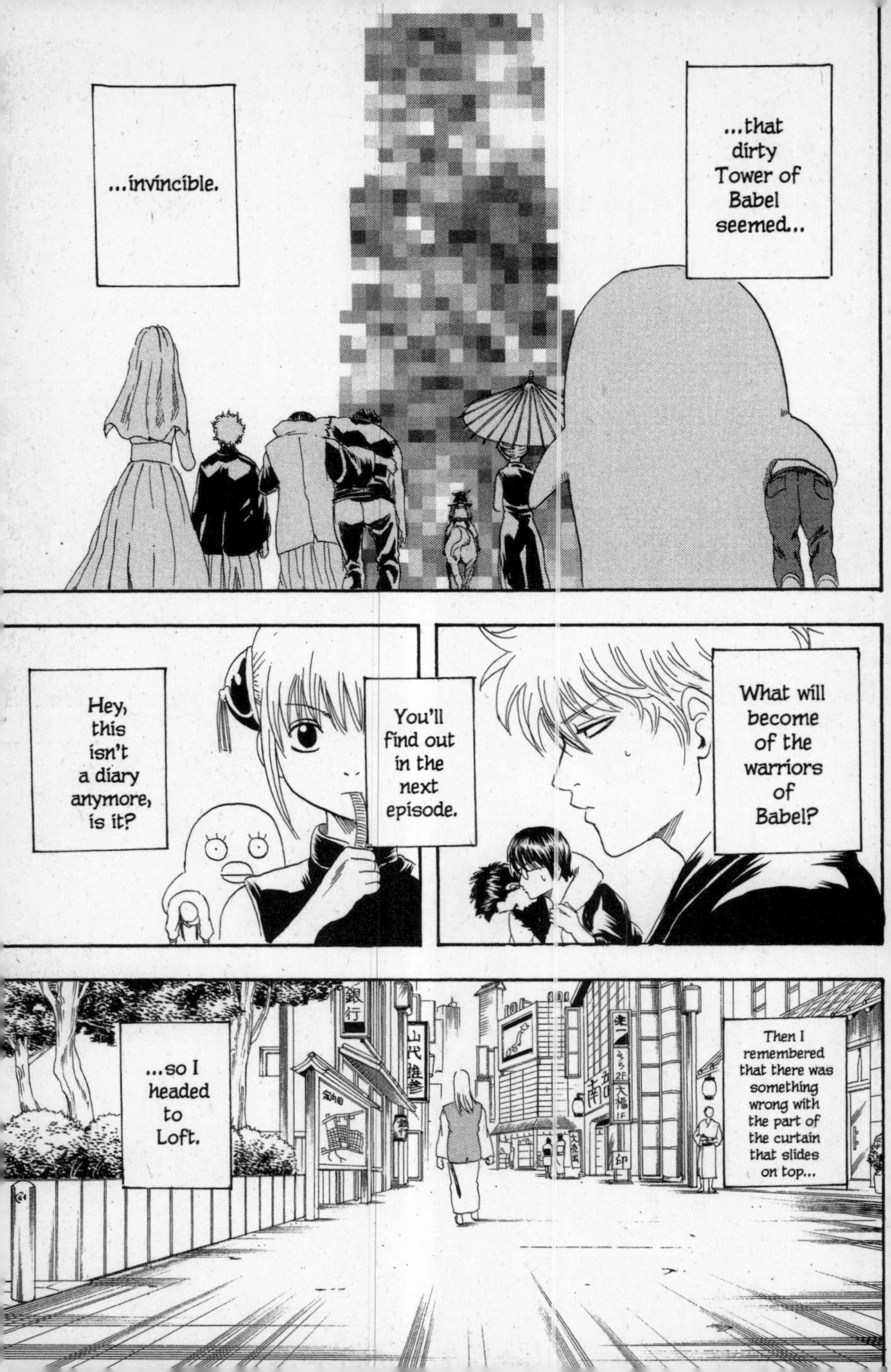

...that dirty Tower of Babel seemed...
...invincible.
What will become of the warriors of Babel?
You'll find out in the next episode.
Hey, this isn't a diary anymore, is it?
Then I remembered that there was something wrong with the part of the curtain that slides on top...
...so I headed to Loft.
銀行

Well, that's it for volume 16. The most important message in this volume is that it's not good to drink too much because it can affect both your head and your butt. For a shy person, this is the inevitable sequence: he gets nervous about talking to a girl he just met; he drinks to overcome the nerves; he takes a crap in his pants. So he has to choose between being a nervous wreck or crapping out. I don't want any of you to make a mistake like that. Those pants weren't the only things I ruined that day...

Send your letters and fan art to:
VIZ Media
Attn: Jann Jones, Editor
P.O. Box 77010
San Francisco, CA 94107

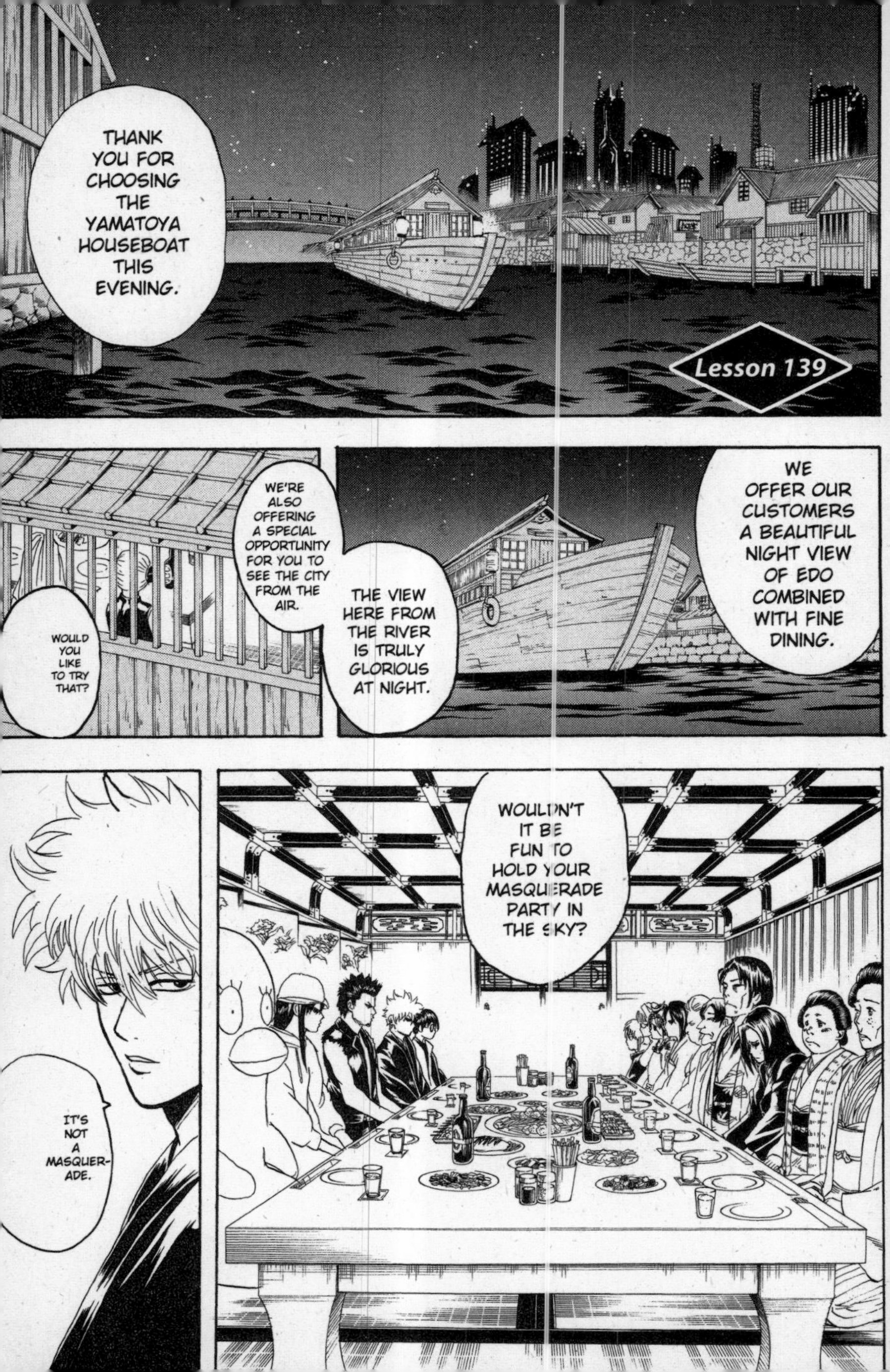
THANK YOU FOR CHOOSING THE YAMATOYA HOUSEBOAT THIS EVENING.
Lesson 139
WE OFFER OUR CUSTOMERS A BEAUTIFUL NIGHT VIEW OF EDO COMBINED WITH FINE DINING.
THE VIEW HERE FROM THE RIVER IS TRULY GLORIOUS AT NIGHT.
WE'RE ALSO OFFERING A SPECIAL OPPORTUNITY FOR YOU TO SEE THE CITY FROM THE AIR.
WOULD YOU LIKE TO TRY THAT?
WOULDN'T IT BE FUN TO HOLD YOUR MASQUERADE PARTY IN THE SKY?
IT'S NOT A MASQUER-ADE.

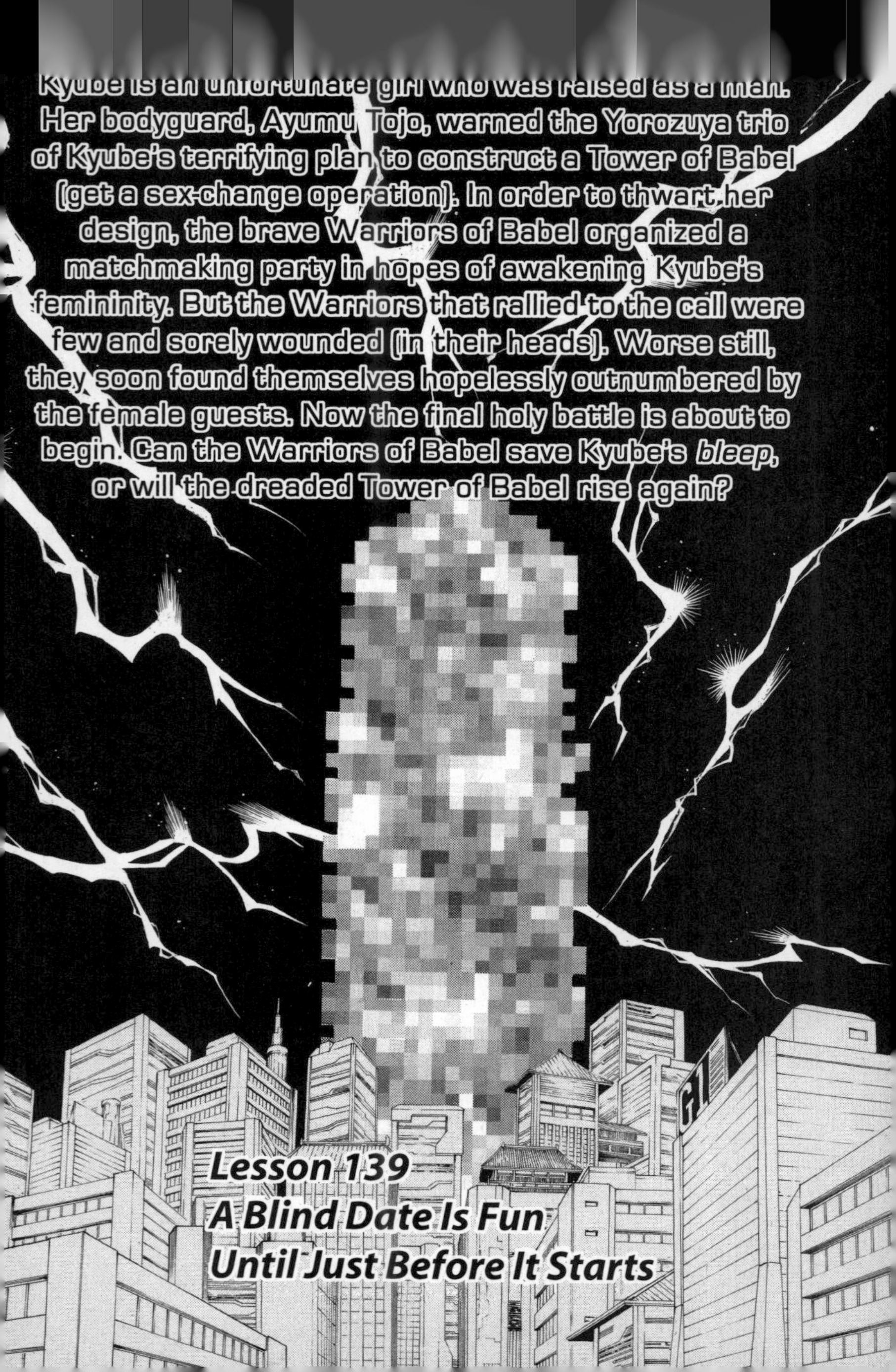
Kyube is an unfortunate girl who was raised as a man. Her bodyguard, Ayumu Tojo, warned the Yorozuya trio of Kyube's terrifying plan to construct a Tower of Babel (get a sex-change operation). In order to thwart her design, the brave Warriors of Babel organized a matchmaking party in hopes of awakening Kyube's femininity. But the Warriors that rallied to the call were few and sorely wounded (in their heads). Worse still, they soon found themselves hopelessly outnumbered by the female guests. Now the final holy battle is about to begin. Can the Warriors of Babel save Kyube's *bleep*, or will the dreaded Tower of Babel rise again?
Lesson 139
A Blind Date Is Fun Until Just Before It Starts
G1

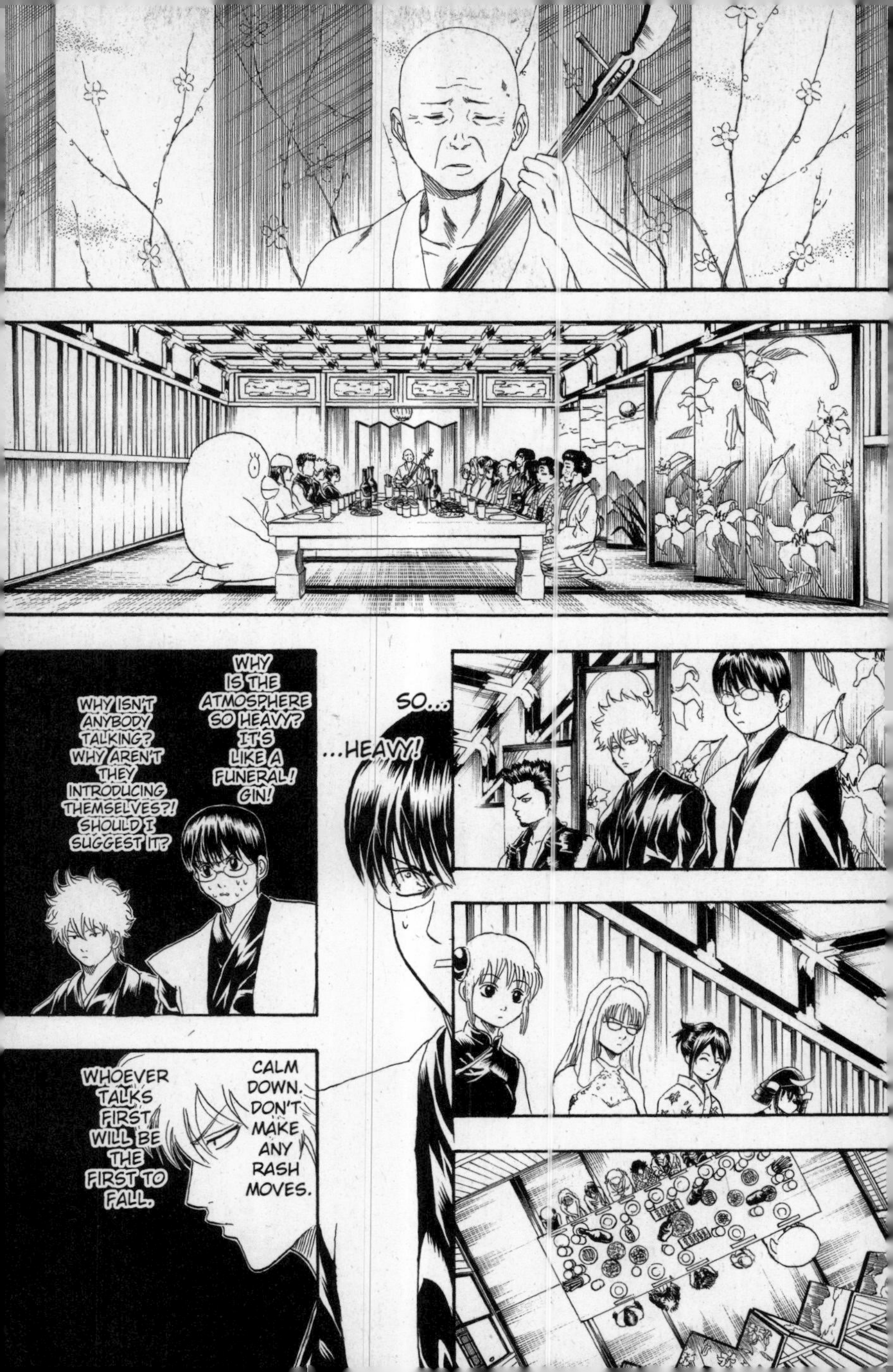
SO...
...HEAVY!
WHY IS THE ATMOSPHERE SO HEAVY? IT'S LIKE A FUNERAL! GIN!
WHY ISN'T ANYBODY TALKING? WHY AREN'T THEY INTRODUCING THEMSELVES?! SHOULD I SUGGEST IT?
CALM DOWN. DON'T MAKE ANY RASH MOVES.
WHOEVER TALKS FIRST WILL BE THE FIRST TO FALL.

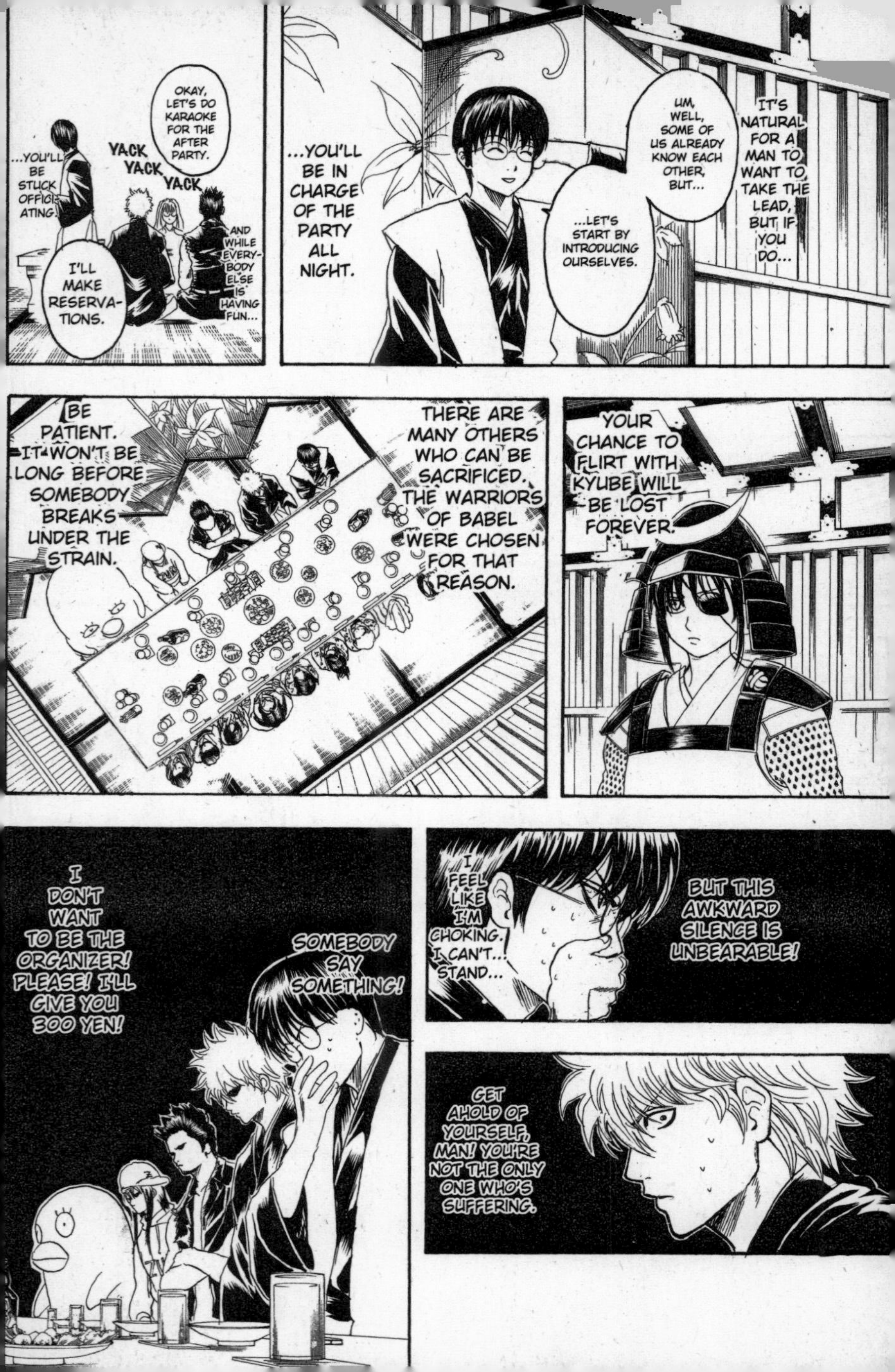
IT'S NATURAL FOR A MAN TO WANT TO TAKE THE LEAD, BUT IF YOU DO...
UM, WELL, SOME OF US ALREADY KNOW EACH OTHER, BUT...
...LET'S START BY INTRODUCING OURSELVES.
...YOU'LL BE IN CHARGE OF THE PARTY ALL NIGHT.
AND WHILE EVERYBODY ELSE IS HAVING FUN...
OKAY, LET'S DO KARAOKE FOR THE AFTER PARTY.
YACK YACK YACK
...YOU'LL BE STUCK OFFICIATING.
I'LL MAKE RESERVATIONS.
YOUR CHANCE TO FLIRT WITH KYUBE WILL BE LOST FOREVER.
THERE ARE MANY OTHERS WHO CAN BE SACRIFICED. THE WARRIORS OF BABEL WERE CHOSEN FOR THAT REASON.
BE PATIENT. IT WON'T BE LONG BEFORE SOMEBODY BREAKS UNDER THE STRAIN.
BUT THIS AWKWARD SILENCE IS UNBEARABLE!
I FEEL LIKE I'M CHOKING. I CAN'T... STAND...
GET AHOLD OF YOURSELF, MAN! YOU'RE NOT THE ONLY ONE WHO'S SUFFERING.
SOMEBODY SAY SOMETHING!
I DON'T WANT TO BE THE ORGANIZER! PLEASE! I'LL GIVE YOU 300 YEN!

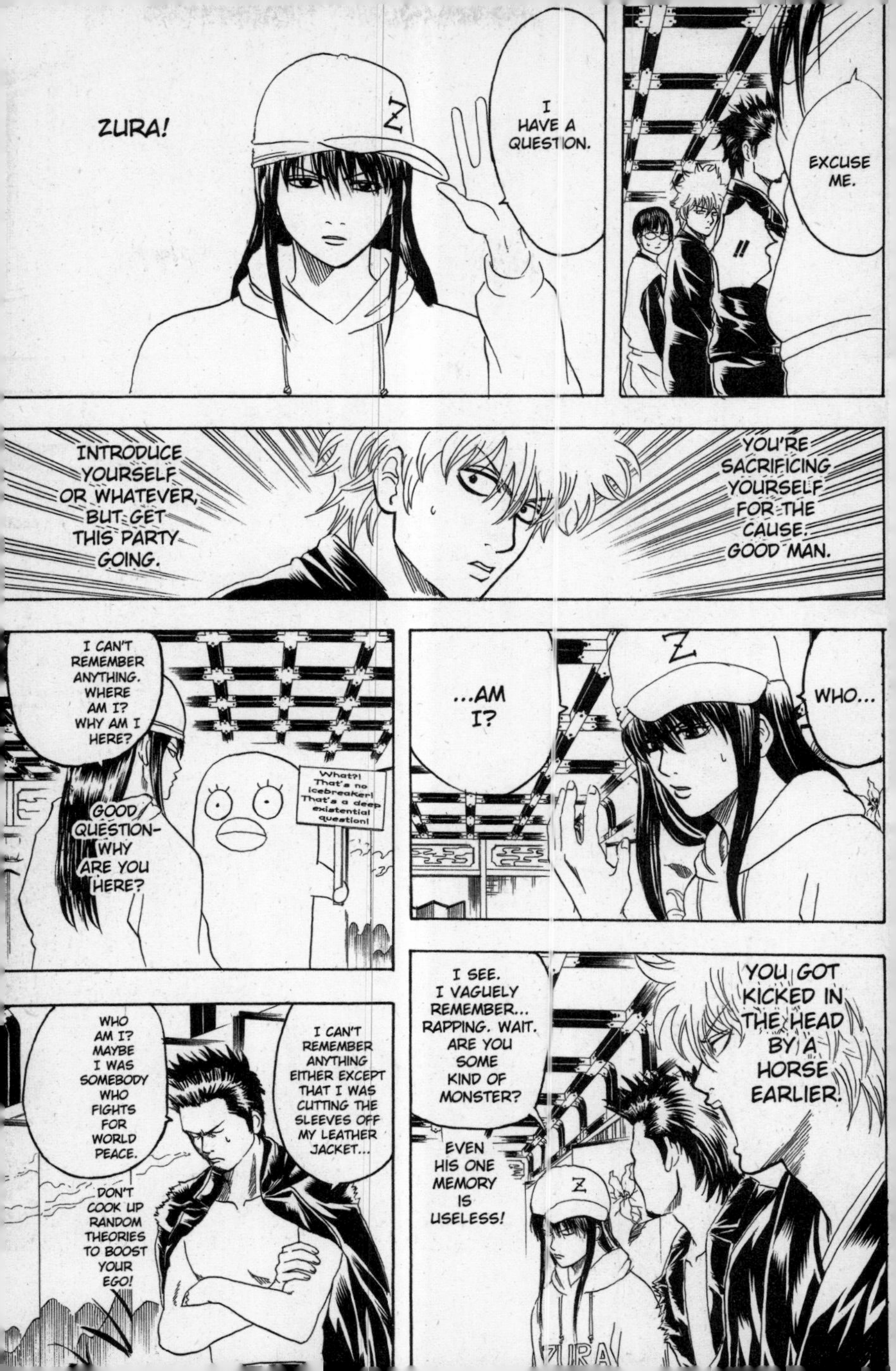
EXCUSE ME.
!!
I HAVE A QUESTION.
ZURA!
YOU'RE SACRIFICING YOURSELF FOR THE CAUSE. GOOD MAN.
INTRODUCE YOURSELF OR WHATEVER, BUT GET THIS PARTY GOING.
WHO...
...AM I?
I CAN'T REMEMBER ANYTHING. WHERE AM I? WHY AM I HERE?
What?! That's no icebreaker! That's a deep existential question!
GOOD QUESTION- WHY ARE YOU HERE?
YOU GOT KICKED IN THE HEAD BY A HORSE EARLIER.
I SEE. I VAGUELY REMEMBER... RAPPING. WAIT. ARE YOU SOME KIND OF MONSTER?
EVEN HIS ONE MEMORY IS USELESS!
ZURA
I CAN'T REMEMBER ANYTHING EITHER EXCEPT THAT I WAS CUTTING THE SLEEVES OFF MY LEATHER JACKET...
WHO AM I? MAYBE I WAS SOMEBODY WHO FIGHTS FOR WORLD PEACE.
DON'T COOK UP RANDOM THEORIES TO BOOST YOUR EGO!

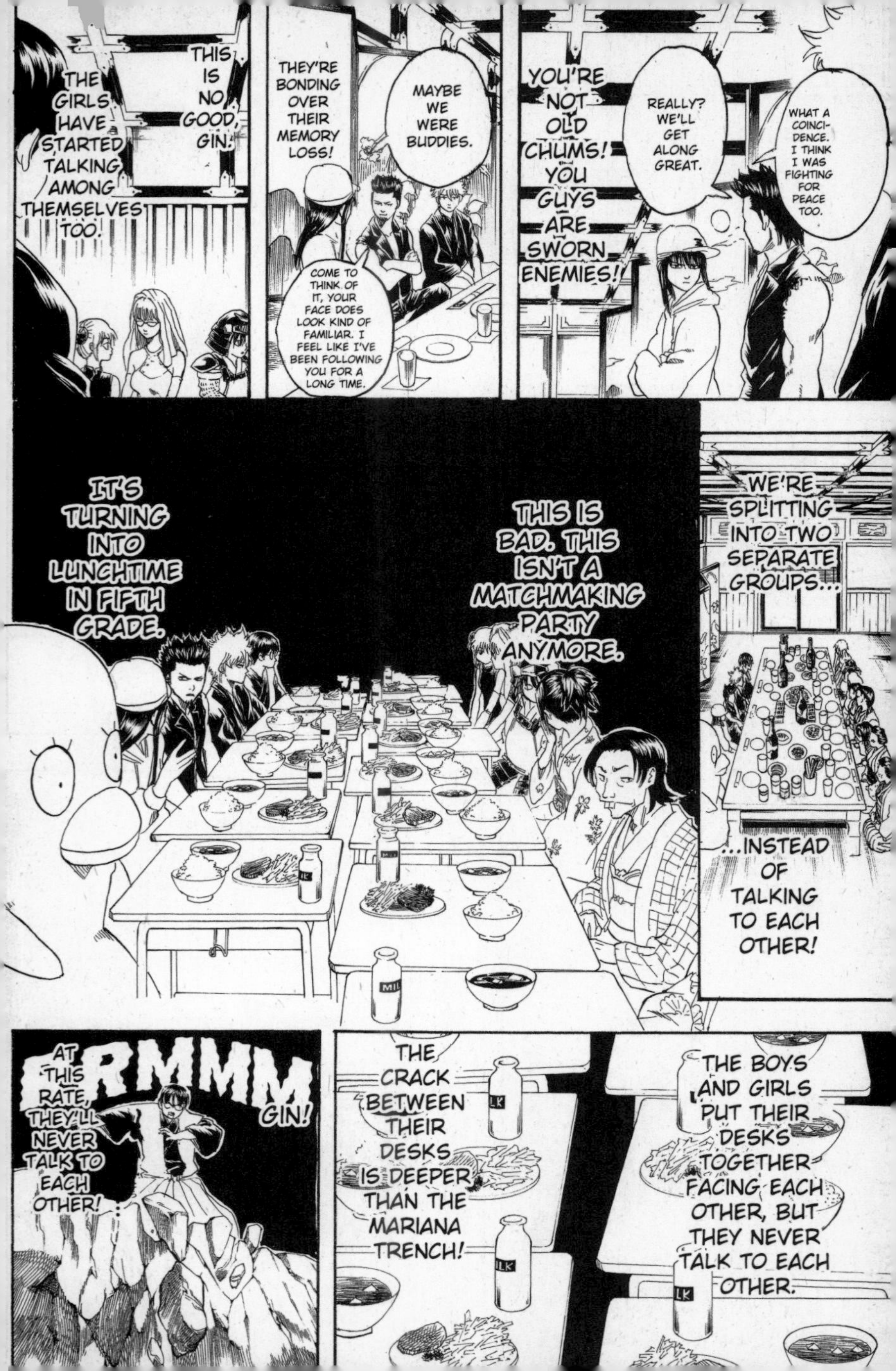
WHAT A COINCIDENCE. I THINK I WAS FIGHTING FOR PEACE TOO.
REALLY? WE'LL GET ALONG GREAT.
YOU'RE NOT OLD CHUMS! YOU GUYS ARE SWORN ENEMIES!
COME TO THINK OF IT, YOUR FACE DOES LOOK KIND OF FAMILIAR. I FEEL LIKE I'VE BEEN FOLLOWING YOU FOR A LONG TIME.
MAYBE WE WERE BUDDIES.
THEY'RE BONDING OVER THEIR MEMORY LOSS!
THIS IS NO GOOD, GIN.
THE GIRLS HAVE STARTED TALKING AMONG THEMSELVES TOO!
WE'RE SPLITTING INTO TWO SEPARATE GROUPS...
...INSTEAD OF TALKING TO EACH OTHER!
THIS IS BAD. THIS ISN'T A MATCHMAKING PARTY ANYMORE.
IT'S TURNING INTO LUNCHTIME IN FIFTH GRADE.
THE BOYS AND GIRLS PUT THEIR DESKS TOGETHER FACING EACH OTHER, BUT THEY NEVER TALK TO EACH OTHER.
THE CRACK BETWEEN THEIR DESKS IS DEEPER THAN THE MARIANA TRENCH!
RMMM
AT THIS RATE, THEY'LL NEVER TALK TO EACH OTHER!
GIN!

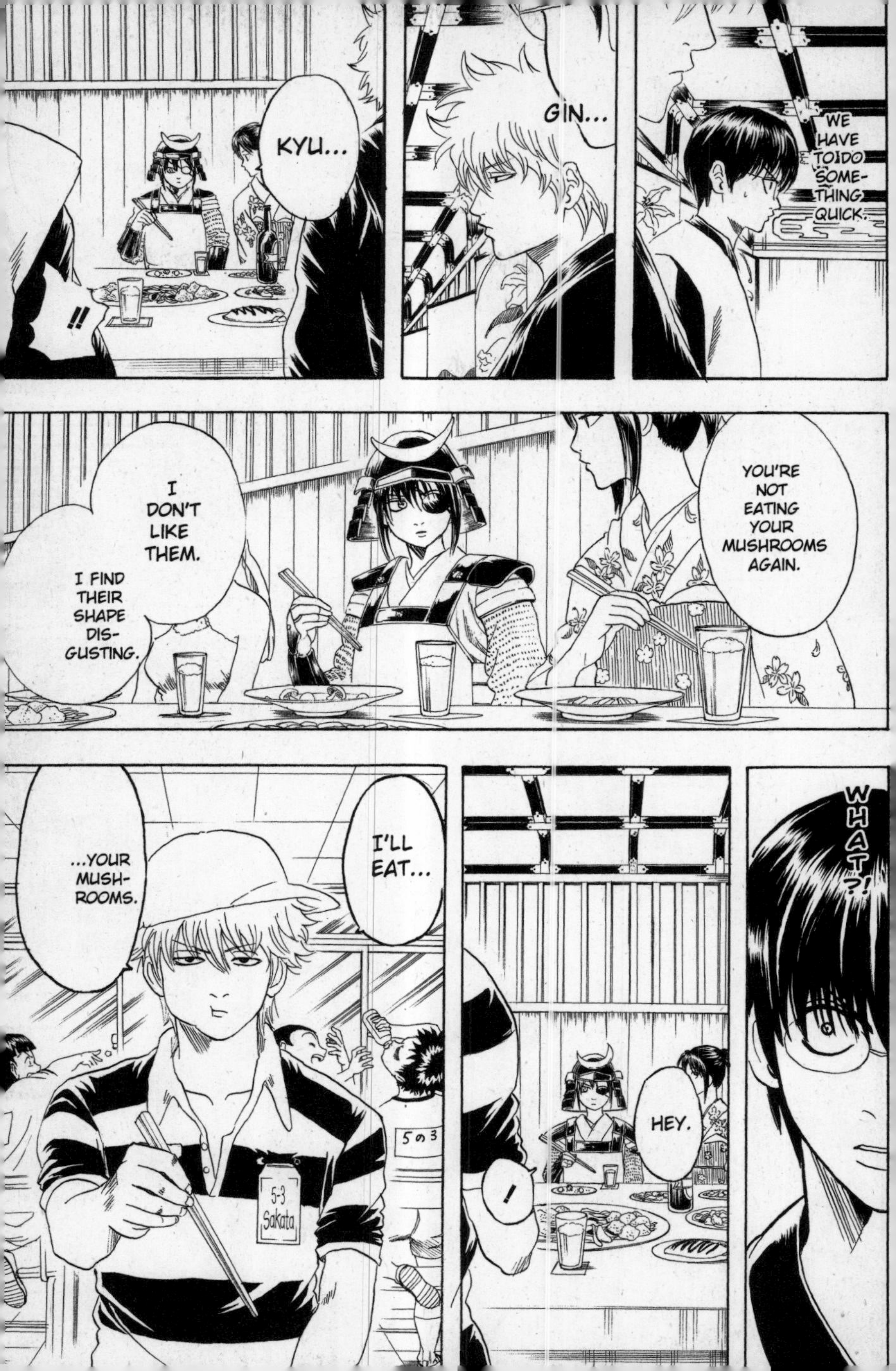
WE HAVE TO DO SOMETHING QUICK.
GIN...
KYU...
!!
YOU'RE NOT EATING YOUR MUSHROOMS AGAIN.
I DON'T LIKE THEM.
I FIND THEIR SHAPE DISGUSTING.
WHAT?!
HEY.
!
I'LL EAT...
...YOUR MUSHROOMS.
5の3
5-3 Sakata

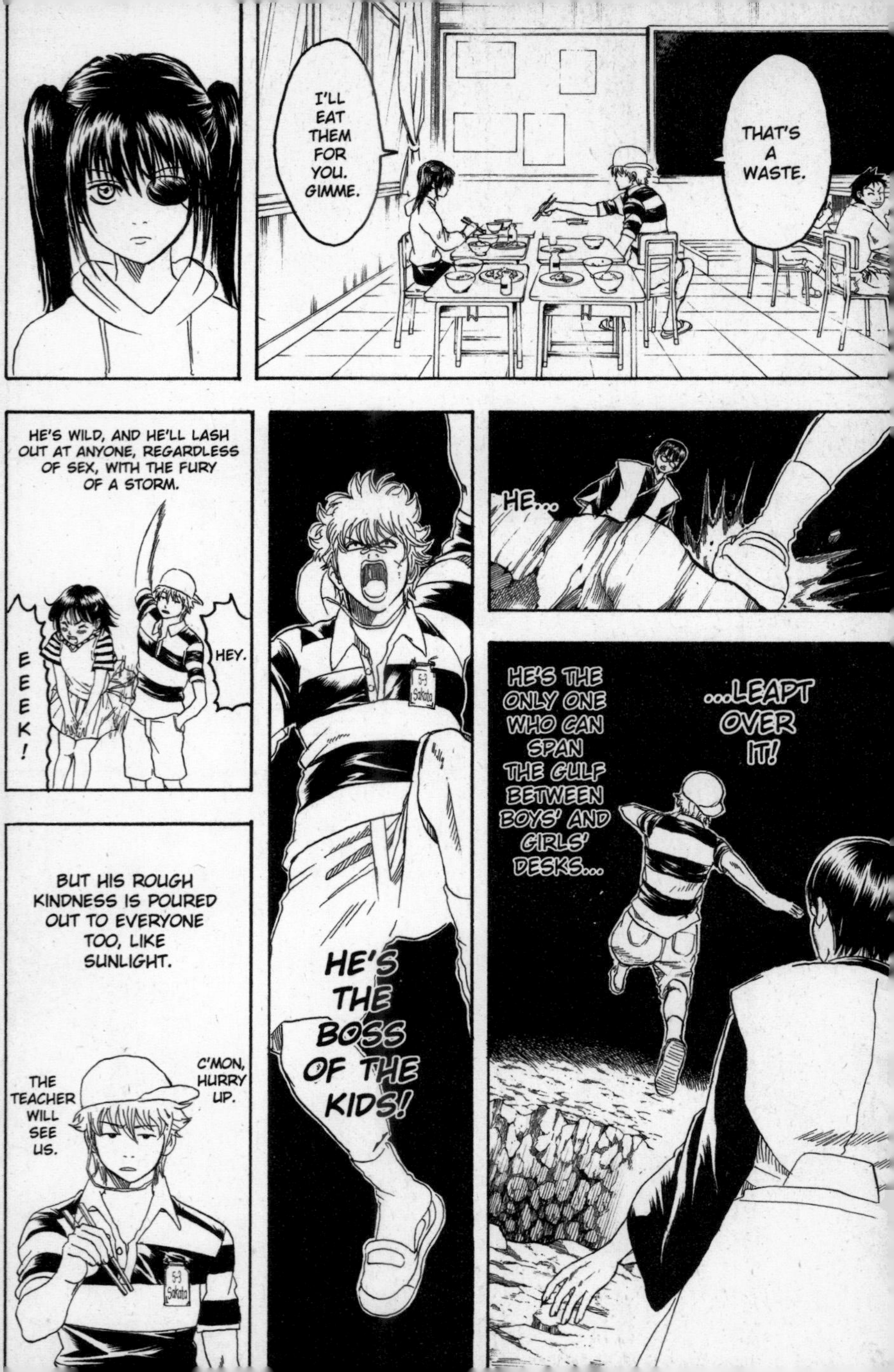
THAT'S A WASTE.
I'LL EAT THEM FOR YOU. GIMME.
HE...
HE'S THE ONLY ONE WHO CAN SPAN THE GULF BETWEEN BOYS' AND GIRLS' DESKS...
...LEAPT OVER IT!
HE'S THE BOSS OF THE KIDS!
HE'S WILD, AND HE'LL LASH OUT AT ANYONE, REGARDLESS OF SEX, WITH THE FURY OF A STORM.
HEY.
EEEEK!
BUT HIS ROUGH KINDNESS IS POURED OUT TO EVERYONE TOO, LIKE SUNLIGHT.
C'MON, HURRY UP.
THE TEACHER WILL SEE US.

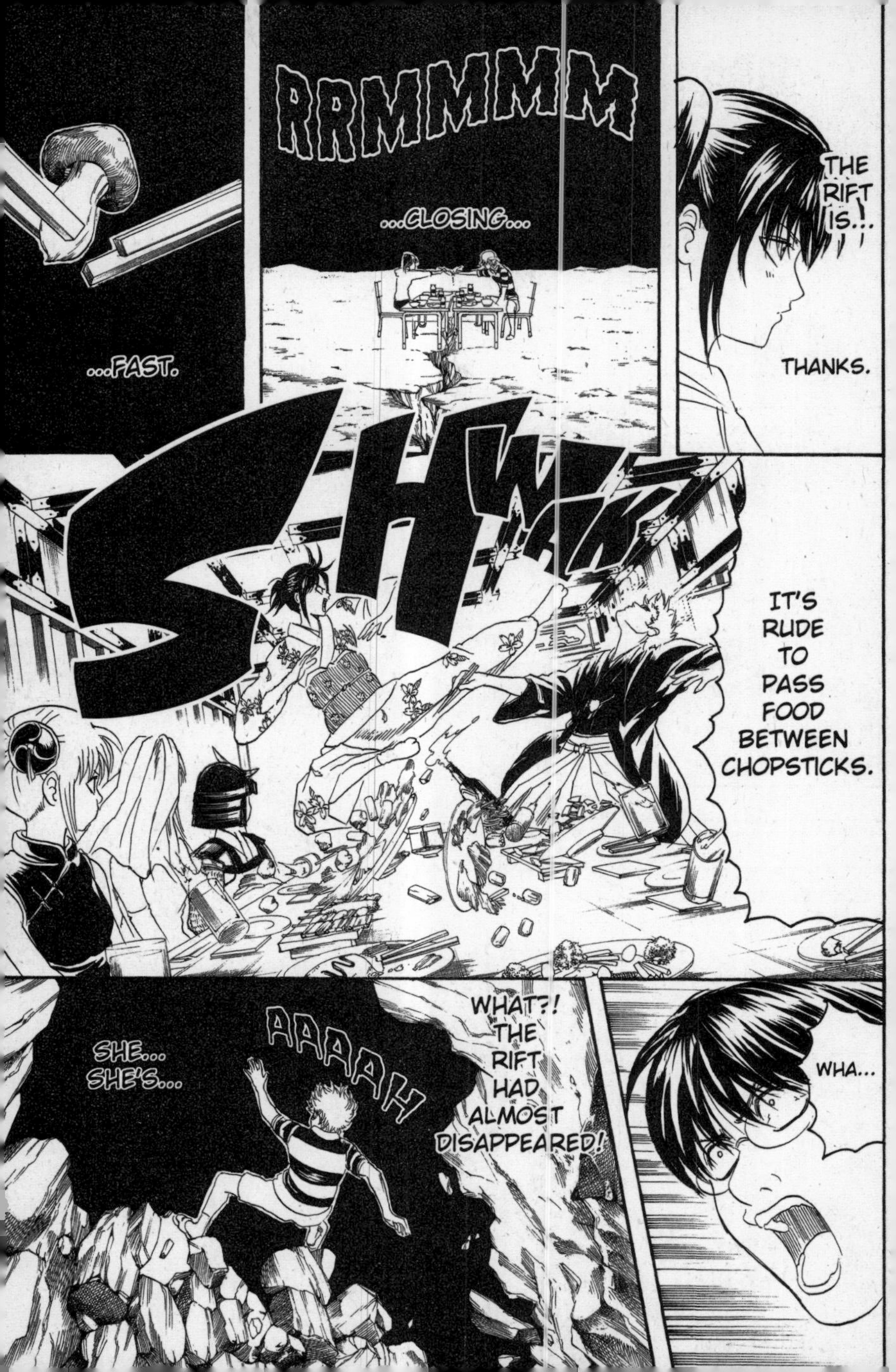

THE RIFT IS...
THANKS.
RRMMMMM
...CLOSING...
...FAST.
IT'S RUDE TO PASS FOOD BETWEEN CHOPSTICKS.
WHA...
WHAT?! THE RIFT HAD ALMOST DISAPPEARED!
AAAAAH
SHE... SHE'S...

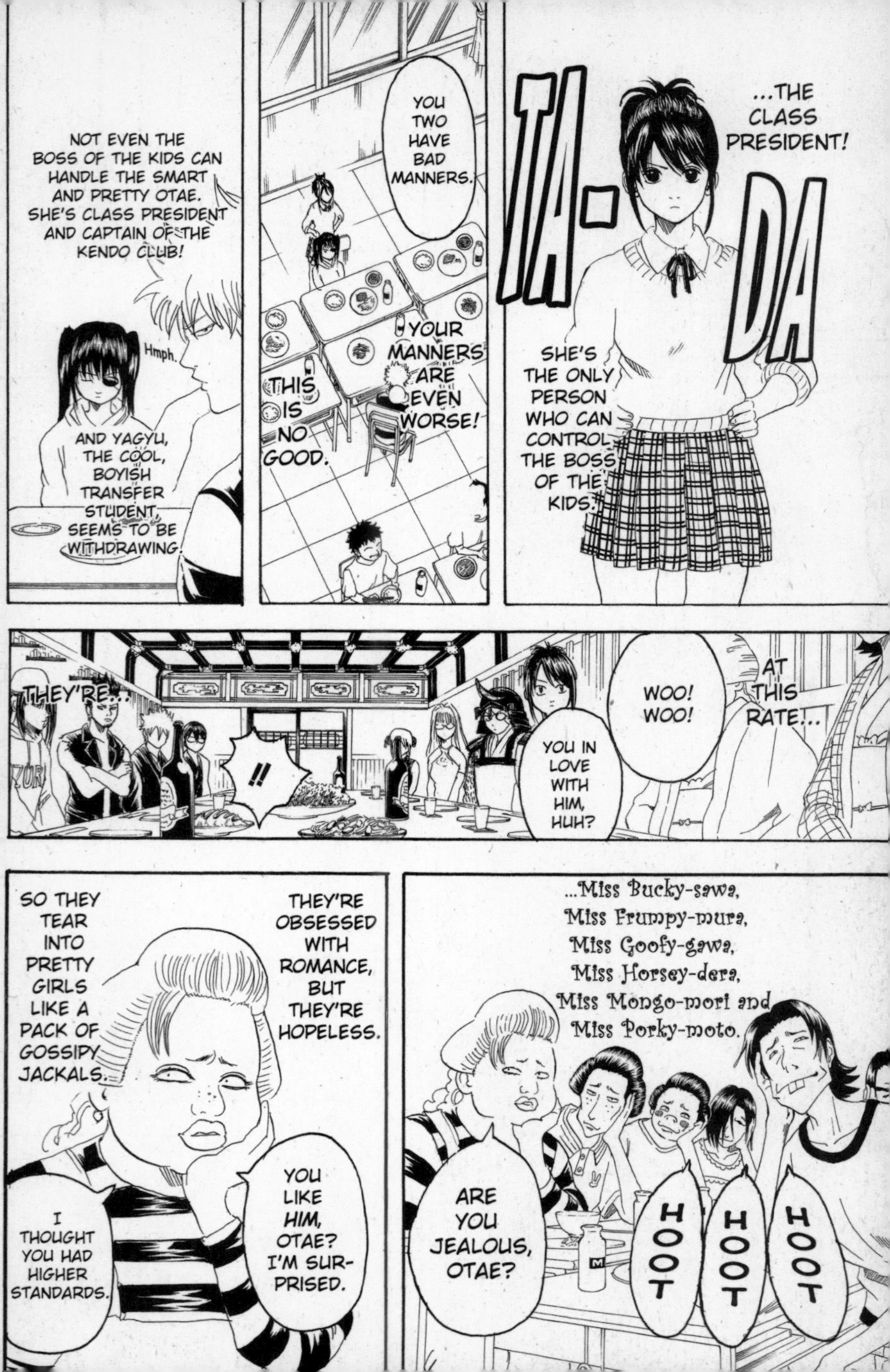
TA-DA
...THE CLASS PRESIDENT!
SHE'S THE ONLY PERSON WHO CAN CONTROL THE BOSS OF THE KIDS.
YOU TWO HAVE BAD MANNERS.
YOUR MANNERS ARE EVEN WORSE!
THIS IS NO GOOD.
NOT EVEN THE BOSS OF THE KIDS CAN HANDLE THE SMART AND PRETTY OTAE. SHE'S CLASS PRESIDENT AND CAPTAIN OF THE KENDO CLUB!
Hmph.
AND YAGYU, THE COOL, BOYISH TRANSFER STUDENT, SEEMS TO BE WITHDRAWING.
AT THIS RATE...
WOO! WOO!
YOU IN LOVE WITH HIM, HUH?
!!
THEY'RE...
...Miss Bucky-sawa, Miss Frumpy-mura, Miss Goofy-gawa, Miss Horsey-dera, Miss Mongo-mori and Miss Porky-moto.
HOOT
HOOT
HOOT
ARE YOU JEALOUS, OTAE?
THEY'RE OBSESSED WITH ROMANCE, BUT THEY'RE HOPELESS.
SO THEY TEAR INTO PRETTY GIRLS LIKE A PACK OF GOSSIPY JACKALS.
YOU LIKE HIM, OTAE? I'M SUR-PRISED.
I THOUGHT YOU HAD HIGHER STANDARDS.

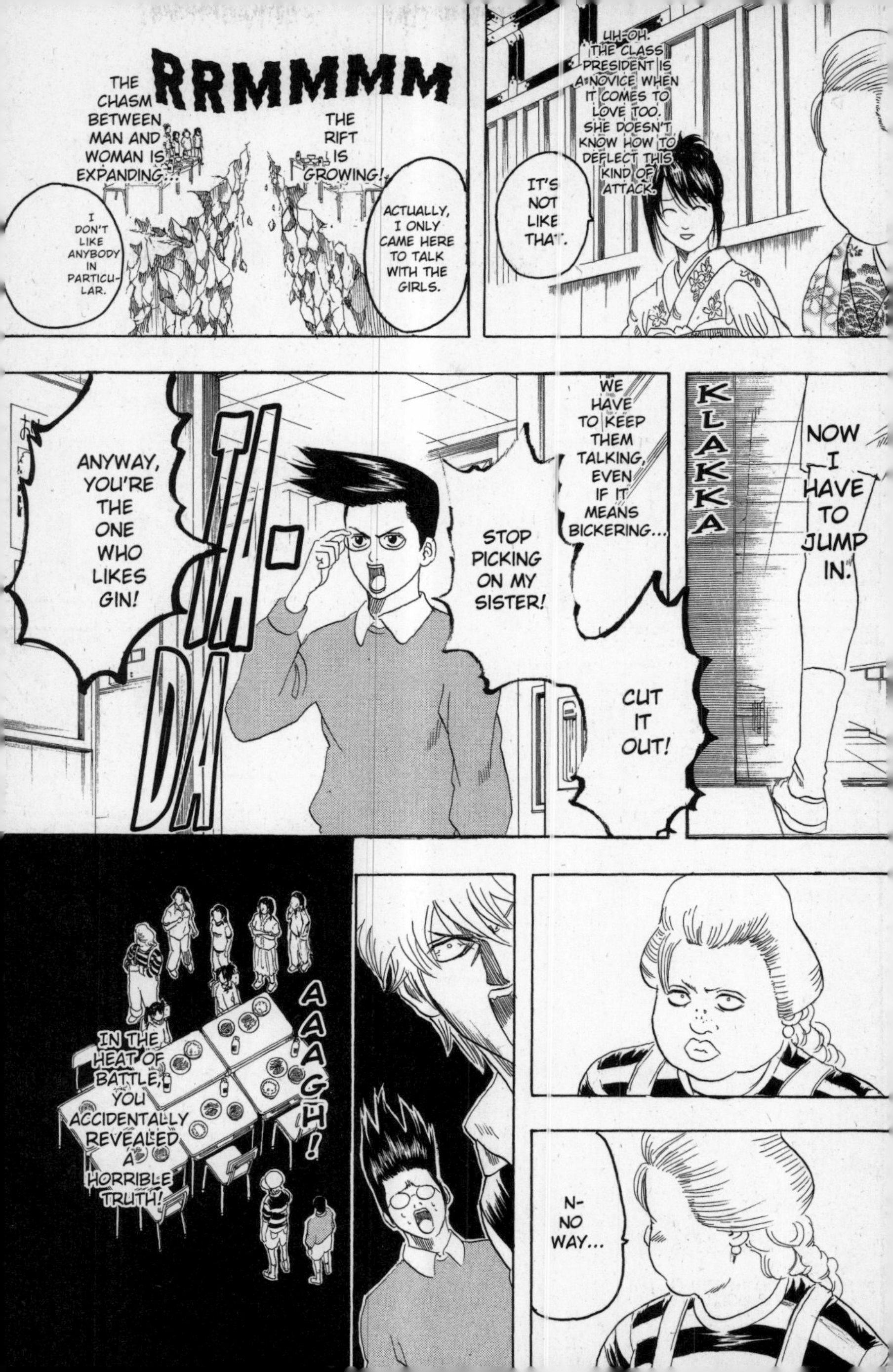
UH-OH. THE CLASS PRESIDENT IS A NOVICE WHEN IT COMES TO LOVE TOO. SHE DOESN'T KNOW HOW TO DEFLECT THIS KIND OF ATTACK.
IT'S NOT LIKE THAT.
RRMMMM
THE RIFT IS GROWING!
THE CHASM BETWEEN MAN AND WOMAN IS EXPANDING...
ACTUALLY, I ONLY CAME HERE TO TALK WITH THE GIRLS.
I DON'T LIKE ANYBODY IN PARTICU-LAR.
KLAKKA
NOW I HAVE TO JUMP IN.
WE HAVE TO KEEP THEM TALKING, EVEN IF IT MEANS BICKERING...
CUT IT OUT!
STOP PICKING ON MY SISTER!
TA-DA
ANYWAY, YOU'RE THE ONE WHO LIKES GIN!
N-NO WAY...
AAAAGH!
IN THE HEAT OF BATTLE, YOU ACCIDENTALLY REVEALED A HORRIBLE TRUTH!

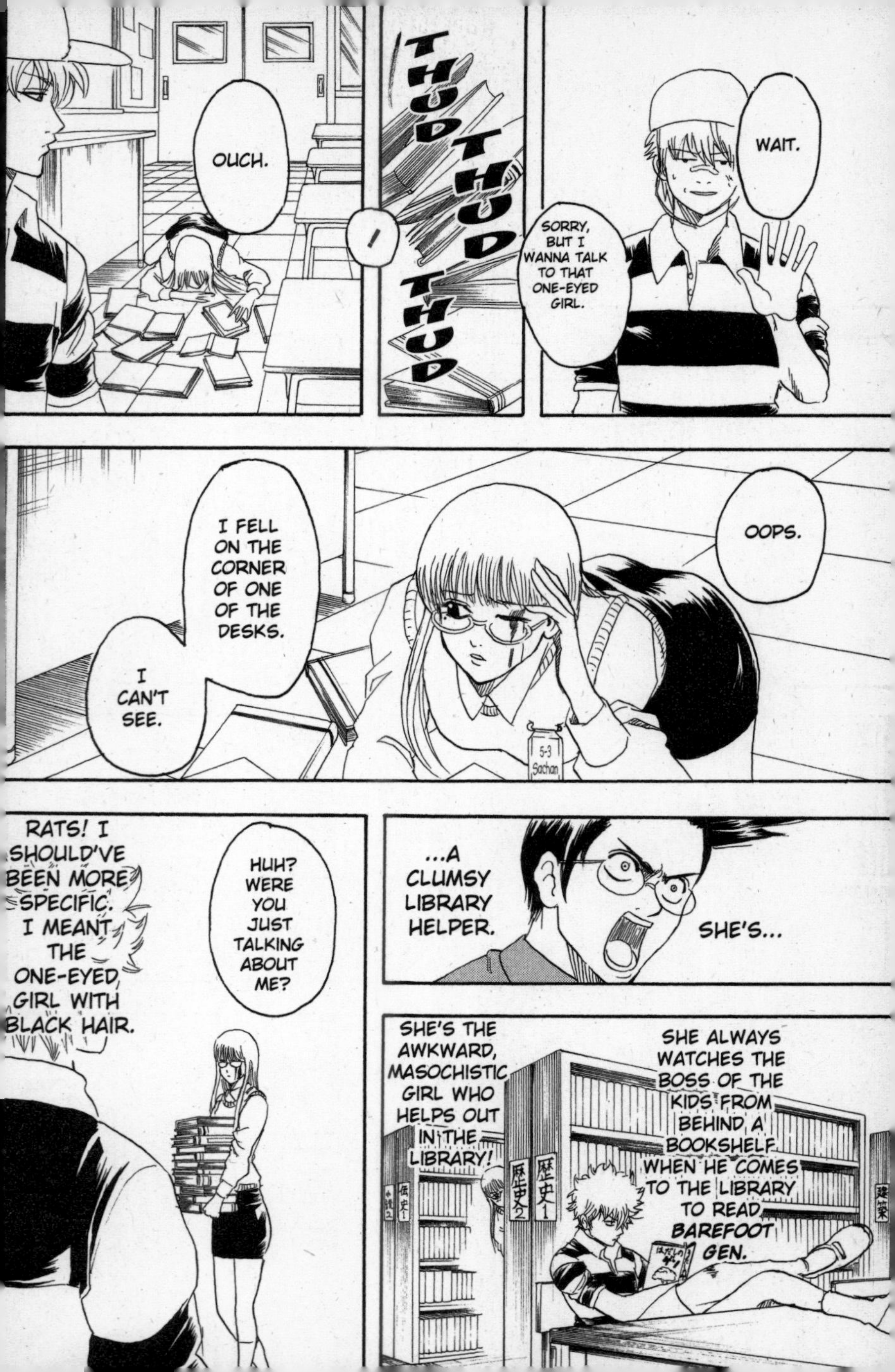
WAIT.
SORRY, BUT I WANNA TALK TO THAT ONE-EYED GIRL.
THUD THUD THUD THUD
!
OUCH.
OOPS.
I FELL ON THE CORNER OF ONE OF THE DESKS.
I CAN'T SEE.
5-3 Sachan
SHE'S...
...A CLUMSY LIBRARY HELPER.
SHE ALWAYS WATCHES THE BOSS OF THE KIDS FROM BEHIND A BOOKSHELF WHEN HE COMES TO THE LIBRARY TO READ BAREFOOT GEN.
SHE'S THE AWKWARD, MASOCHISTIC GIRL WHO HELPS OUT IN THE LIBRARY!
歴史1
歴史2
HUH? WERE YOU JUST TALKING ABOUT ME?
RATS! I SHOULD'VE BEEN MORE SPECIFIC. I MEANT THE ONE-EYED GIRL WITH BLACK HAIR.

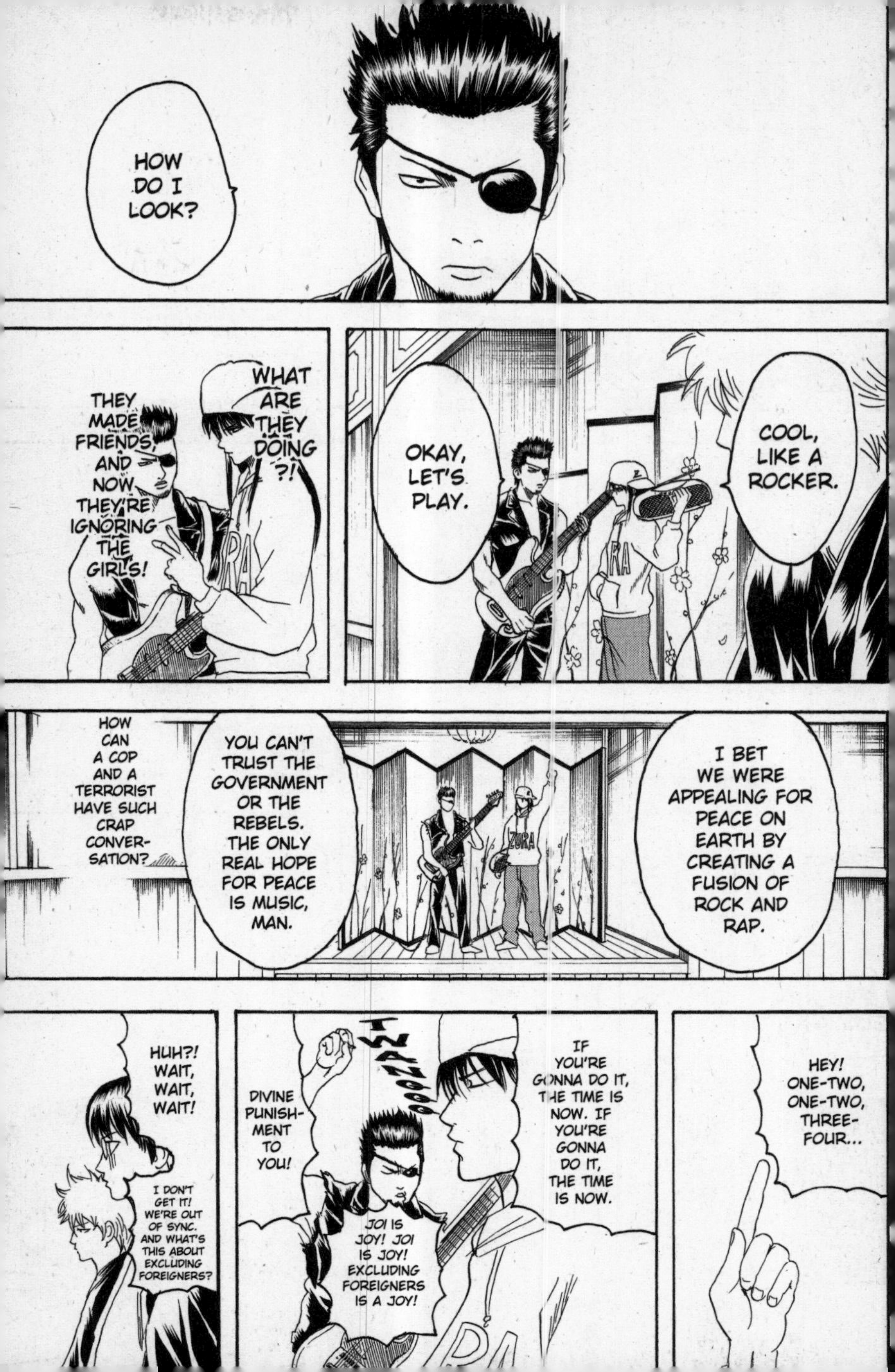
HOW DO I LOOK?
COOL, LIKE A ROCKER.
OKAY, LET'S PLAY.
WHAT ARE THEY DOING?!
THEY MADE FRIENDS, AND NOW THEY'RE IGNORING THE GIRLS!
I BET WE WERE APPEALING FOR PEACE ON EARTH BY CREATING A FUSION OF ROCK AND RAP.
YOU CAN'T TRUST THE GOVERNMENT OR THE REBELS. THE ONLY REAL HOPE FOR PEACE IS MUSIC, MAN.
HOW CAN A COP AND A TERRORIST HAVE SUCH CRAP CONVERSATION?
HEY! ONE-TWO, ONE-TWO, THREE-FOUR...
IF YOU'RE GONNA DO IT, THE TIME IS NOW. IF YOU'RE GONNA DO IT, THE TIME IS NOW.
TWANGGG
DIVINE PUNISHMENT TO YOU!
JOI IS JOY! JOI IS JOY! EXCLUDING FOREIGNERS IS A JOY!
HUH?! WAIT, WAIT, WAIT!
I DON'T GET IT! WE'RE OUT OF SYNC. AND WHAT'S THIS ABOUT EXCLUDING FOREIGNERS?

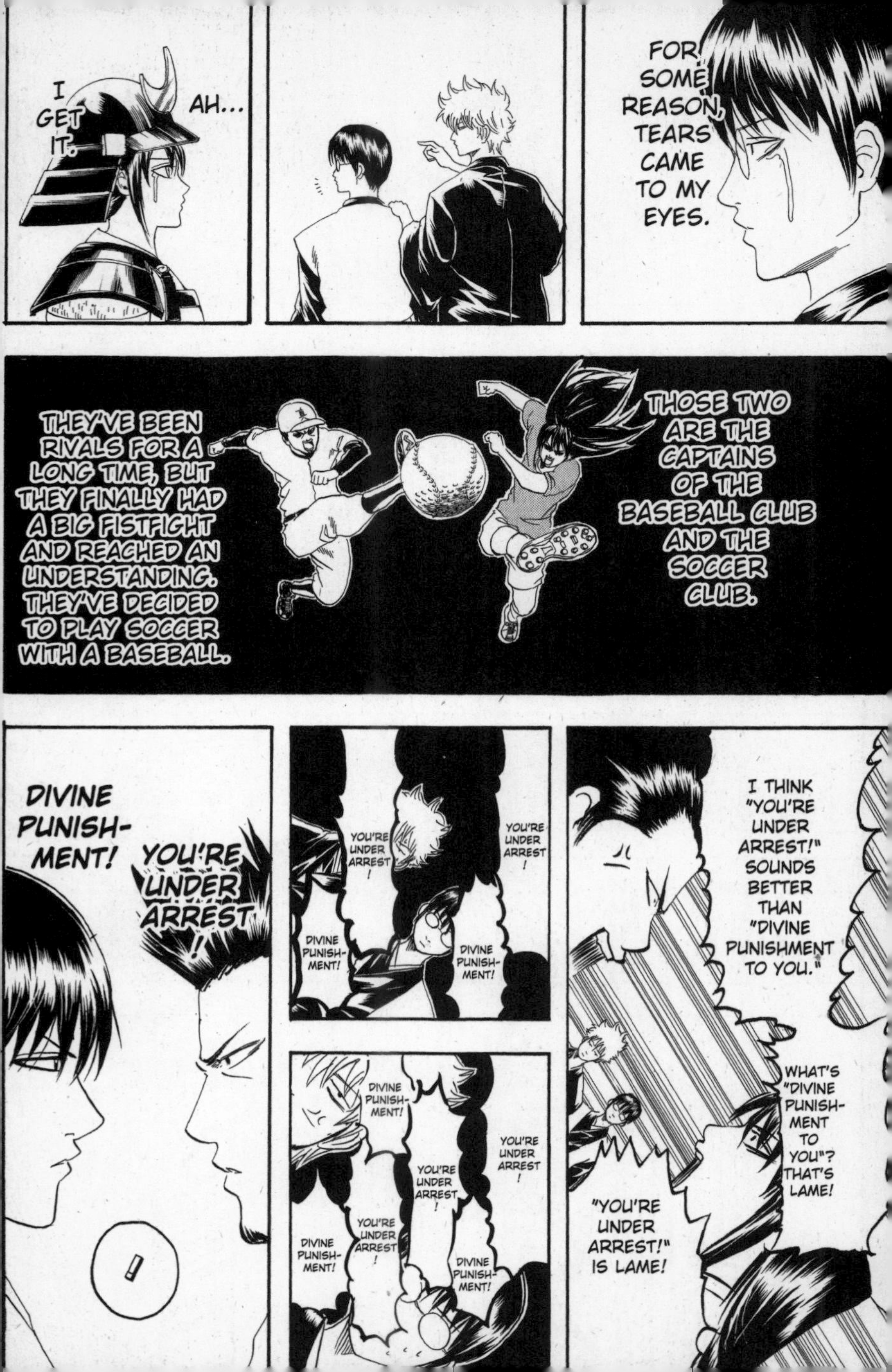
FOR SOME REASON, TEARS CAME TO MY EYES.
AH...
I GET IT.
THOSE TWO ARE THE CAPTAINS OF THE BASEBALL CLUB AND THE SOCCER CLUB.
THEY'VE BEEN RIVALS FOR A LONG TIME, BUT THEY FINALLY HAD A BIG FISTFIGHT AND REACHED AN UNDERSTANDING. THEY'VE DECIDED TO PLAY SOCCER WITH A BASEBALL.
I THINK "YOU'RE UNDER ARREST!" SOUNDS BETTER THAN "DIVINE PUNISHMENT TO YOU."
WHAT'S "DIVINE PUNISHMENT TO YOU"? THAT'S LAME!
"YOU'RE UNDER ARREST!" IS LAME!
YOU'RE UNDER ARREST!
YOU'RE UNDER ARREST!
DIVINE PUNISHMENT!
DIVINE PUNISHMENT!
DIVINE PUNISHMENT!
YOU'RE UNDER ARREST!
YOU'RE UNDER ARREST!
YOU'RE UNDER ARREST!
DIVINE PUNISHMENT!
DIVINE PUNISHMENT!
YOU'RE UNDER ARREST!
DIVINE PUNISHMENT!
!

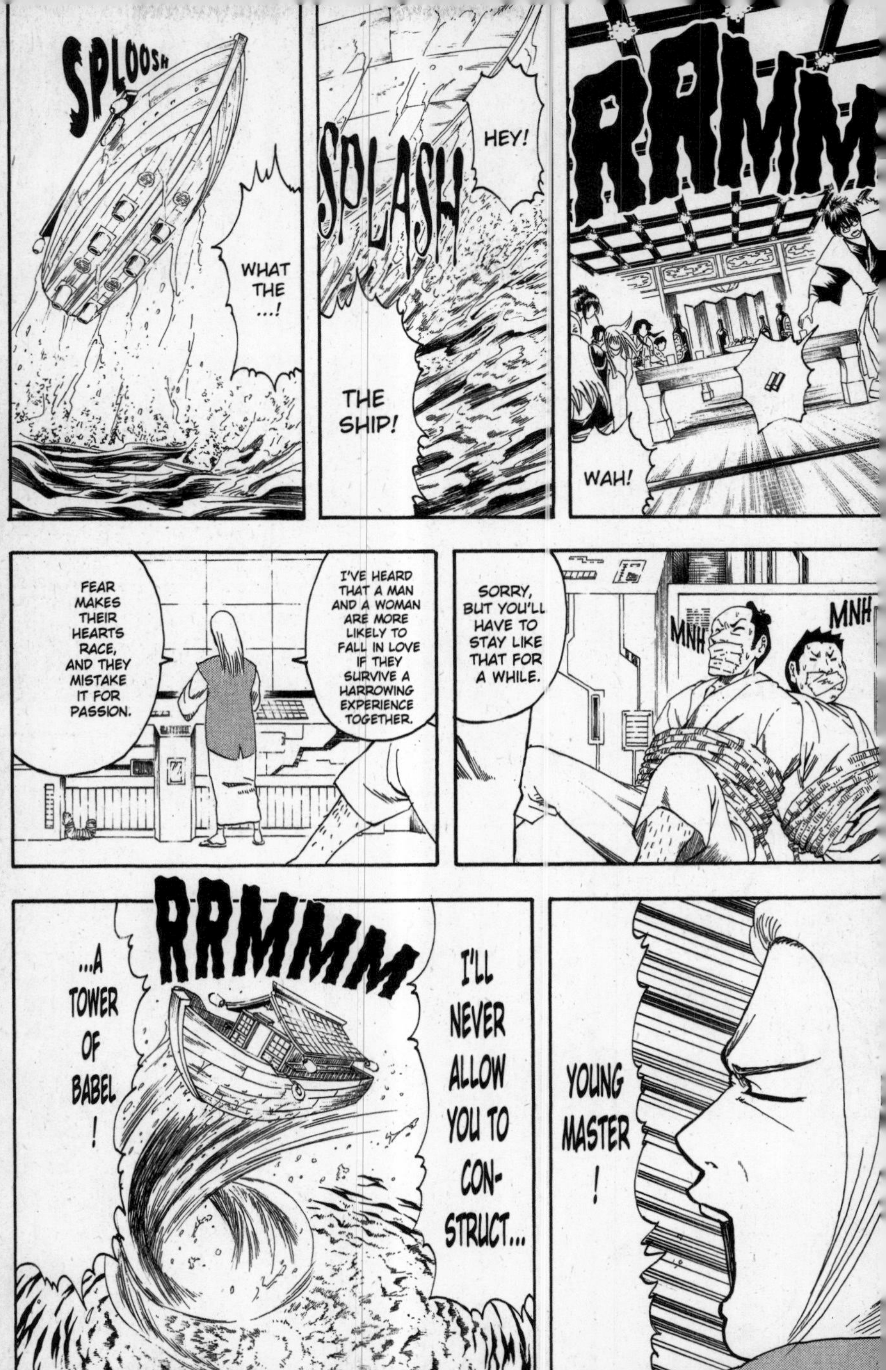
RRAMM
WAH!
HEY!
SPLASH
THE SHIP!
SPLOOSH
WHAT THE ...!
MNH
MNH
SORRY, BUT YOU'LL HAVE TO STAY LIKE THAT FOR A WHILE.
I'VE HEARD THAT A MAN AND A WOMAN ARE MORE LIKELY TO FALL IN LOVE IF THEY SURVIVE A HARROWING EXPERIENCE TOGETHER.
FEAR MAKES THEIR HEARTS RACE, AND THEY MISTAKE IT FOR PASSION.
YOUNG MASTER!
I'LL NEVER ALLOW YOU TO CON-STRUCT...
RRMMM
...A TOWER OF BABEL!
RRM

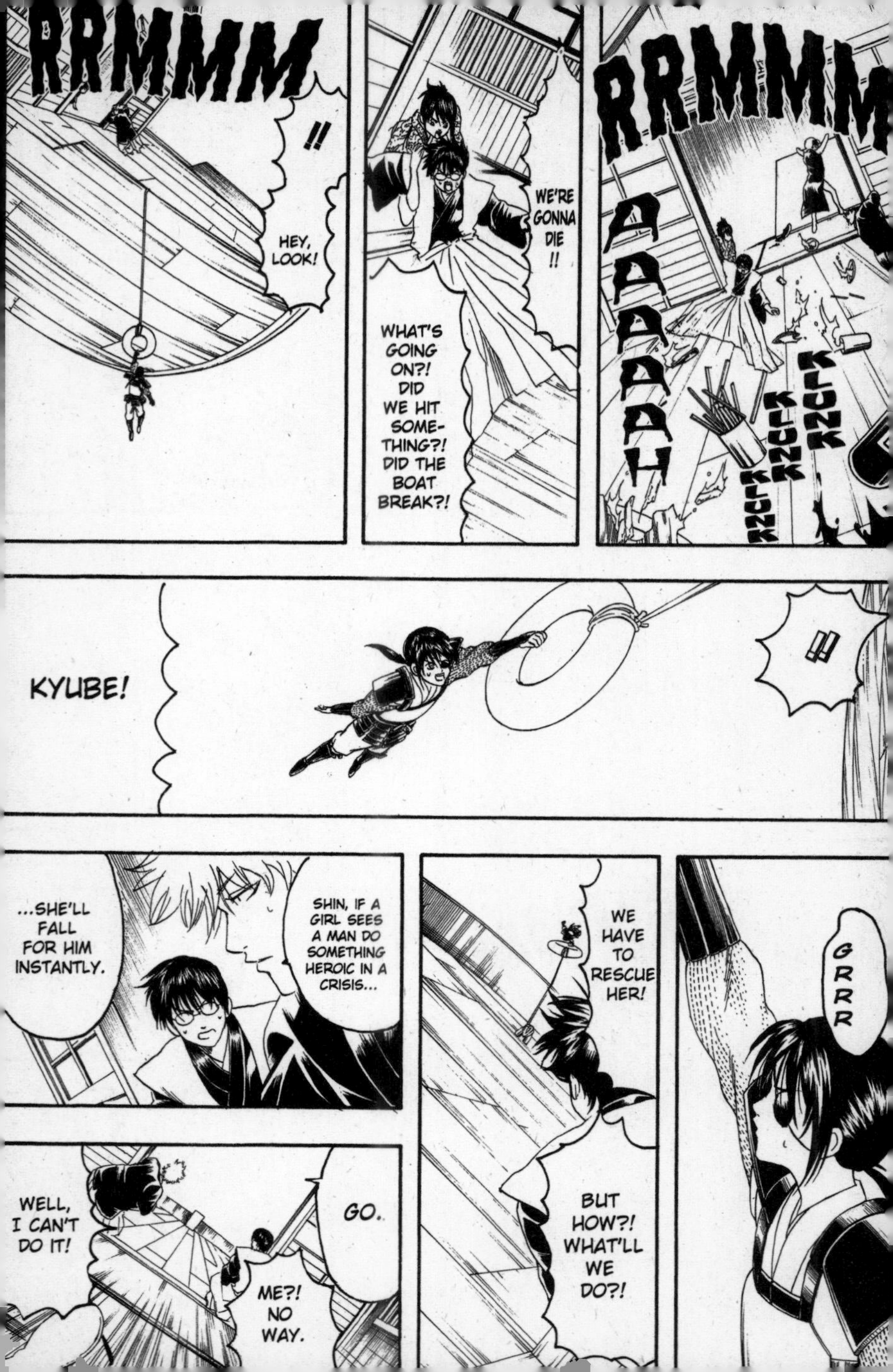
RRMMM
AAAAAH
KLUNK
KLUNK
KLUNK
WE'RE GONNA DIE!!
WHAT'S GOING ON?! DID WE HIT SOMETHING?! DID THE BOAT BREAK?!
RRMMMM
!!
HEY, LOOK!
!!
KYUBE!
GRRR
WE HAVE TO RESCUE HER!
BUT HOW?! WHAT'LL WE DO?!
SHIN, IF A GIRL SEES A MAN DO SOMETHING HEROIC IN A CRISIS...
...SHE'LL FALL FOR HIM INSTANTLY.
GO.
ME?! NO WAY.
WELL, I CAN'T DO IT!

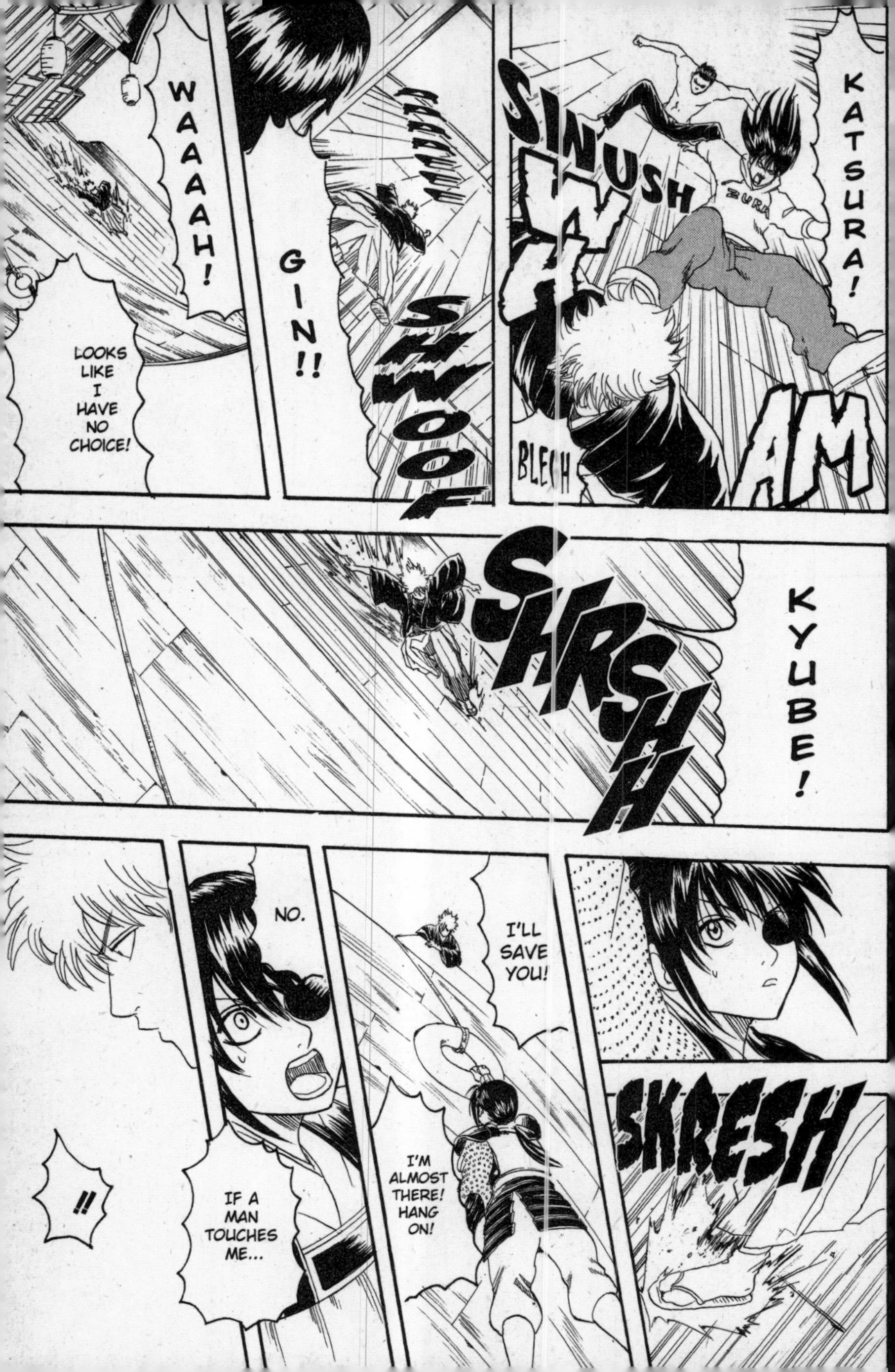
KATSURA!
SINUSH
ZURA
BLECH
AM
GIN!!
SHWOOF
WAAAAAH!
LOOKS LIKE I HAVE NO CHOICE!
KYUBE!
SKRSHH
SKRESH
I'LL SAVE YOU!
I'M ALMOST THERE! HANG ON!
NO.
IF A MAN TOUCHES ME...
!!

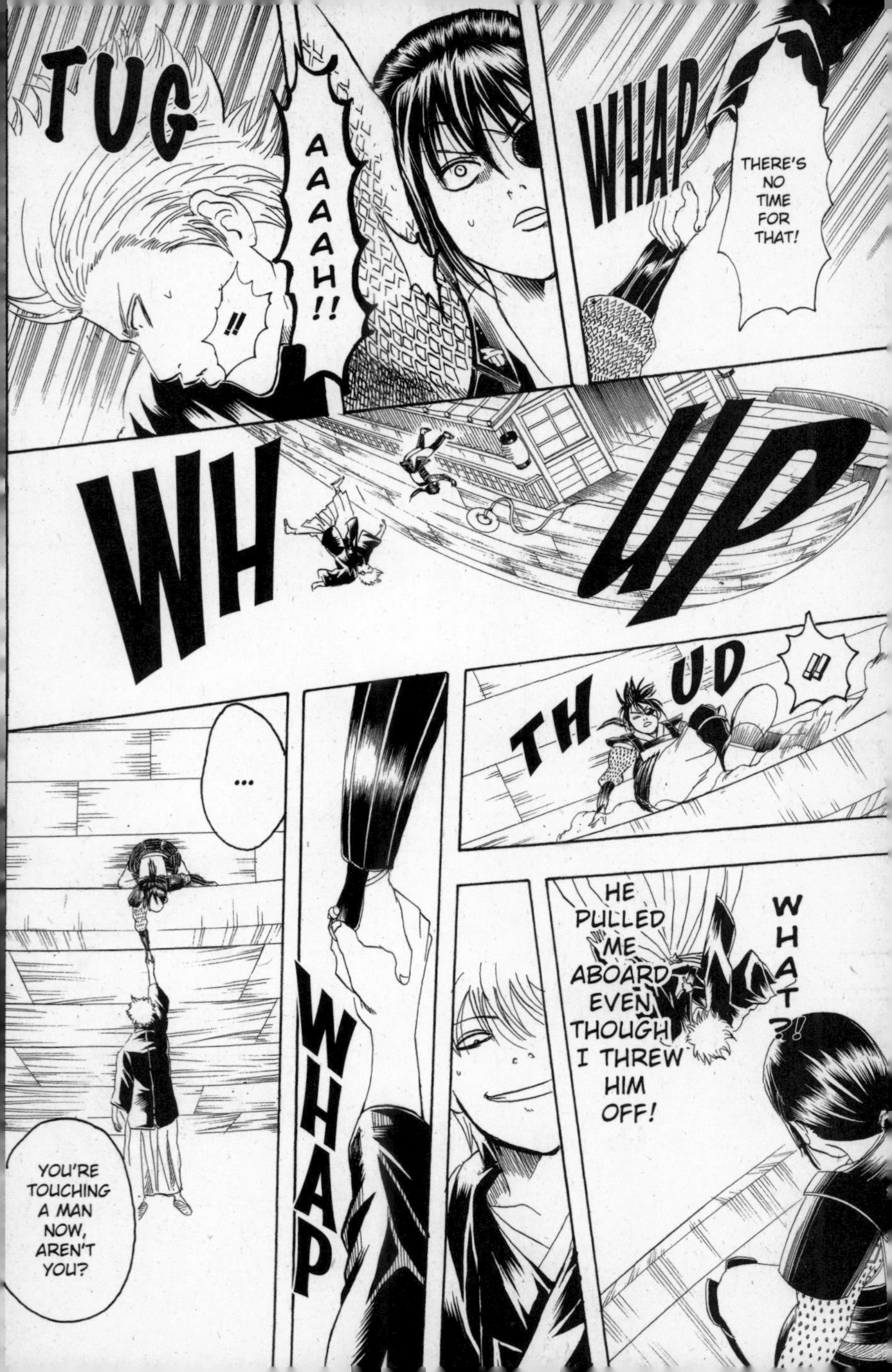

WHAP
THERE'S NO TIME FOR THAT!
AAAAH!!
TUG
!!
WHUP
THUD
!!
WHAT?!
HE PULLED ME ABOARD EVEN THOUGH I THREW HIM OFF!
WHAP
...
YOU'RE TOUCHING A MAN NOW, AREN'T YOU?

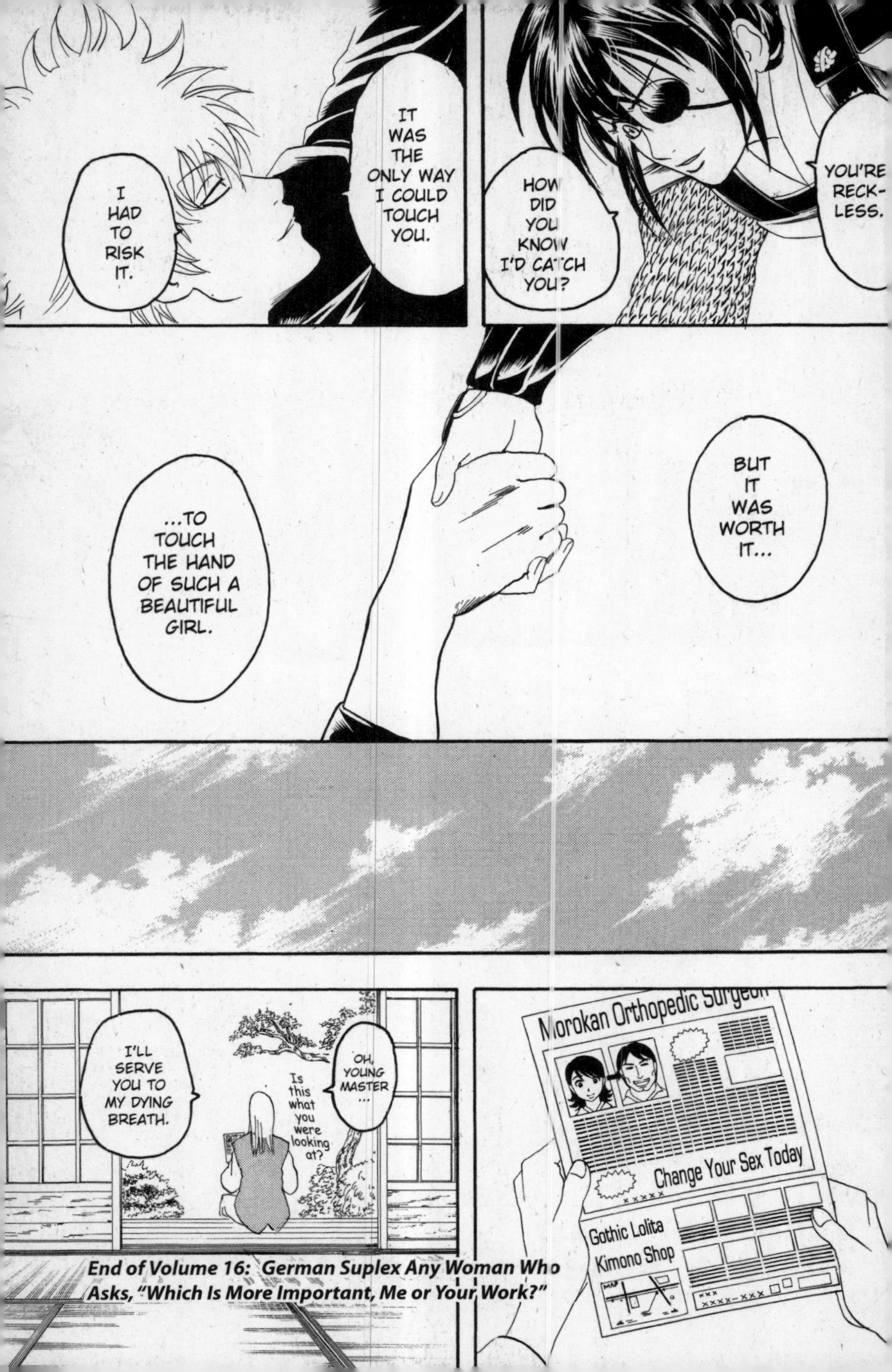
YOU'RE RECKLESS.
HOW DID YOU KNOW I'D CATCH YOU?
IT WAS THE ONLY WAY I COULD TOUCH YOU.
I HAD TO RISK IT.
BUT IT WAS WORTH IT...
...TO TOUCH THE HAND OF SUCH A BEAUTIFUL GIRL.
Morokan Orthopedic Surgeon
Change Your Sex Today
Gothic Lolita Kimono Shop
MAP
OH, YOUNG MASTER...
Is this what you were looking at?
I'LL SERVE YOU TO MY DYING BREATH.

End of Volume 16: German Suplex Any Woman Who Asks, "Which Is More Important, Me or Your Work?"

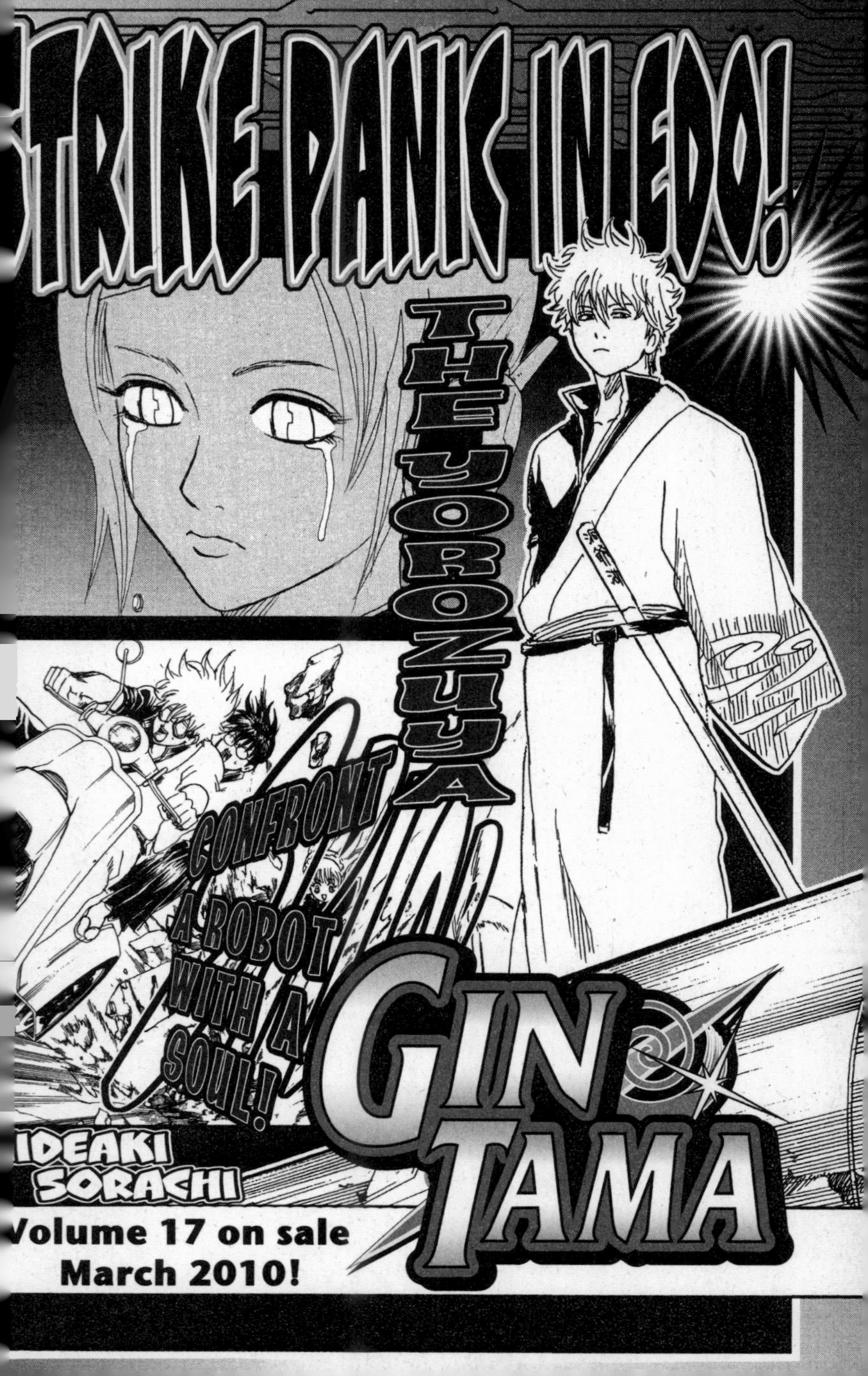
STRIKE PANIC IN EDO!
THE YOROZUYA
CONFRONT A ROBOT WITH A SOUL!
GIN TAMA
IDEAKI SORACHI
Volume 17 on sale
March 2010!

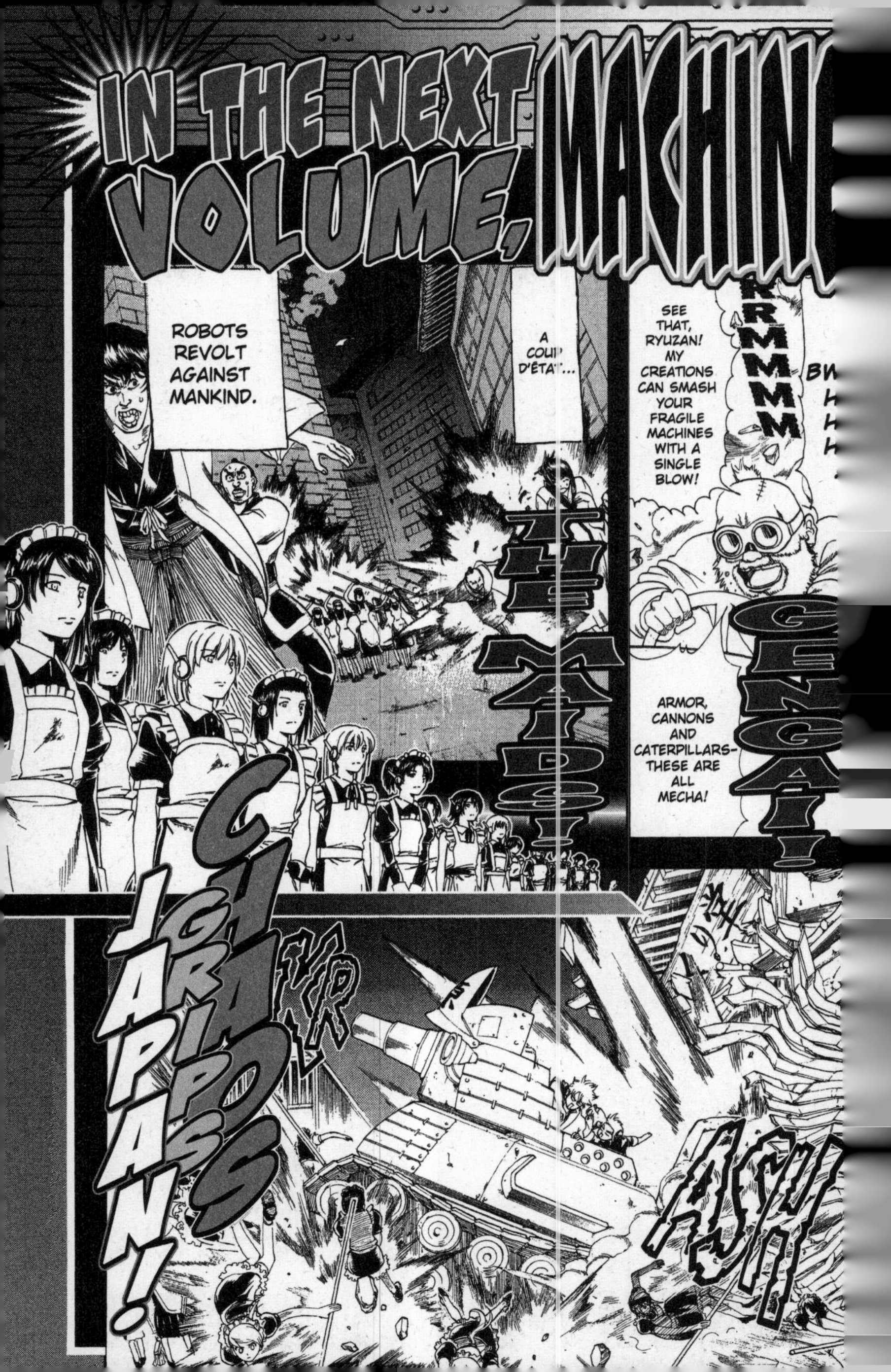
IN THE NEXT VOLUME, MACHIN
SEE THAT, RYUZAN! MY CREATIONS CAN SMASH YOUR FRAGILE MACHINES WITH A SINGLE BLOW!
GENGAI!
ARMOR, CANNONS AND CATERPILLARS- THESE ARE ALL MECHA!
A COUP D'ÉTAT...
ROBOTS REVOLT AGAINST MANKIND.
THE MAIDS!!
CHAOS GRIPS JAPAN!

Tell us what you think about SHONEN JUMP manga!

Our survey is now available online.
Go to: www.SHONENJUMP.com/mangasurvey

Help us make our product offering better!